Introduction

Discovering Ritual Meditation

Transcendental Healing and Self-Realization

By Carlton Brown

Copyright© 2008 Carlton Brown. All Rights Reserved

Please read the detailed copyright notice in the appendices to understand the rights of the author and copyright holder, and the permission(s) granted to the purchaser or user of this book.

Print Edition: Published September 11 2015, 2nd Edition.

ISBN: 978-0992775032

Editor: Jon Harrison

Cover Designer: Jeanine Henning https://jhillustration.wordpress.com/

Please connect with Carlton via www.ritualmeditation.com: to enquire about Ritual Meditation coaching, retreats and eLearning, as well as to schedule potential media interviews and speaking engagements, to access meditation resources, and for blog and social media sign-up links.

Introduction

Would you like to know one of humankind's best-kept secrets?

This secret has the potential to accelerate profound psychological healing and your spiritual awakening. In essence, this secret is the sacred ritual process for accessing altered states of consciousness, a process developed by the ancient Sun god religion priesthoods of ancient Egypt, India, and pre-Colombian Central and South America. I discovered this secret through my interest in pyramid archaeology and the biology of altered states of consciousness.

As a result of this discovery, I have been able to reverse-engineer the ancient priesthoods' sacred ritual process, and use it to develop the **Ritual Meditation** process for sacredly accessing our higher states of consciousness. I also discovered the **Transcendental Self-Inquiry** process for self-realization and profound psychological healing. All of this has been integrated into a **Mind Transformation Plan** to help you spiritually awaken and profoundly heal. Transcendental self-realization, through self-inquiry conducted in altered states of consciousness, is the most profound experience a human being can ever have. Upon achieving this self-realization your need to heal simply vanishes, and you come to realize that the perceived need was an illusion of the imposturous and impermanent ego mind and not of the higher self which is eternal.

Many conditions of the mind are known to significantly benefit from treatment with psychedelics. Conditions such as death anxiety and psychological issues consequent to early life abuse and trauma, or posttraumatic stress, chemical addictions, depression, or anxiety, all face limitations with current treatments, and psychedelics are known to provide significant benefits to those suffering from these conditions, even without sacred, healing, or self-realization intentions. Additionally, if you meditate but have never experienced altered states of consciousness, then this book will show you how adapt your meditation to access these states of consciousness and spiritually awaken and transform your mind.

Psychedelics in medical research settings have shown the potential to help people better manage the psychological conditions mentioned above. Yet psychedelics are illegal and the subject of much misinformation. This makes it virtually impossible for people to safely access improved treatment options that embrace psychedelic medicaments. The impediments to psychedelic access and their safe use will not, unfortunately, disappear anytime soon.

Introduction

What do people in medical or spiritual need do while waiting for the lifting of psychedelic prohibition and for medicine to advance?

Simple. Find another effective process for using psychedelics with a level of "validity" in its use, whilst we await medical and legislative progress. By using Ritual Meditation you gain access to a ritual process that you control. This same ritual process was developed and used by the ancient Sun god priesthoods over more than five millennia to support their religions and empires. This book explores the use of Ritual Meditation (and my Transcendental Self-Inquiry method and Mind Transformation Plan) to help people better manage their psychological and emotional challenges, and for those spiritual-meditation-yoga practitioners wishing to explore their higher states of consciousness and self-realization.

Ritual Meditation involves partaking in a sacred ritual process on the solstices and equinoxes. After undertaking special ritual preparation for a few days beforehand, including fasting, one conducts an eyes closed meditation in sensory silence under the influence of magic mushrooms. Full step-by-step instructions, including how to meditate and how to conduct transcendental self-inquiry, are provided so that you may sacredly prepare and conduct Ritual Meditation in your own home or sacred space. Please remember access to these profound states of consciousness and their experiences are still by the grace of pure consciousness (God), but we can engender that I believe.

Psychedelics work to dissolve our impermanent ego-body consciousness in space and time, shift the seat of consciousness to our eternal higher self, and permit the higher self to merge in Unity awareness with pure consciousness outside of space and time. The ultimate experience is transcendental self-realization in which your window of consciousness shifts to your higher self, and you realize there is in fact nothing that requires healing. Healing, when looked at from the perspective of eternity by your higher self, is seen to be an illusion of the impermanent and imposturous ego consciousness in time.

Transcendental higher self-realization and merging with Unity consciousness, and being able thereby to witness the indescribable bliss-love of Unity consciousness for an eternity, is the most profound awakening and healing experience humans can have. With the seat of consciousness changed to this Unity-transformed higher self, spiritual qualities are afforded their opportunity to innately manifest. By simply resting in the Now, you become effortlessly aware of your higher self's window on consciousness in space and time and the good news is you do not need psychedelics to do this. Meditation is one way to silence the mind and bring it to the Now, and only in the Now will you witness your higher self. Holistically these are simply different aspects of the eternal higher self inside (accessed by meditation) and beyond (accessed by meditation and psychedelic ritual i.e., Ritual Meditation) space and time, which is able to witness itself as all aspects of the higher self, and is also able to witnesses itself (as pure I am awareness without form) merged as Unity awareness of pure consciousness in eternity.

Life's experiences effectively program grooves in our minds, and these can make it hard for us to change our beliefs, emotional responses, and behaviors. The partial promise of psychedelics is to provide accelerated self-inquiry and self-revelation, while creating a more flexible-adaptive mind. Psychedelics, if properly used, are not an escape, but offer us a chance to peek deep inside our minds, and they help reveal the three windows on consciousness (ego, higher self, and pure consciousness) that we humans have been gifted as our birthright. Depending on a person's willingness and capacity to view with honesty and humility their ego's self-image, we are offered powerful tools to assist our self-inquiry, self-revelation, and spiritual awakening, together with elimination of the need to heal.

Introduction

The best way to approach this book is with an open mind and heart. This book will likely shake many of your life assumptions.

One thing is sure. You will receive an education about your human, biological potential to experience altered states of consciousness, as well as your three windows on consciousness (ego, higher self, pure consciousness), how to conduct transcendental self-inquiry, and how you can spiritually awaken and heal. Meaningful knowledge of altered states of consciousness and sacred ritual processes are missing in today's world. This book aims to enlighten, provide you with a sacred ritual process, and then empower you to directly access your higher self and pure consciousness. All of this will help catalyze your spiritual awakening and eliminate any perceived need to heal.

To this end, Chapters 1 to 9 are designed to help you understand the archaeology, art, and science associated with altered states of consciousness. This effectively is an eye-opening and validating exercise that allows you to see the world from which we came, and its awesome achievement in understanding humankind's ability to access higher states of consciousness. And, even more importantly, you will be shown what humanity has forgotten. If science and archaeology is really not your thing, then read the introductions to Chapters 1-9, examine the figures and legends, and then progress to

Introduction

Chapters 9-12 for the Ritual Meditation and Transcendental Self-Realization methods, and the Mind Transformation Plan, and the other important things you need to know about altered states of consciousness, spiritual awakening, and healing.

Chapters 1 to 3 help you see the significance of pyramid alignments in telling sacred time. These dominating solstice and equinox pyramid alignments marked the Sun god religions' most important sacred ritual dates–dates on which sacred rituals dedicated to their Sun gods were performed. Chapters 4 and 5 help you understand how ubiquitous entheogen (psychedelics) use was in the ancient world and you will see how the same sacred ritual process information is symbolically embedded within the pyramid and temple deity art and icons of all these ancient Sun god religions. Importantly, you will come to understand the crucial role that sacredly timed meditation and psychedelics (entheogens) played in achieving higher states of consciousness and in the development of these ancient religions.

Chapters 6 to 8 then help build a bridge between the Sun's cycles of activity and its brainwave voltage supplementing effect on the human brain. When meditation's brain processes are supplemented via sacred rituals, there is a much greater chance to manifest altered states of consciousness than with just meditation alone. In effect, sacred rituals substitute for that rare devotional experience of the true mystic who can experience higher states of consciousness without psychedelics. Sacred rituals therefore provide a shortcut on the path to self-realization and the witnessing of pure consciousness in eternity.

Chapter 9 shows you what altered states of consciousness actually are, and discusses the profound phenomena that can be experienced during these higher states of consciousness. This is explored from the perspectives of transpersonal psychology and the doctrines propounded by the mystic founders of the global religions, as well as my own views on consciousness, transcendental self-realization, and healing. Chapter 10 then provides you with the entire Ritual Meditation process, including its sacred and safety intended set of instructions for use at the solstices and equinoxes.

Ritual Meditation is then integrated into a Mind Transformation Plan in Chapter 11. This combines Ritual Meditation with a healthy and spiritual lifestyle, and daily meditation to help you heal and transform the mind over the yearly time scale. During this, as you progress in transcendental experience and healing, I will show you how to conduct self-inquiry in altered states of consciousness, so that you may permanently shift your window or eye of consciousness to your higher self upon your return to this earthly realm. In experientially awakening to your higher self outside of space and time and conducting self-inquiry, any perceived need to heal will simply vanish. Achieving transcendental self-realization also means that you will escape karmic rebirth after death, and become spiritually immortal. Cognitive self-inquiry, the unlearning of counterproductive beliefs and behaviors, and the learning of new ones are all part of this healing and awakening journey, because you need to know who (ego) it is you will be refuting as your higher self in eternity.

If you do suffer from one or more of the psychological and emotional conditions mentioned above, or if you simply wish to access your higher self and spiritually awaken, then I hope you will find this book of value. If you approach Ritual Meditation in a sacred and safe manner, then positive, safe, and healing experiences should naturally result. That has been my experience. If you would like to explore unique pyramid archaeological discoveries then I hope you will enjoy reading about them here.

If you'd like to explore **Ritual Meditation, Transcendental Self-Inquiry** and **Mind Transformation Coaching** on a **One-to-One basis**, then please contact me via my website **contact form** (http://ritualmeditation.com/contact/). **Please join my blog** (http://ritualmeditation.com/category/blog/) and sign up on my **social media platform** (sign up forms at www.ritualmeditation.com). You can also access a versatile **online meditation calendar** (http://ritualmeditation.com/meditation-calendar/) and know the sun/moon rise or set anywhere in the world, or freely download a **Google Earth pyramid tour** (http://tinyurl.com/qyyp93g) of 450 pyramids and temples and be able to view their sunrises or sunsets and alignments.

Thank you for reading this book. My hope is that you too will be able to realize profound psychological healing and your spiritual awakening, and complete your spiritual journey for self-realization in this lifetime.

My best wishes to you. Thank you.

Carlton Brown

Please connect with Carlton via www.ritualmeditation.com: to enquire about Ritual Meditation coaching, retreats and eLearning, as well as to schedule potential media interviews and speaking engagements, to access meditation resources, and for blog and social media sign-up links.

Table of Contents

Introduction   2

Chapters

1	Ancient Methods for Telling Sacred Time	13
2	Sun God Religions' Sacred Sites Embed Sacred Time Alignments	46
3	Sun God Religions Share the Solstices & Equinoxes as Sacred Time	105
4	Entheogens Generate God Within	148
5	Deity Art & Icons Reveal Priesthood Sacred Ritual Processes	168
6	Sun & Earth Interactions Generate Sacred Time	207
7	Alpha Brainwave Voltages are enhanced by Sacred Time	228
8	The Brain Signatures Of Altered States of Consciousness	243
9	Experiencing Altered States of Consciousness	261
10	The Ritual Meditation Process	298
11	A Mind Transformation Plan for Spiritually Awakening & Healing	339
12	A Bigger Perspective	389

Appendices

Accepting Your Legal, Civil and Moral Responsibilities and Liabilities	408
Biography A Path Less Trodden	411
Dedication	413
Copyright Notice	414
Bibliography & Figure Attributions	416

Chapter 1

Ancient Methods for Telling Sacred Time

Introduction

Before we investigate the sacred real estate of ancient times, we must first understand the concept of timekeeping, and how important this was to ancient societies. However, if you understand how to use the Sun to tell time, and how building architecture can be used to assist this purpose, then you can skip this chapter.

Our ancient ancestors observed the Sun, Moon and stars rise, move across the heavens, and then set every day, and they understood how the Sun's position changed over the course of the year. They built structures—temples and pyramids—to help keep track of these movements and allow accurate time keeping. This was important for society's continued prosperity and to ensure their most important religious ritual and festival dates were secured.

Chapter 1 will introduce concepts of ancient timekeeping and some of the archeological principles used during this project. These archeology methodologies are also discussed to prepare you for Chapter 2. Taken together, these chapters will shed light on those that follow, helping you better understand the archaeology, symbolism, and introductory-level solar-terrestrial physics. This will in turn help to build a bridge from ancient archaeology to the sciences supporting altered states of consciousness.

Earth's Cycles of Rotation in Relation to the Sun

Ancient timekeeping and its imperatives are best comprehended by understanding Earth's three-dimensional rotating, orbiting, and wobbling journey through space relative to the Sun. Concepts like the solstice and equinox, and sunrise and sunset need to be understood beyond dates of the year and times of day. They need to be seen in terms of the Sun's movements along the horizon at sunrise and sunset at these different times of the year.

Earth's three cycles of rotation in space as it orbits the Sun are responsible for the sunrises and sunsets, the seasons, solstices, and equinoxes, and the phenomena called the precession of the equinoxes. These cycles reflect Earth's daily anti-clockwise rotation on its north-south axis and the annual anti-clockwise orbit of the

Sun. The third and less obvious cycle of rotation involves the Earth's very slow clockwise gyroscopic wobbling along its north-south rotational axis every 25,920 years, causing the phenomena known as the precession of equinoxes (apparent counterclockwise movement of the Zodiac in the heavens).

Humankind learned to use these celestial cycles and their earthly phenomena to create calendars, clocks, and stellar observatories. Some of the earliest evidence of timekeeping technology is found in megalithic stone circles dating from before 4000 BCE in Europe, and in ancient sacred temples and pyramids from around the world that date from at least the 3rd millennium BCE. The well-being and prosperity, as well as the religious observances of ancient societies depended on accurate calendars.

A Day & Year Observed from Space

Earth elliptically orbits the Sun in an anti-clockwise manner at an average of 150,000,000 kilometers distance from the Sun, taking 365 ¼ solar days to complete one orbit. As Earth orbits the Sun it rotates anti-clockwise (west to east) on its north-south axis every 24 hours. This makes it appear as if the Sun, Moon, and stars rise in the east and set in the west. Earth's rotational axis is tilted 23.4 degrees relative to Earth's orbital plane around the Sun. This orbital plane is called the solar ecliptic. These daily and annual cycles of rotation are depicted in Figure 1.1.

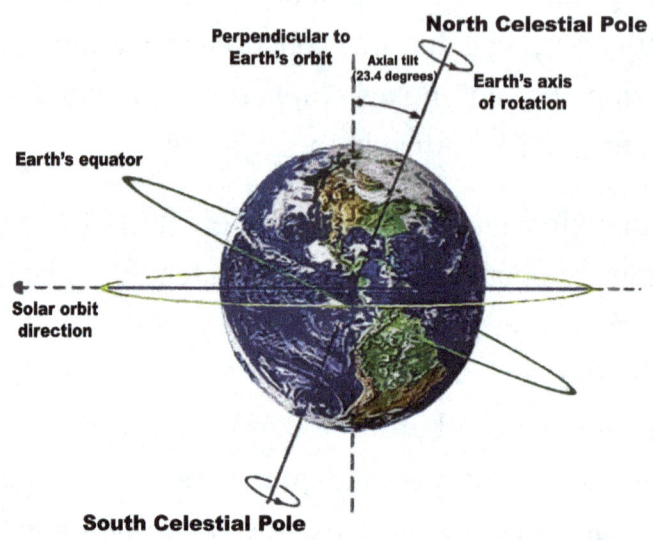

Figure 1.1 Earth's North Pole is tilted 23.4 degrees from the solar system's own North Pole, and rotates counterclockwise about its north south (N-S) rotational axis every 24 hours.[1]

The Solstices & Equinoxes

Earth's N-S axis is tilted 23.4 degrees from the solar system's own celestial N-S axis and currently points toward the star Polaris in the northern sky, maintaining this directional pointing over the course of a day and year. The North Pole therefore faces the Sun to its greatest degree (+23.4⁰) on the summer solstice on the 21st of June, and points the farthest away (-23.4⁰) from the Sun at the winter solstice on the 21st of December. The opposite applies for the southern pole. This generates the longest and shortest days in both the

Northern and Southern hemispheres, with the North experiencing its longest day in June and its shortest day in December, while the reverse applies in the Southern hemisphere. The North Pole is oriented midway between those two solstice extremes on the spring (21st March) and autumn (21st September) equinoxes, providing equal day-night times on the equinoxes (see Figure 1.2).

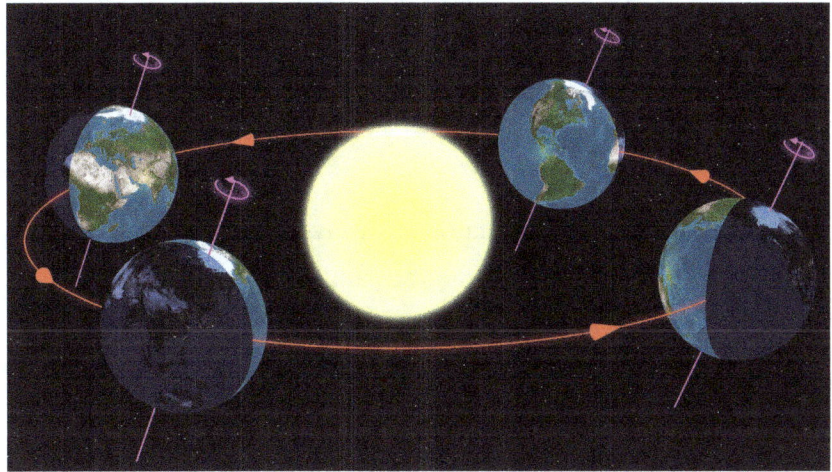

Figure 1.2 Earth orbits the Sun in a heliocentric orbit (slight elliptical orbit) every 365¼ days. The Earth's N-S rotational axis maintains its orientation on the North or Pole Star, close to the north celestial pole as it orbits the Sun.[2]

Combining these two maximal N-S axis tilts from plus to minus 23.4^0 creates a 47-degree V-shape (V47) in the relative N-S axis orientation. I believe this **"V47" degree angular difference was used to symbolize the solstices** in ancient Sun god religion, art, icons, and architecture all over the Sun god world (see Figure 1.3). This will become more obvious in Chapters 2 and 5.

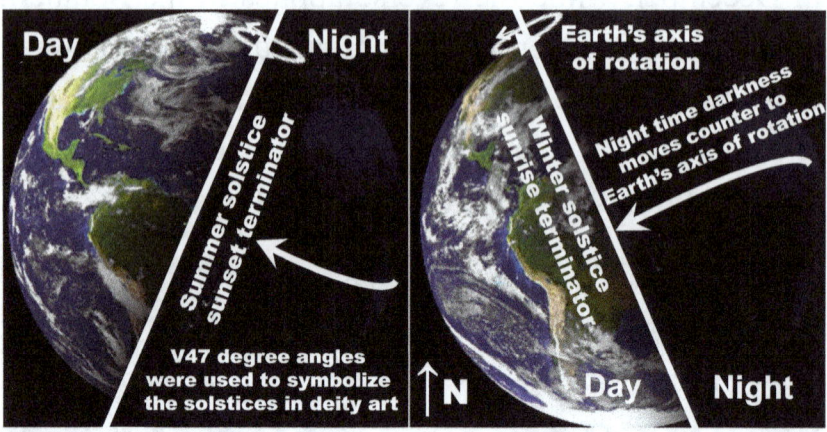

Figure 1.3 The solar terminator line (day-night boundary) as seen from space creates a 47-degree angle between the solstice extremes. The V47 symbol was used to symbolize the solstices as sacred time. **(A)** The summer solstice sunset (21st June in the northern hemisphere), combined with **(B)** the winter solstice sunset (21st December in the northern hemisphere) highlights this solar terminator alignment. The solar terminator angle carved out between these solstice extremes is 47 degrees.[3]

The spring and autumn equinoxes are equally relevant because the Earth's North Pole, which currently points at Polaris, is also pointing in the direction of Earth's orbital path, which is halfway between the N-S axis winter and summer solstice extremes. This is what makes the lengths of day and night equal on the equinoxes. The three-dimensional orientation in space of Earth's N-S axis during the equinoxes is also responsible for aligning the Earth's magnetopauses (funnel-like holes in the Earth's magnetosphere over the poles, which are responsible for the northern and southern lights) with the Sun's interplanetary magnetic field. This will become much clearer and functionally relevant in Chapter 7.

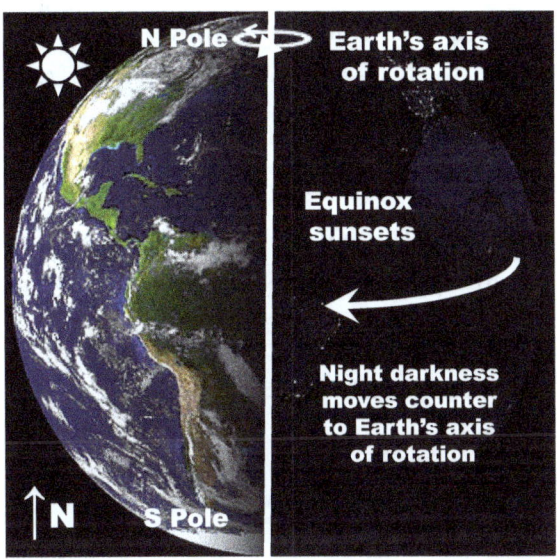

Figure 1.4 The vertical solar terminator lines (day-night boundary) as seen from space on the equinoxes, now match Earth's lines of longitude. The equinox sunsets, on 21st March and 21st September, in the northern and southern hemispheres respectively are depicted.[4]

Sunrise, Sunset and the Midday Sun Over a Year

In viewing the Sun's path over the course of a year, we see that the Sun rises on the eastern horizon and sets on the western horizon. On the winter solstice, the Sun rises and sets at its most southern extremity on those horizons. On the summer solstice it has moved to its most northern extremity on the horizons. Midway between the solstices, or 91 days later, the Sun rises and sets on the spring and autumn equinoxes.

Looking south at the midday Sun, one can observe that its angle of inclination changes in height over the year between the solstice extremes. The Sun is at its peak inclination at midday on the summer solstice and at its lowest inclination on the winter solstice. If one were standing on the equator at midday over the year, it would appear as if Earth rocked backwards and forwards ($+/-23.4°$) on its North-South axis over the course of the year (see Figure 1.6).

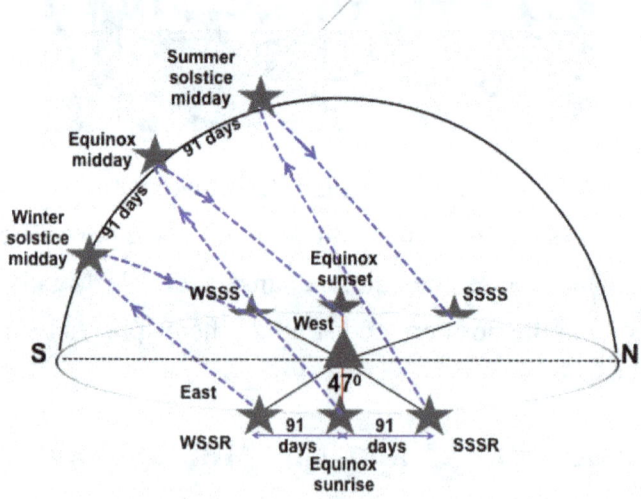

Figure 1.5 From the vantage point of the Northern Hemisphere, Earth's daily rotation and annual orbit around the Sun are observed on Earth as predictable movements of the Sun along the eastern and western sunrise and sunset horizons. As the sun rises

in the east it follows an arc path (solar ecliptic) across the sky to the south, reaching its daily zenith at midday, then descends toward sunset on the western horizon. The Sun rises at its most southerly point on the horizon on the winter solstice (WSSR) and at its most northerly point on the summer solstice (SSSR). If one were standing on the equator the horizon angle between the solstice sunrise/set extremes would be 47 degrees. This combined solstice extreme angle increases the further north or south we go from the equator.[5]

The Solar Terminator or Day-Night Boundary

Given that the Earth is a sphere (more or less) orbiting the Sun, at any one time half of the planet is covered in daylight, while the other half is in darkness. Observed from space, there is a zone of transition between day and night, referred to as the solar terminator. We observe this on Earth as sunrise (dawn) and sunset (dusk) as the Sun rises or falls on the horizon.

Ancient Methods for Telling Sacred Time

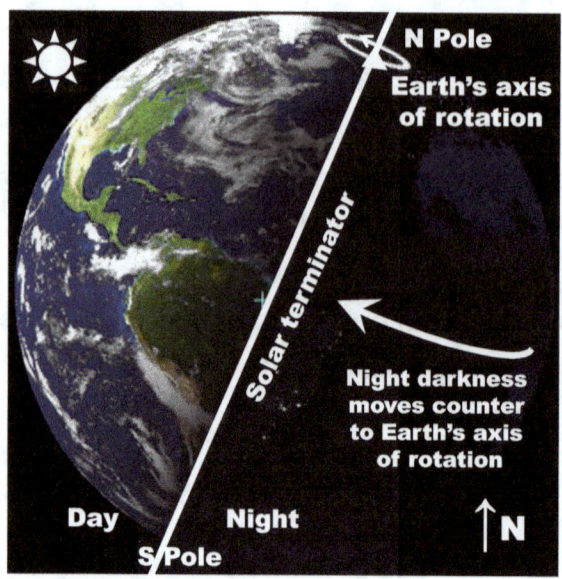

Figure 1.6 Solar terminator as observed from space: the solar terminator (day-night boundary) as observed from space on the northern hemisphere's summer solstice sunset, and the southern hemisphere's winter solstice sunset. The Sun after its long day arcing across the sky sets in the west, with darkness chasing it. Seen from space Earth rotates anticlockwise, yielding an apparent clockwise movement of the solar terminator line across Earth's surface. The solar terminator is experienced as dusk and dawn, around sunset or sunrise respectively.[6]

When observed from space this zone of day-night transition changes its orientation during the year from plus to minus 23.4 degrees relative to the celestial poles (two imaginary points in the night sky where the Earth's axis of rotation, indefinitely extended, intersects the celestial sphere). It is at its maximum angle of plus 23.4 degrees (from celestial north) during the winter solstice sunrise and summer solstice sunset (see Figure 1.4), and vertically aligned with the celestial poles at the equinoxes. The terminator line moves across the sky at approximately 1,600 kilometers per hour at the equator and close to zero kilometers per hour at the poles as the Earth rotates. Solar terminators reveal some very interesting electromagnetic physics associated with ionization/deionization processes in the upper atmosphere. This will be reviewed in Chapter 7 and its relevance to rituals is in Chapters 8-9.

Ancient Calendars Were Utilized By Religion and Agriculture

Organizing time and creating order from the chaos of the ancient world was critically important for ancient societies. These societies were dedicated to knowing important times of the year, and built temples and pyramids that have survived until this day to serve that purpose. Knowing when one solar year ended and another began was crucial to prosperity, and was a key pursuit of priesthoods for millennia.

The commonly held view is that solstice and equinox alignments were related to timekeeping that informed the agricultural calendar. In my view this needs to be expanded to also embrace a religious purpose, i.e., the securing of sacred time. After all, these pyramids and temples were first and foremost important places of religion, and the dates captured by the two most common pyramid and temple alignments (i.e., equinoxes and solstices) represent the Sun god religions' most important sacred ritual dates.

Nonetheless, calendars serving agricultural utility were also critically important. After all, a well-managed community agricultural cycle optimized crop yields, created trade surpluses, maximized the tributes and taxes paid, and permitted the royalty-priesthood partnership that controlled society to prosper. Prosperity allowed these societies to expand their territorial domains and create great empires, which in turn allowed the religions to expand their influence.

Invariably, a 360-day (lunar-solar) or 365-day (tropical or solar) calendar existed alongside a second, agriculturally biased calendar (such as Egypt's record of the annual flooding of the Nile, or the Mesoamerican 260-day calendar).

Temple and pyramid alignments permitted the timekeeping observer a date-fix on the sunrise/sunset horizon, which enabled the observer to accurately determine the important sacred and agricultural dates. It also enabled the time-keeping observer to make adjustments to recalibrate the 360 or 365-day calendars to 365¼ days per year, while also reflecting the precession of the equinoxes.

For example, Uaxactun (Guatemala) offered the time-keeping observer an opportunity to use key site features to accurately tell yearly time, namely the solstices and equinoxes, by standing on the central plaza pyramid platform and looking due east (see Figure 1.9) at sunrise. My observations at Uaxactun gave me the idea that the three queens' pyramids at Giza could be used for a similar purpose.

Figure 1.7 Uaxactun (Guatemala). **(A)** The central plaza platform faces due east. One can observe the sunrise behind the three eastern marker platforms (see B). **(B)** Three marker platforms sit between the eastern sunrise and central plaza platform. The platform to the left marks the summer solstice sunrise (SSSR), the central platform marks the equinox sunrises, and the platform to the right marks the winter solstice sunrise (WSSR).[7]

Annual cycles ended and began at the winter solstice. This was invariably associated with society-wide celebrations and stories relating to the death of the old Sun and its rebirth 3-4 days later on the 25th of December. The celebration of this winter solstice festival was even more widespread than is discussed in this book, which focuses on four ancient Sun god religions: those of Egypt, Mesoamerica, South America, and India.

Introductory Archaeology Concepts

Circles and standing rows of massive stones are found the world over. In addition there are the pyramids and temples of Egypt, Sudan, Central and South America, the ziggurats of Mesopotamia (today's Iraq), the ancient temples of India, and the pyramids and temples found in China and the rest of East Asia. The majority of these sites were once sacred places of worship and the epicenters of communities, states, and empires. Not much else remains of the societies that built these structures, and even less is known of the rituals and other practices that consecrated and enlivened these sacred sites.

By *sacred*, I mean that these sites (sacred spaces) offered a place and a time where humankind–especially the ancient religion's priesthood, leaders, and their societies' elites–could directly communicate with the divine or supernatural realms. They achieved this communion by inducing altered or transcendental states of consciousness, using sacred rituals. These sacred ritual processes have become lost in the mists of time.

So how did this archaeology project begin? In addition to a lifelong interest in pyramid cultures (especially Egypt) I read, while vacationing in Egypt, *The Path of the Pole* by the maverick professor Charles Hapgood.[8] Hapgood's work was endorsed by Albert Einstein as a physically plausible mechanism for causing periodic global cataclysms, which Hapgood saw as the mechanism driving evolutionary change in plant and animal species. His book discussed potential global catastrophe mechanisms linked to partial Earth crust displacement and periodic deglaciation/glaciation of the planet. It reviewed paleomagnetic and carbon dating data and concluded that large movements of the magnetic poles had occurred three times in the last 120,000 years.

Hapgood's work inspired me to look more closely at global catastrophes, the reality of which is supported by pre-biblical flood myths from around the world, as well as stories of lost civilizations and evidence from pyramid cultures that were in existence during the past 12,000 years. When I returned home from my Egyptian vacation, I bought a plastic globe and started sticking pins in it to create a global pyramid map. I also spent considerable time examining the locations of the pyramids, using satellite imagery.

Interestingly, while investigating one question (were Giza, Teotihuacan, Xi'an's and other important pyramids built before or after the melting of the northern ice caps, which supposedly coincided with the last

Ancient Methods for Telling Sacred Time

magnetic pole movement?), certain relationships emerged. Before I knew it, the adventure had begun. My research involved using satellite and aerial imagery, public knowledge and image databases, and scientific publication databases, along with perhaps 150 pyramid, temple and megalithic site visits conducted over two plus decades. Once I had realized the connection between the equinox and solstice alignments of the pyramids (which were clearly linked to important religious ritual and festival dates), I was led to probe the connection between the Sun and the human brain.

Why write about this now? I hope that what I have observed, the provisional conclusions I have drawn, the theories I have formed, and the sacred ritual processes I have discovered may be useful to others. This story also needs to be told because many Sun god religions around the Mediterranean, in the Americas and Europe were eradicated.

The archaeological findings, together with Sun god temple art and icons, reveal the sacred ritual processes of four Sun god religions. These religions were practiced across three different continents during a time span of some 5,000 years. I believe these lost sacred ritual traditions need to become part of our common heritage once again. Humanity could relearn how to use this knowledge to better the world for all, rather than leaving it to the minds and machinations of the few.

Concepts of Archaeoastronomy

Now that we understand how the Earth sits in the cosmos, we need to understand how ancient peoples used this knowledge to observe and measure time. Archaeoastronomy is the field of science that enables us to study ancient methods of timekeeping.

Archaeoastronomy involves the study of how the architectural design of ancient buildings reflects astronomical alignments (Sun, Moon, planets, and stars), celestial lore, mythologies, religions, and the worldviews of ancient cultures. Through this lens, we can see that ancient buildings had secondary functions as calendars, clocks, and stellar observatories. This multidisciplinary, hybrid science functionally embraces architecture, archaeology, astronomy, surveying, navigation, mapping, geomancy, urban planning, calendar systems, cartography, concepts of time and space, and mathematics (especially geometry and counting systems).

For this project I have employed basic and commonly used archaeoastronomy tools and principles to investigate sacred archaeology, in particular the defining of sacred space, sacred time, and sacred ritual specifications at each site. These catch-all categories effectively define the major sub-categories of the religions' sacred ritual processes, which permits us to make standardized comparisons across the different religions. By categorizing sacred rituals in such a manner, one is able to effectively reverse-engineer the entire ritual process, and bring it back to life. This book contains a review of four different Sun god religions, and identifies common elements associated with the process for attaining altered states of consciousness (ASC). These sacred ritual processes were developed by the Sun god religion priesthoods of ancient Egypt, pre-Colombian Central and South America, and southern India, and formed the basis of these religions.

Temple art caught my attention when I realized that it was being used to embed sacred ritual symbols or information. This extended to a basic awareness of deity-associated iconography, e.g., statues, ceramics, pottery, textiles, and murals carved in stone associated with gods and goddesses, ritual utilities, and leaders. Then I realized that the same thematic information was being displayed in the same context around the globe. We have been left important information about the sacred ritual process, and we can decode this information if we approach the investigation in a new way (see immediately below).

Sacred Rituals Embrace Sacred Space and Sacred Time

Every sacred ritual with transcendental intent shares some common components: a person or group of people, a location or space where the ritual is conducted, a time

Ancient Methods for Telling Sacred Time

of the day and year when the ritual is conducted, and specific actions and/or sacraments taken during the ritual. This can be reduced to sacred space, sacred time, and sacred ritual specifications. Each Sun god religion can be viewed using this same investigational framework.

Sun god temples and pyramids (sacred spaces) were important places for the conduct of sacred ritual, and were by and large under the control of priesthoods. Priesthoods of the ancient Sun god religions developed sacred ritual processes for accessing altered states of consciousness. They also developed their religion's deity structures, cosmologies, and mythologies. They used temple art and icons to embed sacred ritual information, which could then be revealed to those undertaking sacred rituals. The information imparted would embrace the art symbolisms, and most likely information contained in the cosmology and mythology of the religion to create a composite whole, or a map of how to access altered states of consciousness on the day of the ritual.

In order to achieve altered states of consciousness one would need to partake in sacred ritual processes. The common theme relating to sacred ritual is the implicit modulation of brain function through a disciplined and coordinated process. The purpose of the ritual process was to modulate the specific parts of the brain that support altered states of consciousness. Science also tells us what external factors have utility in modulating brain function, and what parts of the brain play key roles in generating deep meditative states and altered states of consciousness (this is detailed in Chapters 7 and 8). When doing archeology, I look in the sacred spaces for "brain-modulating" symbols or features that delineate sacred time (i.e., solstices, equinoxes, sunrise, and sunset) or help define how a sacred ritual was conducted (that is, via meditation, body alignments, sensory silence, or hallucinogens).

The brain modulating symbols associated with the Sun gods or goddesses depicted include (see chapter 5 for more detail):

a) *Solstice symbols.* The V47 degree angle was used as a solstice symbol. It served to outline and proportion deity art and was a key design feature in pyramid-temple superstructures for a minority of pyramids, but the majority of India's Divya Desam temples.

b) Sunrise/set symbols were commonly depicted as the horizon deities in art and mythology. Examples include Horus and Hathor in the religion of Ra, Surya and the Ashvin twins in Hindu mythology, and Viracocha and Inti in the Inca and pre-Inca religions.

c) *Earth magnetic field symbols* (i.e., serpents) were associated with the equinoxes, and generally seen alongside the V47 degree angle solstice symbol.

d) *Brain chemicals were symbolized b*y hallucinogens derived from plants, fungi, and frogs. The sacred pink lotus of India, the blue (Egypt) and white (Maya) water lilies a source of dopamine, and psilocybin magic mushrooms, san pedro and peyote, Anadenanthera colubrina (vilca), hallucinogenic toads as providers of 5-hydroxytryptamine-2a serotonin, both critical to the meditation process and accessing altered states of consciousness.

e) Meditation was depicted by the seated posture of deities or a leader, such as Hinduism's Trimurti Sun gods meditating on an upside down pink lotus, or pharaoh seated facing the winter solstice sunrise with his hands on his knees (i.e., as seen at the Temple of Rameses II in Abu Simbel, or the Colossi of Memnon at the Temple of Amenhotep III in today's Luxor).

Sacred space is the physical structure (temple, pyramid, and/or inner sanctums or shrines) used for conducting sacred ritual. This could include caves, underground tunnels, pyramid chambers, or inner temple sanctums where one can achieve sensory silence. Sacred space also includes the dimensions of the physical structure, which might confer specific acoustic properties useful for inducing the brain to generate specific brainwave frequencies. Such spaces would include the angled walls of the Maya Ball courts (where the legendary Hero Twins were said to enter the Mayan underworld), the Kings Chamber of the Great Pyramid at Giza,[9] and the angled circular embankment surrounding the stone circle at Arbor Low in Britain.

Figure 1.8 Examples of sacred space for the conduct of sacred ritual. **(A)** Grutas de Lanquín is a large limestone cave system located one kilometer west of Lanquín (Guatemala), and was used by ancient Mayan shamans. **(B)** The pyramid of Khafre has its main pyramid chamber centrally located beneath the pyramid. Tourist voices are filtered by the descending passageways, which seem to act as waveguides. It's possible to detect auditory and body resonances within the main chamber from this filtered sound.[10]

Sacred space also embraced secondary considerations, such as volcano and mountain solstice sunrise/set alignments, access to bodies of water, and natural defenses.

Ancient Methods for Telling Sacred Time

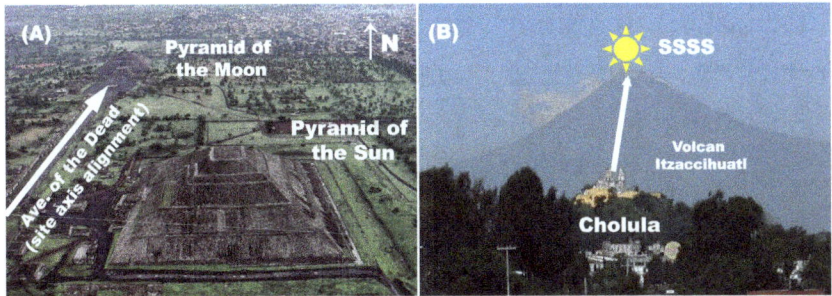

Figure 1.9 Pyramid site plans and alignments typical of ancient Mesoamerica. **(A)** Teotihuacan's (Mexico) site plan aligns with the "Avenue of the Dead". This site is aligned with 15.5 degrees east of north. This Avenue of the Dead may have been aligned with Earth's magnetic axis at the time of its construction. **(B)** The Cholula site (Mexico) aligns with the summer solstice sunset (SSSS), and on this day the sun sets behind the nearby Itzaccihuat volcano to its northwest.[11]

Sacred time refers to the time of day or year, or time of the cycle of a specific celestial body (Sun, Moon, or planet) used to determine when a sacred ritual would be undertaken. This timing would be indicated by the overall site plan, or specific pyramid-temple alignment to the solstice and/or equinox sunrise and sunset horizons, as well as by the V47 degree solstice and serpent equinox symbols in the temple art and icons of the Sun god religions.

Sacred ritual refers to the actions of the divining person (shaman, priest, priestess, or other divine leader) undertaken to specifically achieve transcendental or altered states of consciousness. This could include meditation, ingesting hallucinogens, drumbeats and rattles (as used by shamans for acoustic entrainment), prayer and invocation, repetitive behaviors (chanting, dancing), as well as combinations of some or all of these.

Sacred Site Alignments & their Timekeeping Purpose

Ancient Sun god worshipping societies aligned their temples, pyramids, and urban areas using a number of common alignment principles. Of the 450 Sun god temples and pyramids reviewed for this book, half were aligned with the equinox sunrises and sunsets. Nearly one-third utilized an alignment with the winter solstice sunrise (WSSR) and its corresponding summer solstice sunset (SSSS).

They also held their most important sacred ritual-festivals associated with the Sun gods on these same dates. One could say there was an alignment fingerprint, which included a Sun god temple or pyramid aligned to or demarcating the equinox and/or solstice sunrise or sunset. This alignment principle permitted the accurate prediction of ritual-festival dates, and permitted calendars to be reset for accurate timekeeping.

Common features highlighting sacred space and time elements include the *cardinal alignment* (north-south-east-west; henceforth NSEW), which means that a structure is aligned with the Earth's north-south axis of rotation. This is ideally suited for heavenly observations (Sun, Moon, planet, and star rises, zeniths, and sets), while also allowing one to know the equinox sunrises and sunsets. This is particularly evident with Egyptian Old Dynasty pyramids and India's ancient Hindu temples. *Solstice alignments* are also frequently evident; Egypt's New Kingdom temples and Mesoamerican and South American pyramids were typically aligned with the winter solstice sunrises (WSSR) and summer solstice sunsets (SSSS).

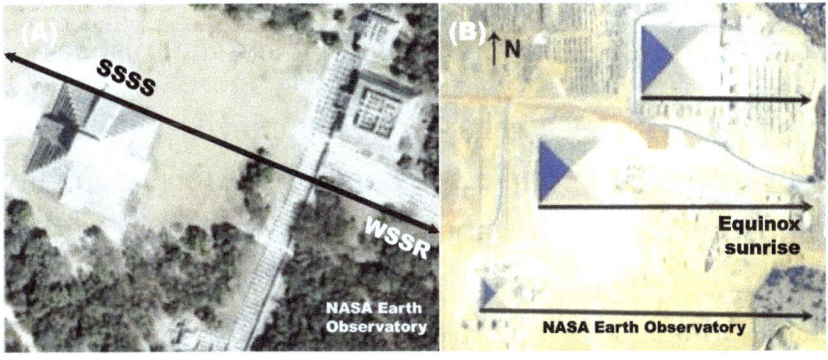

Figure 1.10 Equinox & Solstice alignments. **(A)** The pyramid of Kukulkan and its nearby structures at Chichen Itza (Mexico) align with the winter solstice sunrise (WSSR) and summer solstice sunset (SSSS). **(B)** The main pyramids at Giza (Cairo, Egypt) align with the equinox sunrises and sunsets, while also demarcating the solstice sunrises using a vantage point on the SE corner of the Great Pyramid over the eastern facing queen's pyramids (see Figure 1.14).[12]

Ancient Methods for Telling Sacred Time

The winter solstice sunrise (WSSR) is on December 21 in the Northern Hemisphere and on June 21 in the Southern Hemisphere. This represents the end of the old Sun and the birth of the new Sun. This time was celebrated universally as a sacred moment of the year when the portals to the spirit world became more accessible. This alignment is commonly observed with the Egyptian New Kingdom temples and Mesoamerican and South American temples, pyramids, and pyramid platforms. Only 10 percent of the 108 ancient Hindu temples dedicated to Lord Vishnu (*Divya Desams*) utilize the WSSR/SSSS alignment. But they reveal something else that is highly symbolic of the solstices.

India's Divya Desams frequently utilized a 47-degree V-shaped (V47) temple spire and/or flat-topped, highly ornate pyramid-like structure over the main temple gateways (gopurams). This V47 structural outline is the same angle used in the pyramids at Meroe (Sudan) and Meidum (Egypt), and in Mayan arch design at Tikal! The ubiquitous V47 angle was, I believe, used to symbolize the solstice. As much as three-quarters of these Hindu Sun god temples (Divya Desams) share this architectural feature.

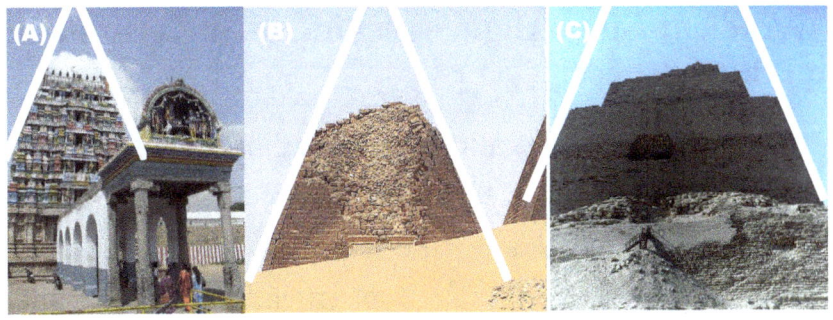

Figure 1.11 Examples of V47 degree solstice symbolizing angles (white lines) in sacred site construction. **(A) The** Brahma temple, like 75% of all Divya Desam temples in India, utilizes the V47 degree solstice symbolizing angle for the gopuram's superstructure outline. **(B)** The winter solstice sunrise-aligned site Meroe (Sudan) contains pyramids with V47 degree solstice angles in their superstructures. **(C)** The NSEW aligned Meidum site (Egypt) utilizes the V47 degree solstice-depicting angle in its inner pyramid superstructure design. Collectively, this knowledge of the equinoxes and solstices delineates sacred time.[13]

Alignment with Earth's magnetic axis involved an alignment of the urban plan, temple, or pyramid with Earth's magnetic axis. The magnetic North and South Pole wander over time, with the magnetic North Pole oriented 11 degrees east of true north today. The principle of geomancy reflects the flow of conscious energy between the Earth and human life. Magnetic axis alignments best facilitate geomancy's biological-brain effects around the equinoxes.

Ancient Sites Align with the Solar Terminator on the Solstices

A common observation is the regional clustering of sacred sites within very narrow geographical ranges. These are delineated by the passage of the day-night boundary (solar terminator) overhead, on the winter solstice sunrise and summer solstice sunset. If we look from space and observe the day-night boundary as it sweeps across the sky at the winter solstice sunrise and summer solstice sunset, we see that between 60-97 percent of a region/religion's sacred sites sit within a 2-7 minute wide geographical bandwidth. This bandwidth sits at an angle of +23.4 degrees over distances of 100 to 1,000 kilometers. This is depicted for each region in Figures 2.2 - 2.5.

Methodology for Sacred Site Observations

Regional Sacred Site Alignment

The methods used to study the alignments of sacred sites included assembling data on the sites from a range of public sources, including their geographical coordinates, accepted dates of construction, and periods of use, as well as a review of scientific knowledge and image databases whenever possible. These sites were viewed using satellite imagery, accepting the potential for parallax errors (+/− 3-5 degrees).

Ancient Methods for Telling Sacred Time

Sacred sites and dominant pyramids, temples, and platforms usually associated with the central plaza area were viewed to check alignments, with a review of other online and academic sources (site maps, plans, and publications), as a double check where possible. I have also visited many sites over the years. Alignment points may become obvious within seconds of centering yourself at these sites, where your vista is largely the same as that of the priests or priestesses who were present all those years ago.

In fact, of the 450 sites examined, representing four Sun god religions spanning more than 5,000 years, half were equinox-aligned and nearly one-third were solstice aligned. While a civilization clearly benefits by maintaining a calendar to ensure agricultural prosperity, the fact remains that these dates also coincided with sacred rituals and festivals dedicated to each religion's Sun gods.

Marking the Solstices and Equinoxes

Marking the solstices and equinoxes typically utilized a building's main foundational/structural lines extended to the sunrise/set horizon to tell that time of the year. This requires knowledge of the Sun's movements over the course of the year, particularly the Sun's position when touching the horizon (sunrise/sunset) as it moves from its northern (summer solstice) to southern (winter solstice) extremities over the course of the year. The key starting-point was the conducting of sunrise and sunset observations by priesthood timekeepers and the temple architects. Once the solstices are marked, one reaches the equinox ninety-one days later and the summer solstice yet another ninety-one days (more or less) further on. This knowledge effectively formed the basis of the solar and/or solar-lunar calendars.

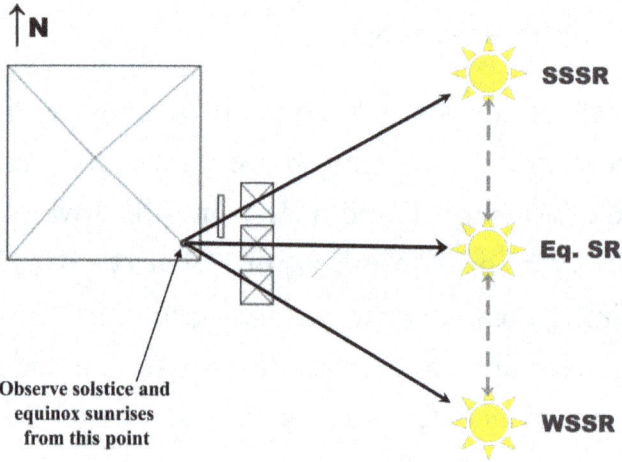

Figure 1.12 Progression of the sunrise during the year observed at Giza (Cairo). Standing on the SE corner of Khufu's pyramid at the height of the three east-facing queen's pyramids permits one to track the sunrise through the year. This can be used to determine the winter solstice sunrise (WSSR), equinox sunrises, and summer solstice sunrise (SSSR).[14]

Imaginary lines drawn perpendicular to an aligned site and the horizon mark the sunrises and sunsets relative to the solstices and equinoxes, enabling the observer to tell the time of the year. This solar horizon marking was important because these ancient cultures typically used either a lunisolar or a solar calendar of either 360 or 365 days. Leap years, or use of a lunisolar calendar, and the precession of the equinoxes meant that the calendars needed to be adjusted relatively frequently to ensure accurate timekeeping over the long term. The alignments afforded the priestly timekeepers the opportunity to assist their leaders in helping to make their societies prosperous.

Gnomons (the vertical piece of a sundial) were also used in ancient times to determine the cardinal points (NSEW). Site planning would have taken time and likely required collaboration between astronomer (often a priest) and architect, both of whom would likely contribute key elements to the sacred space and time planning.

Time-keeping was not a precise art, and the sites show a degree of variability with non-error explanations playing a key role. Anthony Aveni, a pioneering archaeoastronomer, cautions researchers about pinning down any alignment with great precision (+/- 7-10 degrees) because one cannot be sure where the observer stood relative to the sacred site being used as the reference point.[15]

For the purposes of this book, a site was not considered aligned if it was outside +/- 3-4 degrees; in general most sites were within 0-2 degrees of the relevant dates. Additionally, geographical restrictions (e.g., the Andes Mountains or Theban Mountains in Luxor), specific horizon features (e.g., volcano craters), and/or weather (e.g., the likelihood of clouds or mist on the winter morning) might have necessitated a switch, such as marking the winter solstice *sunset* rather than *sunrise*. These observations were a key part of my data reconciliation process.

Other less permanent structural features used for creating visual alignments atop or as part of the sacred site or aligned structure could have been used to further refine observations. I experienced this myself at Tonina in Mexico (see Figure 1.15). When I visited Tonina in 2011, I had to trample the grass down around the marker stones on the plaza platform to make them visible. These reminded me of the mini-megaliths seen in the European stone circles.

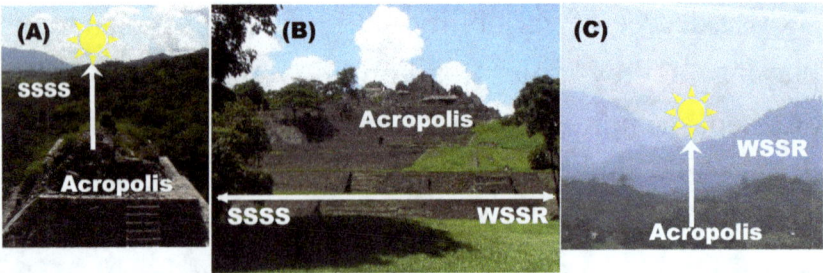

Figure 1.13 Tonina in the state of Chiapas (Mexico). **(A)** Tonina's main plaza platform, situated to the south of the acropolis, has its long axis facing the WSSR and SSSS. Facing east one can watch

the WSSR between the hill cleft–a frequent observation with Mesoamerican sites. The plaza platform has two marker stones on its upper surface which further refine the solstice alignment. **(B)** Looking north from the main plaza platform to Tonina's WSSR and SSSS-facing acropolis one is confronted by a pyramid-like hill as the site's main feature.[16]

If a site marks a winter solstice sunrise, the viewer can turn his or her head 180 degrees to face the corresponding summer solstice sunset (geographical restrictions permitting). Ergo, a site aligned according to the winter solstice sunrise is also aligned to the summer solstice sunset. Likewise a site aligned at 25+/– degrees NE would permit a solstice sunrise observation by turning 90 degrees, or perpendicular, to that alignment. This reflects the common alignment of 14-17 and 25 degrees observed with Mesoamerican town plans, and 25 degrees for some of Egypt's New Kingdom pyramids (which might indicate geomancy principles were used in site planning).

In Chapter 2 we'll examine these regional maps and solar terminator bands and an array of ancient sites from the four religious epochs–a picture, after all, is worth a thousand words.

Chapter 2

Sun God Religions' Sacred Sites Embed Sacred Time Alignments

Introduction

We'll now move straight into the regional sacred real estate maps, followed by a select overview of some of each region's more famous Sun god sacred sites and their timekeeping alignments. A brief historical overview will be provided for each ancient culture, followed by their site alignment summaries. Further detail on each Sun god religion will be provided in Chapter 3.

Regional Maps

Mesoamerican Sites (Maya, Olmec, and Aztec Civilizations)

This Mesoamerican site review considers more than 80 sacred sites, including Tikal, Palenque, Chichen Itza, Uxmal, Calakmul, Tonina, Teotihuacan, and Monte Alban. The Maya sites are mostly located in Guatemala and Mexico's southeast and Yucatan Peninsula (see

Figure 2.2), whereas the Olmec sites are found near modern Mexico City and in Mexico's south and southwest (see Figure 2.2(A)). The Olmecs largely preceded the Maya civilization, with evidence of overlap.

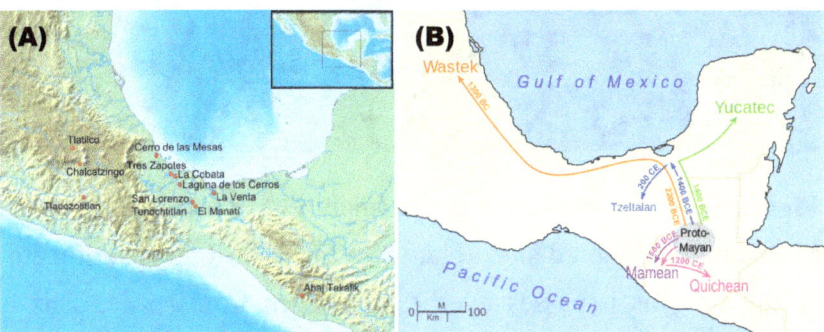

Figure 2.1 Olmec and Maya regional maps. **(A)** Olmec sites are found near Mexico City and to the south of Mexico. **(B)** The Mayan geographical distribution in Central America highlights the possible origination of the Maya around the Guatemalan Highlands, spreading out from there as the civilization developed.[17]

Figure 2.2 highlights a regional map of the ancient Mayan sites. Between 60% and 85% of these sites exist within a 7 to 15 minute wide solar terminator bandwidth, which is 900km in length.

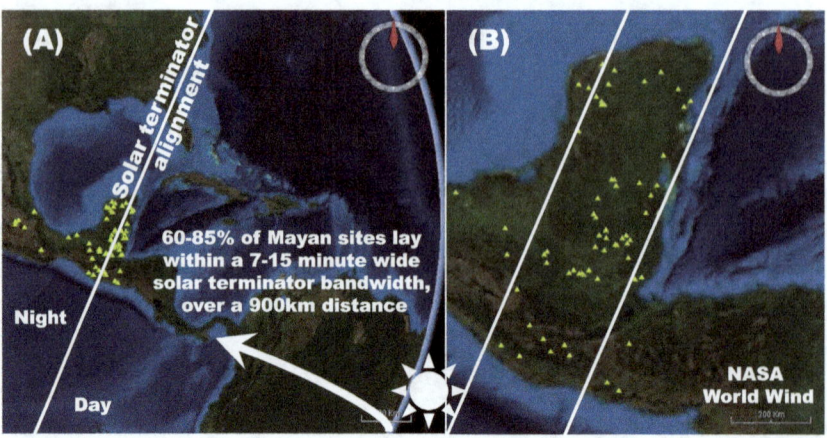

Figure 2.2 Mesoamerican sites (mainly Mayan). **(A)** Ancient Mesoamerican sacred sites relative to the WSSR solar terminator (white line) as it passes overhead, as seen from space. This is observed as dusk-dawn on Earth. **(B)** Between 60 and 85 percent of the important Mayan sites fall within a time bandwidth 7-15 minutes wide respectively, delineated by the solar terminator's shadow on the Earth's surface as seen from space on the winter solstice. This means these sites would have experienced the same peaks of enhanced, extremely low frequency electromagnetic wave fields overhead on the winter solstice sunrise and summer solstice sunset.[18]

South American Sites (Pre-Incan, Incan)

Moving south of the equator to the pre-Inca Kingdoms and the Inca Empire in South America, we flip our perspective to orient with the South Pole; the winter solstice sunrise in the Northern Hemisphere now becomes the summer solstice sunrise in the Southern Hemisphere.

With the exception of Tiwanaku, Sacsayhuamán, Machu Picchu, and Ollantaytambo, which belong to their own narrow terminator band, some thirty-five of thirty-six ancient sites reviewed lie within a <4-minute wide solar terminator bandwidth stretching over 1,000 kilometers along the coast of Peru. These include the likes of Nazca's adobe pyramid cluster at Cahuachi overlooking the Nazca lines, and Peru's ancient solstice-marking pyramids and temple complexes such as Pachacamac (Huacas del Sol and la Luna), Caral (5,000 year-old pyramids), Las Haldas (pyramid mounds), Napena adobe pyramid complex, Chan and Tucume (pyramids).

I'm not suggesting that here, or in any other region, all the sites were contemporaneously active communities, but there certainly was significant overlap in their use by local and regional societies over long periods of time. This regional alignment of sacred sites is depicted in Figure 2.3(B).

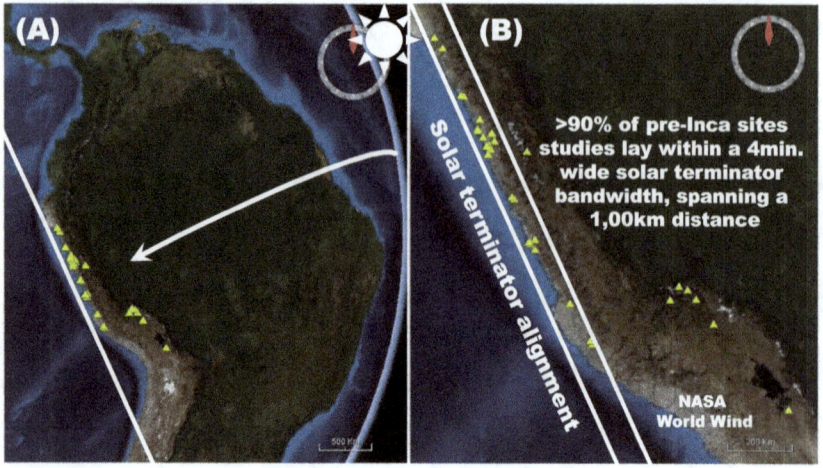

Figure 2.3 Inca and pre-Inca sacred sites of South America. **(A)** The winter solstice solar terminator over South America tracks the Peruvian coastline. Note the change in orientation of the WSSR from southeast to northeast for the southern hemisphere. **(B)** Thirty-five out of thirty-six of the major sites reviewed in this project exist within a <4-minute wide time bandwidth delineated by the WSSR and SSSS solar terminator as it passes overhead, over a distance of more than 1,000km.[19]

It can also be reasonably argued that the alignment of these sites is in large part caused by the geographical challenge of the Andes mountain range and by the shape of the valleys, which provide a resource-rich habitat. However, when compared with other Sun god religions displaying this same cluster alignment feature, I believe we need to withhold the temptation to rapidly reject this regional alignment observation. Both Central and South American Sun god religions followed major fault lines and volcanoes and were located in global lightning centers (regions of high lightning activity).

Additionally, the majority of these sites mark the solstices with their more important temples (huacas) and pyramids, just as we see in Mesoamerica. The third level of detail (discussed in chapter 4), in addition to regional and local alignments, comprises their religious icons and art, which depict embedded sacred time symbols (V47 degree solstice-depicting angles; a serpent as the equinox), as well as hallucinogen symbols. These three levels of solstice marking and symbolism (regional and individual site alignments, art, and icons) is a common fingerprint of Sun god religions.

Egypt's Old & New Kingdom Sites

A unified Egyptian kingdom was founded circa 3150 BCE by King Menes, heralding the beginning of Egypt's dynastic empire, which lasted for nearly three millennia and encompassed thirty dynasties. The Old Kingdom period (c. 2700–2200 BCE) had its capital at Memphis, just south of modern Cairo. The Middle Kingdom of Egypt (c. 2000–1700 BCE) comprised the 11th and 12th dynasties, which ruled from Thebes (Luxor) and el-Lisht (south of Cairo), respectively. The Old and Middle Kingdom dynasties are credited with constructing many of Egypt's major pyramid complexes in Lower (northern) Egypt.

The New Kingdom (c. 1550–1070 BCE) commenced with the 18th dynasty. Egypt's capital was then relocated from Memphis to Thebes (Luxor). Some of Egypt's most famous pharaohs lived during this period, including Hatshepsut, Thutmose III, Akhenaten, Tutankhamun, and Rameses II. The period saw a shift from pyramid to temple building. It was also noteworthy for expansion into Nubia (Sudan) and increased trade and communication networks beyond Egypt's borders.

Egypt fell to the Persians in 525 BCE, and was ruled by them until 404 BCE. The last native ruling dynasty was the 30th (380-343 BCE). Egypt was again conquered by the Persians in 343 BCE, and then by Alexander the Great a decade later.

My study of Egypt reviewed 114 temples and 103 pyramids. I discovered that more than 90 percent of Old & Middle Kingdom pyramids lie between Cairo (Memphis) and Faiyum, some eighty kilometers southwest of Cairo. The temples mostly belong to the New Kingdom, which was centered at Thebes (Luxor) and extended south to Abu Simbel, near Lake Nasser (Middle and Upper Egypt). Other than the Meroe site, Sudan was not specifically studied. These pyramid and temple distributions are highlighted in Figure 2.4. More than 90 percent of pyramids cluster under a winter solstice sunrise day-night boundary bandwidth barely two minutes wide.

Sun God Religions' Sacred Sites Embed Sacred Time Alignments

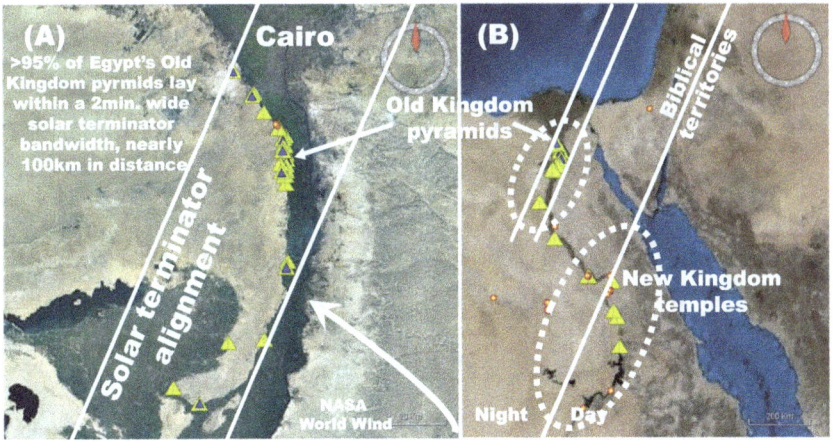

Figure 2.4 Ancient Egypt's sacred site distribution. **(A)** Ancient Egyptian pyramids (yellow triangles = large pyramids, blue triangles = satellite pyramids) shown relative to the winter solstice sunrise solar terminator line. Ninety-five percent of the approximately 130 Old Kingdom pyramids lie within a very tight solar terminator bandwidth <2 minutes wide (yellow lines), and over a distance of 80km from Cairo to Faiyum. **(B)** Moving further south to the New Kingdom, the majority of temples (red-yellow circles) surveyed fall within a second bandwidth approximately five minutes wide. Interestingly, this solar terminator line embraces sacred sites over the ancient Biblical lands in and around Israel, Palestine, Jordan and farther north.[20]

Ancient India's Sun God Temples

The review of ancient India's sacred temples focuses on the 108 Divya Desam temples dedicated to Lord Vishnu. This is because the data is relatively complete, and because we know these temples evolved out of an ancient Sun god tradition. Details about these temples are contained in the works of the Tamil Azhvars (saints), which were written between the 5th and 8th century CE. These temples are largely located in southern India (105 are in India, one is in Nepal, and two are said to be placed outside the realm of perception).

Of the 106 Earthly Divya Desams, three quarters exist within a bandwidth seven minutes wide and 650 kilometers long, as the day-night boundary moves overhead on the winter solstice sunrise and summer solstice sunset. Three-quarters of temples existing within this bandwidth share the V47 degree shaped pyramid gate superstructures, and they nearly all face due east. This data suggests alignment and design logic and, despite the great distances, a collective interconnectedness. Given that these are temples dedicated to Lord Vishnu, who embraced his Sun god heritage, I propose that the V47 degree pyramid gate structures symbolize the solstice as sacred time. We see a similar theme with the 275 Paadal Petra Sthalam temples dedicated to Lord Shiva, embracing his ancient solar origins.

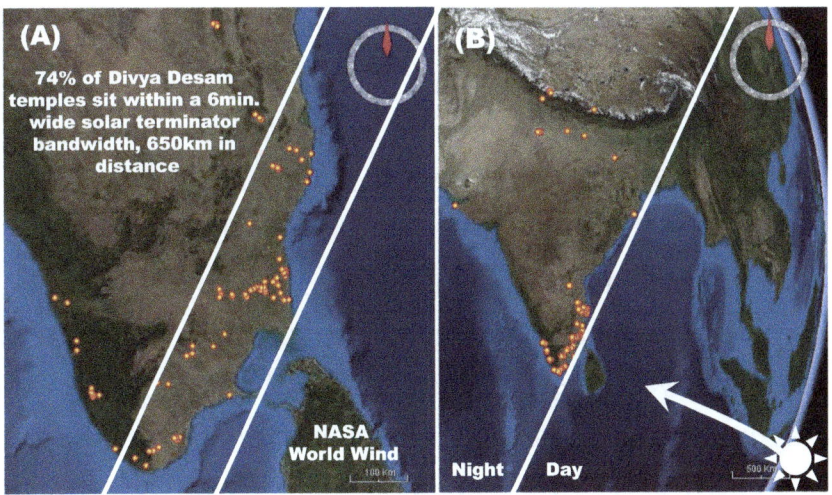

Figure 2.5 A map of Ancient India's Divya Desams temples, dedicated to Lord Vishnu. A similar southern location trend is also seen with the 275 Paadal Petra Sthalam temples dedicated to Lord Shiva. **(A)** The Dravidian style Divya Desam temples are predominantly located within a seven-minute wide time bandwidth. Those temples to the north and west were largely non-Dravidian styles. **(B)** Divya Desam temples relative to a seven-minute wide and 650-kilometer long solar terminator band on the winter solstice sunrise and summer solstice sunset.[21]

Pyramid Alignments and the Solar Terminator

These solar terminator alignments represent a significant amount of sacred real estate sharing a common theme. Although these patterns could have occurred as a result of pure chance or as a function of geographical restrictions such as the Andes Mountains or the shape of a region's landmass or major rivers, there are valid reasons for exploring other potential reasons for the light they may shed.

When one views the alignments from different altitudes (space-eye view, or close-up over a site), combined with the shared ritual symbolism embedded in each religion's temple art and iconography, a composite picture can be drawn. The correlation between sacred site alignments and those times of the year that coincided with the Sun god religions' most important ritual-festival dates, reveals a global fingerprint. This fingerprint begs for an explanation beyond mere coincidence, or the popularly held belief that these sacred alignments were intended to inform a civilization's agricultural and fertility calendars.

An interesting aspect of the day-night boundary's overhead passage, on the winter solstice sunrise and summer solstice sunset, is that these sites (and any people conducting sacred rituals there) would have experienced the same extremely low frequency (ELF) electromagnetic (EM) wave fields overhead. The causes and implications of these enhanced ELF electromagnetic wave fields (Schumann resonances) are reviewed more fully in Chapters 6-8. Suffice it to say here that this would have been beneficial for sacred ritual processes.

The outstanding question is w*hy* and *how* did these ancient civilizations manage to align so many sites over relatively narrow geographical bandwidths? How could they have done so over such great distances (100-1,000km)? Simply put, I cannot yet provide a rational, scientific answer to this question, but it does make me wonder about the concept of non-local communication networks afforded through the simultaneous achievement of altered states of consciousness. The field of transpersonal psychology indicates non-local communication is possible (this will be discussed in Chapter 9).

A Regional Analysis of Sacred Site Alignment

Egypt

The consensus of Egyptologists is that sacred sites were aligned with the Nile River. More recent studies, however, highlight other common alignments, notably the solstices and equinoxes. According to my observations, the more famous temples and all of the pyramids adhere to the solstice and equinox alignment principles.

My interest in archaeoastronomy and sacred site alignments is ultimately about trying to understand *why* these alignments were of importance, and *what* purpose they served for priests, priestesses, pharaohs, and other leaders. Why, too, does ancient Egypt show the same range of site alignments in a high proportion of its sacred sites as the other ancient Sun god civilizations on different continents and from different times (ranging from 1,000 to 5,000 years ago)?

Scientists recently conducted a large study of Egyptian sacred site orientations, involving more than 330 temples.[22] They highlighted a range of astronomical alignment clusters, the two most common being sunrise at the equinoxes and at the winter solstice.

My study covering the main 114 temples and 103 pyramids supports these recent scientific findings. Of the 114 temples reviewed, one-quarter of their entrances face either the winter solstice sunrise or the summer solstice sunset. Some of these are illustrated in Figures 2.6-2.9.

A further seven percent of temples face either 25 to 27 or 205 to 207 degrees of North. This means that if one draws a perpendicular line (or simply turns one's head 90 degrees) to the temple's primary axis (both sides), one would observe the winter solstice sunrise and summer solstice sunset. Therefore, one-third of Egyptian temples (including most of the major ones) offer a solstice marker as a key architectural feature. The 25 to 27 or 205 to 207 degrees site alignments, like their Mayan counterparts, could also reflect alignment to Earth's magnetic axis. This would imply an understanding of the use of geomancy principles. This is discussed later in this chapter.

Egyptian Temples

Sun god temples aligned with the solstices are particularly evident in the 18th and 19th Dynasty temples at Karnak in Luxor, the capital of the New Kingdom. These temples were dedicated primarily to Egypt's solar deity pantheon, particularly Amun-Ra, the supreme Sun god. The Karnak temple complex is composed of four precincts: Amun-Ra, Montu, Mut, and the deliberately dismantled Temple of Amenhotep IV.

Pharaoh Akhenaten (Amenhotep IV) abandoned traditional Egyptian polytheism and urged the people to accept Atenism, a form of solar deity monotheism (honoring a supreme solar deity called "Aten"). His ideas were not popular among the established priestly castes, no doubt because he disbanded their temples, moved the capital further north, and radically changed the priests' roles, undermining their powerbase within society.

The precinct of Amun-Ra, famous for its solstice-aligning colonnade and beautiful grand design, is second only to the Giza pyramids as a tourist destination. Some say it represents one of the grandest temple complexes on the face of the planet. Most of the temples in this complex are aligned with the solstices.

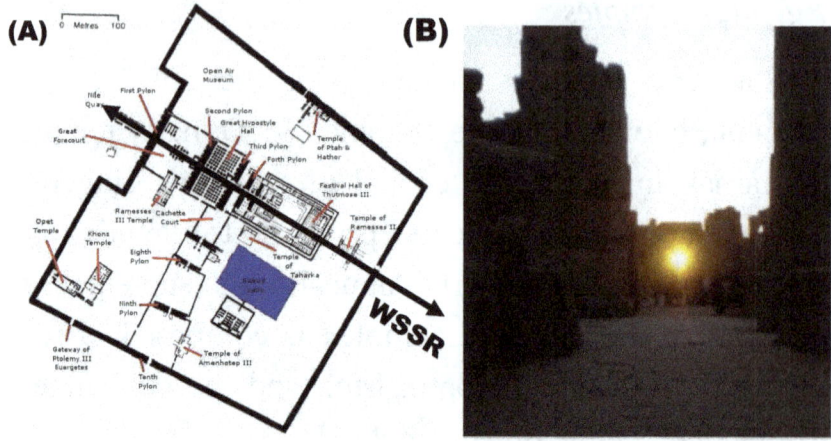

Figure 2.6 Winter solstice sunrise. **(A)** The Temple of Amun (Karnak) site plan and central axis aligns with the winter solstice sunrise (WSSR). **(B)** Looking east along the temple's main axis on the winter solstice sunrise one can visualize the sunrise through a window-like aperture in the temple structure (reprinted with permission of David Furlong.[23]).

The Mortuary Temple of Queen Hatshepsut greets the winter solstice sunrise from the foot of the cliff face at Deir el Bahari on the west bank of the Nile. This temple was dedicated to the Sun god Amun-Ra, and sits alongside the mortuary temples of Mentuhotep II and Thutmosis III, which are also aligned with the winter solstice sunrise.

Figure 2.7 The Mortuary Temple of Queen Hatshepsut. **(A)** This temple faces the winter solstice sunrise, along with other proximate temples, e.g., the Mortuary Temple of Mentuhotep II. **(B)** Temple of Queen Hatshepsut sits at the foot of the cliff face at Deir el Bahari on the west bank of the Nile, with its central axis facing the WSSR.[24]

The Temple of Amenhotep III, located on the Theban necropolis on the Nile's west bank, was the largest of the mortuary temples in the Theban area, even larger than the Karnak temple complex. This temple aligns with the winter solstice sunrise. A little closer to the Nile in front of the temple sit two massive 18-meter statues of Amenhotep III made from blocks of quartzite sandstone, called the Colossi of Memnon. These paired statues of Amenhotep have faced the winter solstice sunrise for the past 3,400 years.

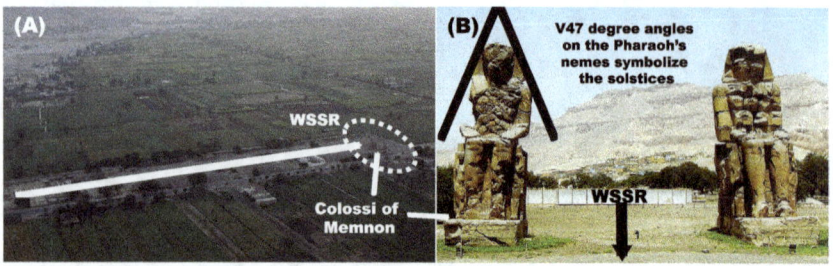

Figure 2.8 Temple of Amenhotep III. **(A)** The temple's central axis is aligned with the winter solstice sunrise and summer solstice sunset. **(B)** The Colossi of Memnon sit on the temple sites central axis facing the winter solstice sunrise (WSSR).[25]

Each statue weights an estimated 720 tons and the quartzite sandstone was transported from near modern-day Cairo (675 kilometers away). Compare this to the King's and Queen's chambers of the Great Pyramid of Khufu at Giza, made of red granite that was transported a similar distance from Aswan to Cairo. Why did the Egyptians build with these materials imported from so far away? What purpose did this specific type of stone serve? Did the ends justify the means? I believe there was a function implied by both these structures, and that the ends did indeed justify the means.

These statues are said to create a resonating, humming sound near sunrise in February and March. This phenomenon piques my curiosity. Quartzite sandstone is known to have piezoelectric properties. This means the quartzite crystals are capable of changing a mechanical force (e.g., mechanical vibrations, sound) into electricity, or an electromagnetic field into a mechanical force (resonating sound). It is conceivable these statues were also resonating sensors of ELF/EM wave fields generated by the sunrise/set and surges in the overhead electromagnetic environment consequent to peaks in sunspot activity around the equinoxes.

Interestingly, the eyes of the massive statues of Pharaoh Amenhotep III look closed, as if he's in a seated meditation posture. They perennially wait for the winter solstice sunrise. On this statue, as with so many other pharaoh statues, you will notice the V47 degree angle formed by the sides of the pharaoh's headdress, or *nemes (*more on this in Chapter 5).

The Great Temple of Rameses II in Abu Simbel dedicated to Amun, Re-Horakhty, and Ptah was built close to the tropic of Cancer (23.4^0 latitude), facing the winter solstice sunrise. Therefore on the summer solstice the midday Sun sits more or less directly overhead, barely casting a shadow on the temple. With one great piece of sacred site selection and planning, Rameses the Great (19th Dynasty; reigned 1279–1213 BCE) made a great symbolic gesture to his Sun gods in marking out the winter solstice sunrise and the midday Sun.

Figure 2.9 The Great Temple of Rameses II at Abu Simbel. **(A)** Pharaohs seated with hands on knees, eyes apparently closed, greet the winter solstice sunrise (WSSR). Does this seated posture depict Pharaohs in seated meditation posture facing the WSSR? Note the Pharaoh's adorning V47 nemes (headdress). **(B)** The temple's central axis faces the WSSR, embedded within the artificial mound housing the structure after its relocation, before Lake Nasser was constructed and filled as a water reservoir.[26]

Of all the temple alignments ancient Egyptians could have used to orient sacred structures, why was the winter solstice alignment so frequently utilized? Given that the solstice marked the end of one solar cycle and represented the birth of a new Sun, many postulate this served the primary purpose of knowing important agricultural and fertility dates.

I would suggest, however, that these sacred site alignments were required so that priests could accurately determine the proper timing of the solstices and equinoxes or, to put it another way, establish sacred time. After all, the solstices and equinoxes represented the ancient Egyptians' most important Sun god religious festival dates. The 365-day tropical calendar and the inexorable precession of the equinoxes meant that calendars became inaccurate. The solstice alignment principle therefore offered the priestly timekeepers the opportunity to adjust their calendars to ensure that they (i.e., the priests) accurately predicted the date for this important ritual festival held on the winter solstice.

We must also account for the ten percent of Egyptian temples that are cardinally aligned, i.e., that face north-south or east-west. Approximately half of the equinox-aligned temples have their primary axis facing north-south, while the other half is oriented east-west. Temples such as Nyuserre-Ini in Abusir, the "solar temple," and the temples of Horus in Edfu and Deir El-Haggar, to name just a few, exemplify this alignment. See Figure 2.10.

Figure 2.10 Cardinally aligned temples with the sites' primary axis facing north-south or east-west. **(A)** Temple of Edfu has its primary axis facing north-south. This alignment permits direct observation of the equinox sunrises/sets if one orients oneself

perpendicular to the primary axis. Picture taken in 1905 CE. **(B)** Plan of the Temple of Edfu highlights its north-south facing primary axis. The inner sanctum is located in the north central part of the temple.[27]

Egyptian Pyramids

The accepted view is that pyramids were built during the Old and Middle Kingdom to function as tombs for the pharaohs. Pyramid texts lining the walls of pyramids at Saqqara during the 5th and 6th dynasties of the Old Kingdom highlight rituals and incantations for the pharaoh that have been interpreted as being used for the pharaohs' afterlife journey.

An interesting question that resonated with me was posed by Jeremy Naydler in his book, *Shamanic Wisdom in the Pyramid Texts*[28]. This question concerned the commonly held interpretation of the pyramids as solely burial places for the pharaohs. Certainly mummified remains have been found; but more frequently that has not been the case. Naydler suggests that the pyramid texts at Saqqara were more likely to have been used by the pharaohs, priests, etc., for journeys into the spirit world during sacred ritual (i.e., the Sed festival), either *before* or *during* the experience of altered states of consciousness (as opposed to after death).[29]

More generally, could not Egyptian pyramids have served the dual purpose of being both "temple and tomb"? Pyramid chambers could easily have provided a rehearsal for journeying into the spirit world (assisted by pyramid texts and other sacred ritual elements). That is, they offered the person undertaking sacred rituals a place of sensory-silence for conducting meditation-based rituals within.

Of the approximately 130 Egyptian pyramids, I have examined 103 using satellite imagery, aerial photos, and other images. I have visited quite a number of them as well. About one-third of pyramids constitute the largest and/or the primary pyramid of a main pyramid site. Much smaller queen and cult pyramids often surround these larger pyramids. Nonetheless, more than 80 percent of all pyramids are cardinally aligned, and a further 10 percent are within five degrees of being cardinally aligned.

When the Great Pyramid (of Khufu) at Giza is combined with the three smaller satellite queen's pyramids to its east, Giza can be used to mark the winter and summer solstice and equinox sunrises (see Figure 2.11). This is not unlike Uaxactun in Guatemala (a Maya city and temple complex), which happens to be where the idea of using satellite pyramids for marking time first entered my mind. An early morning climb to just above the height of the queen's pyramids on the SE corner of Khufu permits this observation.

Similarly, the three satellite pyramids off the southwest aspect of the Menkaure Pyramid could also offer additional utility as a clinometer or gauge to view the Sun and Moon (potentially permitting eclipse predictions), as well as the planets, constellations, and stars of the Milky Way at different times in their cycles.

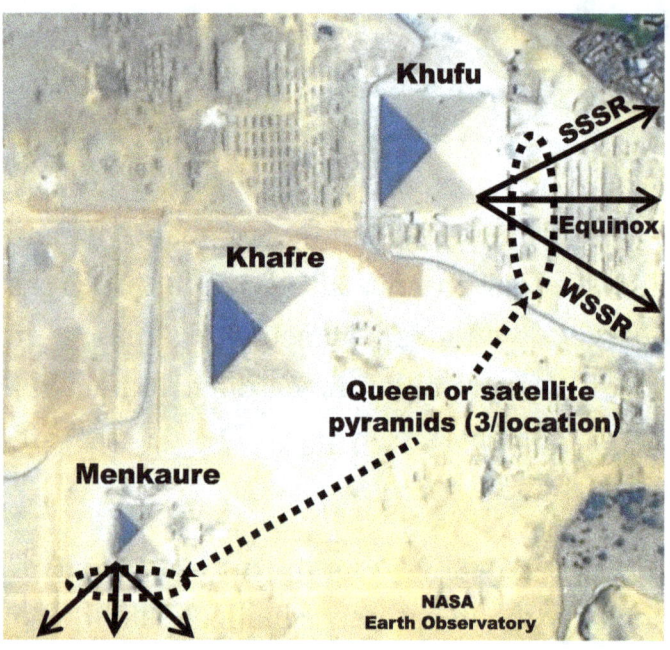

Figure 2.11 The Giza plateau. The Great Pyramid (Khufu) together with the three Queen's Pyramids can be used to mark the solstice and equinox sunrises (red lines). The Menkaure Pyramid has three satellite pyramids to its south. These could have potentially offered heavenly reference points, offering utility as a clinometer (red lines; bottom left). Giza plateau satellite image courtesy of NASA Earth Observatory.[30]

The Giza pyramid complex (Khufu, Khafre) together with the Red Pyramid (Dahshur necropolis) represents the three largest Egyptian pyramids and are amongst its very oldest from the beginning of the Old Kingdom. These are also undeniably the best-preserved pyramids in Egypt. They were built in a golden age of Egypt's ancient past, perhaps further back in time than is commonly accepted. Every pyramid built thereafter was of a much lower construction quality and/or ambition, barely surviving the journey to the 21st Century, or requiring extensive reconstruction to survive.

That's the conclusion drawn using a preservation ranking/rating method I developed for the top 40 primary and/or largest pyramids at all of Egypt's main sites. This method was developed to organize and compare these pyramids, using a scale of 1 (poor) to 10 (excellent) across the group according to age and preservation. The pyramids below scored 8.5/10 (good structural preservation). For context, there is a group of six pyramids scoring an average of 5/10 (moderate structural preservation) while the bulk of the pyramids are in the 2.5/10 (poor structural preservation) group. This tells us that Giza and the Red pyramid were built by advanced architects and builders, and these pyramids were of a much superior build quality relative to Egypt's other pyramid construction (most of which were built after Giza and the Red pyramid).

Figure 2.12 The three largest pyramids in Egypt. **(A)** Pyramids of Giza, Menkaure (foreground), Khafre (midground), and Khufu (background), **(B)** The Red Pyramid, Egypt's third-largest pyramid, is located southwest of Giza on the Dahshur necropolis. The Red Pyramid and Khufu utilize similar corbelled, vaulted spaces for inner design. The Grand Gallery in Khufu and the main chambers in the Red Pyramid portray this feature.[31]

The Pyramid of Ahmose is the only confirmed winter solstice sunrise-aligned pyramid. A second, recently discovered pyramid is also apparently aligned with the winter solstice sunrise (coordinates: 28.36029 N, 30.42419 E).

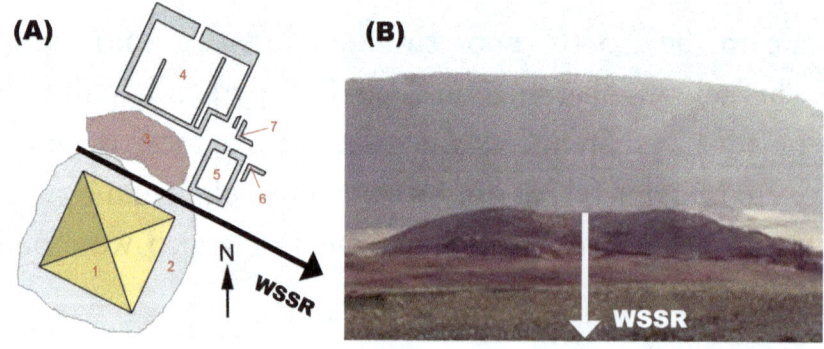

Figure 2.13 The Pyramid of Ahmose. **(A)** The site plan highlights that this pyramid (uniquely among Egyptian pyramids) faces the

winter solstice sunrise. **(B)** The collapsed remains of the solstice aligned Ahmose pyramid.[32]

The pyramid at Meidum is unusual for Egypt because its original or inner structure was designed with an awareness of the V47 degree solstice symbolism (Meroe in Sudan also has this feature).

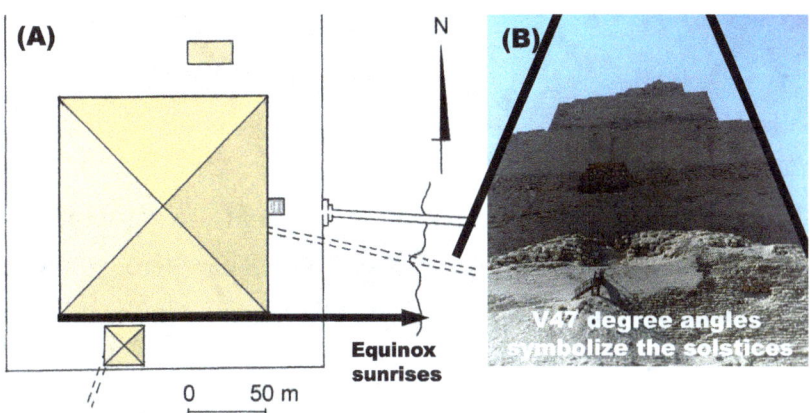

Figure 2.14 The Pyramid of Meidum. **(A)** This pyramid is cardinally aligned and seemingly had an inner and outer structure, as if built according to two different designs. **(B)** The cardinally aligned inner pyramid structure depicts a V47 degree angle, and reminds us of the designer's awareness of solstices and equinoxes, and of their symbolism.[33]

Last but not least is the sacred site at Meroe in Sudan. I mention this because Egypt's borders extended into Sudan during the latter stages of the empire. According to Egyptologists, the winter solstice sunrise alignment represents the most frequently recorded sacred site alignment in ancient Egypt.[34] Meroe is a fantastic example of a multi-pyramid winter solstice sunrise-aligned site. It also uses the V47 degree pyramid shape, in common with the pyramid at Meidum in Egypt.

Figure 2.15 Meroe (Sudan). **(A)** The pyramid site at Meroe faces the winter solstice sunrise (WSSR). **(B)** The Meroe pyramids utilize the V47 degree solstice-symbolizing angle in the design of their superstructure outlines.[35]

Mesoamerica

History

Most of us are unfamiliar with Mesoamerican (Central American) religious history. This is unsurprising given the tragic destruction of the Mesoamerican civilization during the 16th Century Spanish conquest, and the associated religious assimilation by the Catholic Church. Mesoamerica, or pre-Colombian Central America, extended from central Mexico down to Costa Rica and included a number of pre-Columbian societies that flourished over different time periods.

From circa 7000 BCE, Mesoamerica transitioned from an area inhabited by hunter-gatherer tribes to one containing more structured, agricultural-based societies. These societies utilized religious practices with unique mythologies, distinct architectural styles, languages, hieroglyphics, mathematics, astronomy, and sophisticated calendar systems. These societies ultimately became stratified into chiefdoms, with sacred ceremonial centers forming each community's epicenter. These chiefdoms were connected by a network of trading centers and affiliations, and ultimately came under the rule of kings and queens.

In Maya culture, kings were the nexus of power, and they usually built some form of monument (pyramid or temple) to legitimize their power. Maya kings were considered godlike and worked closely with shaman-priests to play an important role in interfacing with their deities. This partnership created shared rituals to help bind their communities together, not unlike other religions in the ancient world. The Maya Formative Period (2000 BCE to 250 CE) saw distinct religious and architectural complexes develop and spread throughout the region.

The Olmecs were the first major civilization in southern Mexico, inhabiting the tropical lowlands in today's states of Veracruz and Tabasco, and flourishing during Mesoamerica's Formative Period (1500 to 400

BCE). The main Olmec sites include San Lorenzo, Tenochtitlán, La Venta, and Tres Zapotes. There is evidence they interacted with earlier cultures at Tak'Alik A'baj, Izapa, and Teopantecuanitlan (located in today's Guatemala). The Maya became established during the Pre-Classic or Formative Period (2000 BCE to 250 CE), reaching their peak during the Classic Period (250 to 900 CE), and covering the southern Mexican states of Chiapas, Tabasco, the Yucatán, Guatemala, Belize, northern El Salvador, and western Honduras. The Toltec culture in central Mexico (800 to 1000 CE) was succeeded by the geographically more expansive Aztec culture, which flourished from the Fourteenth to Sixteenth centuries.

Urban & Sacred Site Planning

Maya urban planning was considered mature by 300 BCE, with sites generally oriented in a NE-SW direction, peaking at 14 to 17 degrees NE orientation.[36,37] A second urban plan alignment peak of 25 degrees is also observed, which aligns with both the winter solstice sunrise and summer solstice sunset (perpendicular to this axis).[38]

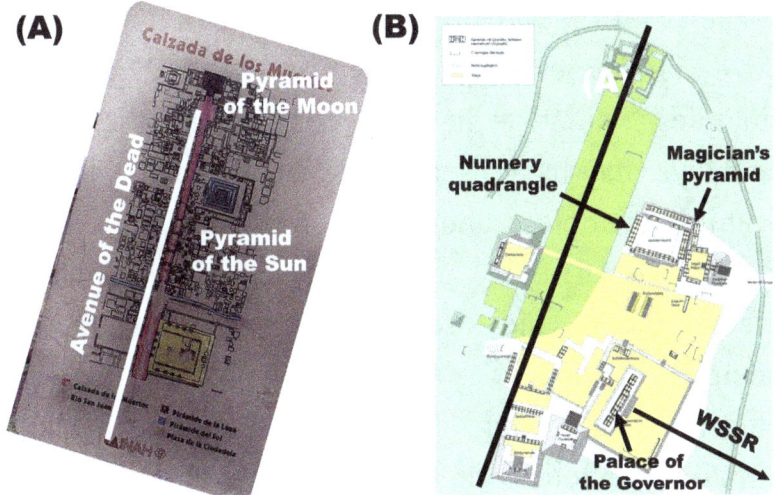

Figure 2.16 Urban plan alignments typical of Mesoamerica (tourist signs of site plans). **(A)** Teotihuacan's Avenue of the Dead represents the site's primary axis, which is oriented 15.5 degrees NE or 195.5 SW. **(B)** Uxmal's principal site axis is similarly aligned.[39]

This general urban site layout and axial orientation was replicated throughout Mesoamerica, indicating the presence of a shared state calendar and architecture.[40] Sites were typically divided into northern and southern sections, whilst also symbolically representing the celestial, supernatural spheres and the worldly and underworld spheres when viewed vertically.[41] Important central buildings (elite residences, pyramids, temples, civic plaza platforms) were astronomically aligned with sunrises and sunsets to mark specific dates of agricultural, civic, and sacred ritual importance to that community.[42,43]

The 14 to 17 degree NE-SW site axis discussed above is interesting in the context of geomancy principles. Scientists have speculated that the Olmecs and Maya may have used a lodestone compass to orient pyramids, temples, and other important buildings to Earth's magnetic poles.[44,45] Scientists using paleomagnetic and archaeoastronomical data have concluded that a site's axial alignment was likely determined by using this primitive type of ancient compass. The lodestone was widely used by the Chinese for *feng shui* ("wind-water"; geomancy) during the past millennia, in order to orient their sacred sites in an auspicious manner. In fact, lodestone artifacts have been found in Olmec sites,[46] and research has also highlighted a possible link between the Olmecs and the Chinese as far back as 1200 BCE.[47]

Geomancy is said to have originated in ancient Asia, seeding other ancient societies as it filtered west along trade routes. Geomancy explores the realm where human consciousness connects with Earth's spirit and consciousness, engendering a harmonious interaction between people and place. The concept of magnetic field reconnections between the Sun and Earth is reviewed in Chapter 7. While science has not yet proven magnetic field connections between Earth and human beings, the principles in operation between the Sun and the Earth might represent a plausible mechanism by which geomancy could operate.

Mesoamerican Sites

A significant body of archaeoastronomical research on Mesoamerican sites has been conducted, reaching back many decades. In addition to a general consensus that Mesoamerican sites incorporate urban plan alignments (NE-SW 14-17 & 25 degrees), there is agreement that the use of solstice alignments for major sacred buildings within these sites was ubiquitous.

Eighty-six sites were reviewed during my Mesoamerican research, of which 80 percent were Maya sites. Important Olmec and Aztec sites account for the balance. Seventy percent of all sites have obvious solstice alignments, with half of these involving the primary site axis (25 or 115 degrees) and the other half involving alignments of important pyramids, temples, or plaza platforms within a site. More than ten percent of site plans are cardinally aligned, and most sites contain one or more buildings that are cardinally aligned.

The city of Teotihuacan, located 48 kilometers northeast of Mexico City, contains some of the largest pyramids in the world. Teotihuacan was given its name by the Aztecs, and means "this is the place where man meets the gods" or "birthplace of the gods." It was established as a new religious center in about 100 BCE, with the pyramid of the Sun completed by about 100 CE. It reached its peak during 400 to 500 CE when the population is believed to have exceeded 125,000.

Teotihuacan's reach extended through much of Mesoamerica before going into a mysterious decline after 600 CE.

Scientists and historians still debate who Teotihuacan's founding builders were, whether it was the center of a state empire, and what caused its sudden downfall. In any case, Teotihuacan exemplifies the common NE-SW urban plan alignment (approximately 15.5 degrees) (Figure 2.17).

Figure 2.17 Teotihuacan's Pyramids of the Sun and Moon. **(A)** The Pyramid of the Sun is one of the largest pyramids in the world, with a base measurement comparable to the Giza (Egypt) and Xi'an (China) pyramids. **(B)** The Avenue of the Dead, seen from the Pyramid of the Moon, is oriented 15.5 degrees east of north and west of south, which might indicate a historical alignment with earth's magnetic axis.[48]

Chichen Itza was built next to a sacred cenote (deep natural well or sinkhole) and literally means "at the mouth of Itza's well." It was a major Mayan economic and sociocultural center of power between c. 600 and

1200 CE (Figure 2.18). The site covers five square kilometers, including such structures as the Great Ball Court, the Temple of Warriors, the Temple of Xtoloc, and El Caracol, among others. Dominating the North Platform is the solstice-facing Temple of Kukulkan (Maya feathered-serpent deity) or El Castillo. This 30 meter high step pyramid contains a 91-step stairway on each facet, and a final step into its top chamber–365 steps in total.

Guarding the base of the stairs on the northern staircase are the carved heads of serpents. On the late afternoon of the equinoxes, a shadow is cast upon the stone railing at the northern side of the steps, which is said to resemble a wiggling serpent's body, which in turn connects to the serpent's head below and moves slowly over a period of many hours. This is believed to depict the feathered-serpent god Kukulkan. Such a theatrical display could not have been designed by a people not attuned to the solar calendar and the Sun's shadow properties.

Archeoacoustic scientists have explored the acoustic properties of El Castillo, where it is known that a handclap in front of the stairs, within a specific range of sound wave angles to the steps, produces a "chirp echo," which is said to sound similar to a Quetzal bird, Guatemala's national bird.[49] The Great Ball Court is also said to have special acoustic properties; a whisper at one end of the open-air court can be clearly heard at the other end, 500 feet away. Was this pure chance or intentionally designed by acoustically-aware architects?

Having spoken informally with a sound engineer and several Guatemalan shamans regarding the Maya ball courts, it seems to me that the tapered walls cone the reverberated sound waves (drum beats) to a central line at head height. This makes me consider the acoustic entrainment of brainwaves to specific frequencies. After all, the Maya believed the ball courts were entrances into the underworld and, therefore, altered states of consciousness. Assuming that you the reader are aware of these structures, have you ever asked yourself why a ball court was nearly always placed close to important, centrally located temples? Were they ball courts, or acoustic waveguides for entraining specific brainwave frequencies required to induce ASC? (This would have helped priesthoods conduct sacred rituals independent of sacred time, i.e., not just during the solstices and equinoxes.)

Figure 2.18 Chichen Itza. **(A & B)** The Temple of Kukulkan faces the winter solstice sunset (WSSR) and summer solstice sunset (SSSS). The columns to the east potentially offer a refining focus for visualizing more precisely the solstice alignments.[50]

Uxmal, located in the Yucatan in Mexico, is one of the most important archaeological sites of Maya culture, along with Chichen Itza and Tikal. Uxmal's major construction took place while it was the capital of a Late Classic Maya state around 850–925 CE, with its distinctive Puuc style architecture and ornate friezes depicting scenes of deities.

Uxmal contains three fascinating buildings: the atypical, oval-shaped Pyramid of the Magician, the solstice-aligned Governor's Palace with its east-west façades revealing an alignment to the WSSR and SSSS, and the Nunnery Quadrangle with its elaborately carved façades featuring V47 degree angled shapes with Kukulkan's serpent head placed in the center (which I believe depicts the solstice and equinox as sacred time– see Figure 5.2).

Figure 2.19 Uxmal (Mexico). **(B)** The unusual oval shape of the Pyramid of the Magician sets its apart from other Mayan pyramids. **(B)** The Governor's Palace faces the WSSR and SSSS.[51]

San Andrés is a Mesoamerican site situated in El Salvador, initially occupied c. 900 BCE and vacated by 250 CE due to an enormous eruption of the volcano of Lago Ilopango (Figure 2.20). San Andres is a great example of a solstice-aligned site situated between two volcanoes. Volcán de San Salvador to the southeast marks the winter solstice sunrise and Lake Ilopango, a volcano caldera, marks the summer solstice sunset. These geographic features are so perfectly placed as to seem preplanned.

Figure 2.20 San Andrés pyramid site (El Salvador). **(A)** One of the main pyramid platforms at this site. This is a solstice-aligned site built between two volcanoes, such that they all sit on a straight line facing the WSSR and SSSS. **(B)** The site uses Volcán de San Salvador as an additional winter solstice sunrise marker,

where the Sun appears to rise out of the volcano crater. **(C)** Lake Llopango is a volcano caldera, now filled with water, and lies toward the SSSS when looked at from San Andres.[52]

Cholula (Mexico City) dates back to at least 300 BCE (Figure 2.21). It became a regional center between 600 and 700 CE and evolved its role throughout the various states that rose and fell during that time. Its immense Great Pyramid has the greatest volume of any known pyramid in the world. This pyramid is aligned with the winter solstice sunrise and summer solstice sunset. One can also observe the sunset behind the Volcan Iztaccihuatl at the summer solstice. The conquistadors built a church atop this sacred site and, not for the first time in Mexico, town planners permanently aligned Cholula's streets with the solstices.

Figure 2.21 Cholula (Mexico). **(A)** The Great Pyramid of Cholula, resembling a hill, is aligned with the summer solstice sunset (SSSS). On the SSSS the sun sets behind Volcan Iztaccihuatl. **(B)** The massive pyramid resembles a small hill adorned with the conquistadors' church. Interestingly Cholula's town planners aligned their town plan to the WSSR and SSSS.[53]

Tikal and Uaxactun are located in the Peten region of Guatemala, about 20 kilometers apart, and exemplify some unique attributes relating to the solstice (Figure 2.20). Tikal, one of the more impressive Mesoamerican sites, dates back to 400 BCE. It reached its peak between 200 and 900 CE, when it was the capital of one of the most powerful kingdoms of the ancient Maya. It occupies 16 square kilometers and contains 3,000 structures, including large royal palaces, pyramids, smaller palaces, residences, administrative buildings, platforms, and inscribed monuments. Temple IV is 70 meters high and can be used with other towering temples to sight both solstice and equinox sunrises.[54]

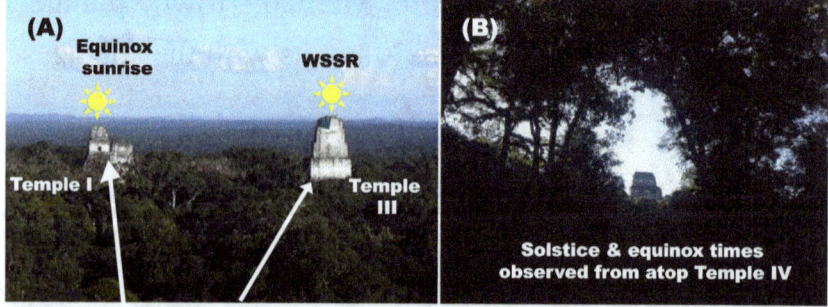

Figure 2.22 Tikal (Guatemala). **(A)** Standing atop Temple IV above the tree canopy, one can utilize a line of sight over Temple 3 to observe the WSSR, and Temple 1 to observe the equinox sunrise. This was the famed spot for observing the end of the Mayan calendar on December 21, 2012. **(B)** Looking due east from atop Temple IV (to the west of the site) one can use the pyramid alignments to determine the WSSR and the equinox sunrise. [55]

Mesoamerican Site Alignments, Volcanoes & Solstices

A quarter of the Mesoamerican sites reviewed used volcano or hill peaks to assist pyramid, temple, or site alignments. This indicates that site planners considered these features important in site selection, along with other amenities such as proximity to a river and naturally afforded protections. Twenty percent of solstice-aligned sites also used volcanoes on the horizon to mark the solstice, meaning that "the great orb of fire," the Sun, either rose from behind or set behind a volcano on the solstices. This same feature is observed for the large Moai stone statues on Easter Island and the ancient Buddhist stupa, Borobudur, located in Java. Some of the Mesoamerican sites highlighting this feature are detailed in Figure 2.23.

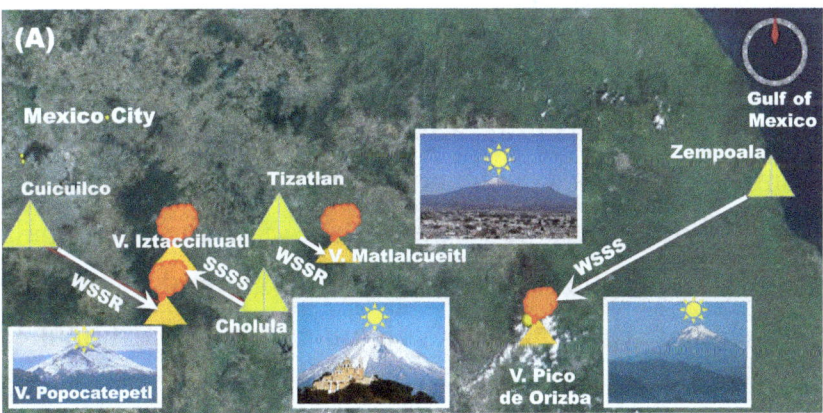

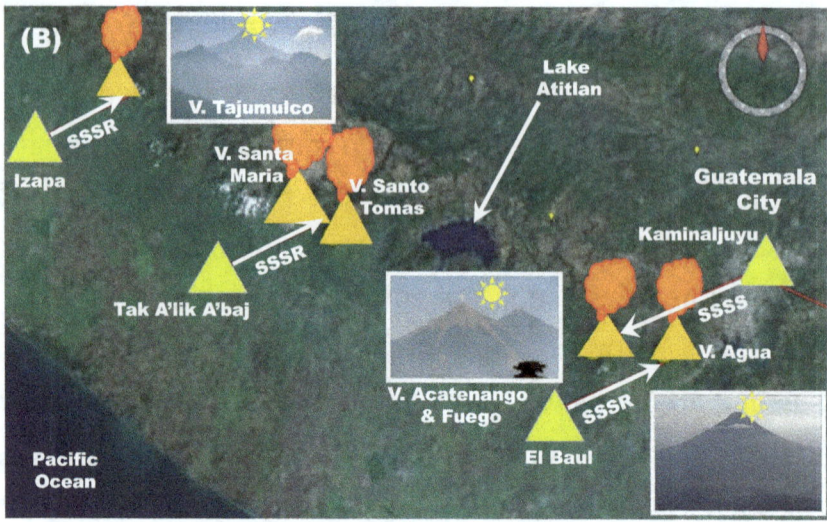

Figure 2.23 Mesoamerican sites and their volcanic alignments. **(A & B)** Mesoamerican sites frequently use a volcano on the horizon to align the site with one of the solstice sunrises or sunsets, i.e., the winter solstice sunrise (WSSR), summer solstice sunset (SSSS), winter solstice sunset (WSSS), or the summer solstice sunrise (SSSR).[56]

The Motagua and Chixoy-Polochic fault complex runs just off Central America's Pacific coast, with Central America's volcanoes lying over the tectonic plate subduction zone further inland, i.e., the Guatemala Highlands. When this fact is combined with the knowledge that active volcanoes and earthquakes (experienced frequently in Guatemala) are associated with extremely low frequency electromagnetic and stronger magnetic field emission signatures in the weeks leading up to activity, I am led to wonder whether there was a functional benefit to these site locations and their volcano-solstice alignments. This will be explored further in Chapter 6.

South American Sites

History

The South American archeological timeline is broadly divided into Preceramic (4000–1200 BCE) and Ceramic (900 BCE–1532 CE) periods. Preceramic urban centers such as Caral (2600 BCE) and others in the Supe Valley of Peru developed at least 1,500 years before other early Mesoamerican societies. Their development was contemporaneous with early Egyptian pyramid societies and the Sumerian-Akkadian societies of Mesopotamia. However, unlike Egypt, Mesopotamia, and India, all of which benefited from networks for the exchange of trade and knowledge, the Peruvian development process is said to have taken place in isolation from other societies on the continent.[57]

During this formative period (900 BCE to 200 CE) important cultures like the Chavin emerged, followed by regional developments (100–800 CE) that included Moche, Nazca, Lima, Tiwanaku, and others. By 600 CE, state-based societies had developed in the central Andes.[58] Three key regions–Moche (northern coastal desert), Wari (Huari; central highlands), and Tiwanaku (south-central Andean high plains)–provide strong evidence of planned urban capitals. They followed expansionist policies. They also developed a widespread road system, utilized intensive agricultural production methods, built dedicated royal tombs in restricted-access temples, and represented a regional polity that extended beyond a single valley.[59] These states eventually formed the basis of the unified Inca Empire (1430-1532 CE), which was later conquered by the Spanish and their hegemonic church agents (1532-1534 CE), just as was done in Mesoamerica.

After reviewing a great number of publications regarding South American sacred sites, it became obvious to me that (as in Mesoamerica) piecing together the evolutionary story of this once rich pre-Colombian society from the scattered shards of evidence would be a tall order. So much was destroyed, looted, and simply lost to time during the era of the Spanish conquest. That said, temple (huaca and ushnus) and pyramid alignments, and a robust field of iconography actually provide a rich data set of alignments and art symbolism. This data set is aligned with the shared archaeological fingerprint from the other Sun god religions.

Bridging the Natural and Supernatural Realms

Huacas were ancient sacred spaces where communication between the natural and supernatural worlds occurred in pre-Inca societies. They also served as astronomical calendars marking religious (sacred time) and agricultural cycles.[60] As these local societies grew, their leaders and priesthoods gained legitimacy in the wider community along the Peruvian coast. In so doing, they created a gravitational pull that attracted faithful worshipers, as opposed to imposing their will on the broader community.[61]

Emerging communities built temples and multi-tiered pyramid-like platforms (referred to as Ushnus), and larger communities coalesced around them. Ushnus functioned as viewing platforms and places where the leading elite and priests conducted important public rituals that helped legitimize their rule.[62]

From the perspective of gathering archaeological data, huacas and ruins within ushnus were my main focus. Not surprisingly, the solstice sunrise and sunset alignments dominate the alignment horizon for these important sites throughout ancient South America.

By the time of the Inca Empire, ushnus were closely associated with veneration rituals dedicated to the Sun. The Inca Empire governed from Cuzco, with its solar cult perpetuated from the *Coricancha*. The Coricancha, located in present-day Cusco, was the Inca Empire's most important temple, dedicated primarily to Inti, their Sun god. This center would be similar in power and influence to Mecca, Jerusalem, or Vatican City in our times. It has been argued that the Inca perpetuated the cult of the Sun as a means of legitimizing and sanctifying divine kingship and primacy over all other religious cults.[63]

South American Sites

Astronomically aligned sites (primarily solstice) emerged early in the evolution of South American societies, beginning with Caral (2600 BCE), the earliest civilization in the Western Hemisphere, and then the Chavin and the state-based societies of Moche, Wari, and Tiwanaku which led up to the Inca Empire. The parallel religious evolution culminated in the appearance of the pre-Inca Creator and Sun god known as Viracocha.

Coordinates for forty South American sites were reviewed. These accounted for the majority of the major sites from northern Peru to Tiwanaku in Bolivia. Nearly ninety percent of these sites are aligned with one or more solstice time points (sunrise and/or sunset). Approximately half of these sites align with the winter solstice sunrise and the other half with the winter solstice sunset. In all cases where the site, pyramid, or huaca is aligned with the winter solstice sunset (rather than sunrise), there are geographical restrictions (Andes mountains) hindering sunrise observation at or close to the sea-level horizon. Three sites in South America were cardinally aligned, notably Tiwanaku, but this site also marks out both solstice sunrises and sunsets.

Caral was a large settlement in the Supe Valley (Peru), 200 kilometers north of Lima, dating back as far as 2600-2000 BCE. There are remains of nineteen other pyramid complexes in an 80-square-kilometer area of the Supe valley, which is said to have supported a very large community. The main pyramid (Pirámide Mayor) covers an area nearly four football fields in area, is 18 meters tall, and encircles a large plaza. The Caral site is aligned with the summer solstice sunrise and winter solstice sunset and is flanked to its northeast by the towering Andes mountain range.

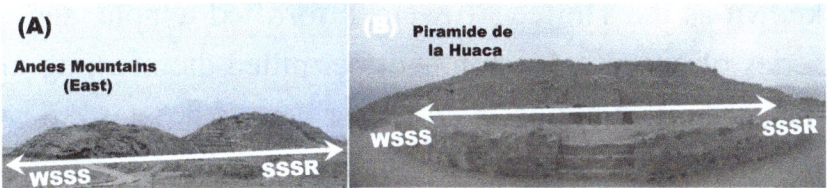

Figure 2.24 Caral (Peru). **(A)** Caral is one of the oldest pyramids in South America (2600 BCE) and aligned its main site axis and plaza pyramid platforms with the summer solstice sunrise (SSSR) and winter solstice sunset (WSSS). **(B)** Pirámide de la Huaca nicely highlights this axial alignment to the described solstices.[64]

Chavin de Huantar is located on the eastern slopes of the Andes, 250 kilometers north of Lima. It was first occupied in 3000 BCE. The Old Temple sits atop an ancient aqueduct from the original site, dating back to 850 BCE, and was built largely of stone. Inside the Old Temple a stairway leads up to a cruciform chamber, where the Lanzon monument is found. The Lanzon was bathed in light at the rising of the Sun on the summer solstice (December) but remained in darkness the rest of the year. It depicts an anthropomorphic figure with hair made of snakes and a fanged mouth, and is identified as a sky god.[65] The Chavin cult believed men could transform into jaguars through the use of a hallucinogen (the San Pedro cactus). Given the Old Temple's solar alignment, it seems likely the jaguar was identified with the Sun.

Chanquillo is a 2300-year-old solar observatory near the Casma Valley. Composed of a group of structures known as the Thirteen Towers, a fortified temple, and a series of observatory points, it permitted the marking of the solstices, equinoxes, and other key solar dates.[66] The proximate plaza and surrounding building structures highlight a general site aligned to the summer solstice sunrise and winter solstice sunset.

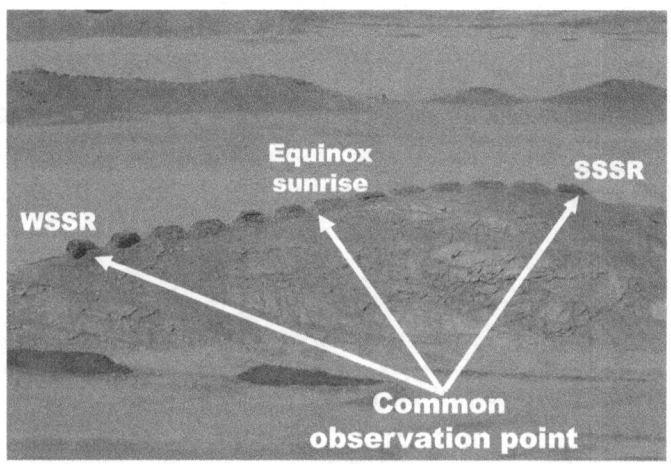

Figure 2.25 Chanquillo's Thirteen Towers calendar (Peru) wall marks out all solstice and equinox sunrises, solar zeniths. Alignments can be visualized from both the Chanquillo fortress and observation points detailed in the picture (not exact).[67]

Further down the Casma Valley are even older ceremonial centers associated with huacas and pyramids (Sechin Alto, Sechin Bajo, and Taukachi-KonKan), all of which are aligned with the winter solstice sunrise. The winter solstice sun rises from the valley without the Andes mountain visual restrictions one sees at Chanquillo or Caral.

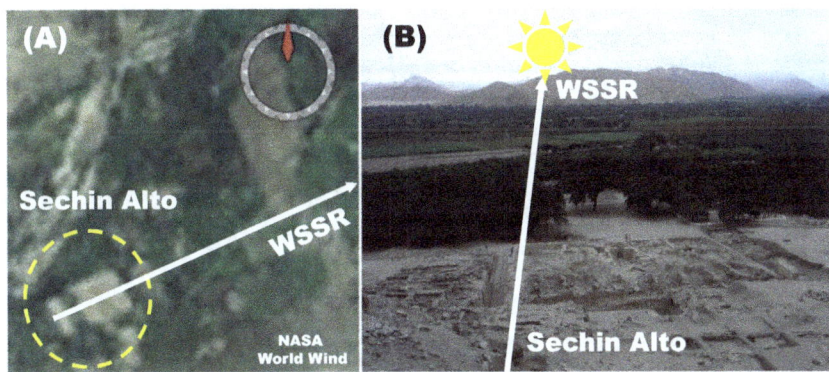

Figure 2.26 Sechin Alto. **(A & B)** Sechin Alto faces northeast up the Casma Valley, and is aligned with the winter solstice sunrise (WSSR) and summer solstice sunset (SSSS). The archaeological site called Sechin Alto was the capital of a pre-Incan culture, occupied between approximately 1800 and 900 BCE. The site is remarkable for its enormous mound, the largest of its time period and measuring some 990 feet long by 825 feet wide by 145 feet tall.[68]

The Moche civilization is considered by some scholars to have been an imperial state, expanding its power up and down the coast. The main Moche site near Trujillo in Peru contains the Huacas del Sol and La Luna pyramid-platform structures. Because these sites are many times larger than any others in the area, it has been suggested that the capital of this polity lay at this site.[69] Both the Huaca del Sol and nearby Huaca de la Luna face the winter solstice sunset with both solstice sunrises blocked by a large hill to the east and by the Andes to the northeast.

Figure 2.27 Huacas of the Sun & Moon. Both Huacas of the Sun and Moon align with the winter solstice unset (WSSS) over the Pacific Ocean. The alignment for both pyramids is best observed from Huaca de la Luna or from the hill behind it.[70]

Pachacamac is an archaeological site 40 kilometers southeast of Lima at the base of the Lurin Valley. The site, composed of at least seventeen pyramids, was originally constructed by the Wari between 600 and 800 CE. After the collapse of the Wari Empire Pachacamac became a religious center for the Ichma state. Most of its buildings were added between 800 and 1450 CE. The Ichma were assimilated by the Inca Empire, which maintained it as an important religious shrine, permitting the Pachacamac priests to function semi-independently of the Inca priesthood in Cuzco. The Inca built five additional buildings including the Temple of the Sun in the main square, which faces the winter solstice sunrise and summer solstice sunset (Figure 2.28).

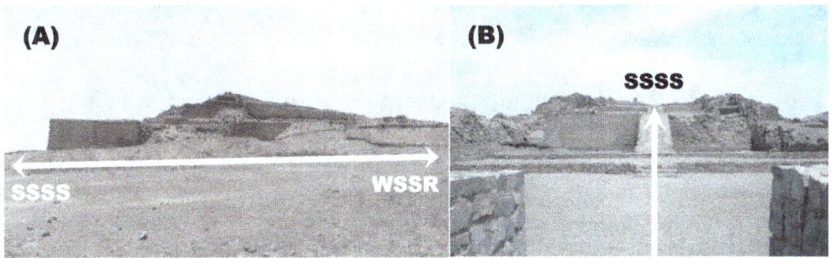

Figure 2.28 (A & B) Pachacamac's Templo del Sol faces the winter solstice sunrise and summer solstice sunset.[71]

Machu Picchu was a 15th century Inca site located 2,430 meters above sea level on a mountain ridge above the Urubamba Valley in Peru. The site was abandoned by the Inca rulers at the time of the Spanish conquest and, fortunately, was never discovered by the conquistadors.

Its three primary structures are the Intihuatana (Hitching Post of the Sun), the Temple of the Sun (Torreon), and the "room of three windows" that was dedicated to Inti, the Inca's Sun god and supreme deity. The Intihuatana stone was arranged to point directly at the Sun during the winter solstice sunrise. Together with the primary site alignment, this highlights the importance of the winter solstice sunrise to Sun god worship for the Inca elite.

Figure 2.29 Machu Piccu faces the winter solstice sunrise with the sun rising between mountain ridge clefts (within the clouds) making the solstice determination easy and accurate –weather permitting.[72]

Cuzco was the ancient Inca capital representing the quintessential nexus of social, natural, and supernatural worlds. Cuzco was built to conform to an elaborate plan with over 400 huacas aligned along 41 ceque lines (straight paths etched into the ground) radiating out from the Coricancha ("Golden Temple"). The Coricancha was originally named Inti Kancha ("Temple of the Sun") or Inti Wasi ("Sun House") and was the most important temple in the Inca Empire, dedicated primarily to Inti, the Incas' Sun god. The conquistadors demolished the Coricancha and the Church of Santo Domingo was built in its place.[73]

Building at Tiwanaku likely began around 200 BCE, and Tiwanaku exercised its main cultural influence through the Middle Horizon period (600–1000 CE). This site contains the Kalasasaya, a low platform plaza (120 by 130 meters) surrounded by high stone walls, which is cardinally aligned. The calendar wall dominates the western face and delineates the equinox and solstice sunsets. The Gateway of the Sun depicts iconography of the Staff-Rayed god, likely the prototype of Viracocha, the pre-Incan creator and Sun god.

Tiwanaku offers a number of observation points from which all solstice and equinox sunrises and sunsets can be seen. One can also determine the time of day and track the nightly heavens from this vantage point. While a calendar-clock and stellar observatory might not be considered its main functions, with a small understanding of celestial movements (sunrise, sunset, moonrise, and moonsets) and with the use of its architectural features, one could readily use the Kalasasaya platform for this purpose—much as Britain's larger stone circles are used.[74]

Figure 2.30 Tiwanaku and its calendrical achievements. **(A)** Site plan reconstruction for Tiwanaku containing a number of structures; the Kalasasaya platform and the ruins of the Akapana Pyramid. The Kalasasaya platform offers the ability to delineate all solstice and equinox sunrises and sunsets, from a single observation point. **(B)** Kalasasaya platform also contains the Gateway of the Sun, Bennet's Monolith (eastern gate) and a Calendar wall (west).[75]

Ancient India

History

The Indian civilization originated in the Indus Valley with the emergence of the Dravidians between 3250 and 2750 BCE. The Dravidians were polytheistic and their beliefs persist in Hinduism to this day. Around 1500 BCE the light-skinned Aryans invaded the Indus Valley, bringing with them the Vedic language (Sanskrit parent language) in which their sacred literature (the Vedas) was written. The Vedic Aryans worshipped nature deities–the Sun god Surya, Agni (fire), and Indra (rain). They absorbed the beliefs and practices of the conquered Dravidians, finding a consensually integrated path forward.

By 500 BCE, a more philosophical faith emerged, with its scriptures depicted in the Upanishads. Brahmanism, India's highest spiritual realm, was a subtle and sophisticated form of monotheism (Brahman as the all-embracing spirit) that tolerated Dravidian beliefs. Consequently, India maintains a deep link to its ancient past, which embraced its peoples' various beliefs to find a long-lasting consensus.

India's Ancient Hindu Temples

Hindu temples are classified into three main orders: the Nagara (northern style, with beehive-shaped towers), Dravidian (southern style, with intricately carved stone pyramid-shaped temples and gateways), and the Vesara (a hybrid style). During the medieval period (sixth to thirteenth centuries CE) temple design took place on a scale comparable to medieval European churches and cathedrals. Invaders in 1100 CE destroyed many of the finest northern temples.[76] As a result, more temples exist in the south today than the north. This perhaps helps to explain the mainly southern India distribution of the 106 earthly Divya Desams, or temples dedicated to Lord Vishnu, and the 275 Paadal Petra Sthalams, or temples dedicated to Lord Shiva, which generally reflect the Dravidian architectural style.

The Hindu temple was said to link the physical world of man to the divine world of God, where God's presence was experienced through rituals, and people were able to access divine knowledge. In so doing, the Hindu temple structure embraced the science and cosmology of the period, symbolizing the outer and inner cosmoses. The outer cosmos expressed its astronomical connections, which linked the temple structure with the movements of the Sun, the Moon, and specific planets. The inner cosmos was symbolically represented and accessed at the temple's inner shrine (sacred space). The various levels of the temple's superstructure (spire or sikhara) are said to correspond to different levels of consciousness.[77]

Such construction was an art *and* a science, blending astronomy, geography, science, mathematics, art, logic, sculpture, music, light and sound, religion, social sciences, and astrology. The construction was choreographed and orchestrated by the chief architect, who was known as a Brahmin, that is, a well-trained architect-priest and leader.[78] According to the treatises, the gods and goddesses always play near rivers, mountains, and springs. Thus these environments typified the locales for temples.[79] This sacred site location resonates with the observations made of sacred temples, huacas-ushnus, pyramids, and pyramid platforms in Egypt, Mesoamerica, and South America.

Temple Alignments and V47 Superstructures

The typical floor plan of a Hindu temple, which was developed over 2,000 years, is a sacred mandala aligned in the cardinal direction (NSEW). The multi-tiered pyramid-shaped sikhara, or temple spire, and gopurams (ornate flat top pyramid-shaped towers at the entrance of the temple complex), frequently use a V47 degree-shaped super structure (Figure 2.31).

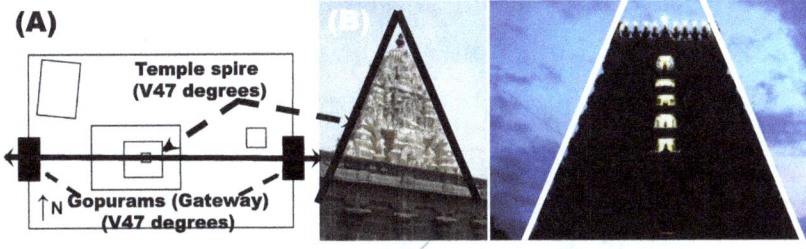

Figure 2.31 Varadharaja Perumal Temple, a famous Hindu temple dedicated to Lord Vishnu located in the holy city of Kanchipuram (India), exemplifies Hindu's Divya Desam temples. **(A)** The Varadharaja Perumal Temple and site plan. In common with 98 percent of Divya Desams, it is cardinally aligned, greeting the equinox sunrise. **(B)** Divya Desam temple spires typically feature a V47 degree angle spire. **(C)** These temple gateway superstructures are typically V47 degree shaped and are ornately decorated.[80]

This Hindu temple review focused on the ancient Divya Desams, or 106 earthbound Hindu temples glorified in the writings of the poet Vaishnava Alvars of Tamil Nadu. While not formally researched, the 275 Paadal Petra Sthalams, or temples dedicated to Lord

Shiva, also share a similar equinox alignment and the same V47 degree angle structural characteristics noted for the Divya Desams.

Of the Divya Desams, more than 80 percent exist within a solstice solar terminator band less than five minutes wide. These temples are aligned geographically over a distance of 600km. Ninety-eight percent of the Divya Desam temples are cardinally aligned, with the majority of these having their main temple gates facing due east to align with the equinox sunrise (Figure 2.31(A)). Seventy percent of Divya Desams temples have a V47 degree angle shaped gopuram (pyramid gateway) (Figure 2.32). By cardinally aligning the sites and using V47 degree angled superstructures, the temple designers implicitly acknowledged sacred time (both the solstices and the equinoxes).

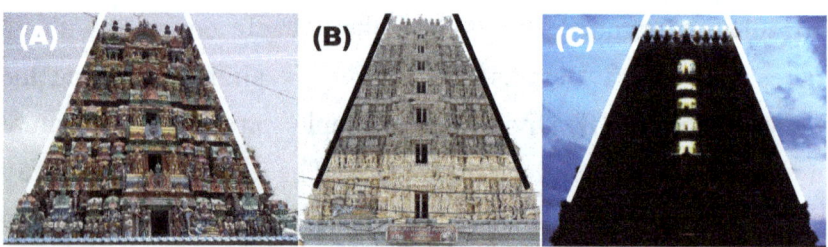

Figure 2.32 Dravidian style temple gopurams (gateways) highlight a common V47 degree solstice symbolizing angle in their superstructure design, as exemplified by: **(A)** Parimala Ranganathar Temple, **(B)** Sri Ranganathaswamy Temple, **(C)** Varadharaja Perumal Temple.[81]

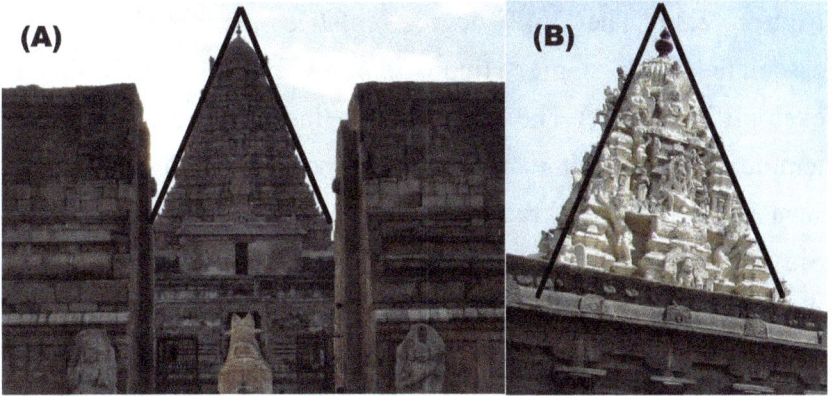

Figure 2.33 Dravidian style temple sikharas (spires) also highlight a 47 degree solstice- symbolizing angle in their superstructure designs, as exemplified by **(A)** Brihadisvara temple spire and **(B)** V47 degree Varadaraja Perumal temple spire.[82]

Before completing this chapter it's worth noting that the V47 degree angle design features are not just confined to Hindu temples in Southern India. This is actually much more widespread within the rest of India, as well as beyond India. The 275 Paadal Petra Sthalams have already been noted, and there are many more examples of V47 superstructure designs throughout Asia (see Figure).

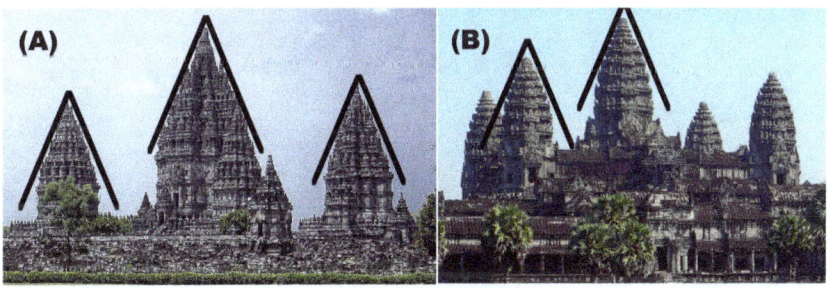

Figure 2.34 The V47 degree solstice symbolizing angles associated with some Hindu temples outside of India, as exemplified by **(A)** The 9th century Hindu Trimurti Prambanan temple, located on the border between Yogyakarta and Central Java province. The three largest temples are dedicated to Lord Shiva in the center, Lord Brahma on the left, and Lord Vishnu on the right. **(B)** Ankor Wat (Cambodia) was constructed as a Hindu temple. The temple was built by the Khmer King Suryavarman II in the early 12th century, as his state temple and eventual mausoleum. Angkor Wat was dedicated to Lord Vishnu.[83]

Chapter 3

Sun God Religions Share the Solstices & Equinoxes as Sacred Time

Introduction

Sun god worship in various forms can be found throughout most of recorded history. A solar chariot traversing the horizon from east to west, and symbolizing the Sun, was depicted on petroglyphs in Neolithic times, and depicted on icons in ancient Egypt (Ra, Horus), in India (Surya, Ashvin twins), and in other proto-Indo-European religions practiced elsewhere. This chariot carried Sun gods such as Surya (Vedic), Sól (Nordic), Helios (Greek), and Sol Invictus (Roman). Sun gods were associated with winged Sun symbols in other parts of the world, including Mesopotamia (Sumeria-Babylonia) and Persia. In the New World there were Sun gods depicted with Sun-haloes. The latter included South

America's Viracocha, his precursors, and the Incan Inti Sun gods.

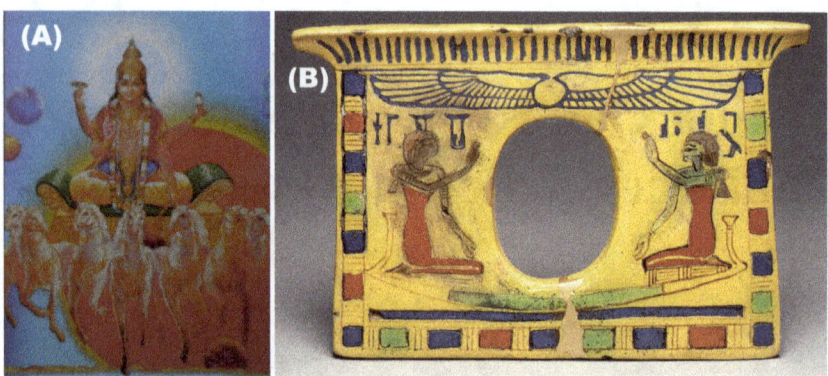

Figure 3.1 Symbols of Sun god religions. **(A)** Surya was the chief early Hindu solar deity. He was said to drive through the heavens in his triumphal chariot led by seven horses, said to represent the rainbow's seven colors and humans' seven chakras. **(B)** The shrine-shaped pectoral (c. 1250 BCE) displays the Egyptian goddesses Isis and Nepthys in a solar barque. An inscribed scarab once lay at its heart, with a winged sun-disk above. Two enthroned gods, falcon-headed Horus and jackal-headed Anubis, supported the missing scarab.[84]

Among some of these ancient Sun god religions are the progenitors of today's global religious faiths. Arguably, the Abrahamic faiths (Islam, Judaism, and Christianity) assimilated or annihilated the ancient religions of Egypt-Mesopotamia, while from the early Aryan-Vedic religion in the Indus Valley evolved Hinduism, which spawned Buddhism and Jainism. From these sources we can see how humankind organized itself into proto-religions that evolved into dominant regional Sun god religions.

Ultimately these Sun god religions present, in the main, a unifying theme: that a supreme Sun god existed in the transcendental realm, beyond this ego-space-time realm. This Sun god was responsible for creating and sustaining all life. An individual's spiritual or consciousness development was accelerated if he or she could experience altered states of consciousness within their lifetime, with the possibility of spiritual immortality (escaping karmic rebirth) on offer for spiritually advanced people.

The Sun gods evolved over millennia, often in association with a hierarchy or retinue of familial deities, and their mythologies and cosmologies did as well. Oftentimes these were a bit far-fetched and allegorically animating. In their cosmologies these religions described different environmental elements (earth, air, fire, and water), celestial bodies (Sun, Moon, Earth, and various planets), the weather, and agricultural, fertility, animal, and plant life.

These myths were associated with Earth's annual celestial cycle, often associating the Sun gods with the constellations, and linked to the solstice and equinox festivals. This was about marking the times of the year when humankind should worship their deities and conduct sacred rituals, i.e., on the solstices and equinoxes. The purpose was to commune with God, honor one's ancestors, and thank God, Mother Earth, and the heavens for making life possible.

Invariably there was a central axis of power-control created by the leaders and priesthoods. These prominent members of society closely associated themselves with the Sun gods, undertaking specialized sacred rituals on society's behalf. Integrated religious and agricultural-fertility festivals and rituals played an important organizing role, binding the community together. It was crucial to know when to conduct sacred rituals, as well as to plan for agricultural cycles to ensure food surpluses.

Surplus taxes (high agricultural yields) from optimized agricultural production made it possible for leaders to invest in waging war against other kingdoms and enemies of the state, which if successful would allow the ancient priesthoods to grow their religious fiefdoms. Ultimately, this partnership between leaders and priesthoods was immensely successful in its society-organizing role, in that it created great empires that thrived for millennia.

The priesthood's effective control of sacred ritual know-how allowed it to create relationships in which leaders were dependent upon the priesthood for access to the spirit world. This placed priests in controlling positions in their societies. Leadership and politics would likely have benefited immensely from this religious control of society. Leaders such as pharaohs, kings, queens, priests, and priestesses enhanced their power by accessing altered states of consciousness.

Meanwhile, the common folk were directed to follow a code of virtuous life conduct that promised a blissful afterlife as a reward for their efforts. Concepts equivalent to today's Hindu and Buddhist principles of Unity states of consciousness, ego death/spiritual rebirth, karmic rebirth, or escape from rebirth (immortality) lay at the heart of advanced spiritual endeavor for many ancient societies' elites. These elites practiced these principles fervently, for their afterlives depended upon it.

Ancient Sun God Religions Shared the Same Sacred Ritual Dates

India and Hinduism

There is merit in reviewing the festival dates observed in India before other regions, because India's highly evolved religion stretches back into deep antiquity and survived its millennial odyssey to exist in the present day. Additionally, when we compare Hinduism's sacred archaeology, its depiction of sacred space and time concepts, its pantheon of solar deities, and its shared sacred ritual dates with the extinct Sun god religions of Egypt, Mesoamerica, and South

America, it's clear that they all share significant themes in common. Perhaps the ancient Sun god religions were regional manifestations of a global phenomenon and organizing principle.

History

Sun god worship in India can be traced to its roots in the Indus Valley during the third millennia BCE. The Sun god was accorded an important place in the Vedas (sacred hymns and texts), in deity symbols, and in Hindu's solstice and equinox festivals. The Hindu religion evolved through various periods in the Indus Valley. The Dravidian culture predominated from 2500 to 1700 BCE, and the Aryan culture appeared around 1500 BCE heralding the Vedic period (1500-900 BCE). This culture is said to have contributed substantially to India's religious, mythological, and cosmological foundations, and its solar (Sûrya, Indra, Ushas) and fire (Agni) pantheons. By 1200 BCE Rigvedic influence in India was widespread.[85]

The Brâhmanical Period (900-600 BCE) emphasized the Almighty (Brahman) as the single, supreme, omnipotent, and omnipresent God, and recast the older Rigvedic gods as manifestations of Brahman.[86] It also witnessed the ascension of the Brâhmans (priests) to the top of the social hierarchy, likely through their control of sacred ritual knowledge.[87]

The Upanishad Period (600-300 BCE) saw the development of the major Upanishads. The emphasis changed to discovering the internal secrets and the path or way of life,[88] and it was believed that the pleasures and attractions of this life could be renounced through ascetic practices (tapas, yoga, and tântra). In so doing one could acquire transpersonal powers and creative energies.

The Purânic Period (300–800 CE) saw further maturation of the Hindu cosmology. This cosmology was characterized by Hindu polytheism on the one hand (centered on Vishnu, Shiva, and Devî (Mother Goddess)) and universalism on the other (all paths lead to the Absolute God, Brahman).[89] During this period the Sun god was merged with Vishnu and linked to the spring equinox festival.[90]

Figure 3.2 Early Hindu deities. **(A)** Surya was ancient India's main Sun god. He was worshipped at dawn and had many temples dedicated to him across India. **(B)** Indra, the god of rain and

thunderstorms, was known to wield a thunderbolt (vajra), as seen at the Ellora Caves. **(C)** Agni, god of fire and immortal messenger, as seen at Rajarani Temple, Bhuvanesvar, Orissa, India.[91]

Ancient Hindu Religion

Hindu mythology gravitated around two systems of worship, namely the Vaishnavite (Vishnu) and Shaivite (Shiva) forms. These complemented each other to cover all aspects of human thought into two systems of Hindu philosophy, Duality and Unity.[92] Brahma created the world, Vishnu maintained it, and Shiva destroyed it. The Trimurti allegorically depicted the cycle of creation, maintenance, and destruction that supported the evolution of life and its development of consciousness.

Figure 3.3 Hindu's Trimurti of deities embraced the cosmic functions of creation, maintenance, and destruction. **(A)** Brahma the creator, from the Prajapati Government Museum in Madras,

India. **(B)** Vishnu the maintainer or preserver, from West Bengal, India. The God Vishnu with Lakshmi and Sarasvati (12th century stone). **(C)** Shiva the destroyer or transformer. Hoysala carving of Shiva from a Belur-Halebid temple.[93]

The Bhagavad Gita, the bible of Hinduism dedicated to Vishnu in his eighth incarnation as lord Krishna, offers a comprehensive portrayal of different paths to human salvation. In Vedic Hinduism, liberation is the attainment of heavenly status and the cessation of karmic rebirth. In the Bhagavad Gita, Krishna refers to earthly souls being able to unite with the supreme entity (God).[94]

From an ancient legacy embracing assimilation, rationalization, and continued development of intellectual thinking, Hinduism evolved into a unity within diversity, with Brahman (the ultimate reality underlying all phenomena) as the supreme god manifested as Lords Brahma, Vishnu, and Shiva. Sacred texts expressed beliefs in the evolution of individual consciousness, the fourfold ends of human life, the laws of karmic rebirth, and Unity states of consciousness.

Hindu Sacred Festivals

Hindus observe sacred occasions with religious festivals, worshiping specific Sun gods and other gods and goddesses, as well as seasonal harvests and fertility.

These festivals are dedicated to Vishnu, Shiva, Brahma, Rama, Krishna, and Surya.

Winter Solstice

For millennia, Indians celebrated the winter solstice as the birth of their Sun god (Vishnu/Surya) and the start of their new year. It is a celebration in honor of the Sun's increasing strength (longer days) and now occurs on January 14. It is considered the "morning of the gods."[95] The next day is named Sun God Day (Surya Pongal), and is dedicated to the Sun god Surya. The shift from December reflects the Hindu religion's use of the lunar rather than solar calendar.

In Vedic times, the winter solstice represented the moment in time when the Sun god (Surya), driving his seven-horse chariot, turned from south to north.[96] Today the "sleep and rise" of Vishnu is celebrated on the solstices, in line with his solar status. A number of authors propose that Krishna and Buddha were born on December 25, or the winter solstice,[97,98,99] as incarnations of the solar Vishnu.

Spring Equinox

The festival of Ratha Saptami falls on the seventh day of the lunar cycle (first quarter of the Moon) following the spring equinox, and marks the birth of Surya (Sun god) and the start of spring. Today this festival is widely celebrated in Sun temples dedicated to Surya.

Holi is one of the most widespread Hindu festivals, and takes place around the spring equinox, particularly in northern India where it is dedicated to Krishna. The spring equinox/full moon celebration represents the solar resurrection, when the day length becomes longer than the night. The association of Vishnu (and Surya) with the winter solstice and Krishna with the spring equinox is comparable to the Egyptian solar myths of Osiris, Isis, and Horus.[100,101]

Chhath is an ancient Hindu festival dedicated specifically to the Sun god Surya, celebrated in March–April on Chaitra Shashti, which occurs a few days after Holi (the equinox). Rigorous rituals are undertaken over four days, including fasting and meditating at sunrise (representing solar birth) and sunset (solar death).

Ancient Egypt

The ancient Egyptian religion went into decline under the rule of Rome, and was subsequently annihilated during the Arab conquest, so few of its sacred texts survive. However, Egyptian architecture honored cults of deities and of the dead with pyramids, temples, and tombs.[102] The rich mythical, hieroglyphic, and artistic achievements of the Egyptians, and the magnificence of their pyramids and temples, reveal a deeply spiritual culture. The difficulty, of course, lies in interpreting the essence of their religion from the remains of their architecture and globally-dispersed art and icons, as well as from their pyramid texts and allegorical myths.

A full understanding of ancient Egyptian culture remains a work in progress. Consensus is yet to be achieved regarding Egypt's historical past, its religion, cosmology, and mythology. A non-mainstream view posits that ancient Egypt's religious cults developed ritual processes that gave practitioners access to altered states of consciousness, such as Unity states of consciousness (mystical unity), ego death/rebirth, spiritual healing, and that this was used in kingship and queenship leadership development. In this vein, the Pyramid texts were used by the pharaohs to assist them to conduct their ritual processes. Over time, these texts became available to the rest of the elite.[103]

Counterpoised to this view is the mainstream perspective that states ancient Egypt's religion was mundane and non-mystical. In so doing, it interprets sacred texts (Pyramid texts) as wholly serving a funerary cult utility. Funerary cults are said to involve the living conferring benefits on the dead in the afterlife through ritual and offerings.[104]

Egyptian Sun Gods

A relatively mature Sun god religion appeared early in Egypt's history, certainly as far back as the Old Kingdom (3rd millennium BCE). This religion was associated with a supreme Sun god called Ra. The chief center of Ra worship was at Heliopolis, where he was identified as Atum-Ra and seen as the progenitor of the Ennead. The Ennead was a group of nine mythological deities comprising Ra and his children Shu and Tefnut, his grandchildren Geb (Earth) and Nut (Celestial heavens), and great-grandchildren Osiris, Isis, Set, and Nephthys.

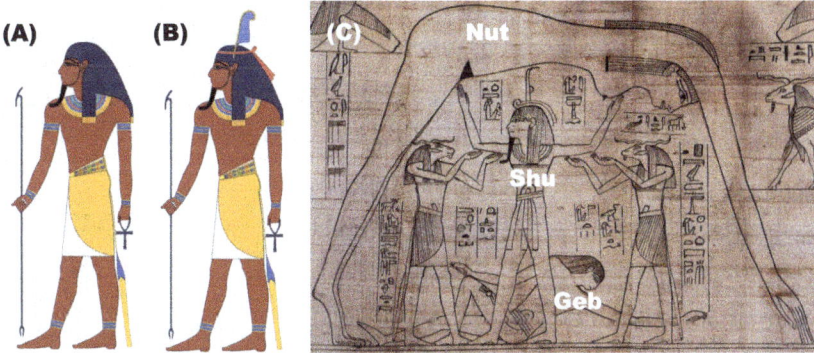

Figure 3.4 Members of the Ennead. **(A)** Atum, was a primordial creator deity, father to the king, and ultimately merged with Ra (Atum Ra). **(B)** Shu (which means "emptiness" and "he who rises up"), was one of the primordial gods and a personification of the air. **(C)** Nut, goddess of the sky, supported by Shu the god of air, and the ram-headed deities, while the Earth god Geb reclines beneath.[105]

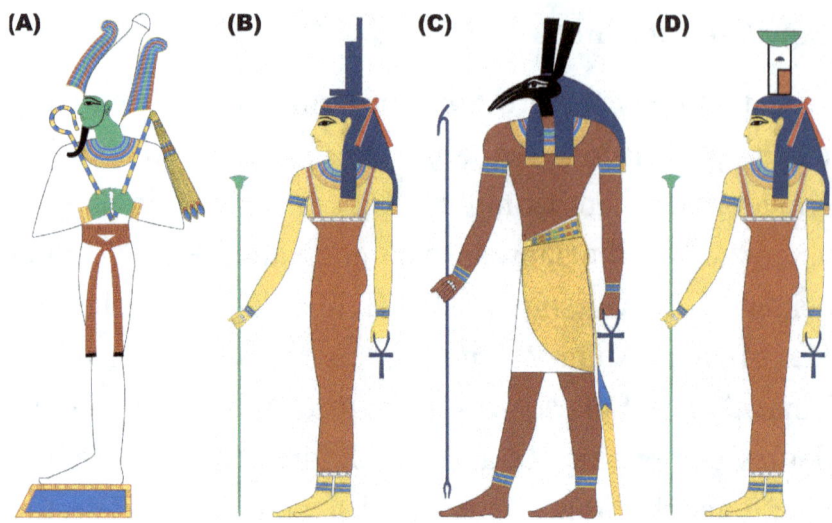

Figure 3.5 The sibling members of the Ennead continued (artistic renditions). **(A)** Osiris, god of the afterlife, underworld and the dead, holding barley. **(B)** Isis, goddess of motherhood, magic and fertility. **(C)** Set, god of storms, the desert, and chaos. **(D)** Nephthys, goddess of death and lamentation, who was typically paired with her sister Isis in funerary rites.[106]

The hierarchy of deities extending beyond the Ennead represented different manifestations of the one Supreme God. Ra was ancient Egypt's Sun god and creator deity. By the fifth Dynasty (3rd millennium BCE), he was the supreme deity ruling in all parts of the created world: the heavens, Earth, and the underworld. During the Old and New Kingdoms Egyptian religion underwent consolidation and evolution. Consequently, Ra merged with other solar deities (Atum-Ra, Amun-Ra, Re, and Re-Horakhty) to become associated with sunrise, the midday Sun, sunset, and the nighttime underworld journey of the Sun to its morning rise on the eastern horizon.

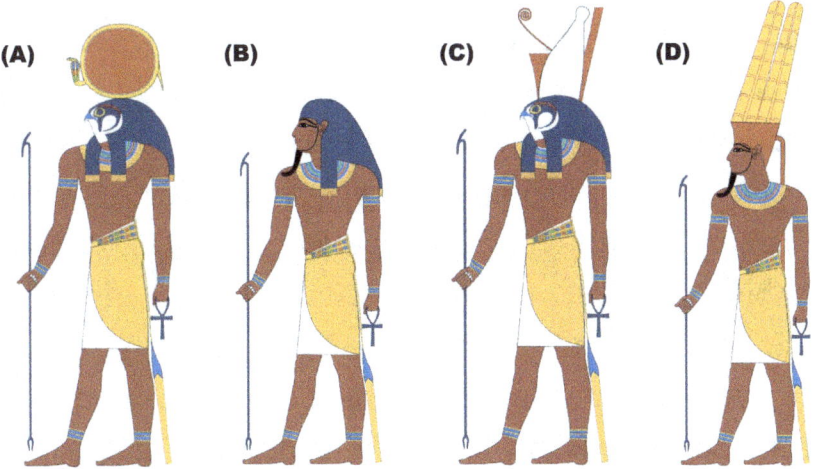

Figure 3.6 Important Sun and Creator deities from early Egyptian history. **(A)** Ra/Re merged with other Sun gods. Ra had the head of a falcon and a serpent sun-disk resting on his head. Re-Horakhty fuses Ra and Horus (of the 2 horizons). Re-Horakhty was also identified with Amun. **(B)** Atum, a primordial creator deity from early times frequently mentioned in the pyramid texts, and father to the king. **(C)** Horus became the ancient Egyptians' national patron god. He was usually depicted as a falcon-headed man wearing the pschent, or a red and white crown, as a symbol of kingship over the entire kingdom of Egypt. **(D)** Amun, with two plumes on his head, the ankh symbol, and holding a scepter.[107]

The pharaohs were seen as Ra's manifestations on Earth, referred to as "Sons of Ra" and their special role in the land of the living was to realize and maintain Ma'at, a virtuous life exemplified by upholding truth, balance, order, law, morality, and justice. Ra is said to have entrusted this activity to the pharaoh, who in turn delegated parts of this responsibility to the priesthoods and administrative officials. The pharaoh, guided by high priests and priestesses, made divine offerings to Ra and mortuary offerings to the deceased on behalf of his subjects during specially timed sacred rituals. The pharaoh's devotion was supported by the priesthood within pyramids and temples, and ritual activities took place away from the public in places of sensory silence, i.e., pyramid chambers and inner temple sanctums.[108] These were areas in which only the pharaoh, queen, and the high priests and priestesses were allowed.

Osiris was an important and popular deity as far back as the Old Kingdom, associated with the afterlife, the underworld, and the dead. The pharaohs of Egypt were associated with Osiris in death and were awarded eternal life through ritualistic processes in which the pharaoh would experience the "Absolute God," Ra, thereby receiving virtuous, divine, and kingship qualities during his lifetime and reign.

Osiris was classically depicted as a green-skinned man with a pharaoh's beard, partially mummy-wrapped at the legs, and wearing a uniquely designed crown. Osiris was considered brother and husband of Isis and father of Horus. His name means "he sees the throne" or "the seat and throne of the eye," and he was the heavenly source of the soul's substance and the heavenly body to which all souls returned.

Figure 3.7 The Ennead in action. Cropped picture; "weighing of the heart scene" from the book of the dead of Hunefer. Hunefer, having passed the test, is said to be presented by Horus to the shrine of the green-skinned, one-legged Osiris, god of the underworld and the dead. Isis and Nephthys accompany him, while the Four Genii Sons of Horus sit atop an opened water lily flower.[109]

Isis was worshipped as protector of the dead, goddess of children, the ideal mother and wife, patroness of nature and magic, and protector of the people. Isis literally means "the power to make Kings" or the "seat and throne of the soul." She personified the throne and was an important representation of the pharaoh's power. Isis was the binding source of the divine soul of Ra's secrets of the universe, and together with Osiris she helped civilize the Egyptian people, via the pharaoh and his upholding of Ma'at.

Horus was the child of Isis and Osiris, and became the intermediary between the living and the dead and the recipient of human prayers for Osiris. Horus literally means "the face of heaven." Horus was also associated with a "twice born," or rebirth/resurrection myth. He was born on December 25th (first birth) a few days after Osiris' winter solstice death, and his rebirth as Horus the elder was celebrated on the spring equinox (second birth). His rebirth as Horus the Elder represented the leadership, intelligence, and longevity of a just ruler. It was said that nothing escaped his watchful eye (eye of Horus, the all-seeing Eye), and he ruled over a unified Upper and Lower Egypt through the pharaoh's kingship.

Hathor was regarded as the divine mother of all reigning pharaohs, and was known as the "Lady of the West," the title referring to her receipt of the setting Sun, which she protected until morning. She was also associated with healing powers. Hathor was depicted as a goddess wearing a headdress consisting of cow horns with a Sun disk placed between them. Her name literally means "House of Horus," in reference to the spring equinox, when Horus was reborn as Horus the Elder.

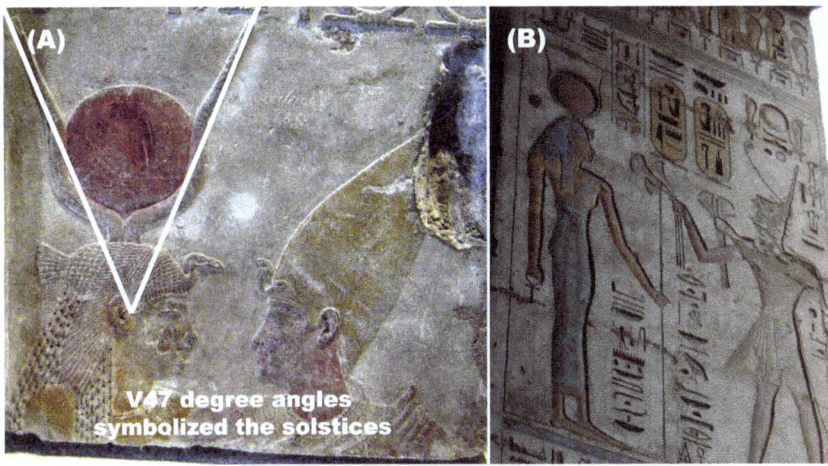

Figure 3.8 Isis and Hathor's cow horn-shaped headgear. Both goddesses were celebrated at the spring equinox. **(A)** Isis and Pharaoh Nectanébo II on a temple relief from Saqqara. The symbolic cow-horned headdress represents a V47 degree solstice-symbolizing angle—the sun as the equinox between the solstices Taurean spars—possibly symbolizing sacred time? Also note Pharaoh Nectanébo wearing a serpent uraeus, indicative of the equinox and Wadjet as sacred time. **(B)** Hathor in the Medinet Habu Temple (Temple of Ramesses III) in Thebes (Luxor).[110]

Ancient Egyptian Sacred Solar Festivals

The winter solstice was a highly significant ritual date in ancient Egypt, beginning many thousands of years BCE.[111] It was celebrated as a Sun god festival involving the death of the old Sun at the solar standstill between December 21st and 25th. This turning point was celebrated with Horus being brought out from the temple before sunrise on December 25th once the Sun had visibly commenced its northward movement on the horizon (third day after the solstice or solar standstill day). Thus the Sun as Osiris died on the winter solstice and was reborn on the December 25th sunrise as his son Horus.

According to Plutarch, a first century Greek historian, a popular festival was held in Alexandria,[112] in which tens of thousands of pilgrims from all over Egypt and the Near East flocked to the Nile delta cities Busirus and Djedu to perform the rites of Isis for the resurrection of Osiris from the dead.[113] According to the Cairo Calendar (an ancient papyrus), a series of elaborate feasts, festivals, and ceremonies dedicated to the Solar pantheon were held in the lead up to the winter solstice. The deities honored included Osiris, Horus, Isis, Sokar and Ptah.[114]

The spring equinox celebrated the dual lunar and solar qualities of both goddesses (Isis and Hathor) and their divine child (Horus). This festival conjoined the influences of the new Moon and spring equinox as closely as possible, much like the Christian Easter of today. The celebration of fertility linked to lunar cycles and longer days, and associated with the spring equinox, was almost universal in the ancient world. Nine months later, at the winter solstice, a divine child was born. In Egypt's case this was Horus. The feast dedicated to Hathor and Isis was celebrated at the Temple of Edfu.[115] Plutarch stated that a second festival for Horus in his adult form followed on the spring equinox.[116] In the run up to this there occurred a series of feasts and celebrations dedicated to the solar pantheon (Re, Osiris, and Horus) and other Gods (Thoth, Bastet).[117]

Figure 3.9 Other Sun god-supporting deities from early times. **(A)** Ptah was god of creation, the arts and fertility. **(B)** Thoth, god of knowledge, hieroglyphs and wisdom, was almost always depicted holding a rod symbolizing power in one hand, and ankh (the key of the Nile symbolizing life) in the other. His wife was Maat, goddess of truth and justice. **(C)** Bastet, the goddess of cats, Lower Egypt, and the Sun and Moon.[118]

The summer solstice was a celebration of the birth of Ra (the supreme Sun god). Ra entered the world again at this time to oversee his annual cycle as played out by members of the Ennead. Lords Osiris, Horus, Set, Lady Isis, and Hathor were all born around the summer solstice.[119] On the final day of celebrations, ritual prayers were spoken just before sunset. Note the link to the summer solstice sunset, which is also indicated by temple alignments. The summer solstice also coincided with the Nile inundation, which marked the commencement of the year for the Nile Rising Calendar.[120] This was the ancient Egyptian agricultural calendar (distinct from the 365-day solar-sacred calendar); thus the solar (sacred) and agricultural calendars converged around the summer solstice when the agricultural year was said to begin.

Osiris and Set as brothers represented the light and dark, respectively, of life's duality principle, and they battled during the course of the year as days changed in length. Around the autumn equinox, a balance was achieved between them: day and night were equal in length. For the three days of the autumn equinox ceremony, they divided the world equally. Equinox celebrations involved Set, Osiris, Isis, and Horus, with rulings between the feuding Set and Osiris adjudged by Ra, Thoth, and Ptah.[121]

Pre-Colombian South America

In contrast to Old World religions, we know of the Inca and pre-Inca Andean religions only through archaeological remains and Spanish post-conquest accounts. These cultures never developed a writing system, so there exists no formal body of documentation or glyphic texts to delineate their religion or its evolution.[122] Couple this with the disappearance of native languages, and we can better comprehend the loss of shamanic traditions and rituals. It no doubt required many years of education to master such esoteric knowledge, ritual practice, and daily discipline. Thus we have only a limited account of pre-Colombian religion and its rituals, with some general agreement on its origins, evolution, and geographical spread.[123,124]

Andean iconography (e.g., sacred artifacts, ceramics, and textile symbols) provides interesting clues to the evolution of pre-Incan Andean religions. Apparently, by the end of the Early Horizon era (900–200 BCE), after a centuries-long regional and cultural odyssey, the symbol of the staff-bearing god emerged out of the older Rayed Head symbol. By the Middle Horizon (600–1000 CE) this staff god achieved religious supremacy among the closely interacting and widespread Wari and Tiwanaku cultures, which were later conquered by the Incas.[125,126] Viracocha, the staff-rayed, pre-Incan, solar-creator deity, emerged pre-eminent from this millennial journey.

The Inca civilization arose in the Peruvian highlands sometime in the early thirteenth century CE. During the ascendancy of the Inca, Viracocha was integrated into their deity pantheon, albeit subordinated to Inti, the Inca's supreme Sun god. The key to understanding pre-Colombian Andean religious evolution is, in my view, recognition that both Viracocha and Inti had different primordial origins, yet embraced the same solar qualities. These converging Sun god-based religions also captured the same solstice alignments within their sacred sites (temples, pyramids, ushnus, huacas, etc.), which certainly adds support for the concept of Viracocha's Sun god connection across pre-Columbian and pre-Inca South America.

Figure 3.10 (A) Depiction of Viracocha as a sun-rayed, staff-holding creator and solar deity on the upper section of the Gate of the Sun, in the ancient city of Tiwanaku (Bolivia). **(B)** A representation of Inti, the Inca Sun god.[127]

Cosmology and Mythology

The Andean worldview split the cosmos into three interconnecting realms, each occupied by deities: Hanan Pacha, the celestial world; Ukhu Pacha, the inner earth (Pachamama/Earth-mother representing fertility, reproduction, motherhood); and Cay Pacha, the Earth's surface, which included humans and where deities intervened and mediated between the realms. This worldview embraced concepts of duality (Sun-moon, sky-earth, night-day, etc.) and gender with an animating or vitalizing force imbuing all aspects of life.[128]

The male forces of the cosmos vitalized the earthly, feminine, regenerative-procreative forces. These forces were drawn into cyclical systems: the rain nourished the earth and water was then drawn up into the clouds. Other meteorological deities such as lightning and rainbows joined the celestial and earthly realms, permitting the inflow of life-giving forces. The thunder and lightning deity, via storms, returned the life-giving force (water and the global weather circuit) back to the Earth.[129] Given the Sun's role in weather, lightning, and thunder, it could be argued that Viracocha was a solar deity work-in-progress, while Inti was the usurping Sun god.

According to Andean beliefs, human history was divided into various epochs: the first epoch of humanity ended with a catastrophic flood, the second when the vault of the sky fell from the heavens, and the third was destroyed by a great wind. The fourth catastrophe was the Spanish Conquest, said to resemble the physical return of Viracocha to the Inca lands. Each of these forms of world destruction (Pachacuti) meant a change in the most fundamental divisions of the cosmos from which the Andean peoples' world was recreated.[130]

Andean Deities and Religion

The name Inca means "people of the Sun." They regarded the Sun as their creator and supreme deity. Sun god worship was introduced by Pachacuti Inca after the Sun appeared to him in a dream and addressed him as "child." Pachacuti Inca ascended to the throne after his successful battle with the neighboring Chanca tribe. This conflict likely reflected a struggle between the Viracocha and Inti cults, as well as differences between their priestly classes, who were said to be opposed to Pachacuti's reforms.[131]

Pachacuti reorganized and reformed much of Inca society, promoting the cult of the Sun (Inti) over the combined creator-solar deity Viracocha. Pachacuti Inti assumed the role of patron, renovated the Temple of the Sun in Cuzco (Coricancha), assigned lands to the Sun cult, and constructed temples of the Sun beyond Cuzco (e.g., Pachacamac). Thus, the cult of the older Viracocha deity was replaced by a new religious focus, the Sun (Inti). As the conquests of the Inca extended their empire, the latter became known as the "Land of the Sun.[132]

The Inca religion and deities were superimposed onto popular, widespread Andean deities such as Pachamama

(Earth Mother) and Mamacocha (Mother Sea). Cuzco aside, two huacas were venerated above all others in the Empire: Titicaca and Pachacamac. The Incas honored this connection. The Sun god cult itself may have originated near Lake Titicaca. The Incas also built a solar cult temple, the winter solstice sunrise aligned Pachacamac, alongside an oracular cult center just south of present-day Lima. Here, the Incas co-opted the fame and power of the existing famous regional cult shrines, thus facilitating religious and societal assimilation and integration.[133]

The Inca ruler presided over public ceremonies as son of the Sun and, together with the high priest (Villac Umu), thereby connected with the supernatural realm.[134] Public ceremonies were regulated by the Incas and were associated with cosmological (solar, lunar) and agrarian cycles. The most important celebrations were dedicated to the winter solstice, equinoxes, summer solstice, lunar phases, maize harvest, and unexpected climatic changes and volcanic eruptions as well.[135] However, many other celebrations were performed in private by the Inca elite.[136]

Viracocha was recognized by the Inca as the creator deity and given other titles such as "foundation of the Earth". Viracocha and Inti sat alongside the god of lightning, forming a triad of solar-themed deities.[137] Later Viracocha became known as Pachacamac, originally the name of a sky god of the Lurín Valley in central Peru. In pre-Incan times the Aymara-Quichua race worshipped Viracocha as the great creator god and possessor of all things, and believed Viracocha made both the Sun and the Moon.[138]

Viracocha was the creator deity who emerged in a time of primeval darkness and created the celestial bodies (including the Milky Way), as well as the world and all its living things. The Quechua term *Viracocha* likely referred to a creative-vitalizing force and function rather than to a divine personage. Viracocha was associated with prayer at sunrise and was assisted in his divine endeavors by other creative aspects or "alter egos." One such alter ego, Imaymana Viracocha, was associated with the medicinal jungle botanicals that were essential for ritual practice. In the Aymara-speaking society around Lake Titicaca the words *vira* and *cocha* were, and still are, associated with the preparation of herbs and aromatic plants used for offerings in rituals. The Antisuyu people identified Viracocha with the shamanic or priestly order. Viracocha's influences over the Andean world included a civilizing and instructive role in which he taught correct moral and ethical behavior as well as skills such as agriculture and crafts.[139]

The Inca's Sacred Festivals

Given this evolutionary odyssey of local-regional godheads combined with the impact of the conquistadors and associated religious assimilation, little is known of sacred festivals prior to the Inca. Given that the pre-Incan sacred sites (pyramids, huacas, and ushnus) are largely solstice-aligned (with a minority equinox-aligned), we can reasonably deduce that prior to the Inca ascendancy sacred festivals were held on the solstices and equinoxes.

The priests were responsible for observing the celestial heavens, particularly the Sun and Moon, and maintaining the calendar. The Inca religious festivals typically revolved around the rhythms of the Sun and Moon. As in other regions and epochs, the winter solstice was pre-eminent among the religious festivals. Inti Raymi (Feast of the Sun) was celebrated at the winter solstice as the start of the New Year,[140] honoring Inti as the pre-eminent Sun god of the Inca religion.[141] This festival was associated with the birth of the new Sun, which signaled the start of the New Year. Viracocha also played a central role in worship as the creator god of the universe. Viracocha was depicted wearing the Sun as a crown, holding thunderbolts in his hands, and with rain pouring down from his eyes like tears.[142]

Sun god worship during Inti Raymi lasted several weeks. A rigorous fast was observed for three days prior to the festival, and no fires were lit. On the morning of the fourth day, the Inca, followed by the people *en masse*, gathered at the great plaza in Cuzco to hail the rising Sun. After sunrise, they marched to the Coricancha (golden temple of the Sun).[143] Facing the rising Sun, the Inca drank a toast of aqha (a fermented drink) to the Sun. Only the Inca performed this ritual, after which they entered the Coricancha (Golden Temple). A subsequent toasting ceremony took place between the Inca and non-Inca elites in front of the masses in the plaza. This was likely used to legitimize the non-Inca elite in the eyes of their people, while representing a socio-political gesture that helped to facilitate the integration of the empire. Similar segregated cult-festivals took place elsewhere within the empire.[144,145] Teenage Inca boys completed their initiation rites and were accepted into adult society at this festival time.[146]

Coya Raymi (Moon feast) was the official imperial ceremony honoring the Moon as queen of all planets and stars of the sky, as well as wife to the Sun.[147] Coya Raymi coincided with the spring equinox and marked the start of a new agricultural cycle. It was considered an auspicious occasion in which fertility and the start of the agricultural season were honored. Coya Raymi lasted for one month.

This was followed by the summer solstice's (Capac Raymi) Glorious Festival, in which the Sapa Inca led the people in Sun worship. The autumn equinox was celebrated as the harvest festival (Pacha-puchuy), during which animal sacrifices were offered to the gods. Other sacred and agricultural festivals such as praying for rain, honoring the dead, harvesting, and making sacrifices were interspersed among the key solstice and equinox sacred festivals.[148]

Pre-Colombian Maya (and Mesoamerican)

Similar to pre-Colombian South America, we only know pre-Colombian Maya and Mesoamerican (Aztec, Olmec) religious beliefs and cosmology through archaeological remains, iconographic evidence (pottery, carved stone stelae), and ethno-historic accounts written around the time of the Spanish conquest. This information is supplemented by a limited number of Postclassic books (Dresden, Madrid, and Paris codices, and the *Popul Vuh*),[149,150] that survived the Spanish conquest.

The Maya were not a single empire but represented numerous political-religious regions. Despite this regional diversity, many religious traits were shared across the various post-classic Maya polities. This sharing also extended to the Aztecs, who had close political and economic ties to the Maya region. The vast majority of major Maya deities known from the Yucatan codices were already worshipped among the Classic Maya.[151]

Cosmology and Mythology

The profound influence on Mesoamerican life of the movements of the Sun, stars, planets, and other celestial bodies was reflected in their mythology. The Maya cosmos consisted of the sky, the Earth, and the underworld. Their world was ordered by time as measured by the movements of the Sun, Moon, planets, and stars. With this knowledge the culture developed various calendars, the most important being a 260-day cycle (agricultural, fertility, solar zenith/antizenith) and a 365-day cycle (solar/tropical), which approximated the solar year and recorded cycles of the Moon and Venus.[152]

The Maya creation myth, the Popol Vuh, tells of three generations of deities who created the world, humans, and other life. The creator grandparents of the sea and lightning gods of the sky were the first generation of gods and goddesses. The second generation comprised the creator grandparents' sons Hun and Vucub Hunahpu. Hun Hunahpu had two wives and two sets of sons. Hunahpu and Xbalanque, the Hero Twins, were the youngest sons and were associated with the establishment of the celestial cycles.[153] The journey of the hero twins and their father through dark Xibalba was said to play out annually in the procession of constellations across the ecliptic horizon. The Maya refer to the Milky Way as Xibal Be, or the road of Xibalba. It seems that, as in many other old world mythologies, the apparent movements of the stars and planets across the skyward heavens may have served as a basic template for the development of Mesoamerican mythology[154] (not unlike the Osiris myth for the ancient Egyptians).

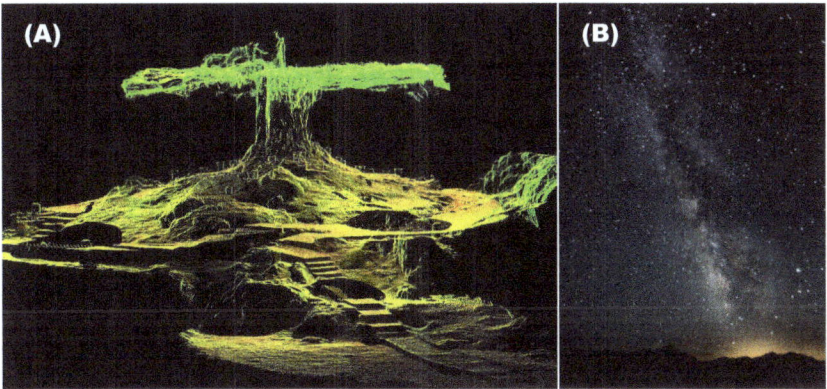

Figure 3.11 Mayan cosmology. **(A)** The entrance to Xibalba, the ancient Mayan underworld, was traditionally held to be a cave. Composite 3D laser scan image shows staircases and artifacts surrounding the great limestone column of Balankanche. Balankanche is a cave located at the Chichen Itza World Heritage site in Yucatan (Mexico). Stretching from floor to ceiling and resembling the ancient Maya conception of the World Tree (Ceiba), this cave like many others was a sacred place to the ancient Maya and was used as a temple for ceremonial purposes. **(B)** The ancient Maya understood the heavens and how they created life. They knew the sun would rise in a dark cleft in the

Milky Way on the winter solstice 2012; they termed this the end of the Mayan calendar.[155]

Like the Aztec myth of the Five Suns, Mayan religion told of multiple creations and destructions.[156] Maya and Aztec myth indicate that a flood immediately preceded the creation of the present era. The date associated with this was the beginning of the last great Baktun cycle in 3114 BC (144,000 days long). The cycle was predicted to end on December 21, 2012. Myths of world creations and destructions are frequently couched in terms of calendric events, that is, the completion of the 365-day year and the Katun cycle (Mayan end of world).[157]

The Sun was the most important unit of order and was reborn daily from the underworld at dawn in the east. Following its ecliptic arc across the sky, the Sun then descended into the underworld at dusk on the western horizon. During the night the Sun would make its journey through the underworld, to re-emerge on the eastern horizon at sunrise.[158] According to the Maya, the Earth was flat with a four-cornered surface demarcated by four mythological mountains indicating the cardinal points and their sunrises and sunsets.[159] The sides represented a protective perimeter preventing supernatural forces from entering and harming humans.[160] The sky was supported by four world trees, and in the center was a Ceiba tree that connected the underworld (its roots) to the sky (its branches).[161]

Mayan (& other Mesoamerican) Deities and Religions

The notion that a Maya deity could have multiple aspects or manifestations is well established. Many of the major gods and goddesses had four different aspects, one for each cardinal direction, with different responsibilities or traits associated with each direction.[162] Each world direction had its own god (Bacab or Sky-Bearer) and color. The East was called likin and was the direction of sunrise (red); the West was called chikin where the sun sets (black). Here the word *kin* signifies the important nature of the sunrise and sunset and is associated with the Sun god. The Sun's association with important gods and goddesses indicates the importance of sunrises, sunsets, and cardinal dates (solstices and equinoxes) as portals to the supernatural realm.

The qualities of the gods and goddesses and their attributes changed with time, and were influenced by other Mesoamerican religions. The gods were one and yet three; each was creator, preserver, and destroyer, resembling Hinduism's Brahma, Vishnu, and Shiva. An important characteristic of Mesoamerican religion was the duality among the divine entities; the gods and goddesses represented the confrontations between opposite poles: the positive, exemplified by light, comprised the masculine, force, war, and the Sun; and the negative, exemplified by darkness, the feminine, the Moon, and peace.[163] Mayans made no distinction between the natural and supernatural realms or between the animate and inanimate, because they saw everything as being imbued with the same spiritual life force.

Additionally, gods and goddesses may present a combination of aspects: of humans, various animal species, and other deities, as well as a counterpart of the opposite sex. Combinations of young and old, and of benevolent and malevolent attributes, reflected the fundamental Mesoamerican principle of duality.[164] The names, ages, appearances, attributes, and even genders of Maya divinities changed over time, as did their domains of influence.

Mayans believed in a solar paradise reserved for those who could overcome the gods and goddesses in the Underworld. Evidence from the Classic period indicates that the kings and high nobles could look forward to a return to the dwelling place of the gods and goddesses,[165] known as Flower Mountain. This was considered a paradisiacal place of creation and origin.[166] The rulers were intermediaries between their people and the gods and goddesses, but were not believed to directly control the supernatural. Instead, humans worshiped and petitioned the gods and goddesses through ceremonial offerings and rituals.[167]

Ancestor worship and human and blood sacrifices were also an important part of Mesoamerican religious ritual.[168] The Maya gods and goddesses reigned over the Sun, other celestial objects, the seasons, agriculture, fertility, rain, water, fire, and war. There was no one set of common gods and goddesses venerated by all pre-Colombian Maya, but rather a series of localized regional cults, composed of deity combinations specific to particular polities or dynasties within a polity.[169] There may have been as many as 166 gods and goddesses in total.[170]

Pan-Maya deities existed as well. By the time of Spanish conquest, Hunab-Ku was considered the supreme god and creator of the Maya, and was either father of or the same as the god Itzámna. The other gods and goddesses were aspects of Itzámna who looked after the everyday affairs of humans and their world. Itzámna was the Maya sky and Sun god, and was perhaps the god most worshipped by the Maya.[171] To some Maya he was lord of all the gods and goddesses. He was said to have brought writing, knowledge, and calendrics to the Maya. Itzámna was the god that the priests paid special attention to at the beginning of the New Year. Blood sacrifices were often made in his honor. He was married to the goddess Ix Chel (representing the Moon, rainbows, fertility, and birth) and was father of the Bacabs, the gods who stood at the four corners of the world and held up the heavens.[172]

Figure 3.12 Representation of Ixchel as jaguar goddess of midwifery and medicine, and possibly as the Moon goddess (left), and Itzámna (right), seated at the Holy Mountain prior to the creation of the world. Carved in limestone at the Usumacinta River Basin, Chiapas (Mexico).[173]

Kinich Ahau (Sun-faced Lord) was the ancient Maya Sun god who moved across the sky during the day (as Itzámna) and transformed into a jaguar during his nightly journey through the underworld to the eastern horizon.[174] The Sun god, like the maize god, also symbolized rebirth and resurrection. Kukulcan was the feathered serpent god; in the Yucatan he was considered a creator deity with solar and sky aspects. The Maya represented him with the body of a serpent, feathers of the quetzal, and the teeth of a jaguar. He held a human head in his jaws. As part of his creator-god status, he controlled the four elements — earth, air, fire, and water

—which were associated with corn, lizard, vulture, and fish iconography respectively.[175]

Figure 3.13 (A) At the Kohunlich pyramids in Mexico, the Sun god mask of Kinich Ahau flanks both sides of the main pyramid. **(B)** The serpent head of Kukulkan at the bottom of the northern steps on the temple of Kukulcan.[176]

The behavior of the deities was a model for appropriate human conduct. This justified and provided rationalizations for elite activities, the social hierarchy, and the political structure.[177] Maya rulers explicitly linked themselves with the Sun god (Kinich Ahau) in both life and death. Conversely, the Maya Sun god often wears the accouterments of kingship, including the cloth headband, indicating either his rule of the heavens or the imparting of kingship qualities upon the ruler. Upon death, rulers were said to merge with the Sun god and continue to rule in the heavens. Dynastic succession was linked to the cycle of the Sun, with the inauguration of a new ruler occurring at the dawn of a new Sun (winter solstice).

Maya (and other Mesoamerican) Sacred Festivals

The Maya represented their cosmos symbolically, using a planogram (see figure 3.19). This planogram symbolizes the four solstice corners depicted by the god N Bacabs (the Sun god). To the east the young Moon goddess sits on the equinox position.[178]

Religious ceremonies were held at the end of each Maya calendar month and on the cardinal dates (solstices and equinoxes). Different deities presided over these times of the year. The ancient Maya viewed the solstices as sacred portals. Shamans and priests used this planogram symbolism for establishing ceremonial altars, and to demarcate sacred times for rituals that served as entrances to the spirit world. The central stone of the planogram was regarded as the center of the cosmos and was the equivalent of the World Tree through which shamans communicated with beings in the spirit world.[179]

Figure 3.14 Replica of the Madrid Codex in the Museum of the Americas (Madrid). The four pillars of the world represent the solstice extremes and the boundaries of the sky. This planogram, when appropriately placed, would demarcate the cardinal directions and solstices underpinning Mayan cosmology.[180]

The Tztotzil of Chenalhó, a town in the Chiapas region in southern Mexico, say the Sun changes its path twice a year; at the transition points the old men stand at dawn to undertake a ritual devoted to the Sun. Yachilan was a sacred Maya ceremonial site, and important sacred ceremonies and rituals were celebrated there during three days around the summer solstice. A similar phenomenon occurred at Palenque, an important Maya city in what today is southern Mexico, which flourished in the 7th century CE. Solstices also represented important dates for transitions in political and religious leadership.[181]

The resurrection of the Sun on the winter solstice was also a primary component of Aztec belief systems, just as it was for the Maya. Huitzilopochtli was an important Aztec deity on a par with Quetzalcoatl, and was considered a Sun god. Huitzilopochtli was said to be in a constant struggle with the darkness, and required nourishment in the form of sacrifices. Panquetzaliztli was the Aztec month dedicated to Huitzilopochtli, and was one of the most important Aztec festivals (December 7th to the 26th; ending a few days after the winter solstice).[182] As the battle between day and night progressed, the Aztec recognized his victories over darkness with each new sunrise.[183] On June 24, the Aztecs marked their yearly summer solstice festival with fire ceremonies.[184]

Sacred Rituals—But Not for Everyone

We must ask who conducted and partook in sacred rituals. I would argue that there were two tiers of sacred ritual embedded within societies that worshipped Sun gods. Tier one ritual was associated with a society's elite and involved sacredly-timed pyramid or temple-based rituals with advanced meditation practices. These practices were taught within elite circles of education. The key ritual protagonists were the king, queen, or pharaoh and the high priests and/or priestesses. The priesthood held and controlled ritual knowledge. Together this partnership between royalty and the priesthood had a special responsibility to worship the gods and conduct rituals on society's behalf.

The second tier was religion for the masses. Public religious festivals, ceremonies, and their own special rituals were conjoined with the king-queen and priest-led sacred rituals. These second-tier rituals and ceremonies did not involve the active pursuit of altered states of consciousness. Access to altered states of consciousness was tightly controlled, because it was a source of leadership power.

These societies held their inaugural ceremonies around the solstices, and engaged in rituals that allowed the new leaders to accelerate their consciousness development, thus imparting benevolent leadership qualities. A theme common across the Sun god religions was the pursuit by elites of access to altered states of consciousness in which they experienced such things as Unity states of consciousness (merging with God), ego death/rebirth, and the ultimate prize of life, that is, the escape from karmic rebirth (i.e., spiritual immortality).

Chapter 4

Entheogens Generate God Within

Introduction

Entheogens (hallucinogens, psychedelics) are psychoactive substances that mimic chemicals naturally produced by the brain. They are derived from plant, fungi, and frogs. The word literally means "generating god within" (en: within; theos: god; gen: to generate). For thousands of years entheogens have been used in religious, shamanic, and other spiritual contexts to supplement practices of sacred ritual, healing, and divine revelation. Their religious significance is well established.

Some of the more common entheogens include the *Psilocybin* and *Amanita* magic mushrooms, blue and white water lilies, the sacred pink lotus, peyote and San Pedro cacti, mandrake, Syrian rue *(Peganum harmala)*, ayahuasca, vilca (*Anadenanthera colubrina*), morning-glory seeds, *Salvia divinorum*, bufotenin (bufo toad skin secretions), datura, angel trumpets, belladonna, uncured tobacco, and cannabis.

Entheogens Generate God Within

Figure 4.1 Flowers associated with the Sun gods. **(A)** Sacred pink lotus (*Nelumbo nucifera*). **(B)** Blue water lily (*Nymphaea caerulea*). **(C)**, White water lily (*Nymphaea ampla*).[185]

Figure 4.2 (A) Syrian rue (*Peganum harmala*). **(B)** Datura (Angel trumpets) from my garden — a very strong scented flower. **(C)** Mandrake (drawing).[186]

Figure 4.3 (A) Magic mushrooms (*Psilocybin cubensis*). **(B)** Fly agaric magic mushrooms (*Amanita muscaria*). **(C)** Banisteriopsis

caapi vine (Ayahuasca component containing monoamine oxidases).[187]

Entheogens in the Ancient World

A cross-cultural survey of literature conducted by experts in the 1970s and involving nearly 500 societies around the world highlighted that nearly 90 percent of these societies practiced culturally institutionalized access to altered states of consciousness, aided by the consumption of psychoactive plants and fungal substances.[188,189]

One of the first scholars to highlight the use of psychoactive substances by ancient societies was Philippe de Felice. He considered such substances central to the development of ancient religions (1936).[190] He believed that the use of naturally derived psychotropic substances represented a most basic human instinct to realize higher states of consciousness, an instinct which was deeply embedded in the culture of humankind and was, perhaps, at the root of all religions. Since then, many academic and private scholars have conducted research and built upon his original thesis.[191,192,193,194]

What we are exploring here is nothing less than the progressive rediscovery and reacceptance of humankind's lost heritage, while at the same time

Entheogens Generate God Within

recognizing the human species' instinctive drive to experience altered states of consciousness.

First, we should consider one of the world's oldest profession, that of the shaman. The shaman was the ancestor of both the doctor and the priest.[195] The shaman's knowledge of plants and fungi was useful for accessing altered states of consciousness, for calling on the spirit realm for healing, and for manipulating the gross body in the physical realm.[196,197]

Shamanism is the world's oldest form of religion and involves a belief in the forces or essence of nature imbuing all life. Shamans possessed (and still do today) the sacred ritual knowledge that permits one to access altered states of consciousness, though without necessarily believing in distinct Gods.[198] During the Holocene period, when the northern ice caps were melting, humans spread out into new regions of the world, taking with them their innate behaviors, culturally-inspired motivations, and an instinct to seek out entheogens. Arguably, this led to the spread of shamanism and sowed the primordial seeds of the ancient world's religions, at the same time providing those early religions with ritual process know-how.

Moving forward in time, the ancient Indo-Iranian people, who originated in Central Asia, are thought to have been progenitors of the ancient world religions in Mesopotamia, India, and other parts of Asia. This early

Indo-Iranian culture divided into ancient Iranians and Indo-Aryans about 4,000 to 5,000 years ago, with the Indo-Aryans migrating south into the Indus Valley. Both groups preserved extensive religious traditions that were ultimately rendered into sacred texts such as the Rig Veda (Indo-Aryans) and the Avesta (Zoroastrian scriptures of Iran).

The sacred rituals of both the Indo-Aryans and ancient Iranians involved the consumption of entheogens. The Indo-Aryans used soma; the Iranians used a substance called haoma. Evidence of entheogen use in early Mesopotamia has been discovered on ritual vessels from approximately 2000-1000 BCE found in temple shrines. These contained residual traces of psychoactive plant materials (ephedra, opium, and cannabis). Physical evidence has also been found in Egypt and other countries around the Mediterranean.[199]

Psychoactive plants were also prominent in the urban cultures of pre-Colombian America: those of the Aztecs, the Maya, and the Inca. According to some religious scholars, the three global monotheistic religions of today (Christianity, Islam, and Judaism) have their mystic founding roots in the consumption of psychoactive substances.[200] Both Gordon Wasson (an independent American researcher and author who made pioneering contributions to the fields of ethnobotany, ethnomycology, and anthropology) and Albert Hoffman (the Swiss chemist who is remembered as the man who synthesized LSD) believed that a psychoactive brew containing fungal-derived hallucinogens (ergot alkaloids) was at the heart of the Eleusinian mysteries of ancient Greece.[201]

Entheogens in the Modern World

Asserting that ancient religions used entheogens is still somewhat controversial, particularly as society in general thinks less than positively about such matters. How and why did such a stigma become attached to hallucinogens? After all, humans and entheogens co-evolved together over millions of years, to the point that entheogens specifically mimic naturally produced brain chemicals and fit perfectly into specific receptors within specific parts of the brain known to be associated with the brain processes involved with meditation and those required to switch our state of consciousness from being awake to altered states of consciousness.

The rise of civilization and then monotheism eliminated most of these ancient world traditions and indigenous religions.[202] Ritual knowledge was ultimately lost and entheogens outlawed. It would seem that ancient societies' controlling elite and priesthoods did not want the masses to control their own access to the spirit world or spiritual destiny. That would, after all, have undermined the elites' control of the general populace, from which taxes and therefore religious institutional wealth and power were generated.

We live in a different world today, one in which chemicals are used all the time to alter our mental and physical states. We should be inured to the chemical manipulation of our brains and minds by now; after all, we have caffeine, alcohol, cigarettes, and other stimulants, and tens of billions of dollars are spent on pharmaceutical drugs and nonprescription over-the-counter health products to modulate brain and mind activity. And let's not forget the billions of dollars spent on mind-altering recreational drugs.

21st Century humans are no strangers to manipulating the brain or mind. In fact, I would say it's a fundamental human trait that was naturally selected in protohominids on their long march to becoming sentient, social, innovative, creative, and loving beings. Addictions to alcohol and drugs are said to represent, in part, a craving for the experience of altered states of consciousness (and for unconditional love as well). Seen in this way, it becomes obvious to ask the question: What have we done? We have replaced entheogens and the sacred rituals of our ancestors with brain-stimulating chemical alternatives such as alcohol, nicotine, and drugs in order to live our 21st century life.

We should celebrate the collective intelligence and achievements of our ancient ancestors, and derive great joy and humility from knowing that they understood things about spirituality and the evolution of consciousness that our modern societies have long since forgotten. I, personally, am humbled by and in awe of that.

Ancient Sun God Religions' Entheogen Trail

We shall now chart the entheogen trails for ancient India, Egypt, Mesoamerica, and South America. With the exception of ancient Egypt, the archeological and anthropological record clearly indicates entheogens were used by ancient societies as part of their sacred religious processes.

Ancient India

The Rig Veda is considered one of the most important sacred texts in the Hindu religion. Soma, an unknown entheogen, is mentioned over 1,500 times in its 10,500 verses, indicative of the important role this sacrament played in the ancient Hindu religion.

The Rig Veda tells us that soma was prepared by pressing soma stalks; the milky juice was collected and purified by draining it through a wool sieve. The soma juice was drunk alone or mixed with milk, curds, grain, or honey.[203,204] The soma ritual usually lasted for three or more days, with the soma being consumed at sunrise within a ritual context.

What was the identity of soma, as depicted in the Rig Veda? This specific question is not an easy one to answer. The Rig Veda scriptures are a tough delight, a forest of words, containing many secrets. It is refreshing that the scholarly community (see next paragraph) entertains the possibility that entheogens were used as a means of connecting with higher states of consciousness and deities. While the scholarly consensus is building, it is just as important that we recognize soma was an entheogen and was integral to soma rituals conducted by priests.

Some twenty or more plant or fungal species were put forward as putative soma candidates during the nineteenth and twentieth centuries.[205] Gordon Wasson's *Soma: Divine Mushroom of Immortality* (1968) associated *Amanita muscaria* (fly agaric magic mushroom) with soma.[206] Two decades later, David Flattery and Martin Schwartz argued the case for Syrian rue (*Peganum harmala*) as soma.[207] Terence McKenna in *Food of the Gods* built the case for another type of magic mushroom (*Psilocybe cubensis*) from which soma could have been made.[208] David Spess more recently built an interesting case for the sacred lotus as soma in his book *Soma: The Divine Hallucinogen*.[209] As you can see, there is no shortage of candidates.

The Effects of Soma

When imbibed, soma was said to induce a divine state of ecstasy with powers to heal, rejuvenate, and regenerate the physical body and to extend lifespan. Soma was associated with psychogenic creations, levitation, and walking on water, as well as the expansion of consciousness beyond the physical realm.[210] This ecstatic or transcendental state induced Unity states of consciousness, where one would experience pure consciousness (God). These ecstatic effects bestowed holiness and spiritual immortality on the user of soma. Additionally, in these ecstatic states, knowledge about the universe and creation could be imparted.

Pre-Colombian Mesoamerica

Hallucinogenic plants and fungi were commonly used to induce altered states of consciousness in healing rituals and religious ceremonies throughout pre-Colombian Mesoamerica, just as they are used today in ritual ceremonies in Guatemala and Mexico. Mushroom stones dating from 1000 BCE have been found in ritual contexts in Mesoamerica. Peyote use also dates back to over 5,000 years ago.[211]

Perusing some of these descriptive and often-cited books below, one observes a common, consistent subject matter relating to ancient Mesoamerican societies and the ritual use of entheogens within a religious context. Here is a list of titles:

"Transcultural Use Of Narcotic Water Lilies In Ancient Egyptian And Maya Drug Ritual";[212] *The Hallucinogenic Fungi Of Mexico—An Inquiry Into The Origins Of The Religious Idea Among Primitive Peoples;*[213] *The Influence Of Psychotropic Flora And Fauna On Maya Religion;*[214] *Plantae Mexicanae II, The Identification Of Teonanácatl, A Narcotic Basidiomycete Of The Aztecs;*[215] *Hallucinogenic Drugs In Pre-Columbian Mesoamerican Cultures;*[216] *Hallucinogenic Mushrooms In Mexico—An Overview;*[217] "Waterlily And Cosmic Serpent: Equivalent Conduits Of The Maya Spirit Realm."[218] Just to name a few.

Entheogens commonly used by pre-Columbian Mesoamerican societies included magic mushrooms (*psilocybin spp.*), white water lily (*Nymphaea ampla*), bufo species of hallucinogenic toad containing bufotenin, peyote, datura, morning glory seeds (Ipomoea species), *Salvia divinorum*, ololiuhqui seeds (Turbina corymbosa), and wild tobacco.[219]

Figure 4.4 Some of Mesoamerica's hallucinogenic flora and fauna. **(A)** Morning glory flowers (morning glory seeds are hallucinogenic). **(B)** Peyote (*Lophophora williamsii*). **(C)** *Bufo marinus*, a toad native to Central and South America.[220]

The Psilocybe mushroom was known as *Teonanacatl* to the Aztec, meaning "flesh of the gods." Teonanacatl use was outlawed and suppressed by the post-conquest Catholic Church.[221] The magic mushroom aspect of the Maya sacred ritual survived and made its journey into the 21st Century within shamanic communities over most of Central America. Richard Schultes and Gordon Wasson discovered the magic mushroom's sacred ritual use, and brought this knowledge back to the Western world around the middle of the 20th century.[222,223] Since then many researchers have been active within these fields of research (i.e., ethnobotany, anthropology, iconography) such that the ritual use of entheogens by pre-Colombian Mesoamerican societies within a religious context is widely known today and is generally accepted by academia.

Pre-Colombian South America

We know, based on iconographic and archeological data, that certain entheogens played an important role in the evolution of Andean religious rituals.[224]

San Pedro cactus was considered sacred and its name was derived from the postcolonial Christian saint San

Pedro. It was said to hold the keys to the gates of heaven, indicative of its entheogen status. The entheogenic and healing use of San Pedro cactus dates back to the second millennium BCE in northern Peru at Chavín de Huantar, and similarly at sites north of Lima. It is still used today by indigenous communities and within spiritual tourism. Its depiction on pottery and textile icons and in rock art in association with deities and rituals provides good evidence for its use in the past.[225,226]

Figure 4.5 San Pedro cactus (*Echinopsis pachanoi*) grows up to 8m tall and was used for over 5,000 years in sacred rituals in South America. On the Inca trail en route to Machu Picchu.[227]

Anadenanthera colubrina (vilca) was also widely used in sacred and healing rituals. The tree's seedpods are the source of the active compound bufotenin, which is a dimethyltryptamine (DMT)-like substance. Evidence of vilca's widespread use in sacred ritual ceremonies by pre-Incan societies along the Andean coastline and also inland comes from its frequent identification in ancient snuffing paraphernalia.[228] These snuffing utensils were used to deliver vilca up the nose during sacred rituals. The antiquity of snuff tablets and their evolution as symbols in pre-Incan, Andean societies indicates that snuff tablets were an important artistic means for disseminating ritual processes.[229] *Anadenanthera colubrina* is still widely used today by lowland Amazonian shamans who continue this ancient tradition.

Figure 4.6 Anadenanthera colubrina tree. **(A)** Known as Vilca, it grows 5-20 meters tall. In Chile bean pods are produced from September to December. **(B)** Mimosa leaves grow up to 30cm in length, and the bean pods provide bufotenin, a DMT-like chemical substance.[230]

Ancient Egypt

In Chapter 3 I mentioned that mainstream Egyptology does not accept that entheogens played an important role in the conduct of sacred rituals associated with the religion of Ra. This contrasts with scholarship concerning other regions of the ancient world (Mesopotamia, pre-Colombia Meso- and South America, and Greece) with a similar level of evidence. Therefore, we face a hurdle in building the argument that entheogens underpinned ancient Egypt's mystical traditions and their spiritual practices.

What is the evidence for the ritualistic use of entheogens in the ancient Egyptian religion? Medical papyri detailing therapeutic know-how, entheogen samples retrieved from temples and tombs, and temple art depicting psychoactive plants and known hallucinogens employed in the interface between Sun gods and elites are the main sources that support this thesis. This is detailed below.

Figure 4.7 Ancient Egypt's art frequently depicted hallucinogens and psychoactive flowers. **(A)** Blue water lily (*Nymphaea caerulea*). **(B)** Datura. **(C)** Opium poppy (*Papaver somniferum*). The poppy is the source of numerous opiate narcotics, including morphine. **(D)** *Psilocybin species* of magic mushrooms.[231]

The ancient Egyptians developed one of the earliest medical recording systems in the ancient world. Twelve medical papyri exist today dealing with a variety of remedies to treat a range of illnesses and physical conditions.[232] The texts reveal that blue water lily was the medicinal plant prescribed most often. The use of opium and mandrake are also described.[233,234]

Ethnobotanical experts have found sample evidence for Syrian rue, blue water lily, pink lotus, mandrake, magic mushrooms, opium, datura, claviceps (a fungus), and cannabis in temple artifacts belonging to early civilizations in the Fertile Crescent (including Egypt).[235,236] Similar evidence from other regions has proven sufficient to convince scholars that entheogens were an important sacred ritual component in those civilizations.

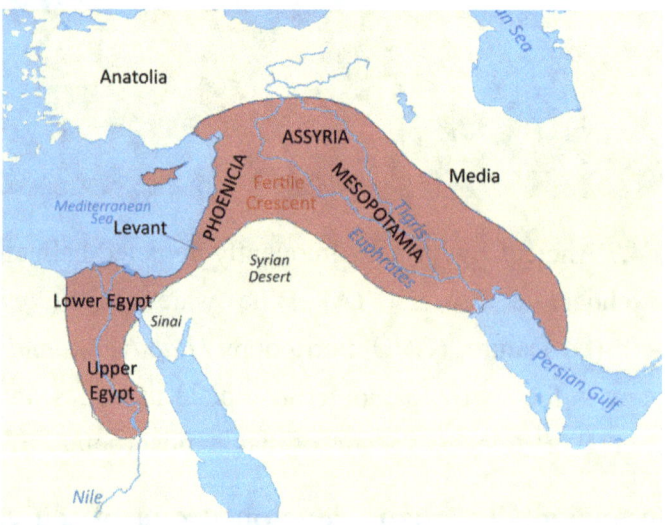

Figure 4.8 The Fertile Crescent is a crescent-shaped region that contained the comparatively moist and fertile land of otherwise arid and semi-arid Western Asia, and the valley and delta of the Nile River in northeast Africa. This part of the world was once fertile land before desertification processes subsequent to climate change transformed it into desert.[237]

In addition, Egyptian art and iconography commonly depict blue water lily (*Nymphaea caerulea*), mandrake

(*Mandragora* species), magic mushrooms (*Psilocybin sp.*), and opium (*Papervum somniferum*), across the dynasties. Most importantly, these psychoactive plants are placed between Sun god and an elite human in temple art scenes, especially murals (see the next chapter).

Entheogen Pharmacology

There is an extensive scholarly and medical literature on the psychogenic and hallucinogenic properties of psilocybin and amanita magic mushrooms, mandrake, datura, ayahuasca, Syrian rue (*Peganum harmala*), and vilca (*Anadenanthera colubrina*). Additionally, know-how for the use of mandrake and other psychoactive plants for anesthesia, pain relief, and sedation is contained in Byzantine texts, likely reflecting a broader use throughout the earlier empire of Rome.[238]

These plant and fungal hallucinogens fall into three main pharmaceutical modes of drug action. These include; **(i) 5-hydroxytryptamine-2a (5-HT2a) serotonin receptor stimulators** (*magic mushrooms, Anadenanthera colubrina, morning glory seeds, Bufo toad*), **(ii) dopamine receptor stimulators** (*blue and white water lily, pink lotus; after metabolism*), and **(iii) muscarinic acetylcholine receptor stimulators** (*datura, mandrake*).

The Pink Lotus, Blue and White Water Lilies

The pink lotus and the blue and white water lilies were the most commonly depicted flowers associated with the Sun gods of ancient India, Egypt and the Maya lands respectively. However, there is academic discussion regarding the entheogenic properties of these flowers. In my view this is due to the lack of irrefutable clinical data, the fact that a well-structured comparative pharmacology argument has not been assembled from the data at hand (where it could be better assembled), and also because there is a relatively poor understanding of altered states of consciousness (versus non-specific hallucinations) and its associated pharmacology (dopamine, 5HT2a, glutamate pathways; see Chapter 9) from within the social sciences.

Sacred pink lotus is rich in bioactive compounds, supporting a wide array of human uses.[239] A dopamine receptor blocker or antagonist (nuciferine) accounts for approximately one fifth of the extracted plant mass.[240,241,242,243,244] What is not commonly appreciated about the pink lotus and the blue and white water lilies is that nuciferine is broken down in the body into a chemical called atherospermine, and this is a dopamine *agonist*.[245] As a therapeutic drug category, dopamine agonists similar to atherospermine are used in the treatment of Parkinson's disease and hyperprolactinemia, and are frequently associated with hallucinations when given in high doses or overdose.[246,247,248]

Manufacturers of bulk supplies (1kg to multi-ton quantities) of the pink lotus, blue water lily, and white lily extract detail the nuciferine content in their wholesale water lily product extracts.[249] This is an obligatory part of the manufacturing quality control compliance for these products which underpins the ability to sell such products for human use. We therefore know that they all contain the dopamine agonist after the nuciferine has been metabolized.

Additionally, numerous scientific publications and books highlighting the mind-altering properties of blue water lily (*Nymphaea caerulea*) indicate the plant and/or its extracts have psychoactive and/or hallucinogenic properties.[250,251,252,253,254]

Chapter 5

Deity Art & Icons Reveal Priesthood Sacred Ritual Processes

Introduction

Temple art and religious icons from ancient India, Egypt, Mesoamerica, and South America impart important information in symbolic form for the learned eye. This information occurs as a triad of symbols comprising the Sun god/goddess and/or leader, entheogen (hallucinogen), and sacred time (V47 degree solstice symbolizing angles; serpent as the equinoxes).

According to the thesis of this book, this ritual symbol triad is an important part of a broader *shared archeological fingerprint* associated with the Sun god religions. This fingerprint defined important elements of the ancient priesthood sacred ritual processes for accessing altered states of consciousness i.e., meditation, sensory silence, sacred time, entheogens, and geomancy. This fingerprint includes pyramid and temple alignments (equinoxes, solstices), the triad of ritual symbols embedded in their deity art and icons (deity, V47 solstice and serpent equinox, and entheogen symbols), and artistic/iconographic evidence that meditation (in sensory silence) played a central ritual role, which sacred rituals supplemented (see Chapter 8).

That shared archeological fingerprint crops up across three continents and more than 5,000 years of human history. This raises some very big questions (beyond the scope of this book) concerning how this could have happened. Given that this art was associated with pyramids and temples, it brings the priesthoods into focus, simply because they would have had control over the temple art.

This book proposes that priesthoods of the ancient Sun god religions commissioned art, murals, and icons that symbolically embedded information in a veiled format detailing their sacred ritual processes. The embedding of ritual information had numerous benefits; as a recording medium it permitted priesthoods to instruct leaders and the elite, and to teach new priests and priestesses in the absence of writing material or a written language. The fact that this know-how remained undiscovered until now indicates the effectiveness of art and icons as an encryptable medium for selective communication.

Reading and Interpreting Temple Art & Sacred Icons

Some of the concepts discussed above will be demonstrated in this section before examining each religion's deity art.

The V47 degree angle is frequently embedded in Sun god temple art and icons, and was used to symbolize the solstices as sacred time. V47 degree angles are used to create symmetrical outlines and proportions for the images, or key lines/cruxes within the image to position entheogen elements. This is observed on Sun gods, on leaders' headgear, and adorning the superstructures of sacred site buildings. It is invariably combined with serpents as equinox symbols, further strengthening the sacred time link.

We see such representations when we consider ancient Egypt's pharaohs, whose heads were adorned with the nemes. This stylized V47 head cloth was often combined with the uraeus, a form of the Egyptian cobra that symbolized the protection of Wadjet (cobra goddess; serpent-equinox). In real life Wadjet provided another link to sacred time because of her association with both solstice and equinox festivals (i.e., the going forth of Wadjet on December 25th).

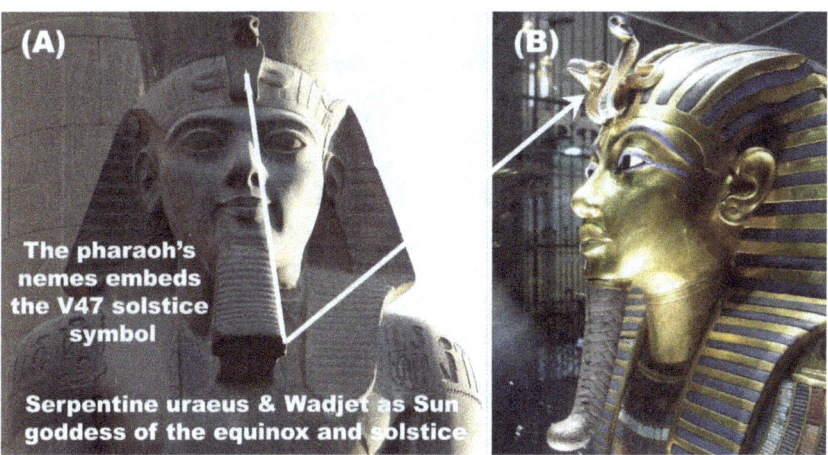

Figure 5.1 Pharaohs' statues symbolically depict their heads being under the influence of sacred time, symbolized by V47 degree solstice depicting angles and serpent depicting equinox. **(A)** Close up of Ramesses II Colossus in Luxor Temple. **(B)** Mask of Tutankhamun's mummy featuring a serpentine uraeus. The cobra image of Wadjet was associated with the solstices and equinoxes.[255]

Serpents similarly are used to symbolize the equinox. The serpent equinox theme is depicted on Uxmal's Nunnery Quadrangle exterior walls (Yucatan, Mexico), where it is placed mid-way between the V47 degree solstice symbols. Here, Kukulkan's head was represented by the "feathered serpent."

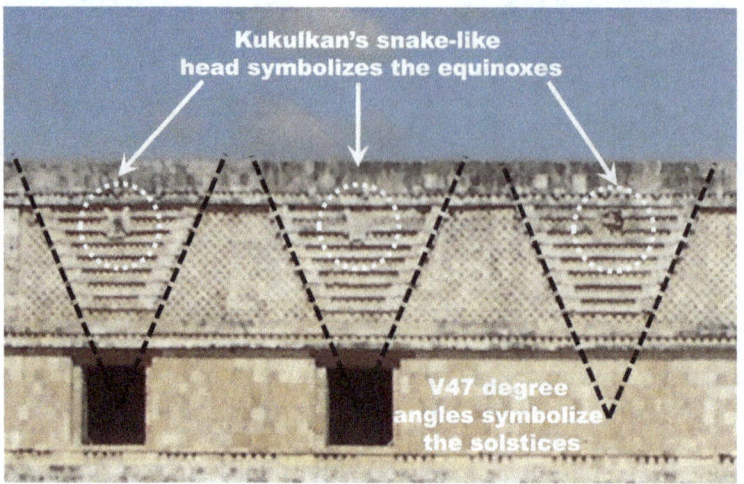

Figure 5.2 Uxmal nunnery quadrangle with mosaic-like wall design; V47 degree angle solstice symbols are depicted with a centrally placed serpent head (Kukulkan) denoting the equinoxes.[256]

With a little knowledge of the deity's or co-appearing deities' role(s) and association(s), one is able to appreciate a greater level of implied communication in the art. For example, if we examine Figure 5.3 with its statue of Surya, we can infer a number of sacred time and ritual associations. Surya was worshipped at dawn and on the solstices, which is also when the lotus flower opens atop a lake or pond (i.e., morning). Surya is also depicted in association with snakes, and is often accompanied by the Ashvin twins (his sons) who symbolized the sunrise and sunset gateways. That combination of Surya-Ashvin-Lotus, when decrypted, tells us rituals were conducted on the solstices and equinoxes, at sunrise or sunset, under the influence of pink lotus.

Figure 5.3 Surya standing atop the upturned lotus, accompanied by his sons the Ashvin Twins who symbolized the sunrise and sunset gateways. Sacred lotuses are captured within two V47 degree solstice angles, one triangle guided by the three hats worn (Surya, Ashvin twins), indicating an awareness of sacred time.[257]

Sun God Religion Temple Art & Icons

Ancient India & Soma's Identity

The lotus flower has been a divine symbol for thousands of years, and the pink lotus (*Nelumbo nucifera*) in particular is widely depicted in Hindu temple art and icons (and Buddhist also). Hindus revered the pink lotus in association with the Sun gods Surya, Brahma, Vishnu, and Lakshmi. The pink lotus was the most commonly depicted flower in the temples dedicated to Lords Vishnu (Deva Desams), Shiva (Paadal Petra Sthalam temples), and Surya. All are frequently portrayed holding lotus flowers in their hands or standing or sitting atop an upside-down, pink lotus flower.

Figure 5.4 The prominence of the sacred pink lotus as the Sun god's and Trimurti's entheogen. **(A)** Surya holds lotuses in his

arms. **(B)** Vishnu holds them in his hands, stands atop an upside-down lotus, and is haloed behind the head with a lotus flower. **(C)** Brahma's lotus association: seated on an upside down lotus flower, foot resting similarly, associated with his V47 degree angled and cardinally-faceted head.[258]

Surya is often seen standing atop an upside-down lotus flower, replacing its stalk. It is this reason why I believe Surya, and later the Trimurti, were pointing to the lotus stalk as soma, from which the mildly opaque soma juice was extracted and the deity made manifest during the ritual (see Chapter 4).

Soma's recognized scarcity most likely induced plant cultivation and prohibitions to protect the supply. Most Sun god temples have large ponds that are deep enough to promote the growth of long lotus flower stalks. These deep ponds also offered the ability to increase the water depth, as evidenced by their graduated levels. This likely offered the grower an opportunity to generate longer flower stalks containing more soma liquid, which, according to the Rig Veda, was extracted on the full moon.

Deity Art & Icons Reveal Priesthood Sacred Ritual Processes

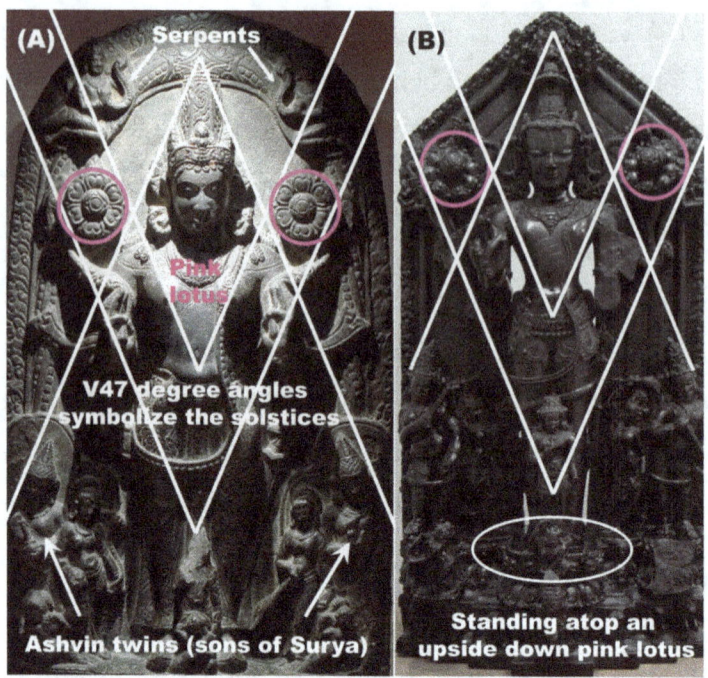

Figure 5.5 Sculptures of Surya, the Vedic Sun god. **(A & B)** Statues of Surya also depicting the Ashvin twins (sunrise/set horizons), V47 degree solstice angles, serpent-depicting equinoxes, and entheogen symbolism (lotus flowers).[259]

Surya is also depicted with ornate, flare-like symbols emanating from the sides of his head. In my view the Sun god religions recognized high solar activity (i.e., solar flares and coronal mass ejections) as the serpent, and as a time of enhanced cosmic consciousness enabled by the sun's activity, which in turn was useful for the ritual process. This will become clearer in Chapter 6, where I consider Earth's magnetic field and how it is influenced by solar activity. Chapter 8 will detail the significance of enhanced magnetic fields on the brain's activity through their enhancement of alpha brainwave voltages over the frontal brain.

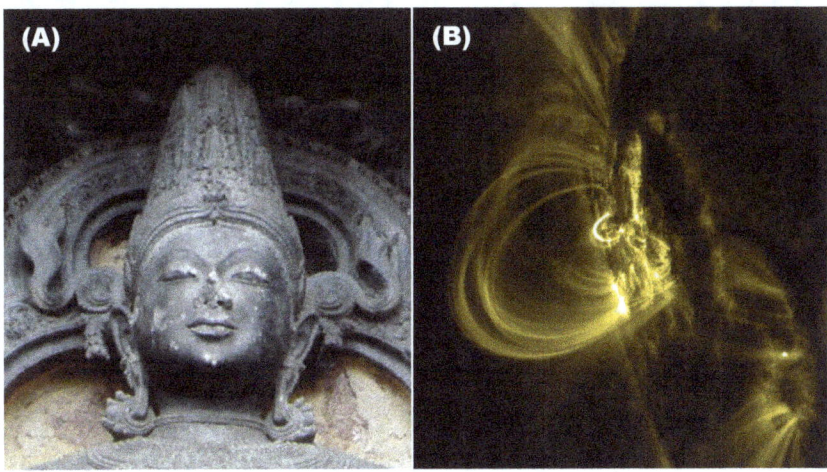

Figure 5.6 Surya's depiction of solar themes. **(A)** Statue of Surya the Sun god at the Konark Sun Temple (Orissa). A closer look reveals unusual solar symbolism on the sides of Surya's head– resembling magnetic loop symbols emanating from the sun's surface? **(B)** Depictions of magnetic loops above the Sun's surface.[260]

Lord Brahma was said to be "self-born" in the lotus flower, and is commonly depicted sitting on a lotus flower connected to the navel of Lord Vishnu. Brahma, creator of the universe, was the first member of the Hindu Trimurti. The V47 degree solstice angle symbolism is frequently depicted in Lord Brahma's torso outline, as well as in his four cardinally directed faces. This collectively depicts the solstices and equinoxes as sacred time, and the lotus as the entheogen.

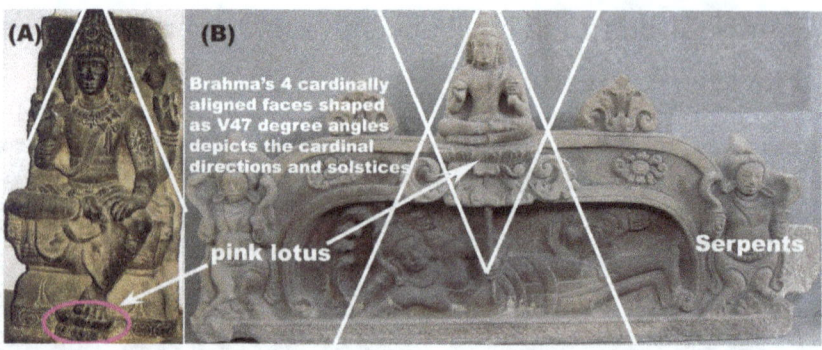

Figure 5.7 Iconographic depictions of Lord Brahma. **(A)** As the creator deity he displays the V47 degree angle solstice symbolism in torso outline, while seated upon an upside-down lotus flower. **(B)** A 7th century sculpture shows Lord Vishnu lying at the bottom of the ocean with a lotus plant growing from his navel and connected to Lord Brahma, who was born from the lotus. Lord Brahma sits atop a sacred pink lotus with his head portraying four cardinally aligned faces each depicting the V47 degree angle solstice symbolism in their outline.[261]

Statues, art, and murals of Lord Vishnu consistently highlight sacred time and entheogen themes. Lord Vishnu is often portrayed in a reclining posture as Padmanabha (Lotus-navel) with a lotus stalk emanating from his navel connected to a lotus flower on which Lord Brahma meditates. In another frequent depiction, Lord Vishnu stands atop an upside-down lotus flower.

Figure 5.8 Lord Vishnu as the Sun god in two common forms—depicting sacred time and entheogens (pink lotuses). **(A)** Representation of Vishnu as Padmanabha reclining on the serpent Shesha, the king of all Nāgas (serpent deities) and one of the primal beings of creation, also an avatar of the Supreme God known as Narayana. From Vishnu's navel sprouts a lotus flower on which the god Brahma sits or meditates. **(B)** A statue of Lord Vishnu with Consorts Lakshmi and Sarasvati. India (Bengal), Pala Dynasty, 11th century, in black chlorite. Lord Vishnu stands atop a sacred lotus, while depicting the V47 degree solstice angle proportions (i.e. forearms) and with the lotus entheogens placed in his hands.[262]

Shiva, the third member of the Trimurti, is known as the destroyer, the God of War and of thunderstorms. Shiva evolved from the deities Indra and Soma as the Hindu religion underwent rationalization. Indra and Soma were known for their thirst for soma. The ancient Vedic deity Soma evolved into a lunar deity, with the full Moon identified as the time to collect and press the soma stalk. Perhaps the gravity pull of the Moon caused (as with ocean tides) more sap to rise in the stem, giving greater amounts of extractable soma juice to the experienced harvester. The Moon was also the cup from which the gods drank soma. It is said that a waxing Moon meant Soma was recreating himself, so that soma would be ready for drinking at the next full Moon.

Shiva's standing atop an upturned lotus flower suggests, as with other members of the Trimurti, that he is the lotus' stalk with the V47 degree solstice angle demarcating the solstices and equinoxes. The large wavy projections to the sides of Shiva's head are thematically similar to those of Surya.

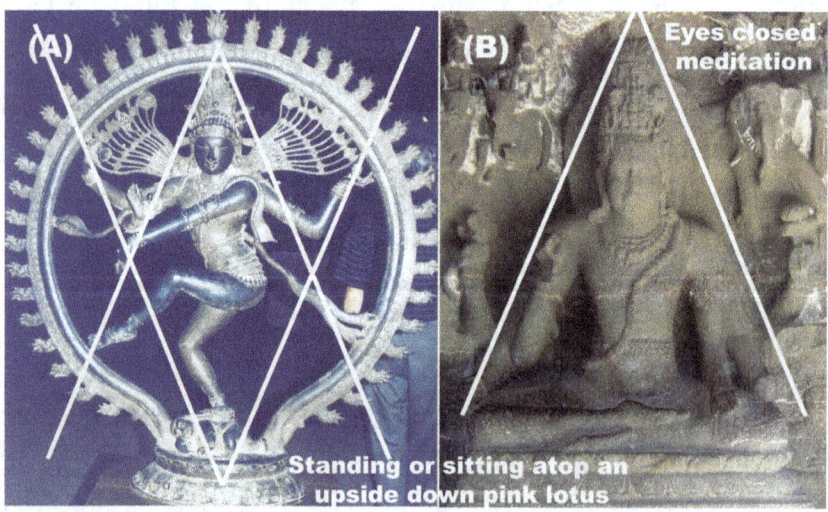

Figure 5.9 Art and icons depicting Lord Shiva. **(A)** As Nataraja, Lord of Dance, Shiva performs his divine dance of destruction as he prepares for Brahma's creation. Standing atop a lotus, Shiva marks out the solstices and equinoxes. **(B)** A panel from the Kailash temple (Cave 16) at Ellora depicting Lord Shiva

meditating (eyes closed) atop a sacred pink lotus, also depicting the V47 degree solstice symbolism to proportion his body outline.[263]

Hindu Sun god temple art and icons are a rich source of sacred ritual information that exists right in front of our eyes. There is a strong link between all the Trimurti Sun god deities and the sacred pink lotus. Typically they are depicted sitting or standing atop an upside-down lotus flower, that is, on the spot where one normally finds the stalk from which soma was extracted and then consumed, whereupon the deities manifested themselves. These deity icons (Surya, Trimurti) also embed sacred time symbols depicting the V47 degree solstice angle(s) and serpent (Naga) equinox symbolisms to depict sacred time, that is, the solstices and equinoxes.

Ancient Egypt

In Chapters 2 and 3 I highlighted the fact that mainstream Egyptology appears unwilling to accept that ancient Egypt's mystical traditions used entheogens in sacredly-timed rituals. Instead, there exists a more mundane explanation for rituals connected to the ancient religion of Ra. Therefore, a discussion of sacred rituals for accessing altered states of consciousness needs to overcome this explanation provided by mainstream Egyptology. From my perspective, ancient Egypt offers a rich smorgasbord of sacred ritual delights in its temple art, icons, and sacred texts (such as the Book of the Dead).

A review of Egyptian temple art and icons highlights three main concepts. First, pharaoh statues from the Old and New Kingdoms symbolically depict the pharaoh's head under the influence of sacred time. Second, the headgear worn by Sun gods and the Egyptian elite commonly depicts entheogen symbols. These observations drive the concept of heads or minds under the influence of sacred time and entheogens. And third, the frequent depiction in temple art of Sun gods and human elites with psychoactive plants or entheogens placed between them introduces the concept that entheogens were the means of connecting the human mind with the Sun god or divine consciousness (hence the term "generate god within" as applied to entheogens).

Pharaoh's Mind under the Influence of Sacred Time

Old and New Kingdom pharaohs were often depicted wearing a nemes. This was a striped headcloth that covered the crown of the head and nape of the neck with two large flaps that hung down behind the ears and in front of both shoulders (figure 5.11-5.12). This was said to symbolize the pharaoh's power and status.

A consistent finding across the Old and New Kingdoms reveals that the nemes have a silhouette outline depicting the V47 degree solstice angle. This is frequently combined with the uraeus on their foreheads. The uraeus was a stylized form of the Egyptian cobra symbolizing the protection of the goddess Wadjet, associated with both solstice and equinox festivals. I conclude that the nemes and uraeus associated with the pharaohs symbolize "heads under the influence" of sacred time.

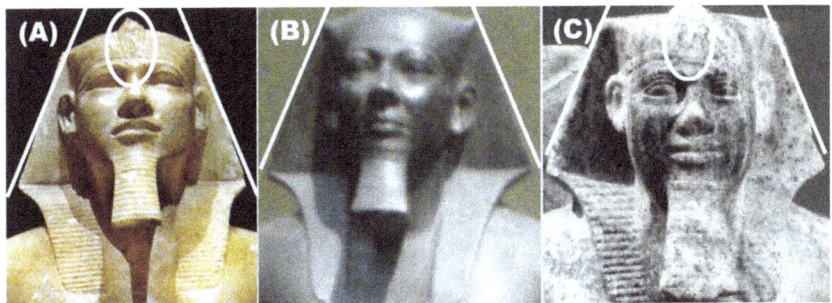

Figure 5.10 Old Kingdom pharaoh nemes depict the V47 degree angle, with a serpentine uraeus on the center of the forehead —"heads under the influence of sacred time". **(A)** Sitting portrait of pharaoh Khafre from the fourth dynasty (c. 2558-2532 BCE). **(B)** Menkaure statue from the Giza Valley Temple of Menkaura (c. 2548-2530 BCE). **(C)** 5th dynasty pharaoh Sahure's statue (c. 2487-2475 BCE).[264]

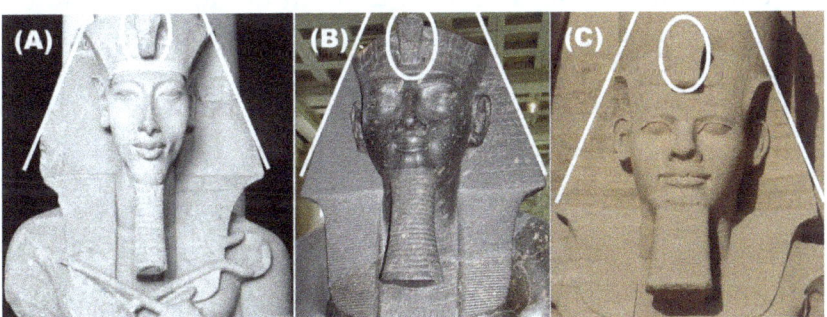

Figure 5.11 New Kingdom pharaohs depict the V47 solstice angled nemes and a serpentine uraeus on the mid forehead —"heads under the influence of sacred time". These sacred time symbols occurred across Old and New Kingdom dynasties. **(A)** Akhenaten's V47 degree angled, solstice-symbolizing nemes from a statue at Aten's temple at Karnak. This temple also provides an alignment on the winter solstice sunrise. **(B)** Seated statue of Amenhotep III adorning his V47 degree angled nemes and serpentine uraeus. This denotes "under the influence of sacred time". **(C)** Pharaoh Ramesses II faces the winter solstice sunrise at Abu Simbel with eyes apparently closed. Pharaoh statues symbolize the head under the influence of sacred time. Is he in seated meditation facing the WSSR?[265]

The Wadjet cobra symbol became associated with the Eye of Hathor, Horus, and Ra. This fortified the link with the solstice celebrations via the "going forth of Wadjet" festival celebrated on December 25th and on other solstice and equinox celebrations. Wadjet became associated with Isis, whose role was to assist the pharaoh in obtaining divine kingship qualities and the attributes of the all-seeing eye.

The pharaoh, of course, was the maintainer of Ma'at, and the spiritual conduit to the realm of the Sun god. This stylized pharaoh nemes-uraeus sacred time symbolism occurs through both the Old and New Kingdoms, suggesting it was an important and foundational component of ritual. Hence the phrase "minds under the influence of sacred time." The pharaohs are frequently depicted in a seated position with their eyes closed. Could this imply meditation under the influence of sacred time?

Even when we consider the heretic Pharaoh Amenhotep IV from the New Kingdom (1336 BCE), who temporarily changed the Egyptian religion to a monotheistic form (Atenism), the same sacred ritual symbolism becomes even more overt. One readily observes the V47 degree angle solstice and uraeus equinox symbols emanating from the solar disk (Aten). Interestingly, entheogens (blue water lily) are placed between the pharaoh and the God (Aten). This temple art depicting Pharaoh Amenhotep IV constitutes some very rich Sun god ritual symbolism.

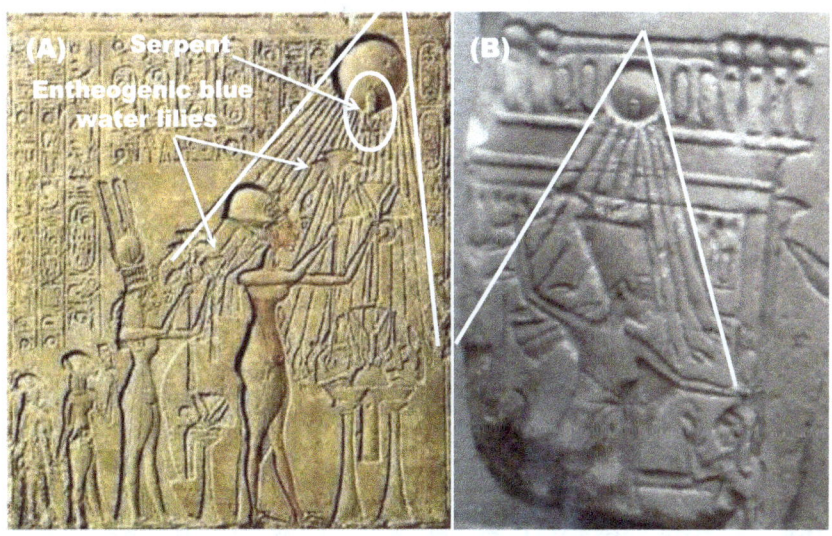

Figure 5.12 Pharaoh Amenhotep IV (Akhenaten). **(A)** Depicted worshiping the Sun disc of Aten, the supreme Sun god deity of Atenism. Note the V47 degree solstice angled spread of solar rays

emanating from the solar disc. The serpentine uraeus placed midway between completes sacred time. The pharaoh and queen Nefertiti stand with entheogenic blue water lilies placed between them and the Sun god Aten, a legacy of symbolic information from the preceding dynasties. **(B)** Detailed close-up of a limestone relief of Queen Nefertiti from Hermopolis during the reign of Akhenaten (c. 1353-1336 BCE) symbolizing sacred time.[266]

Entheogens in Egyptian Temple Art

Mid-twentieth century Egyptologist Arpag Mekhitarian once said that when viewing Egyptian temple art, even without any apparent religious connection, it was obvious to him the art was always guided by ritual considerations.[267] In a similar vein William Emboden, a strong proponent of the idea that Egyptian and Mayan temple art contained embedded entheogens, declared that religious cults dealing in sacred elements did not explicitly reveal their ritual secrets.[268] We should be aware of this when viewing temple and pyramid art, icons, and hieroglyphic texts.

The counterargument used by Egyptology to refute ethnobotanists/pharmacologists is this: just because an entheogen is depicted in the art does not imply ritual consumption. In my view, we need to dig deeper than this. A fundamental question we must all answer in viewing temple art is: In what theoretical circumstances could a Sun god and human coexist within the same scene, as implied by that piece of art?

This boils down to two ideas. You're either dead and therefore in a so-called mortuary temple scene (Osiris, mummy, mummification process, weighing of the heart). Or you're in a transcendental state of consciousness where ego boundaries have disintegrated, in which case the artist could legitimately depict the Sun god and elite human in the same scene or context. In an after-death scene, one would also expect to see Osiris more often (as god of the afterlife), while Ra or Horus would appear less frequently.

The following scene (figure 5.13) depicts Horus with Lady Taperet. Chains of datura flowers connect Re-Horakhty's solar disc headpiece to the Lady's head, and this symbolizes her connection with divine consciousness at sacred time. Also evident, and placed between them, are blue water lilies, and an unguent jar wrapped with the blue water lily bud.[269] Datura is a potent hallucinogen that provides the user with extraordinary powers of mystical flight.

Figure 5.13 This scene on a painted wooden stele of Lady Taperet (10th to 9th century BCE, 22nd dynasty) in the presence of Re-Horakhty (Ra, Horus) is heavily laden with entheogens and sacred time (V47 solstice and serpent representing the equinox [white circles]). Datura flowers are potent hallucinogens associated with mystical flight, and are seen here placed between her head and his. Blue water lilies are placed between them, with unopened buds, and an unguent jar wrapped with an unopened blue water lily is at their feet. This scene communicates all the key ritual elements, that is, sacred time and entheogens placed between the elite's head and the Sun god.[270]

The Papyrus of Ani (*The Book of the Dead*) was a manuscript written in hieroglyphics during the Nineteenth Dynasty (c. 1240 BCE). It is said to contain declarations and spells for a person's journey in the afterlife. This papyrus includes funerary prayers for Ani, a Theban noble, "to assume the form of a water lily." Ani requests that the water lily provide visions and soul flight. This indicates the power of the water lily to provide transcendent experiences.[271] Jeremy Naydler has suggested the *Book of the Dead* actually depicts mystical or shamanic rituals for achieving mystical or altered states of consciousness.[272]

Figure 5.14 Flowers or entheogens mediating transcendental co-appearance? **(A)** From the Papyrus of Ani. Monopodial, mushroom-shaped headgear is worn by Osiris, who is holding a crook & staff depicting the V47 degree solstice angle, while seated in front of the Theban noble Ani. Blue water lily flowers take up the space between them. **(B)** An 18th dynasty wooden stele depicting Re-Horakhty wearing his Sun & serpent head gear in front of a kneeling supplicant, blue lilies populating the space between them, and overseen by the eyes of Ra.[273]

Figure 5.15 (A) The Semenkhara relief in the tomb of Menna at Thebes depicts Princess Meriton, daughter of King Akhenaten and Queen Nefertiti, offering two mandrake fruits and a blue water lily bud to someone supported by a crutch. This scene is said to represent a ritual healing. A blue water lily is inserted between two mandrake fruits and on Princess Meriton's corona. She is said to wear a golden yoke bearing the emblems of water lily petals and mandrake fruits.[274] **(B)** Ancient Egyptian wooden stele depicting Lady Djedkhonsuiwesankh in the same scene as Re-Horakhty with blue water lilies taking up the space between them.[275]

According to William Emboden, an expert ethnobotanist who undertook an extensive review of Egyptian temple art, some common observations can be made in the portrayal of entheogens in temple art. His analysis of 18th Dynasty temple-tomb scenery (Thebes; Luxor) identified the blue water lily as the most frequent flower depicted; it is commonly depicted as a half-opened flower flanked by two unopened buds. This combination appeared in scenes of ritual healing and the approach of the soul of the dead to Osiris. The second most frequent depiction is a solitary, partially opened flower over a vase, an offering to Horus, placed before the nostrils or on the forehead. The third most frequent depiction is a single flower bud and stem, often wrapped around the leg of a royal chair or vessel, or in a food offering.[276]

This frequent juxtaposition of deity (Ra or Horus, combined with sunrise/set horizons), entheogen (blue water lily, mandrake, datura), and elite human in the same scene indicates that connection to the divine was mediated by entheogens, and that these scenes represent altered states of consciousness rather than afterlife scenes. Supporting this thesis is the fact that one would have expected to see Osiris depicted as the primary deity if this were an afterlife scene.

Magic Mushrooms and Headgear

The concept that pharaoh and deity headdresses symbolize "heads or minds under the influence" is introduced in this section, and particularly with reference to those crowns said to resemble the psilocybin magic mushroom species as a ritual entheogen.

The Egyptian white crown (Hedjet) of Upper Egypt and the red crown (Deshret) of Lower Egypt have their origins in the Predynastic Period. The earliest image of the Hedjet is dated to around 3500-3200 BCE, indicating kingship's early presence within Egyptian society. After Egypt's unification (c. 3100 BCE) the white and red crowns were merged to form the Pschent, symbolizing the pharaoh's power over a unified Egypt. Appended to its front were the uraeus, symbolizing the goddess Wadjet, and a white vulture symbolizing the goddess Nekhbet, said to represent purification. None of these crowns have physically survived, so we only know of their physical form through Egyptian temple art. The Atef worn by Osiris was a feathered white crown. The feather has been linked with the goddess Maat, underpinning the kingship concept of Ma'at: law, order, truth, balance, morality, and justice. That's a large amount of implied information obtained just by looking at headgear.

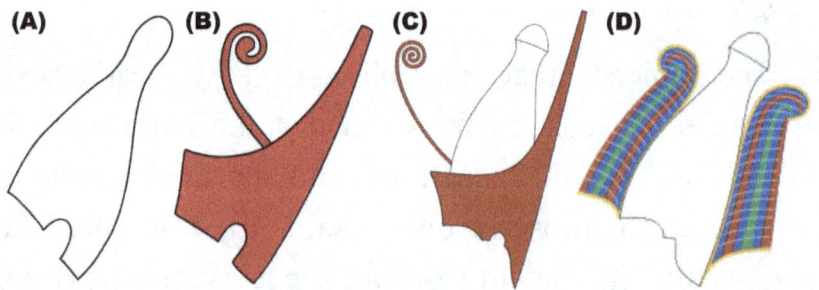

Figure 5.16 Deity headgear depicting "minds under the influence" in order to manifest the deity. **(A)** Hedjet (white crown) said to resemble a young magic mushroom. **(B)** Deshret

(red crown) with its electromagnetic symbol being communicated. **(C)** Pschent (red & white combo) brings the best of young magic mushroom together with an electromagnetic symbol. **(D)** Atef, with feathered symbol of Ma'at adorning the mushroom shaped hedjet, are said to represent the development of kingship. [277]

Research published in the *Journal of Ethnopharmacology* puts forth an interesting ethnomycological perspective that magic mushrooms were the symbolic basis of the white crown, pschent, and atef. These symbolized the concept of "heads under the influence." According to this article, the crowns worn by pharaohs and important Sun gods (Osiris, Horus) resemble pin-stage (young) magic mushrooms (*Psilocybe cubensis*).[278]

According to the research referenced above, Osiris was said to personify the magic mushroom with a white crown, one-legged body, and arms united holding a crook and staff. Further scrutiny by me identified V47 degree solstice angles used in proportioning Osiris's torso, while he wears a young magic mushroom crown (atef). The Egyptians also regarded Osiris as the personified spirit of barley.[279,280] Osiris, with the help of Hapy, the Nile god of the inundation, was revived after his annual murder by Set. Osiris was said to return each year with the barley.[281]

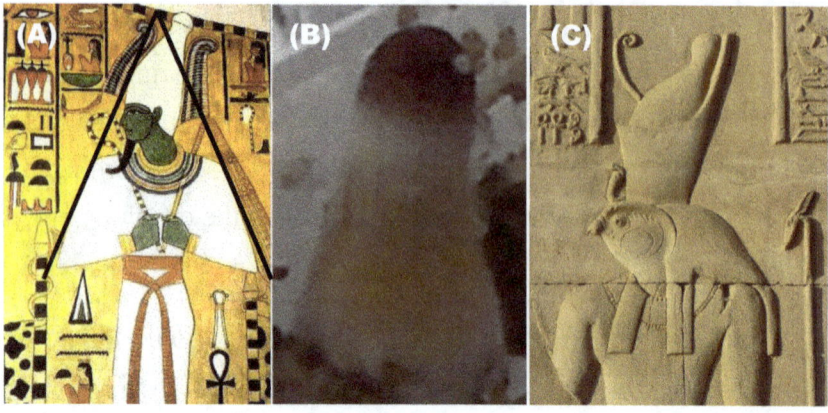

Figure 5.17 Visual similarities between a young magic mushroom (Psilocybe cubensis) and Egyptian crowns containing the Hedjet (mushroom primordium shape). **(A)** Osiris wearing his Atef on the wall of Nefertari's tomb (1295-1255 BCE), personifying a magic mushroom incorporating V47 degree solstice symbolizing angle. He was also patron deity of the barley adorning his V47 degree solstice angled crook & staff. This depiction of Osiris is obviously rich in ritual symbolism. **(B)** A Psilocybe cubensis primordium with its hedjet-shaped, bulbous base and demarcated brown top with a zone of transition in the primordium's neck— these grow naturally on sterilized barley (i.e. after lightning strikes). **(C)** A pschent crown worn by Horus on a wall of the Kom Ombo Temple. [282]

According to the Egyptian allegory "Cheops and the Magicians," crowns were bestowed on Egypt's new 5th Dynasty kings by deities who initially hid them in barley that was exposed to a storm and later left in a storeroom for two weeks.[283] It is more than possible that those magic mushroom crowns, or the crown's spores, grew into new magic mushroom crowns. Osiris's association with the summer solstice, the V47 degree angle solstice symbolism associated with Osiris's upper body with folded arms, and his headdress form, which is said to depict the young magic mushroom, yield much ritual information.

Pre-Columbian Mesoamerican Entheogen Trail

According to scholars, three Maya art motifs commonly appear in pre-conquest Mesoamerica temple, palace, or pyramid art and icons: the white water lily, psilocybin magic mushrooms, and bufo hallucinogenic toads (which secrete bufotenin, a DMT-like molecule). All three motifs represent entheogens which are known to contain psychoactive compounds. The close association of the white water lily with underworld entry, and the Sun god aspects of important Maya deities represented in temple murals and icons (as waterlily jaguar, waterlily serpent, and quadripartite god) imply knowledge of their ritual use by the shaman and priests.[284]

Magic mushrooms were the most frequently depicted entheogens in Mesoamerica.[285,286] Hundreds of mushroom stone effigies dating between 1000 and 100 BCE incorporate a human face or an animal image such as a toad or jaguar. The jaguar was the Sun god variant of the night and underworld. In the mushroom stone effigies, jaguars or toads are depicted projecting from the mushroom's stem. This coassociation of symbolic ritual elements is not unlike what is observed with respect to the Maya's waterlily jaguar and waterlily serpent deities (see below). In 1961 Stephan de Borhegyi, an archaeologist, proposed that the mushroom idols were connected with the Nine Lords of Xibalba and the Cult of Sacred Mushrooms.[287,288]

Various Mushroom Stones (approx 1 ft tall - 1000 B.C. to 500 A.D.)

Figure 5.18 Were these mushroom stones, like those originally discovered by Stephan de Borhegyi, possibly connected with the Nine Lords of Xibalba and the Cult of the Sacred Mushrooms?[289]

The white waterlily is also well represented artistically in Maya netherworld art,[290] and is a unifying mythological symbol. Various Maya aquatic and netherworld gods, including the waterlily serpent, waterlily jaguar, and quadripartite god, depict waterlily stalks and flowers emanating from their eyes, ears, and mouth, perhaps indicating sensory hallucinations.[291] The white water lily (*Nymphaea ampla*) is cousin to Egypt's blue water lily (see Chapter 4).

Maya temple art and icons (e.g., ceramics) from important Maya religious sites, together with the Maya codices, reveal that the white water lily was ubiquitously and frequently associated with different forms of the Sun god (jaguar, serpent, quadripartite god). These deities are juxtaposed with entheogens (white water lilies, toads). These depictions ultimately linked Sun gods, entheogens, and sacred time with kings-queens, chiefs, the ruling elite, and priests and priestesses.

The waterlily jaguar was associated with the Maya's jaguar god of the underworld and the white waterlily. The jaguar god was the nighttime aspect of Kinich Ahau (Maya Sun god and god of the underworld), ensuring unhindered passage of the Sun to its eastern horizon.[292] The flower of the waterlily rises above the surface of the water for a few days, opening at sunrise and closing at sunset and finally closing and being pulled underwater into the jaguar god's underworld by a recoiling flower peduncle. Depictions of waterlily jaguar can sometimes tell us even more if we understand how artists can use V47 degree angles to proportion and position items within the art, as detailed below in Figure 5.19.

Figure 5.19 Ceramic depiction of the waterlily jaguar. V47 degree angled solstice lines can be drawn connecting the base of the waterlily flower stalks, thus demarcating sacred time. The equinox is depicted by the water lily held in his left hand. This completes the triad of Sun god, sacred time, and entheogen symbols. Originally published in McDonald and Stross 2012; used with permission.[293]

White waterlilies are also recurrently associated with cosmic serpents. In my view, cosmic serpents symbolize the equinoxes. As specialized aspects of the Sun god, the waterlily stalk and solar serpent oscillate between the underworld after sunset and the sky during the day. Not much information is available about the water lily serpent as a deity, but inner temple sanctums frequently employ a serpents' wide-open mouth at the entrance, symbolizing a doorway to the underworld realm and the realm of the Sun gods.[294] The cosmic serpent was also identified with Itzamna and the Sun god K'inich Ajaw (Kinich Ahua).

Figure 5.20 Waterlily serpent. **(A)** An anthropomorphic deity cradles a peccary within the coils of a waterlily serpent. Note the apposing water lily (gray shading) and iconographic white flower ear flares on the serpent, and plumes emerging from a water lily on the serpent's backside. This combines serpent (sacred time) and entheogen themes and involves important Maya gods. **(B)** A long-nosed Waterlily Serpent with the white waterlily symbolized (gray shading). Originally published in McDonald and Stross 2012; used with permission.[295]

The quadripartite god embraced the Sun god as his aquatic underworld representative, and was closely associated with the white waterlily. He is represented by a skull resembling a waterlily monster wearing a headdress called the "Quadripartite badge" (Figure 5.22). This displays prominent symbols embracing the k'in glyph (Sun) and waterlilies. This badge was said to be associated with rulership or kingship, much like a king's crown or emblem.[366] Worn by rulers, it embraced Sun god connections, solstice associations via the cruciform glyph, and entheogenic themes via the waterlily.

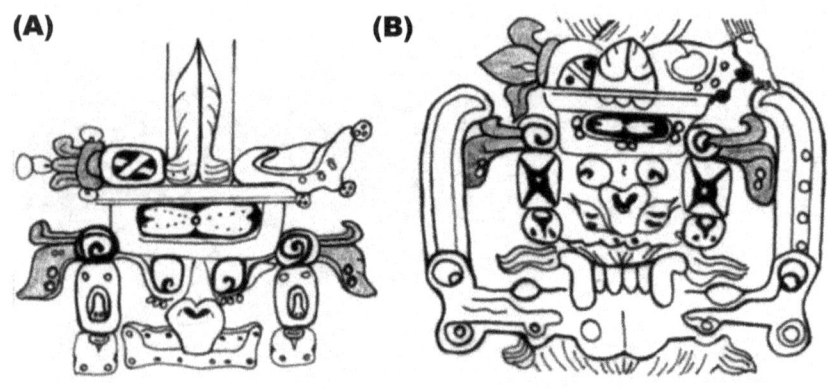

Figure 5.21 The quadripartite god, depicted as a badge worn atop a Waterlily Monster, with white water lilies shaded gray. **(A)** A frontal view of Quadripartite God's face resembles that of the Waterlily Monster. **(B)** Pakal falls into the plate of Quadripartite god. The Kan cross (ear rings) indicates a port of entry to the land of the water lilies (Xibalba). Palenque, Mexico. Originally published in McDonald and Stross 2012; used with permission.[296]

Kukulkan, the Feathered Serpent, should not be forgotten as an important Maya god. He was a creator god who established the four elements (earth, air, water, and fire), resurrection and reincarnation, terrestrial waters, and the annual cycle of time—namely the 360-day *tun* period and the nameless five days, called Wayeb, at the end of the annual calendar. Maya calendars start on the winter solstice, a time that was recognized as more conducive to entering the spirit world. The combination of water lily and serpent blends cosmic connectivity and/or the spirit doorway with entheogens at the equinoxes (represented by the serpent).

Figure 5.22 Serpents adorn important Maya buildings. **(A)** Uxmal, House of the Governor, corner molding (Yucatan, Mexico). **(B)** Ballcourt marker from the Postclassic site of Mixco Viejo (Guatemala). **(C)** The Nunnery Quadrangle murals depicts Kukulkan, jaws agape, with a warrior emerging. Kukulkan's head is placed midway between the V47 degree solstice symbol depicts the equinox.[297]

Kukulkan, K'inich Ajaw, and Itzamna were Sun gods, and as such were associated with the solstices, which is when they were worshipped. The art can be more clearly understood with knowledge of these deities and their roles, associations, and characteristics, which are similar to those in the ancient Egyptian and Hindu religions.

The toad motif is also commonly found in Mesoamerican art, frequently in combination with the water lily (figure 3.21).[298,299] Certain toads secrete bufotenin, a powerful hallucinogen containing a variant of dimethyl tryptamine, a known potent hallucinogen released by the brain during near death experiences.[300, 301]

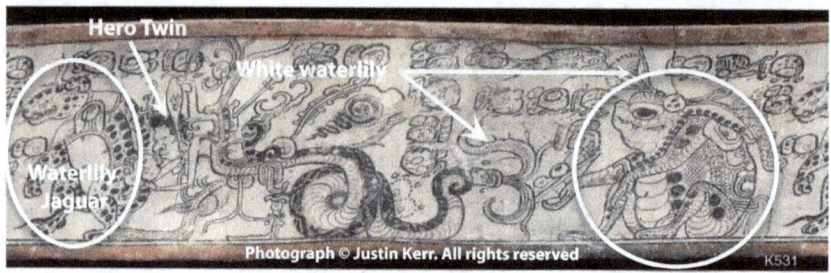

Figure 5.23 The toad and waterlily are sacred entheogen symbols. Ceramic vase art depicts a toad with a waterlily on its head, God K, Waterlily Jaguar, Serpent, and the Hero twins Hunahpú & Xbalanqué. This vase depicts sacred time, the underworld, and multiple entheogens known to be used by the Maya i.e., the waterlily, hallucinogenic toad, and cacao (the fish by the waterlily on the toad's head), that helped make that journey into the underworld possible.[302]

Pre-Columbian South America

We know hallucinatory experiences played an important role in the evolution of Andean religious rituals, which were displayed in religious icons as far back as the second millennium BCE.[303] We can also see a continuity of entheogens (*Anadenanthera colubrina*,

San Pedro cactus) as well as solar (lightning staffs) and sacred time (Sun rays, V47 solstice, and serpent equinox) symbols in pre-Incan deity art. This triad of symbolic information is seen in the Raimondi Stela at the Chavín de Huántar temple (2ⁿᵈ millennium BCE) and continues right through to the Middle Horizon period (600–1000 AD) as exemplified by Viracocha, the staff-holding, Sun-rayed creator deity.[304]

San Pedro's widespread use is inferred from its frequent iconographic depictions on Cupisnique and other ceramic pottery, on textiles, and in rock art recovered throughout Peru.[305] One of the most widely published San Pedro cactus depictions, detailed in Figure 5.24(A), is the Raimondi Stela granite carving. This shows a huachumero shaman in the Old Temple of pure consciousness at Chavín de Huantar in northern Perú, which dates back to the second millennium BCE. This fanged-serpent (equinox) deity-shaman holds two staffs of San Pedro cactus in each hand. The multilevel stacking of V47 degree angled solstice symbolisms with spiral tips attached to an elaborate headdress of fanged serpents provides rich solstice-equinox sacred time symbolism.

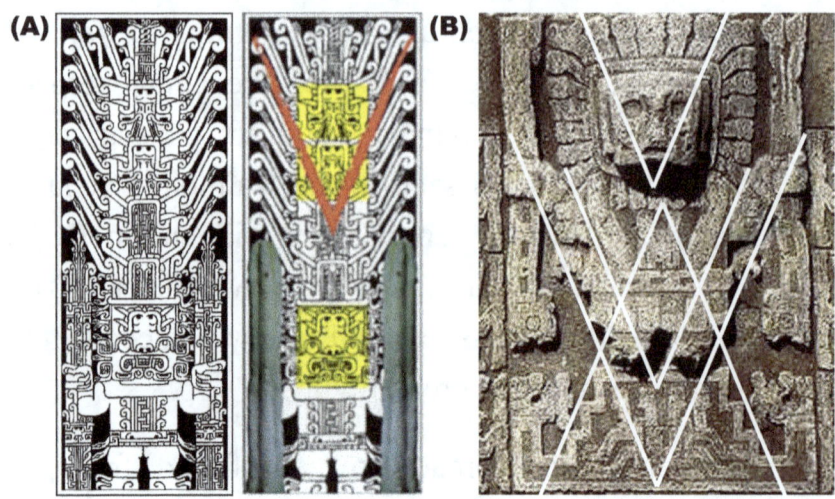

Figure 5.24 Sun gods, sacred time, and entheogens communicating across time. **(A)** A print of the Raimondi Stela from Chavín de Huantar represents an early version of a fanged serpent deity holding staffs symbolizing the San Pedro cactus. Right diagram: this deity is rich in sacred time (V47 degree solstice angle, three serpent heads for the equinoxes) and entheogen symbolism (San Pedro cactus). **(B)** Viracocha created the universe and civilization and was god of the Sun and of storms. Here the Sun-faced, V47 degree angled outlined, staff-holding Viracocha, who wears the Sun as his crown with rain descending from his eyes as tears. This is a little more difficult to interpret, as it is uncertain if the stalked items emanating from the deity's head are vilca seed symbols (Ananandathera colubrina) as depicted in earlier Rayed Head deities.[306]

The deity Viracocha is said to have emerged from an evolutionary process. Viracocha's ancestors likely included the Staff god and Rayed Head deity's antecedents. The precursor deities evolved during the

Early Horizon period (c. 900–200 BCE) and the Middle Horizon (600–1000 CE).[307] This deity and icon evolution became possible as a result of the cultural and trade interactions between different regions that were facilitated by the vast road networks existing throughout the Andes.[308]

One thing is clear: precursors of both the rayed head and staff god displayed sacred time and entheogen symbolisms (Vilca; *Anadenanthera colubrina*). We see V47 degree angle solstice symbol lines and equinox symbols interspersed among those perimeter lines (see Figure 5.25 for specific depictions). *Anadenanthera colubrina* symbols populate both types of deity icons. And, in both cases, the deities' faces depict tears flowing. Vilca, as it was commonly prepared, was incredibly painful to snuff (snuffing being its method of delivery). Perhaps the tears symbolize the pain of intranasal administration.

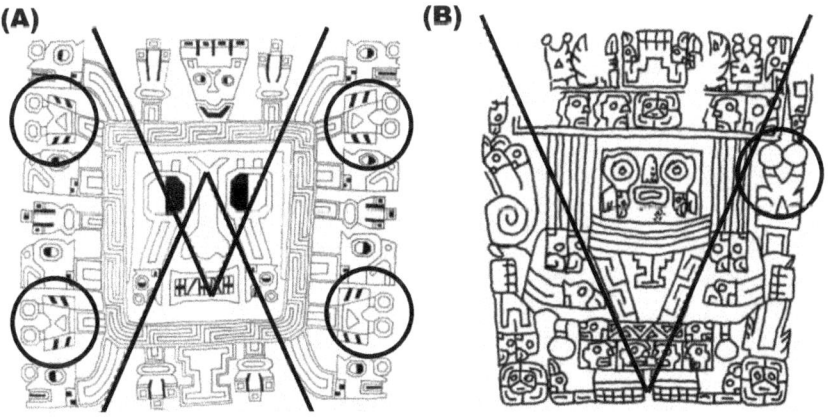

Figure 5.25 Andean icon artifacts depict rayed head and staff gods: **(A)** *Anadenanthera colubrina* symbol on a "fire textile" rayed head snuff tray from San Pedro de Atacama. The Rayed Head deity depicts solstice angles, equinox eyes and a liberal use of hallucinogen symbols (red circles). **(B)** Staff god deity depicting *Anadenanthera colubrina* symbols (red circles) on a snuff tray from San Pedro de Atacama. Original drawings by Dr. Patricia Knobloch in Andean Archaeology, Vol. III.[309]

We should remember that these pre-Incan deity icons belonged to religions which built solstice-aligned huacas and ushnus (temples; sacred space). Right from their primordial beginnings, the ancient pre-Inca Chavin, Moche, Wari, and Tiwanaku societies were communicating sacred time and entheogen symbols in their deity art, thereby revealing to future generations their ritual secrets.

Chapter 6

Sun & Earth Interactions Generate Sacred Time

Introduction

The concept of Sun god worship raised a question in the project's early stages. What did the word "Sun" in Sun god have to do with the religions of ancient Egypt, India, and pre-Colombian Central and South America?

The data in hand at that time was quite clear. Priest-architects from these ancient Sun god religions aligned their pyramids and temples with the equinoxes (50% of the time) or the solstices (30% of the time), and conducted their most important sacred rituals and festivals dedicated to their Sun gods at those same times of the year.

Life is starting to open my eyes to the fact that if you dare to ask the Universe such a big question, it will be answered if you are prepared to listen in unusual ways. The unorthodox answer to this question came to me when I was flying to Denver from London one day in late 2008. My plane was struck by lightning over the

Sun & Earth Interactions Generate Sacred Time

Rocky Mountains, causing the engines to sound as if they were failing (and many passengers to scream). As it happened, we were flying over the backyard of Nicola Tesla, the famous scientists and inventor. Tesla was one of the greatest scientific minds of the 20th Century. He developed AC voltage, ionosphere lightning conductors, and even wireless electrical transmission through the ionosphere. That lightning strike preceded a flash of deep insight that said "solar-terrestrial physics holds the answer to your question" i.e., What does the word Sun in Sun god have to do with these ancient religions?. A wry smile lit up my face, as I realized I was listening with my intuitive mind to the Universe's rather unorthodox answer i.e., "Here's your next clue."

Ultimately, solar-terrestrial physics creates our cyclical electromagnetic and magnetic environments here on Earth (via lightning, twice daily solar terminators, and geomagnetic activity). As the Earth rotates daily and orbits the Sun annually we observe twice-yearly peaks in the strength of the terrestrial electromagnetic (EM) and magnetic (M) fields. These peaks occur around the winter solstice sunrise (EM), summer solstice sunset (EM), and at both of the equinoxes (M). These times of the day and year also coincide with the most important sacred ritual dates of the Sun god religions discussed in this book, which are referred to here as sacred time. And, as previously mentioned, pyramids and temples were typically built with an alignment to the sunrise or sunset of one of these dates/times.

The above dates and times are significant in that they are periods when one can optimally increase or supplement the voltages of the brain's alpha brainwaves over the forehead region (see Chapter 7). This part of the frontal brain contains some important structures involved in supporting the meditation process and accessing altered states of consciousness (see Chapter 8). Therefore, I conclude that solar-terrestrial physics provided favorable conditions for augmenting meditation-based rituals for switching one's state of consciousness.

If the scientific details are not particularly of interest to you, then please proceed to the next chapter with this summary in mind.

The Sun's Activity

The Sun is the center of our solar system and generates its energy by nuclear fusion. We perceive this as sunlight and heat here on earth. In addition to generating heat and light, the Sun also generates a magnetic field that reaches far out into the solar system. The sun's magnetic field waxes and wanes according to the various solar cycles.

Figure 6.1 Our Sun in motion. A burst of solar material leaps off the sun, captured on March 23, 2013. The resulting coronal mass ejection (CME), or solar flare, is captured using special telescopes. Large CMEs are visible through polished obsidian. This may be the source of the serpent and flame-breathing dragon symbols of the ancient world.[310]

Due to the incredibly high temperatures (1 million° C) in the sun's outer layer (the corona), plasma is ejected from the Sun's surface (a phenomenon commonly known as a solar flare) and becomes associated with the interplanetary magnetic field as solar wind. The solar wind carries the Sun's magnetic field into the solar system, forming the interplanetary magnetic field (IMF), which eventually reaches the Earth.

Solar Cycles and Sunspot Activity

Sunspots are regions on the Sun's surface of intense magnetic activity driven by the Sun's magnetic cycles. Sunspots cause heating in the corona, which in turn creates active regions that are the source of intense solar flares and coronal mass ejections.

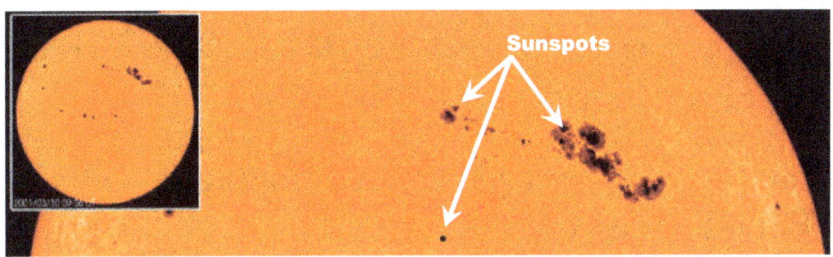

Figure 6.2 Sunspots' intense magnetic activity seen up close.[311]

The number of sunspots visible on the Sun varies over an 11-year period known as the solar cycle. At a solar minimum, few sunspots are visible. As the solar cycle progresses, sunspot numbers increase, and they converge toward the Sun's equator. Figure 6.3 below demonstrates Sunspot activity since the year 1880, and highlights its 11-year periodicity.

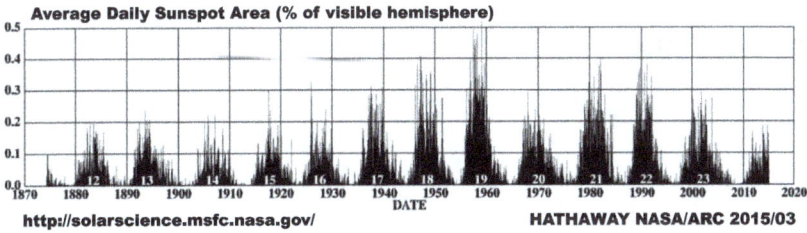

Figure 6.3 Sunspot area over different solar cycles. These cycles have displayed an 11-year periodicity since observations began in 1880. Sunspots typically appear at higher solar latitudes first, and progress toward the Sun's equator as the Sun's cycle peaks.[312]

The net outcome of solar activity and sunspot cycles is to modulate the intensity and power of Earth's electromagnetic and magnetic fields. The impact of sacred time on sacred rituals would be enhanced toward the peak of the solar cycle.

Earth's Magnetosphere, Geomagnetic Activity & the Equinoxes

Earth generates its own magnetic field, which extends from Earth's inner core outward for tens of thousands of kilometers into space, where it meets the magnetized solar wind. Earth's magnetosphere is the area of space surrounding Earth where the magnetized solar wind's charged particles (plasma) are controlled by the Earth's magnetic field.[313] This is graphically depicted in Figure 6.4. The magnetosphere essentially acts as a solar wind shield on Earth's sunny side, preventing solar wind plasma from entering our atmosphere and destroying life on the planet.

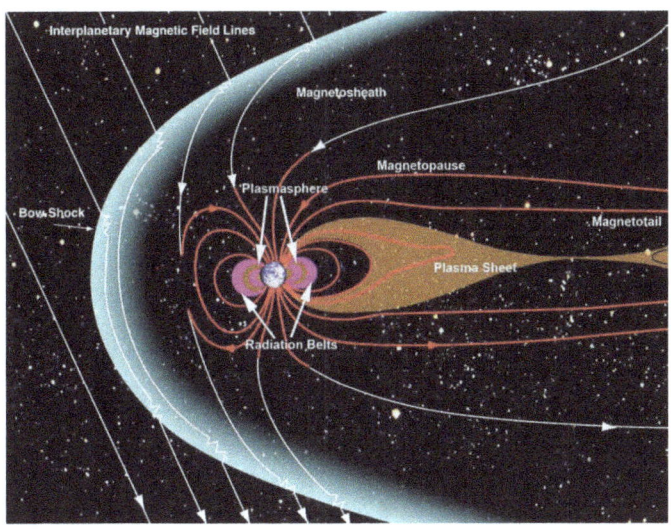

Figure 6.4 Artistic renditions of Earth's magnetosphere. Earth's magnetic field interacts with the interplanetary magnetic field (IMF) to create the magnetosphere. The magnetocusps are two regions in and around Earth's magnetic north and south poles where the IMF contacts with Earth's magnetic field and transfer the Sun's charge and energy. The IMF changes the magnetosphere's size, shape, and energy depending upon the level of solar activity.[314]

Geomagnetic Activity & the Equinoxes

The Sun's interplanetary magnetic field (IMF) is not readily able to reconnect with the magnetosphere's magnetic field. Physical reasons normally prevent this reconnection. However, around the equinoxes, Earth's three-dimensional orientation in space is in an optimal alignment for permitting magnetic field reconnections between the Sun's IMF and the magnetosphere. These reconnections permit the inflow of solar wind plasma and the charging of the Earth's magnetic field, which is registered as geomagnetic activity (GMA).[315,316,317]

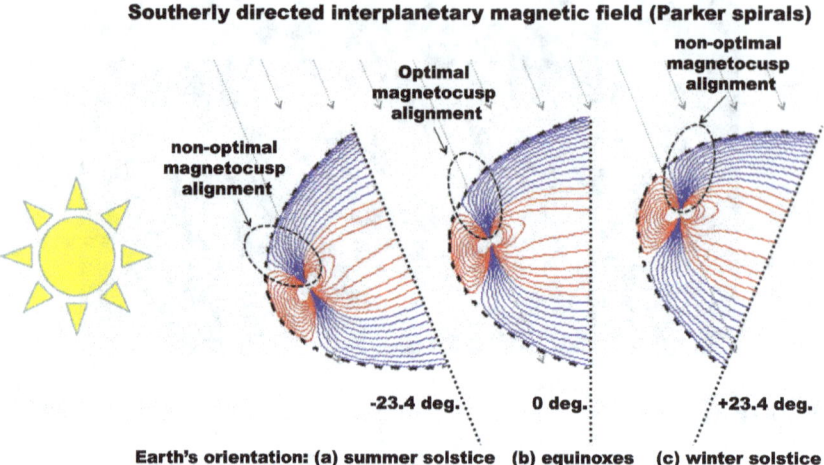

Figure 6.5 Depiction of the southerly-directed interplanetary magnetic field relative to the North Pole and how it reconnects with Earth's magnetic field at the magnetocusps. This magnetic field reconnection happens optimally around the equinoxes.[318]

The strength of Earth's magnetic field varies according to surges in solar wind caused by coronal mass ejections and solar flares.[319,320,321] Increased geomagnetic activity due to solar activity around the equinoxes is seen as an increased visibility and intensity of the northern and southern lights in the polar regions.

Figure 6.6 Northern lights (Aurora Borealis) flowing over the fjord into Tasiilaq (Greenland, September 2005).[322]

An international and planetary scale index (Ap Index) is used to measure the average level of geomagnetic activity and its fluctuations caused by the Sun's activity. Figure 6.7(A) highlights a seven-decade relationship between sunspot numbers and geomagnetic activity. Figure 6.7(B) also highlights a seven-decade relationship between the number of magnetic storms and the twelve months of the year, which demonstrates that geomagnetic activity peaks around the equinoxes (March and September).[323,324,325]

It's these twice-yearly peaks in geomagnetic activity around the equinoxes that are of importance to sacred ritual processes. This is because increased geomagnetic activity enhances the voltages of human alpha brainwave frequencies over the forehead region of the brain, via a process of brainwave entrainment. This will be explained further in Chapters 7 and 8.

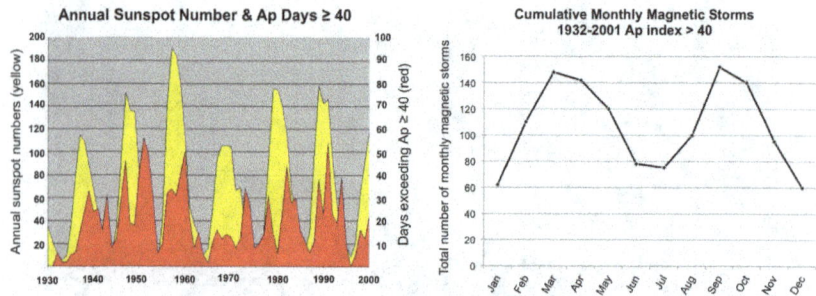

Figure 6.7 (A) Graphical relationship between annual Sunspot numbers (yellow) and geomagnetic activity (Ap ≥ 40; red). **(B)** Seven decades of geomagnetic activity data highlight twice yearly peaks of GMA around the equinoxes. These equinox peaks are twice the magnitude of the solstice minimums.[326] Taken together, both solar activity (sunspot activity) and Earth's solar orbital 3D configuration (equinoxes) impact geomagnetic activity experienced on Earth.

The Ionosphere, Schumann Resonances, and the Solstices

The ionosphere is an ionized part of the upper atmosphere created by solar ionizing radiation, and extending from about 85-1,000 kilometers above the Earth's surface. The ionosphere consists of multiple concentric layers composed of different gas molecules, electric currents, and their associated magnetic fields. These atmospheric gases naturally organize into different altitude layers, which become ionized, and are referred to as the D, E, and F layers.

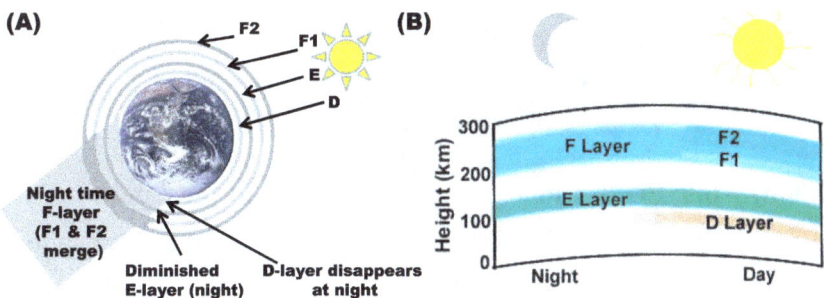

Figure 6.8 (A&B) A two-dimensional depiction of Earth's ionosphere layers: from D, E to F1 and F2 layers being present by day to E and F1 & F2 merged together by night. During the day, a D-layer forms and the E and F layers become much stronger.[327]

The D-layer is the innermost layer, 80 to 90 kilometers above Earth's surface. The appearance of the D-layer around sunrise and its disappearance around sunset depends on the lower ultraviolet light frequencies that appear with sunrise and disappear at sunset, or surge after solar flares and coronal mass ejections. The D-layer also represents a key component of the Earth-ionosphere waveguide, an invisible structure that guides electromagnetic waves, i.e., radio waves and Schumann resonances, around the Earth. These electromagnetic waves are formed between the Earth's surface and the inner surface of the daytime ionosphere.

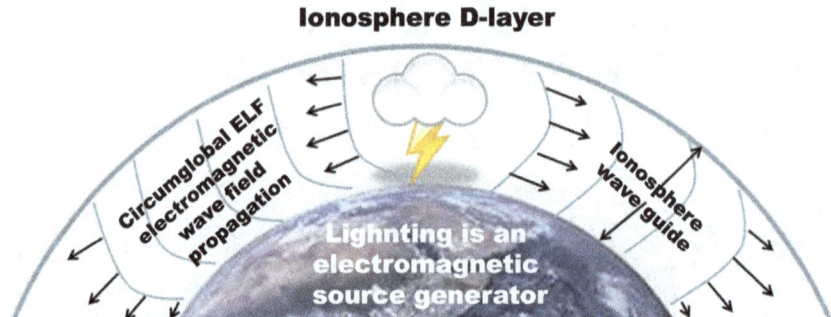

Figure 6.9 Earth's ionospheric waveguide formed between the Earth's surface and the inner D-layer of the ionosphere. Extremely low frequency electromagnetic fields (lightning, solar terminator) propagate well in this cavity.[328]

Extremely low frequency (ELF) electromagnetic fields (which are generated by lightning and the solar terminator), especially the 7.8-hertz Schumann resonance frequency, are propagated most efficiently within the Earth-ionosphere waveguide with little loss in signal intensity.[329,330]

Elevations in the ionosphere's inner D-layer electron density through atmospheric ionization processes are associated with the generation of enhanced Schumann resonance (SR) signal intensity (wave amplitude, power, or voltage).[331] We typically observe a ten-fold increase in D-layer electron density within an hour of sunrise/sunset, during solar flares and storms[332], and seasonally around the solstices. These increases in electron density are enhanced still further toward the peak of the various solar cycles (i.e., 27 day, 11-year cycle, etc.).

Enhanced Schumann resonances are of importance to the sacred ritual process and it's timing, as will be explained in Chapter 7. You will note in this chapter how Schumann resonances (especially 7.8 hertz frequency) peak during the day at sunrise and sunset, and twice annually at the solstices, specifically the winter solstice sunrise and summer solstice sunset. As the solstice peaks of Schumann resonances coincide with the ancient Sun god religions' most important sacred ritual dates/times, I refer to these dates/times as *sacred time*. Recall also that all the Sun god religions depicted their deities, mythologies, and cosmologies linked to these same times (see Chapter 3). The biological or ritual relevance of this is detailed in Chapters 7 and 8.

Schumann Resonances

Schumann resonances (SR) are a set of naturally generated electromagnetic wave peaks in the extremely low frequency (ELF) portion of the electromagnetic wave field spectrum (less than 60 hertz frequencies). The most important SR frequency within this spectrum is the 7.8 hertz frequency, because it matches the human alpha brainwave frequency (see Chapters 7 and 8). An EM frequency of 7.8 hertz has a corresponding wavelength approximately as long as the Earth's circumference (which is just under 25,000 miles, or 40,000 km), making it the fundamental EM frequency of this planet. This 7.8 hertz frequency is typically of the greatest intensity in the SR spectrum.[333]

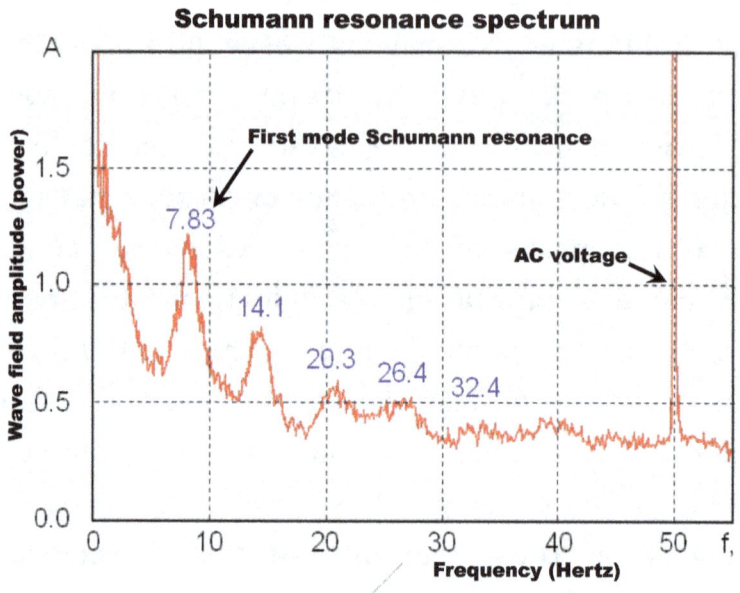

Figure 6.10 Schumann resonance electromagnetic spectra. This spectrum is a series of stable electromagnetic frequencies generated by lightning and the solar terminator. The first mode SR (7.8 Hz) attains the highest intensity.[334]

Earth's Main Sources of Schumann Resonances

Lightning and solar terminators (day-night boundaries) are the most important natural generators of Schumann resonances.[335,336] SR wave amplitudes (voltage) increase at dawn and dusk, seasonally (solstices), geographically (lightning centers; see below), during solar storms (CMEs and solar flares), and at the peaks of the different solar cycles.[337,338,339] All of these timings and locations (lightning centers; see below) are, interestingly enough, associated with the various Sun god religions as sacred time and these ancient religions' geographical locations.

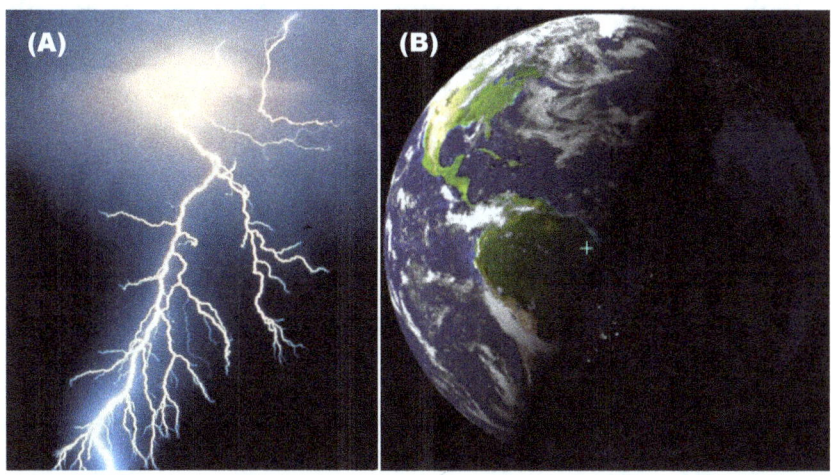

Figure 6.11 Earth's natural Schumann resonance generators. **(A)** One of the 50-100 lightning strikes that hit Earth every second. Lightning is Earth's largest generator of SR wave fields.[340] **(B)** The winter solstice sunrise (solar terminator) occurring over South America and the Atlantic Ocean.[341]

Global Lightning Centers and the Summer Solstice Sunset

Lightning occurs 50-100 times a second worldwide, and is the biggest generator of Schumann resonances and other naturally generated low frequency electromagnetic fields worldwide.[342,343] Global lightning activity is concentrated in three major thunderstorm regions, namely, Southeast Asia, Central-East Africa, and the American Continent (SE USA, Central and South America). These three lightning centers are the biggest global generators of Schumann resonances (SR). Interestingly, all the Sun god religions reviewed here existed within these lightning centers or close by on the same longitude (Egypt).

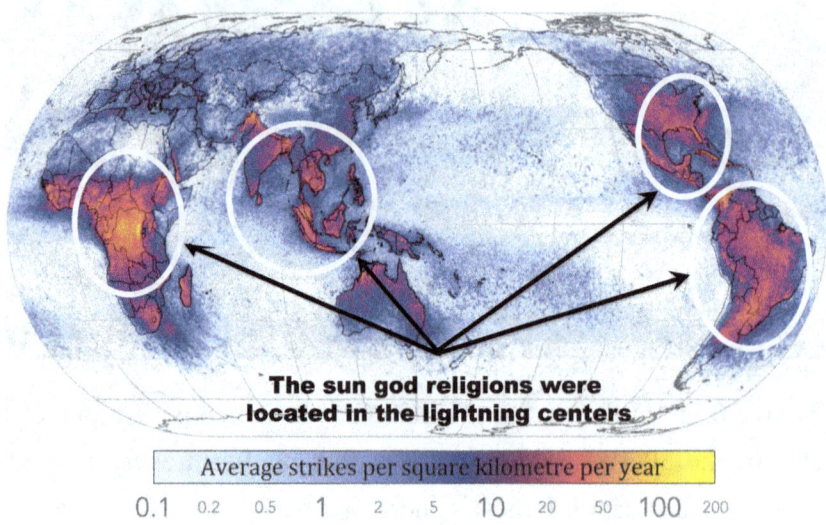

Figure 6.12 Lightning activity concentrates into three main mid-latitude regions and is responsible for generating ELF/VLF wave fields as lightning's by-product. This world map shows the frequency of lightning strikes (flashes per km² per year) from 1995–2003.[344]

Global lightning activity is the most important factor affecting global Schumann resonances (wave amplitudes or power). Thunderstorm activity migrates daily as the Earth rotates, from one lightning center to the next. This thunderstorm activity also migrates north-south annually as the Earth's north-south axis tilts from plus to minus 23.4 degrees. What this means is that Schumann resonance wave amplitudes (voltage) peak during the late afternoon, [345] and annually during mid-summer (June-July, Northern Hemisphere) (see Figure 7.14).[346,347,348] Interestingly, the summertime Schumann resonance maxima coincide with the ancient Sun god religions' summer solstice sunset ritual-festivals.

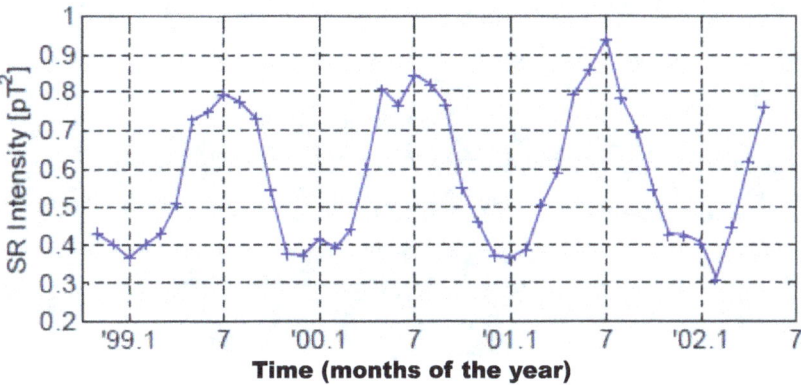

Figure 6.13 Seasonal variations of absolute Schumann resonance intensity from 1998 and 2002. The first three frequency (7.8, 14, 20Hz) intensities were collected at Moshiri Observatory (Japan). One observes a +/–2 pT² (picoTesla) variance due to lightning, which peaks around the summer solstice.[349]

The Solar Terminator and the Winter Solstice Sunrise

In Chapter 2, four satellite image regional views were presented of the different Sun god religions' sacred sites. These were largely located within narrow time bandwidth clusters delineated by the passing overhead solar terminator on the winter solstice sunrise and summer solstice sunset. In fact, 60-97 percent of a religion's important sacred sites were located within time bandwidths two to seven minutes wide, and spread over distances between 100-1,000 kilometers long.

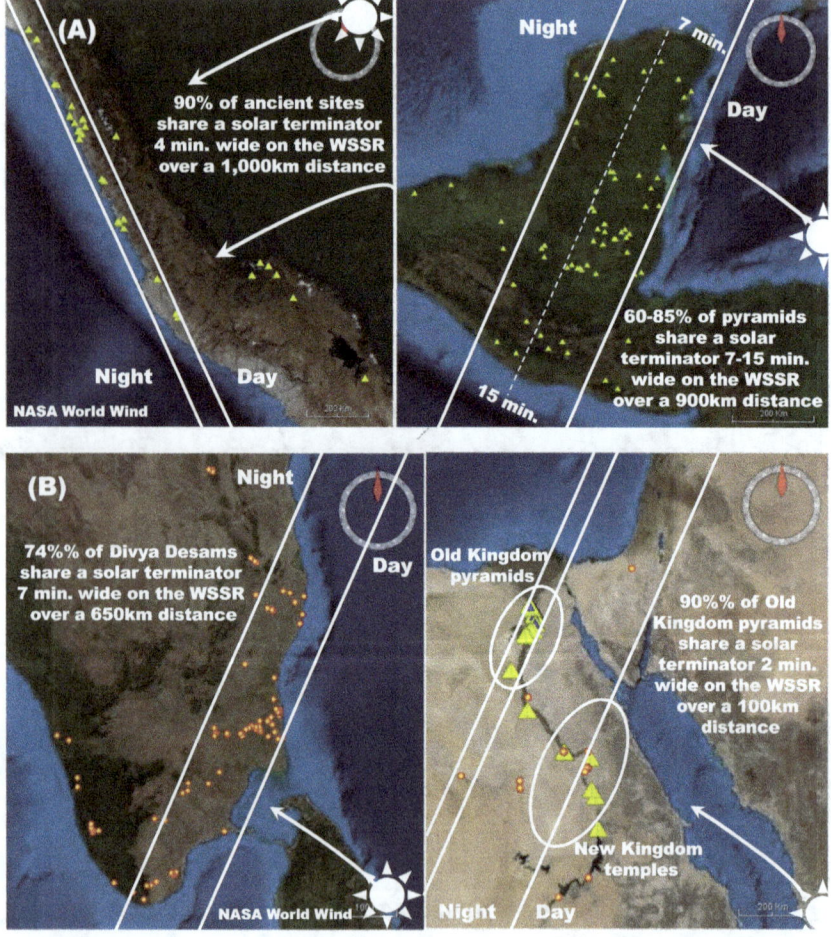

Figure 6.14 Regional maps of ancient Sun god sacred real estate. **(A and B)** Solar terminator alignments over ancient South and Central America's, Southern India's (Divya Desams), and Egypt's pyramids. Sixty to ninety-seven percent of these sacred sites align

within narrow terminator bandwidths 2-7 minutes wide and between 100-1,000km long relative to the solar terminator passing overhead on the winter solstice sunrise and summer solstice sunset.[350]

The solar terminator's twice daily passage causes peaks in local Schumann resonances, particularly the 7.8 hertz frequency. These SR wave fields peak around the winter solstice sunrise and summer solstice sunset on a yearly timescale.[351,352]

When we reflect on the above regional alignment clustering we see that most sites belonging to a Sun god religion would more or less simultaneously experience the same enhanced Schumann resonances overhead, on the winter solstice sunrise and summer solstice sunset. This is due to the solar terminator's overhead passage at these times and dates. This corresponded with the most important sacred ritual dates for all the Sun god religions reviewed in this book.

This in turn raises two big questions in my mind. First, how could these Sun god religions have established this clustering alignment pattern over such long distances? Second, could these regional alignments have represented non-local communication networks accessed through altered states of consciousness at sacred time? I'm going to leave you to ponder these two enigmatic questions, because the possible answers are speculative, and moreover are not central to the main theme of this book (which is the discovery and use of ancient sacred ritual processes for accessing altered states of consciousness).

Fault Lines and Volcanoes Generate Electromagnetic Anomalies

Recall that one-fifth of surveyed Mesoamerican sacred sites (especially the Guatemalan highlands), as well as other sacred sites around the world (Borobudur, Easter Island), are aligned with volcanoes on the solstice sunrise or sunset horizon(s). I ask this question: were intermittently active volcanoes and fault lines, generating enriched EM/magnetic fields, of benefit to sacred rituals at non-equinox/solstice times? The science seems to indicate that this question has merit.

Earthquakes and active volcanoes are important local generators of low frequency electromagnetic wave fields and magnetic fields. Data indicate that earthquake epicenters emit ultra low frequency (ULF), extremely low frequency, and very low frequency electromagnetic wavefields prior to an earthquake.[353,354,355,356] ULF wavefield emissions (defined as <10Hz) become detectable 3-4 weeks before an earthquake, and peak a few days before the earthquake occurs.[357,358] Local magnetic field strengths also increase for about 5-12 days before an earthquake, followed by quiescence, and then a sharp increase three to four hours before the earthquake occurs.[359]

The fact that ULF emissions are emerging as promising predictors of earthquakes at a distance of up to 70-80 kilometers from the earthquake's epicenter indicates that these emissions represent significant wave fields. The fact that animals are known to be behaviorally sensitive to volcanic eruptions and earthquakes (i.e., dogs bark without apparent cause) makes me ask if these enriched EM/magnetic fields could also potentially influence human biology, (i.e., be of use in augmenting ritual processes).

Chapter 7

Alpha Brainwave Voltages are enhanced by Sacred Time

Introduction

In the previous chapter we saw how the Sun's interaction with Earth creates our cyclical electromagnetic and magnetic environments. The result of this interaction is that we observe peaks in Schumann resonances and geomagnetic activity around the solstices (winter solstice sunrise, summer solstice sunset) and equinoxes respectively.

What this chapter highlights is that increases in Schumann resonances (esp. 7.8 hertz), other extremely low frequency electromagnetic fields, and geomagnetic activity cause an enhancement of alpha brainwave voltages (8-10 hertz brainwave frequency band) as detected by EEG over the forehead region. This enhancement of brainwave voltage happens via a natural process called brainwave entrainment. This entrainment process I believe was used to supplement meditation's alpha brainwave-generating processes during sacred rituals. This helped the ritual meditator reach specific

Alpha Brainwave Voltages are enhanced by Sacred Time

voltage thresholds required to trigger a switch in the state of consciousness. The significance of this becomes clearer when we see in Chapter 8 that increased alpha brainwave voltages over the forehead region are the most important brainwave signature naturally generated by persons in deep meditation and transcendental states of consciousness.

For the purposes of this book I define meditation as a "gateway process" for accessing altered states of consciousness. By that I mean meditation is the core ritual process which sacred rituals supplement. With this perspective, it becomes clear that peaks in Earth's EM/magnetic fields, associated with sacred time, further supplement meditation's natural enhancement of alpha brainwaves over the forehead. Likewise, meditation's associated elevations in specific brain chemicals (dopamine, 5HT2a serotonin) are further supplemented via entheogens containing concentrated sources of those same brain chemicals.

We know, based on the archaeological evidence of temple art and icons (depictions of the Hindu Trimurti deities and ancient Egypt's pharaohs would be examples), that meditation was a core ritual process. Indeed, meditation (plus yoga) is still used today by Eastern spiritual traditions (i.e. Hinduism and Buddhism) as a core ritual process. We also know from spiritual and scientific literature that highly accomplished spiritual-meditation practitioners (i.e., mystics, yogis) are able to access altered states of consciousness without requiring psychedelic or entheogen supplementation. This indicates meditation's natural capacity to act as a gateway process for providing access to altered states of consciousness.

The corollary of the above is that less experienced meditation practitioners can achieve, using sacred rituals (i.e., alpha brainwave voltage and brain chemical supplementation), what the mystic adept naturally achieves through dedication to a spiritual life and a high level of meditation skill.

With the framing provided by the above information, the science detailed in this chapter highlights the possibility of naturally supplementing the alpha brainwave-generating process in the frontal brain. The opportunity for entraining enhanced alpha brainwave voltages over the forehead region is maximized when meditation-based rituals are conducted at sacred time. This is because the environmental electromagnetic and magnetic signals are at their peaks during sacred time. Electromagnetic fields peak during winter solstice sunrise and summer solstice sunset in both hemispheres, and earth's magnetic fields peak during the equinoxes. Based on personal experience, I believe the timing of sacred rituals was arrived at both intuitively (you can feel the sunrise, sunset, and solstice impact on meditation versus other times of the day and year) and via awareness imparted during altered states of consciousness.

Another important concept to understand is that humans are gifted with four main states of consciousness. These are: being awake, asleep, dreaming, and altered states of consciousness. Humans, by and large, regulate being awake and asleep via the brain receiving daylight signals from the natural environment. Dreaming of course is dependent upon being asleep. So, ultimately, three of our four states of consciousness are regulated by electromagnetic signals derived from daily planetary rotation (sunrise, sunset, length of day). The potential to experience altered states of consciousness (i.e., by using meditation-based rituals) is linked to Earth's cardinal positions in the heavens as it orbits the Sun (that is, on the solstices and equinoxes).

Humans discovered those dates and their ritual utility, and enshrined them within sacred rituals the ancient world over. We observe this ritual timing within shamanic traditions, the Sun god religions, and in many other ancient religions.

Again, I would say that if the scientific details are not particularly of interest to you, then please proceed to the next chapter with this summary in mind.

Brain Entrainment Regulates the Body's Rhythms & Cycles

The regulation and control of bodily function across the animal kingdom evolved under the influence of day and night, the Moon's cycles, severe thunderstorm activity, and geomagnetic field fluctuations. In so doing, the body evolved to regulate itself using regular environmental electromagnetic and magnetic signals, referred to as zeitgebers. Normal states of consciousness like sleep-dreaming-awake cycles all derive their electromagnetic cues (light-dark) from Earth's daily rotation.[360]

Naturally-derived zeitgebers provided life periodic electromagnetic and magnetic signals with daily (solar), annual (solar) and monthly (lunar) periodicities. Underpinning this periodic body regulation is a natural biological process called physiological entrainment, whereby the physiological rhythm (i.e., awake, asleep) within the body is matched to a naturally occurring zeitgeber from the environment, i.e., increasing or decreasing daylight length, triggering specific thresholds resulting in physiological change.

Alpha Brainwave Voltages are enhanced by Sacred Time

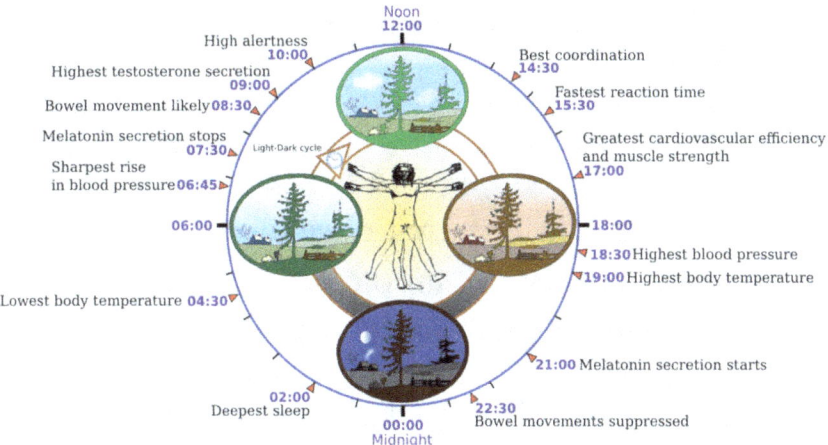

Figure 7.1 Human circadian clocks affect the daily rhythm of many physiological processes. This diagram depicts the circadian pattern typical of someone who rises early in morning, eats lunch around noon, and sleeps at night (10 pm). Circadian rhythms (sleep, awake, metabolism) tend to synchronize with cycles of light and dark via a process of physiological entrainment.[361]

The concept of physiological entrainment becomes important to our understanding of how the solstices and equinoxes could augment the meditation process to access altered states of consciousness. Why is this so? Because some important brain structures located in the frontal brain (the prefrontal cortex and angulate cingulate cortex) are those that govern the meditation process and naturally generate alpha brainwaves when activated (see Chapter 8).

According to the science of this chapter, physiological entrainment is likely implicated in supplementing meditation's alpha brainwave-generating processes that are housed in the prefrontal cortex and the angulate cingulate cortex. This alpha brainwave voltage supplementation helps to trip the voltage threshold switch required to change one's state of consciousness. This I believe is why sacred rituals were conducted at sacred time, so as to maximize meditation's alpha brainwave voltage supplementation.

More on this in Chapter 8, but please note this key fact: *sacred time naturally supplements the meditation process.*

The Human Body & Electromagnetic Fields

All living organisms on our planet are surrounded by a self-generated electromagnetic field, which is detectable as radiating heat and ultra-low and extremely low frequency electromagnetic fields of between 0.5-30 hertz frequencies. The brain, heart, muscles, and cells throughout the body generate these electromagnetic fields as a consequence of their functioning, and these are detectable using a wide array of medical diagnostic instruments, i.e., the electrocardiograph (ECG), electroencephalograph (EEG), and magnetic resonance imaging (MRI). [362,363]

The human brain emits extremely low frequency electromagnetic wave fields (i.e., brainwaves) that closely approximate the frequency bands of Earth's Schumann resonance generators (i.e., lightning and the solar terminator).³⁶⁴ This means Earth provides naturally occurring electromagnetic wave fields that can interact with the body's brainwaves (see below). This is of relevance to the process of brainwave entrainment (enhancing voltages) and switching states of consciousness via sacred rituals. This comparability in brainwave frequency bands and the Schumann resonance spectrum is highlighted in Figure 7.2.

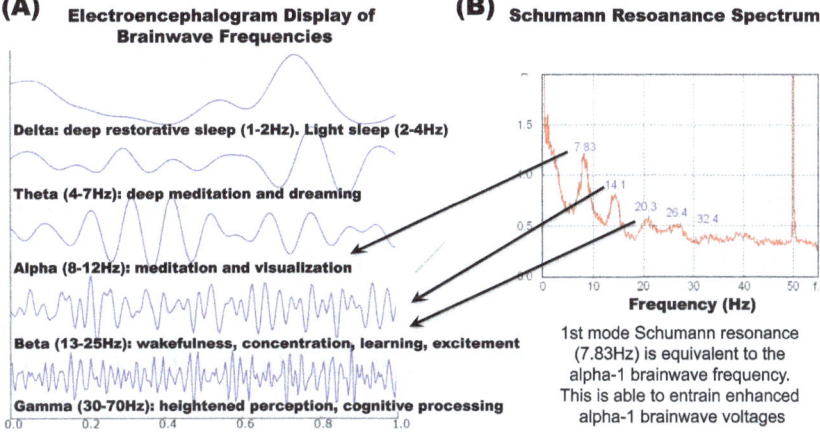

Figure 7.2 (A) Brain wave frequencies each displayed as an encephalograph (delta, theta, alpha, beta, and gamma). **(B)** The highest amplitude first mode Schumann resonance (7.83 Hertz) corresponds in frequency to alpha-1 brainwaves.³⁶⁵

The field of acupuncture highlights the skin's incredible properties for preventing entry of electromagnetism above certain frequencies. This prevents interference with internal electromagnetic signaling-communication processes, which the skin ultimately protects.³⁶⁶ The skin achieves this by providing windows, called acupuncture meridians, whereby electromagnetic frequencies corresponding to the Schumann resonance frequency range (<20 hertz) can pass through relatively unperturbed and entrain those same frequencies in the body, while higher frequencies are impeded.[367] This highlights a living/responding connection between the human body and its electromagnetic environment.

Within the body electromagnetic frequencies below 300 Hertz behave as if their electric and magnetic field components are decoupled. This decoupling explains why humans are sensitive to both Schumann resonance (SR) wave fields as well as magnetic fields corresponding to those same SR frequencies. The body is then able to entrain its frequency outputs to both electromagnetic and magnetic fields of the same or similar frequencies.[368] This explains how electromagnetic and magnetic fields produce a similar effect on the brain, and therefore why peak Schumann resonances at the solstices and peak magnetic fields around the equinoxes could be used during sacred rituals to entrain enhanced alpha brainwave voltages over the frontal brain.

Human Sensitivity to Solar Terrestrial Physics
Entraining Brain Electrical Activity

To give further context to brainwave entrainment, we need to understand the role of the thalamus. The thalamus is located in the midbrain and acts as the brain's central command and control and communication center. The thalamus organizes bundles of nerve cells and triggers their collective 'firing' to produce brain waves, which are then propagated to other parts of the brain and body. The thalamus needs time to recover after generating a brainwave; this recovery process is referred to as nerve repolarization. During this repolarization phase, the brainwaves previously generated are no longer controlled by the thalamus. It is during this repolarization moment that brainwaves can be affected or entrained by electromagnetic or magnetic fields from outside the body.[369] This fact is important to the concept of brainwave entrainment (supplementing voltages) during ritual processes.

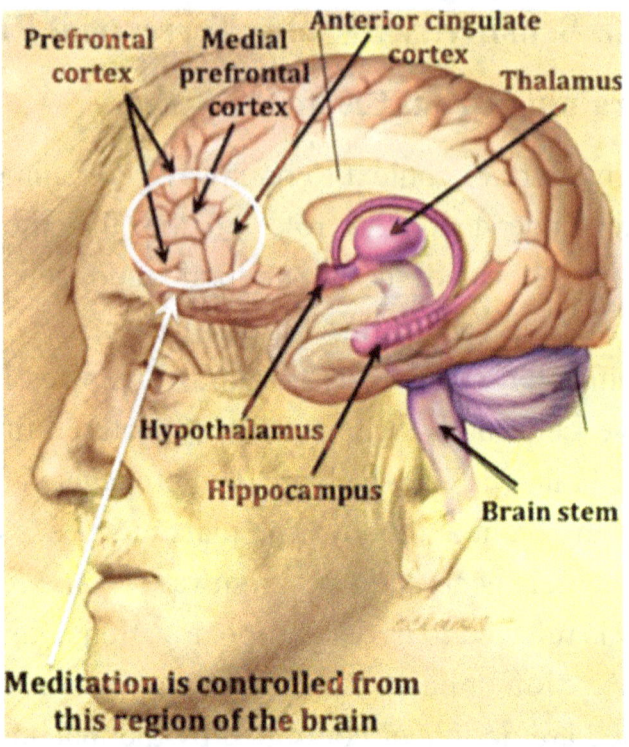

Figure 7.3 Some of the important brain structures associated with deep meditation and transcendental states of consciousness.[370]

Brain electrical activity can be selectively entrained to external electromagnetic signals, both naturally generated SR fields (lightning, solar terminator) and manmade, extremely low frequency electromagnetic fields (i.e., AC voltage). Numerous clinical studies have demonstrated that both naturally generated and artificially pulsed electromagnetic fields change brain electrical activity. One observes significant increases in alpha-1 (8-10 hertz), alpha-2 (10-12 hertz), and beta-1 frequency bands over the frontal cortex (forehead), and significant decreases in alpha-1 and/or alpha-2 bands in the parietal and occipital areas (side and back of head).[371,372,373]

The human brain at rest naturally synchronizes with Schumann resonances generated by the external environment. This is exemplified in Figures 8.4 and 8.5 where correlations are observed, over a one and ten day period respectively, between brainwave amplitudes (voltage) and the environmental SR frequencies in the 6–16 hertz range. The correlation is greatest at the sunrise and sunset hours, and during solar wind-induced geomagnetic activity (Figures 7.4 and 7.5).[374,375,376]

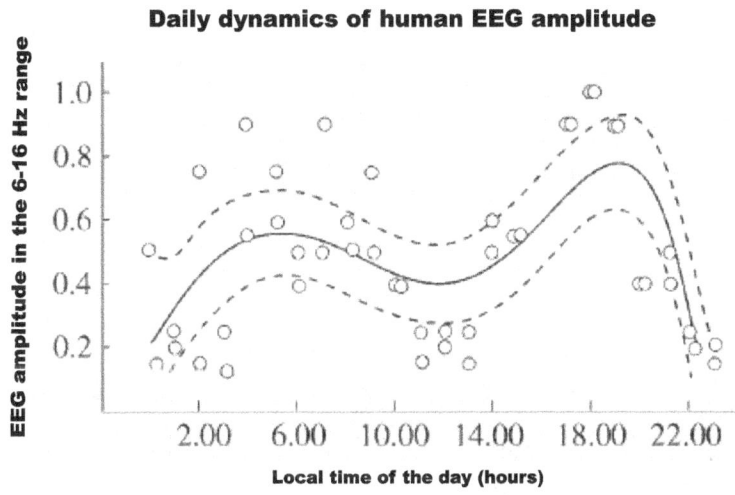

Figure 7.4 Daily variation of the average human electroencephalogram (EEG) output (15 subjects) in the 6–16 Hz frequency range over a 24-hour period. The horizontal axis shows local time in hours and the vertical axis the average subject brainwave amplitudes (6–16 Hz). **Conclusion**: human alpha and

theta brainwaves are naturally boosted around sunrise and sunset, when naturally generated Schumann resonances peak.[377]

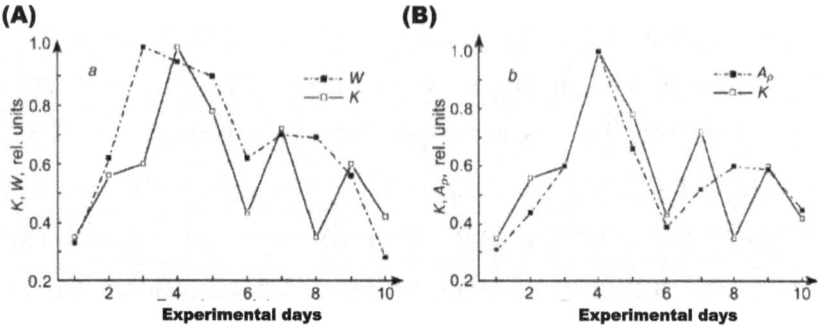

Figure 7.5 Averaged correlation coefficient (K) between EEG and SR frequencies in the 6–16 Hertz range with the: **(A)** index of sunspot numbers (*Wolf index, W*) and **(B)** Geomagnetic activity (measured by the Solar Geomagnetic Ap Index) during the ten-day study period with 15 volunteers. Correlation coefficients between 0.2–0.8 exist for EEG-SR (K) and solar activity or geomagnetic activity indices. **Conclusion**: This data indicates that the human EEG in the theta-alpha-low beta frequency ranges correlates with the Sun's activity over numerous days.[378]

Oscillations in Earth's magnetic field having similar frequencies to alpha brainwave rhythms are also known to entrain enhanced alpha brainwave voltages.[379] Severe geomagnetic activity is known to lead to malaise, weakness, and the occurrence of localized headaches. This was observed in most study participants on days when severe geomagnetic storms took place (see Figure 8.6). Participants also synchronized their alpha-1 and alpha-2 brainwaves into the lower alpha-1 range on days with severe geomagnetic storms.[380,381]

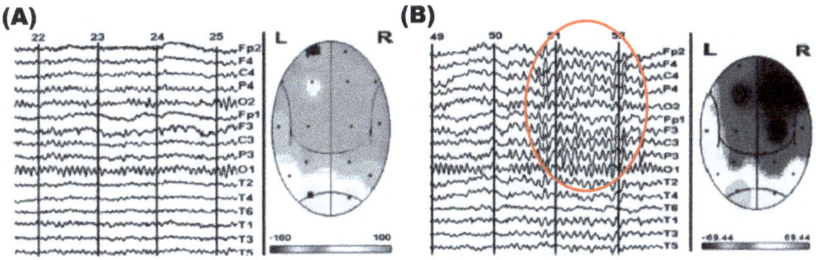

Figure 7.6 EEG during quiet and geomagnetic storms. **(A)** An EEG and total amplitude cartogram during relatively quiet geomagnetic conditions. **(B)** An example of an EEG and total amplitude cartogram during a severe geomagnetic storm. Flashes of sharp pointed alpha and theta brainwaves in the right cerebral hemisphere were registered during severe geomagnetic storms. One also sees a reduction of brainwave frequencies of dominating rhythms and a strengthening of synchronization of activity processes.[382]

This daily and multi-day responsiveness of the brain's EEG outputs to environmental Schumann resonance and geomagnetic activity fluctuations tells us that the human brain responds (i.e. entrains its brainwave outputs) to naturally-generated peaks in our electromagnetic and magnetic environments. These induce increased alpha-1 (8-10 hertz) brainwave voltages over the frontal brain.

This entrainment process becomes important in understanding that increased alpha-1 brainwave voltages (in the frontal brain/forehead region) are an important consequence of deep meditation and transcendental states of consciousness (see Chapter 8). By placing the meditating brain in sacred space (sensory silence), during the solstices and equinoxes, one is able to naturally augment the frontal brain alpha brainwave voltages.

Taking this a step further; by conducting sacred rituals at sacred time and ingesting entheogens at the right time before the ritual commences, one is able to coincide a state of deep meditation with the peak voltage-supplementing effect of sacred time and brain chemicals provided by meditation and entheogens. Ultimately, this collectively triggers a switch in the state of consciousness from deep meditation to altered states of consciousness.

Chapter 8

The Brain Signatures Of Altered States of Consciousness

Introduction

Brain-imaging technologies such as functional magnetic resonance imaging (fMRI), electroencephalography (EEG), and other methods are being used to map the human brain during specific states of consciousness such as being awake and asleep, engaging in specific tasks, during dream states, meditation, altered states of consciousness, etc. This has given science the opportunity to define the brain structures and processes involved in supporting these states of consciousness. These can be grouped together and termed the brain signature or neurological correlates for that specific state of consciousness. Over the last decade or so science has progressed a great deal in preliminarily defining the important brain signatures for deep meditative and transcendental states of consciousness.[383,384]

What this chapter highlights is that the preliminary brain signatures for deep meditative and transcendental states of consciousness are similar. These similarities involve activations of frontal and mid-brain structures associated with emotional regulation and executive control functions (decision making), and deactivations of most other brain regions in order to quiet both the brain and the body's physiology (i.e., heart and breathing rates, metabolism).

The preliminary brain signatures of deep meditation are a lowering of the average brainwave frequency, the generation of enhanced alpha brainwave voltages over the frontal brain, and increased levels of dopamine and 5-hydroxytryptamine-2a serotonin (5HT-2a) brain chemicals. Interestingly, meditation's brain signatures closely mirror the putative physiological consequences of sacredly-timed meditation conducted in sensory silence and under the influence of entheogens.

To recap, the shared archaeological fingerprint detailed in this book highlights a series of archaeological findings commonly associated with the pyramid/Sun god religion cultures. That is, solstice or equinox aligned sacred sites (i.e., demarcating sacred time) offered places of sensory silence (i.e., tunnels, chambers, sanctums) within, above or underneath these structures. These sacred sites once contained (or still do contain) deity art and icons that frequently embed a triad of sacred ritual symbols (i.e., Sun god, sacred time, and entheogens), as well as art and icons that depict people or deities in meditating postures. Let me explain this further because this is both very interesting and important.

1) Meditation as a ritual activity is implied by its presence in temple art and icons especially for the religions of ancient India, Egypt, and Central America. Even today the Hindu religion, and its Buddhist offshoot, continues to use meditation (and yoga) as a core ritual process.

2) Pyramid tunnels and chambers, and inner sanctums provided places of sensory silence. This permits the brain to be quieted and the average brainwave frequency lowered. Try meditating in these spaces and see for yourself.

3) Enhanced alpha brainwave voltages over the frontal brain are observed during meditation. Sacred time offered peaks in electromagnetism and magnetism (see Chapter 7), and the opportunity to entrain enhanced alpha brainwave voltages. Peaks in Schumann resonances occur around the solstices and are known to enhance alpha brainwave voltages. The V47 degree angles embedded in deity art symbolize the solstice as sacred time. The solstices provide peaks in Schumann resonances

which maximally enhance alpha brainwaves such as those produced by meditation.

4) Likewise, alpha brainwave voltages are maximally stimulated by peaks in geomagnetic activity, which occur around the equinoxes. The serpent depicts the equinoxes and accompanies the V47 solstice symbolism in the deity art. Enhanced alpha brainwave voltages are implied by the equinox's serpent symbol.

5) The depiction of floral-fungal-fauna entheogens in temple art and icons indicates that brain chemicals such as dopamine and 5HT-2a were important to the ritual process because they coappear with the deity and sacred time symbols. That is to say, the pink lotus, and blue and white water lilies indicate concentrated sources of a precursor of dopamine (nuciferine), whilst Psilocybin magic mushrooms, San Pedro cactus, and DMT-containing toad secretions and Anadenanthera colubrina indicate concentrated sources of 5HT-2a serotonin stimulators.

In other words, sacred rituals supplement what meditation naturally generates as its key brain signatures, i.e., enhanced alpha brainwave voltages, and elevated levels of brain dopamine and 5HT-2a. These brain signatures are also the physiological consequence of supplementing the brain with sacred time (i.e.

enhancing alpha brainwave voltages) and entheogens. I have taken these symbols to imply supplementation. This is because they are a concentrated source and a natural means for supplementing alpha brainwave voltages and meditation related brain chemicals.

Again, I would say that if the scientific details are not particularly of interest to you, then please proceed to the next chapter with this summary in mind.

Brain Activations and Altered States of Consciousness

Few clinical studies focused specifically on altered states of consciousness have been conducted, and often these are designed with statistical and other shortcomings. As a result we must also review clinical studies involving experienced meditators in deep meditative states, because meditation is a gateway process for accessing altered states of consciousness, i.e., it is a precursor state to our higher states of consciousness.

Nonetheless, as a "proof of concept," the EEG findings are consistent across both deep meditation and altered states of consciousness. Increased alpha brainwave voltages are detected over the frontal brain, oftentimes including increased alpha brainwave coherence with other brain regions (stable correlations of brainwave frequencies between different brain regions).[385,386,387]

Two of the studies reviewed involved subjects who accessed altered states of consciousness (transcending body-space-time boundaries). Professor Frederick Travis at the Maharishi University of Management in Iowa (USA) conducted both of these studies. One study involved 30 subjects with an average of 5.4 years of transcendental meditation (TM) experience, all of whom undertook specific mind tasks or meditation for the same duration. EEGs and other physiological parameters were monitored, and the subjects completed subjective experience questionnaires. In this case, transcending was subjectively characterized by the absence of space, time, and body awareness. Transcendence was associated with statistically significant lower respiration rates, increased skin electrical conductivity, higher EEG alpha brainwave voltages (at the front, central & side regions of the head), and higher alpha brainwave coherence.[388]

A second study assessed experienced long-term meditators (25 years practice on average) who experienced continuous transcendence (continuous TE) during waking and sleeping states. This continuous transcendence is not unlike that which Eckhart Tolle, author of the books *Power of Now* and *A New Earth*,[389] and one of the most influential spiritual people in the world, experienced before his career as a spiritual leader commenced. These rare Continuous TE subjects were EEG-compared during both study-specific tasks and meditation with experienced meditators (eight years average experience), meditators who occasionally transcended, and with non-experienced meditators who rarely or never transcended. Transcendental experience was assessed using validated scientific methodologies and all subjects were "blinded" to the specific experimental hypotheses.[390]

The key findings of this study were that the Continuous TE subjects experienced stable and elevated frontal alpha brainwave (6-12 hertz) voltages, and that these voltages were higher than the Occasional TE group, which in turn were higher than the Rare TE group. Transcendence integrated with waking states was correlated with increased frontal brain alpha brainwave voltages and coherence.[391]

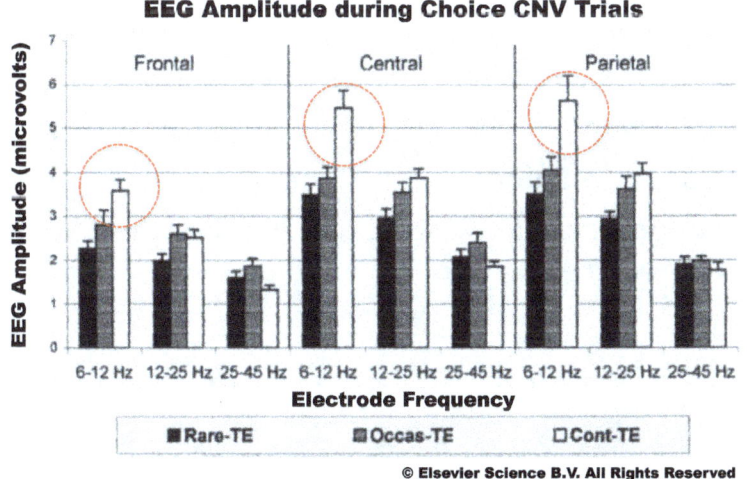

© Elsevier Science B.V. All Rights Reserved

Figure 8.1 EEG monitoring theta-alpha, beta, and gamma wave amplitudes at the frontal, central, and parietal (side of the head) EEG leads during study specific tasks. Mean EEG amplitude data is plotted by group: Rare-TE group, Occasional-TE group, and Continuous-TE group. **Conclusions**: Alpha brainwave amplitudes are significantly increased across frontal, central and lateral scalp surfaces during permanent transcendence, and are higher than the Occasional TE and Rare TE groups.[392]

Brain Activations Associated with Experienced Meditators

Meditation is initiated in the frontal brain, within the prefrontal cortex (PFC) and angulate cingulate cortex (ACC). Experienced meditators generally increase their frontal alpha brainwave voltages, which signify activation of their executive control functions and emotional regulation.[393,394] The PFC is richly and reciprocally connected with the limbic system (hippocampus and amygdala), midbrain (thalamus and hypothalamus), and other brain regions. These structures drive meditation's initiation and maintenance. Meditation's outcome consists in being calm and relaxed, with a quieting mind, detached nonreactive awareness, emotional regulation, modulation of self-perception, and a slowing of the breath and heart rates.[395,396,397]

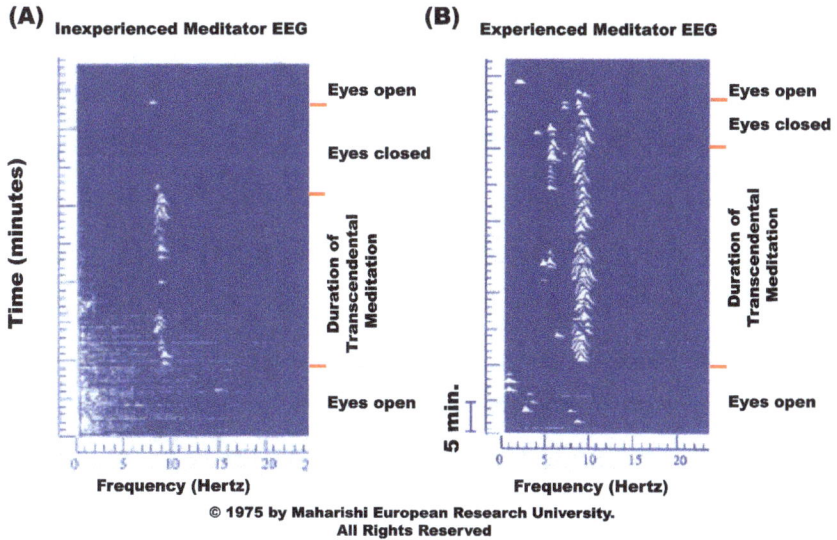

Figure 8.2 Impact of Transcendental Meditation™ experience on alpha-theta brainwaves. **(A)** The appearance of alpha brainwave coherence specific to the Transcendental Meditation (TM) technique in a new meditator highlights the immediacy of observable EEG effects with the TM technique. **(B)** Alpha and theta brainwaves with high alpha coherence in the central and frontal EEG leads. This individual's meditation fingerprint is alpha brainwaves with central-frontal coherence. **Conclusion**: This displays the impact of meditation experience on alpha brainwave generation, and the abrupt decrease in alpha coherence at the end of meditation. Reproduced with permission from Maharishi European Research University.[398]

Increased alpha brainwave voltages are associated with the active inhibition of sensory information processing during internally directed tasks such as meditation.[399] Frontal alpha-1 (8-10 hertz) brainwave voltage increases during meditation.[400] Experienced meditators demonstrate an overall 1-Hz slower mean brainwave frequency, and they selectively lower their alpha frequency band by 0.8 Hz.[401]

Meditation studies also highlight, though less regularly and consistently, that alpha, theta, and gamma brainwave coherences can increase with deep meditation. Scientists are beginning to suggest that multi-brainwave coherence (alpha, theta, and gamma) is part of a coordinated brainwave integration mechanism. This putatively links different brain regions into integrated patterns able to support the meditative, transcendental, and ultimately transcendental-awake states.[402,403]

Neurotransmitters Supporting Transcendental States

Deep meditation has an impact on a number of brain chemical pathways involved in multiple brain systems and processes. Dopamine and serotonin ($5\text{-}HT_{2A}$) pathways are the most important.[404,405] These two brain chemicals dominate both meditation and hallucinogen pharmacology. Additionally, these two brain chemicals consistently show up in Sun god temple art and icons, implied by the artists' portrayal of entheogens, specifically dopamine (white and blue water lilies, pink lotus) and serotonin 5HT2a (psilocybin magic mushrooms, Anadenanthera *spp.*, San Pedro cactus, frog bufotenin) stimulators.

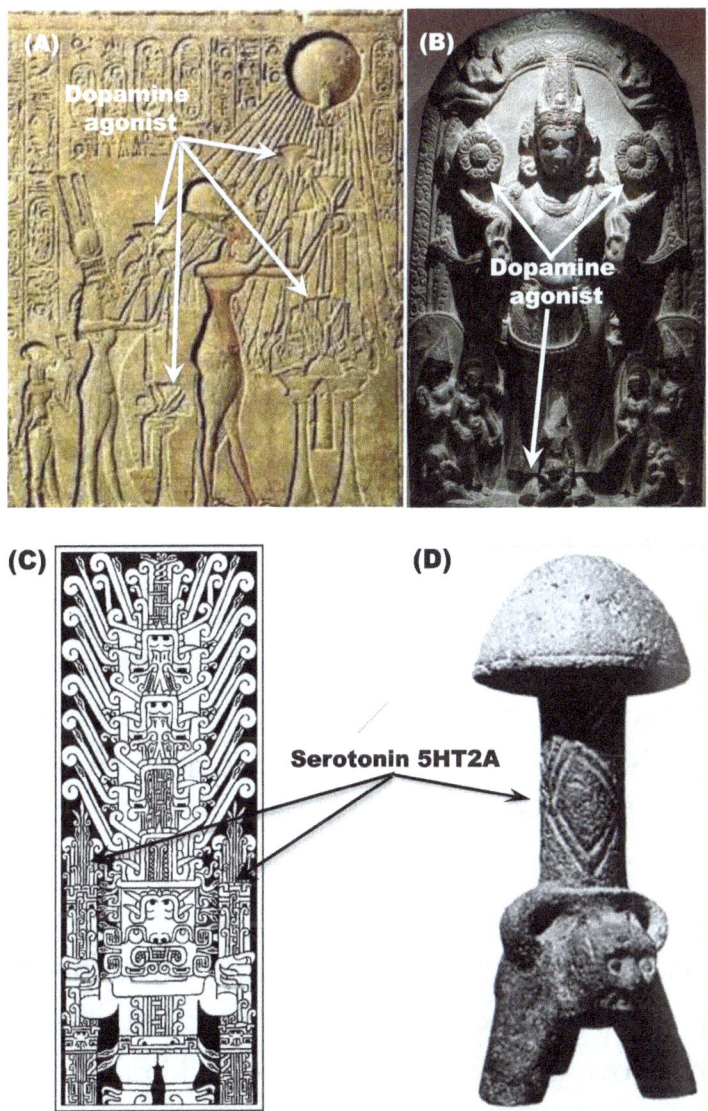

Figure 8.3 Sun god art and its depicted hallucinogen mode of drug action. **(A)** Egypt; Blue water lily provides dopamine (after nuciferine's metabolism). **(B)** India; sacred pink lotus provides dopamine (after nuciferine's metabolism). **(C)** Chavin; San Pedro cactus provides 5 hydroxytryptamine-2a serotonin (5-HT$_{2A}$). **(D)** Maya; the magic mushroom provides 5-HT$_{2A}$. Dopamine and

serotonin (5-HT$_{2A}$) are two of the most important neurochemicals supporting deep meditative and transcendental states.[406]

Under certain circumstances, meditation may cause a powerful brain chemical, dimethyltryptamine (DMT), to be released by the brain (by the pineal gland). DMT has been associated with a variety of transpersonal experiences, including out-of-body experiences, distortion of time and space, and interaction with supernatural entities.[407]

Brain Circuits Involved in Meditation

It would be unrealistic to say science knows how the brain fully works in supporting consciousness and altered states of consciousness, but data is accumulating and study designs are progressing. Various models have and will be proposed and will continue to evolve. One recently proposed model that caught my attention was that of Professor Frederick Travis, which integrated the dominant frontal brain changes and alpha brainwave signatures observed during deep meditative states. One can then overlay this with the increased brain chemicals (dopamine, 5-HT-2a, glutamate) observed in the frontal brain. The frontal brain interconnects with the midbrain and other brain regions to create a map of the key circuits and their brain signatures.

Travis proposed a two-stage model to explain the electrical and autonomic differences during meditation versus eyes-closed rest. The initial phase involves frontal brain structures (prefrontal cortex; PFC and angulate cingulate cortex; ACC) shutting down inputs from the thalamus to the cortex to quiet the mind and body. A second phase maintains this quiescence via automatic circuits, the signatures of which are enhanced alpha brainwave voltages. This involves funneling inputs from the cortex (upper brain) and midbrain (amygdala, hippocampus) to the thalamus (midbrain), then back to the frontal cortex via a dual highway brain circuit (input/output). This in turn modulates the level of activation seen in the brain cortex (upper brain surface region).[408]

What's important to note here is that these alpha brainwave-generating meditation circuits require voltage thresholds to be reached before the circuits are activated. As I've indicated, these alpha brainwave voltages can be supplemented by conducting meditation at sacred time, which we know enhances the alpha brainwave voltages via physiological entrainment. The consequence of this is a tripping of the voltage threshold switch and a change in the state of consciousness, allowing one to proceed from a deep meditative state to altered states of consciousness.

The general process of damping down non-essential brain activities and directing attention internally is facilitated by meditation in sensory silence.[409] In my view this was the function of the inner temple sanctums, pyramid chambers, tunnels, and caves used by the priests of the ancient Sun god religions.

The key points to understand are, first, that meditation-based rituals conducted by experienced practitioners in sensory silence drive enhanced alpha brainwave voltages over the frontal brain (i.e., the forehead), and second that alpha-1 brainwave voltages can be supplemented by environmentally-generated Schumann resonance and magnetic fields (which peak at sacred times).

The Practical Implications of Sacred Ritual Processes

An important conclusion of this project is that meditation is a physiological gateway process for accessing altered states of consciousness. We see meditation's central ritual role implied by its depiction in temple art and icons associated with deities and leaders (see Chapters 3 and 5). Even today, we can see that meditation still plays a central role in Hindu and Buddhist rituals, and we know that highly experienced and devout meditation practitioners are able to access altered states of consciousness without using entheogens. We therefore know that altered states of consciousness are a natural outcome of meditation, albeit a relatively rare one. More indirectly, we can see that pyramids and temples offered priesthoods a sacred space (tunnels, chambers, and sanctums) which provided a sensory-silencing environment for the conduct of meditation rituals.

I therefore have come to the conclusion that humans have a natural, inbuilt capacity for experiencing altered states of consciousness using meditation-based rituals, and that ancient priesthoods learned this millennia ago.

The hurdles are set high for manifesting this consciousness-expanding capability of our fourth state of consciousness, as only a small percentage of humans can access these higher states of consciousness via meditation without the help of entheogens. This chapter's science highlights that deep meditation and altered states of consciousness are associated with enhanced alpha brainwave voltages and brain chemical (i.e., dopamine, 5HT2a) signatures that can be supplemented via sacred rituals. Interestingly, these brain signatures are a physiological consequence of conducting sacredly-timed meditation in sensory silence under the influence of entheogens.

By conducting meditation in sensory silence one is able to quiet the brain and generate increased alpha brainwave voltages over the frontal brain. Conducting meditation at sacred time permits one to supplement meditation's self-generated alpha brainwave voltages. Reaching certain voltage thresholds is required to trip meditation's gateway process switch, thus enabling one

The Brain Signatures Of Altered States of Consciousness

to access altered state of consciousness. The use of entheogens, i.e., dopamine and/or serotonin 5HT-2a stimulators, supplements those produced naturally by the frontal and mid brains during meditation. This supplementation of the meditation process permits voltage and brain chemical thresholds to be reached, whereupon the switch to altered states of consciousness occurs.

Normally, these enhanced alpha brainwave and brain chemical signatures are generated using highly-evolved meditation practices, which take many years to develop to a level in which higher states of consciousness are possible. Today's mystics, ascetics and highly-evolved spiritual practitioners typically achieve this after one or more decades of devoted practice, or very rarely in spontaneous occurrences, as in the case of Eckhart Tolle (a recognized spiritual guru).

This dedication to the mystic-yogi-ascetic way of life and its meditation (and yoga) ritual practices was not a full-time option for busy empire- building pharaohs, kings, queens, high priests, and other elites. At the heart of Sun god religious rituals lay a practice of supplementing meditation's process to ensure that optimum levels of alpha brainwaves and meditation-related brain chemicals were attained. In all likelihood, priesthoods obtained this ritual knowledge from their precursor religions (historical learning), by trial and error, and from knowledge attained in altered states of consciousness. Consequently, these Sun god priesthoods developed rituals that placed the meditator in sensory silence (inside inner temple sanctums, pyramid tunnels, or chambers) at sacred times, and provided brain chemicals by using entheogens to supplement those naturally produced during meditation. This supplementation ensured that biological thresholds were reached for the important brain signatures, such as alpha brainwave voltages and specific brain chemicals (dopamine, 5HT2a). With the ego dissolved, higher states of consciousness are witnessed. This is perceived as a switch in the state of consciousness.

In contrast, the Yogic traditions (Buddhism, Hinduism, and Jainism) and Taoism evolved their ritual processes for achieving altered states of consciousness by making meditation a central and sacred ritual in their devout practitioners' lives. This required long-term commitment and practice, along with a spiritual education and way of life. The fact that their important deity art depicted the sacred lotus (representing dopamine neurochemicals), and often times sacred time symbols, suggests that their full ritual process has been lost to time.

Whatever the means, all these traditions sought the same outcome: to achieve altered states of consciousness where Unity states of consciousness, ego death/spiritual rebirth, chakra and kundalini activations, and other spiritual experiences were achieved. The outcome of this was to heal deep psychological wounds, accelerate one's consciousness development by transcendentally changing the seat of consciousness to the higher self, and the spiritual awakening or transformation of the practitioner. The consequence of this, in turn, would be an escape from karmic rebirth, or the attainment of spiritual immortality (which was seen as the ultimate goal of life).

Chapter 9

Experiencing Altered States of Consciousness

Introduction

The main objective of this book is to create a bridge between the shared archaeological fingerprint I discovered in the pyramid archaeology (sacred ritual processes; chapters 1, 2, 3, and 5) and the science supporting altered states of consciousness (chapters 4, 6, 7, 8, and 9) as part of our natural biology. Why does the book aim to accomplish this?

First, to help you comprehend what altered states of consciousness actually are, without obfuscating dogma. This chapter therefore describes altered states of consciousness both scientifically and through the words of the mystic founders of today's global religions.

Second, to provide you with a sacred ritual process that has been reverse-engineered from this archaeological fingerprint discovery (see Chapter 10). You will then have the choice and the opportunity to access your higher states of consciousness and to conduct transcendental self-inquiry on your own without anyone having control over you. The reasons you might want to do this are detailed in Chapter 11; suffice it to say that a mind-transforming opportunity is on offer, with transcendental self-realization, spiritual awakening and healing, and spiritual immortality being the ultimate prizes.

I've deliberately adopted a more scientific and rational approach to this discussion because I believe religion, at the leadership and sacred ritual process levels, lost its way a long time ago. Our global religions at their simplest level invariably worship a great mystic founder from thousands of years ago who experienced profound states of consciousness, such that the founder's life was spiritually transformed. After their deaths these mystics and the examples of great spiritual leadership they provided became packaged as religion.

Just reflect on this simple fact: the mystic founders did not write the sacred texts of today's global faiths. Other people wrote those sacred texts decades (in the case of Islam) or centuries (Buddhism, Christianity, and Judaism) after the mystic founder's death (Lao Tzu being the sole exception). In my view there are differences between the sacred texts of these religions and the actual teachings and ritual processes used by their mystic founders. This is why I went in search of my own answers. Reflect on this also: why would you worship without question someone who once, millennia ago, had a spiritual experience, when you could have a spiritual experience yourself—and do so while still honoring, following, and respecting the spiritually inspiring leadership of that long-ago figure?

The truth is that all humans have the biological capability to experience these higher states of consciousness, if they only knew how. And that's the problem; we've simply not been taught how to use ritual processes effectively, because these got lost to time, religious assimilation, or quite possibly have been deliberately withheld from mainstream society because they were a source of great power.

By the end of this book you will better understand what altered states of consciousness are, and I will provide you with a ritual process that will allow you to access these higher states of consciousness (see Chapter 10, *Ritual Meditation*), and to conduct *Transcendental Self-Inquiry*. Further, I will show you how you can integrate this into a life- and mind-transforming plan (see Chapter 11 and my *Mind Transformation Plan*) designed to help you spiritually awaken, profoundly heal, and become transcendentally self-realized—that is, enlightened. You can then become spiritually immortal after your death.

Altered States of Consciousness

The purpose of this section is to provide some expert clinical insight into altered states of consciousness, and the phenomena one can experience while in these states. This will be followed by a discussion on the unifying theme underpinning the world's global faiths, through the words of some of the mystic founders. Ultimately you will see the overlap between the scientific and mystic-esoteric perspectives, and realize they say and describe the same thing.

Transpersonal Psychology Provides Perspective

Transpersonal psychology puts forth the idea that religious, spiritual, transpersonal, or transcendental experiences are a natural phenomenon associated with one's consciousness development. It promotes the healing, transformative, and consciousness development potential of non-ordinary or higher states of consciousness.

In the late 1960s, a small group of scientists including Stanislav Grof, Abraham Maslow, Anthony Sutich, James Fadiman, Miles Vich, and Sonya Margulies created a new psychology movement that honored the entire spectrum of human experience, including various non-ordinary or higher states of consciousness. The groundswell of interest in Eastern spiritual philosophies, mystical traditions, meditation, ancient and shamanic wisdom, and psychedelic experimentation during the 1960s highlighted a need for a more comprehensive and cross-culturally sensitive psychology that embraced the entirety of human endeavor. This new discipline was named "transpersonal psychology" (the Fourth Force of Psychology).[410]

More recently, important recognition of transpersonal psychology and its endeavors was demonstrated by the inclusion of a new coding in the Diagnostic and Statistical Manual IV (DSM-IV). DSM-IV is published by the American Psychiatric Association and is used in the United States and other parts of the world to diagnose and manage psychiatric, personality, and other mind phenomena. The new coding via section V.62.89, "Spiritual and Religious Problems" in the V-category "other clinical relevant problems"[411] are now recognized as clinically important but distinct from psychological or personality disorders.

Transcendental Experiences & their Phenomena

Scientific literature associates mystical experiences or altered states of consciousness with different causations, including spontaneous occurrence, entheogen use, meditation, shamanic practices (drumming), religious practices (prayer, austerities), sensory deprivation, holotropic breathing, epilepsy, and near-death experiences.[412,413,414,415]

An epidemiological study carried out by researchers using specific criteria in line with clinical study questionnaires (concerning mystical experiences and altered states of consciousness), which specifically defined these states of consciousness, found that less than 1% of those surveyed reported having had a profound experience. The profound experiences defined were characterized by "awesome emotions, a sense of the ineffable, feelings of oneness with God, nature, or the universe, altered perceptions of time and space, and a feeling of 'knowing' coupled with a reordering of life's priorities".[416] So we can see that the incidence and prevalence of these experiences in humans is rare.

A principal characteristic of these experiences is the transcendence of one's personal identity and the dissolution of the primary consciousness grounded in one's ego. Another frequently described experience is the perception of merging or identification with the source of being, known as God, Unity, Absolute, Lord, Divine, etc. Accordingly, this experience is most commonly described as both transpersonal and transcendental. In such situations, ego identities disintegrate and one's awareness can expand to encompass the entire universe. It is possible, paradoxically, to perceive all forms as emptiness pregnant with form. Ultimate wisdom and knowledge of the cosmos such as the creation of the phenomenal world and concepts of karmic rebirth are imparted.[417]

Such experiences are said to have a profound impact on one's life thereafter. According to Stanislav Grof, one of the founders of the transpersonal psychology field and a leading expert in the use of psychedelics for accelerated psychological healing, these transpersonal experiences are the province of the world's shamans, founders of the world's great religions, spiritual teachers, mystics, and saints. Mystical literature the world over describes these crises as the hallmark of the spiritual path and confirms their transformative healing potential.[418]

Grof paints a most vivid picture of the transpersonal realm from LSD sessions with subjects undergoing psychotherapy. These realms can include the reliving of various life events, psycho-spiritual (ego) death and rebirth, episodes of mystical rapture, sense of oneness with God, and feelings of cosmic unity. Encounters with suprahuman spirit entities such as spirit guides, teachers, and protectors represent one of the most valuable transpersonal experiences. Spirit entities perceived on higher planes of consciousness are a source of light or energy. In this context, the subject's ego identity is preserved, relating dualistically to these spirits with varying degrees of fusion and unifying awareness.

Encounters with coexistent universes and their inhabitants are also possible. Bizarre physical forms, incomprehensible laws that defy our Cartesian-

Newtonian paradigm of understanding, and fundamentally different body functioning may be experienced. Ultimately, the hallucinogens catalyze the experience, which reveals unconscious insight into pure consciousness. How these hallucinogens generate such intricately-changing imagery or such rich philosophical, universal, and spiritual insight is unclear.[419,420]

Most deities appearing in LSD sessions fall into two main categories: those associated with the forces of good and light, and others associated with darkness and evil. Blissful and benevolent divinities such as Isis, Osiris, Bodhisattvas, Krishna, Ahura Mazda, and Apollo are widely represented. Wrathful deities such as Set, Satan, Huitzilopochtli, and Hades are equally well known and still feared to this day. Occasionally, subjects act out and recount entire culturally-inspired cosmological dramas, such as the creation of the Universe and the Earth, global deluge, and Armageddon. Sometimes experiences will range from ecstatic rapture and divine bliss to metaphysical terror and feelings of being insane. [421] This is a very important reason why hallucinogens must be treated with the utmost respect, and only used within a broader context of accelerated spiritual development and psychological healing.

Consciousness of the universal mind is considered one of the most transformative and profound experiences observed in spiritual crises, as well as in patients undergoing LSD psychotherapy. The illusions of space, time, matter, and infinite subjective realities are completely transcended to experience this boundless, unfathomable, and ineffable cosmic awareness of divine unity.[422]

According to Stanislav Grof, in normal states of consciousness we experience ourselves existing within perceptive boundaries facilitated by the ego. These boundaries include one's physical body and mind as the subjective self. In so doing we are discreetly separated from the rest of the world through our perception of subject-object dualities and the belief that we are separate from everything. This happens because of the way in which the ego mind interprets the sensory inputs (sight, sound, smell, touch, and taste), mixed with our feelings and perceptions, which in turn have been impacted by our previous experiences. We become aware of the space we physically occupy, how we interface with the external world, and our body image and boundaries. Our perception of our environment is largely confined to our external five senses. Internal and external perceptions are subject to specific space-time limitations. Transpersonal experiences, on the other hand, are experiences involving an expansion or extension of consciousness beyond the usual ego boundaries and beyond the limitations of space and/or time.[423]

Organizing the Phenomena of Transpersonal Experiences

Two main categories of transpersonal experiences are derived from Stanislav Grof's pioneering work in LSD psycholytic therapy. Here, transpersonal experiences occur "within and beyond" a framework of objective reality.[424]

Transpersonal experiences within the framework of objective reality have three subgroupings:

(1) *Temporal expansion* of consciousness to include prebirth (being in the womb or birth canal), ancestral experiences, evolutionary memory, previous incarnations, precognition, clairvoyance, and time travel;

(2) *Spatial expansion* of consciousness in which one experiences ego transcendence in interpersonal relationships, identification with other persons, group consciousness, animal-plant-matter identification, a feeling of oneness with all life, planetary, and extra-planetary consciousness, out-of-body experiences, traveling, clairvoyance, space travel, and telepathy.

(3) *Spatial constrictions* of consciousness at the level of organ, tissue, and cellular consciousness.

During transpersonal experiences beyond the framework of objective reality people can encounter spiritual entities, or travel to other universes and have encounters with their inhabitants, experience complex mythological and archetypal sequences, have experiences with deities, gain intuitive insight into universal symbols, experience the activation of various chakras, or the arousal of Kundalini energy, or consciousness of the Universal mind, or achieve awareness of the metacosmic void.[425]

Spiritual Emergencies as a 21st Century Fact of Life

Spiritual emergencies represent crises during which the process of spiritual growth and change becomes utterly overwhelming for the person experiencing it.[426] Included in spiritual emergencies are spiritual emergence, mystical experiences, near-death experiences, meditation and spiritual practices, psychic and visionary experiences, shamanic crises, and demonic possession experiences.[427]

Spiritual emergencies can also be viewed as a natural part of the process of human development, albeit in an accelerated fashion in which the subject moves beyond ego identity into the transpersonal realm. This involves an increasing awareness and connectedness to a higher awareness or pure consciousness (God). It has been suggested that many conditions which were/are diagnosed as psychotic in the West and are treated with suppressive medications are not psychotic at all. If correctly understood and supported, these psycho-spiritual crises can result in emotional and psychosomatic healing, remarkable psychological transformation, and accelerated consciousness evolution.[428,429]

Clinical Questionnaires Capture Mystical Experiences

Spiritual, mystical, exceptional, or peak experiences are a recognized occurrence in the human population, according to scientists developing mystical experience questionnaires.[430] Researchers studying mystical and transpersonal experiences have empirically defined and validated broad categories of mystical experience using a number of tools, particularly mystical experience questionnaires such as the Hood's Mysticism Scale, Mystical Experience Questionnaire, and APZ questionnaire.

These questionnaires quantifiably categorize important experiential aspects of mystical experience, including concepts of unity, transcendence of time and space, and noetic qualities like sacredness, peace-joy, ineffability, and paradoxicality. Others capture similar parameters within different categories like oceanic boundlessness (positive aspects of ego-dissolution), anxious ego dissolution (negative aspects of ego-dissolution), and visionary restructuralization, which is defined as illusions of sense and meaning, such as hallucinations.[431]

While we may not fully understand or even appreciate mystical experience, science can empirically define its phenomena and consequences and can objectively say these are "real" human experiences that should be considered normal rather than pathological.

Knowledge Acquisition

We can obtain information about the universe in two very different ways. First, as we do today, we can use conventional means of learning by deploying our sensory perceptions and scientific methods to accumulate data from which we generate knowledge, innovation and construction. Or, secondly, we can find awareness, knowledge, connectivity, and insight into our world as well as the divine universe within altered states of consciousness.[432] When we marvel at the accomplishments of our ancient ancestors and their apparent knowledge, we should acknowledge the fact they may have accessed knowledge and know-how in altered states of consciousness.

Mysticism and Divine Unity as Religion's Unifying Theme

There is a common core of mysticism shared by Buddhism, Hinduism, Islam's Sufism, China's Taoism, Christian Mysticism, and Judaism's Kabbalah. A unifying principle places the transcendental divine, as divine Unity, in the midst of genuine mystical experience.[433,434] There is a near-universal human desire and an unmistakable human potential to experience union with the divine. A seeking and longing for divine unity is the keystone of mystical experience.[435] The interrelationship of all things derived from a single reality implies total interconnectedness, everything in totality imbued with God's essence and consciousness.[436]

It has been said that no words can adequately describe divine unity, yet a single word would suffice: One. Mystics have described it as the One underlying the many, the real within everything and yet beyond any of this apparent reality. This dimension of unity is one of the most common characteristics of mystical experience. Even though the experience may be short-lived in this realm, one's life will never be the same thereafter. The mystic usually reevaluates his or her life; there is a life before and a different life after one has experienced Unity in altered states of consciousness.[437]

Religion and Mysticism Basics

True mystics live in the radiance of divine love and the unity of divine reality. They were not chosen; rather, they *chose* themselves to study, practice, and actualize the divine in their lives. Spiritual liberation is said to be the ultimate objective across all religions. It is sought in stages, bringing together meditative-based ritual, spiritual wisdom, and appropriate ways of living and conducting one's life in harmony with all. Our ego attachment to the outer world is said to blind us to our unconscious ability to experience divine unity.[438] Without attaining enlightenment, one will continue in the karma-samsara cycle and experience karmic rebirth again and again. So, ultimately, we have a choice to make in our lives: this one, or another...?

Buddhists see spiritual enlightenment as the realization of Buddha mind; in Hinduism, it's known as Moksha; in Taoism, it is the Tao; in Sufism, enlightenment is called the Fanaa; in the Kabbalah it's known as Devekut; and in Christian mysticism it's called Unio Mystica. The word God is used in Christianity, Brahman in Hinduism, al-Haqq or Allah in Islam, Dharmakaya or Nirvana in Buddhism, the Tao in Taoism, and Ein Sof in the Kabbalah of Judaism.[439] Most commonly, God is referred to by a number of other names—the One, Absolute, Almighty, Deity, Lord, Supreme, Divine—and is described as omniscient and omnipotent.

Most religions speak of God as a spiritual omniscience or an all-pervading life force. Beyond today's global religions we see this in Native American, tribal African, aboriginal, and shamanic traditions, as well as with other faiths like Confucianism, Shinto,

Sikhism, Jainism, Bahá'í Faith, Cao Đài, Cheondoism, Tenrikyo, Wicca, Church of World Messianity, Polynesian spirit worship, and many others. Global religions, like smaller regional religions, all have their origins in mysticism. Ergo, all of us are linked via the house of divine Unity, each faith a different path to that same house.

Eight major esoteric traditions have been previously identified: the shamanic traditions, Eastern mystical traditions, Western mystical traditions, mystery school traditions, Kabbalistic tradition, gnostic traditions, brotherhood traditions, and new age or neopagan traditions. These traditions are said to preserve secret wisdom on transcendental themes.[440]

The Indian mystic Shankara (8th century) and others, including the Germans Rudolph Otto (1926–1971; a Lutheran theologian and scholar of comparative religion) and Eckhart von Hochheim (1260–1328; a theologian, philosopher, and mystic) differentiated between the soul-mysticism of Eastern spirituality and the God-mysticism of the Western theistic traditions.[441] Theistic mysticism seeks union with God, whereas Eastern soul mysticism seeks a disintegration of ego boundaries to experience divine unity and enlightenment. Whatever the pathway, the outcome is the same: a unitive or mystical experience.[442]

Mysticism's History of Challenging Religious Dogma

Throughout the history of the three monotheistic religions (Christianity, Islam, and Judaism), autotheistic language has been used by mystics and frowned upon by these religions' institutions. This autotheistic language, such as "I am God, God is I," has caused periodic tension and debate. Frictions occur between religious authorities and mystics associated with those faiths.[443] Every major global religion's primordial roots were in mysticism; yet somehow they grew into or ended up as politics, dogma, law, and ethics.[444]

In the beginning, a religion's doctrine more closely represented the mystic's earliest words and interpretations. Over time, religion reinterprets its mystic founder's words to fit life's changing context. Iterative doctrinal commentaries were amassed and with each new interpretation, religion moved further and further away from its primordial experiential source (the mystics' teachings). The result is that the ancient mystics' doctrines became fossilized into mainstream religious dogmatism, law, ethics and ceremony in other words the religious world we experience today.[445]

Islam and Sufism yield no shortage of such instances of public rebuke of important mystics. For example, Al-Hallaj was martyred in Baghdad (10th CE) for his insistence that, ultimately, he and God were one. Meister

Eckhart's writings invoked condemnation by Pope John XXII as heretical (1329) for their use of autotheistic language.[446] Mystics experience communion with the ultimate reality, and subsequently may begin to sense discrepancies between their version of the ecstatic religious experience and the dogma preached by their religious institutions. Look to your religion's mystic foundations if you wish to understand the potential of your faith, as well as that of your journey in life.

All religions have an exoteric (outer) and esoteric (inner) path. The exoteric is religious dogma: formal religious doctrines, ethics and rituals, or the public face of the religion. The esoteric, on the other hand, is concerned with the hidden, mystical, symbolic, and/or initiatory ways of communing with pure consciousness or God. Esoteric religion comprises meditation, gnosis, secret teachings, initiation, and physical austerities. It embraces the mystical, transcendental, or unitive states of consciousness experienced by its mystics.[447]

A mystic and scholarly insight holds that while exoteric paths differ immensely, their esoteric paths converge to common principles and outcomes, namely primordial sacred traditions, secret wisdom, forgotten knowledge, ancient theology, ageless wisdom, and a life-living pathway to divine unity, enlightenment, and the escape from karmic rebirth.[448]

Our Great Religions' Mystical Traditions Converge on Unity

Mystical death is the esoteric concept that one must experience ego death and spiritual rebirth in order to experience divine Unity. To "die before you die" is one of the most important common denominators of these great mystical traditions.

Traditions such as Hinduism, Buddhism, Taoism, Kabbalah, Sufism, and Christian mysticism all describe the long and arduous road to enlightenment. Mystics describe how we can deconstruct our empirical world to unveil a spiritual or unitive reality. Mystics in different traditions describe ego death and spiritual transformation as the goal of their physical life. These spiritual practitioners use a wide array of spiritual practices or techniques to alter their field of awareness and subdue the ego mind, such as meditation, prayer, isolation, fasting, and other austerities or combinations thereof. These techniques lead to an inhibition of the ego's adaptive, defensive, and mediating functions whereby higher states of consciousness can be experienced.[449]

Moksha and Nirvana (liberation) are key life goals for Hindus and Buddhists alike. Liberation is sought from the cycle of rebirth (samsara) and suffering. At physical death, it is said that the unrealized self passes diverse after-death experiences where karmic debts are reflected, with rebirth occurring in the form and context generated by one's previous life karma. The karma-samsara cycle continues endlessly until moksha or nirvana is attained.[450]

It has been said that the nature of Nirvana is a great challenge for Buddhist philosophy. Buddha himself refused to speculate on it, saying that if you want to know what nirvana is, then attain it. Nirvana is probably best characterized as the realization that there is no "self." Buddha was said to have described nirvana as "consciousness without distinguishing mark, infinite and shining everywhere, untouched by material elements, and with obeisance to no power".[451]

Meditation and/or other ritual techniques are required to disintegrate the ego-self boundaries. It is said that the "perfected one" who has attained Nirvana is as deep, immeasurable, and unfathomable as the mighty ocean.[452]

For Buddhists, consciousness is conditioned, and arises due to the five aggregates coming together: the physical form, feelings, perceptions, mental functions, and consciousness. The self and our reality are an illusion of interaction between these aggregates. In attaining Nirvana one achieves liberation from samsâra (karmic rebirth) and becomes enlightened to the unifying truth that there is no separate self. One's own existential suffering ceases and compassion for others becomes paramount. This is a defining characteristic of enlightenment.

The ineffable nature of Nirvana arrived at through insight and meditation is the ultimate goal of the Buddha way. Following the Noble Eightfold Path, which operates within the elements of wisdom, ethics, and morality (as well as meditation), one can attain Nirvana. By negating the existence of "I" or "self," a horizon beyond the confines of individuality can be achieved, offering the ultimate possibility of Nirvana.[453]

Hindu's Shankara (Advaita Vedanta) stresses Brahman as an infinite, omniscient consciousness that transcends subject-object duality. Brahman (absolute God) is the One without a second, for there is nothing outside it.[454] Satcitananda represents the subjective experience of Brahman, literally meaning "being consciousness bliss." This sublime blissful experience of boundless, pure consciousness is a glimpse of divine unity.[455]

Moksha is associated with self-knowledge and ego-consciousness disintegration, whereupon the veil drops and one realizes that Atman (oneself) has always been Brahman.[456] Enlightenment engulfs one in a transformed world that encompasses nondual awareness of one's self as Brahman. No longer is "I, me, my, myself" the locus of consciousness; rather, the self-luminous nature of reality is unveiled as non-dual consciousness. There is no longer a duality between an observed object and a conscious subject that observes it, or between the external world and the self that experiences it.[457]

The Tao is the undivided Great One who cannot be named or known but can be experienced through mystical union. The Tao embraces both the source and the driving force imbuing everything that exists, and is ultimately ineffable. It is said that by clinging to quietness and pushing out into the void, practitioners of Taoism can uncover the layers of consciousness so as to arrive at pure consciousness, seeing the inner truth of everything.[458]

Sufism, a form of Islamic mysticism, seeks to attain union with God through the suppression of the ego and special insight into mystical processes. Sufi doctrine teaches that in addition to the rules of religious life there is another level of spiritual meaning, revealed to those who have been instructed in its secrets.[459] Ibn 'Arabi (1165-1240 CE) was a remarkable man whose stature in the Sufi-Islamic world is such that he is renowned as al-Shaykh al-Akbar, or the Greatest Master. The term "Oneness of Being" was Ibn 'Arabi's primary mystical philosophy.

In Sufism, God's manifestation is described as a self-disclosure in which the real discloses itself to itself. The disclosure by the One to itself in the form of a singular other reflects God's beauty and grandeur in what is called the perfect human, or the insān i-kamīl. Ibn 'Arabi constantly reminds us that every human is possessed of the potential for a "complete heart." The heart is considered the epicenter and the only faculty able to unify and integrate the incessant succession of states and revelations. When the heart has been opened, all faculties seamlessly align to it in complete conformity with the One's revelation. Ibn 'Arabi suggests the usurper that oppresses the heart is one's ego: a simple lack of knowledge, ignorance of the real situation, and a failure to recognize duality's illusion.[460]

While Christianity and Judaism differ greatly, they are both theistic mysticisms. Both are grounded in a reality that the union between humans and God results from divine grace and God's initiation of the mystical experience. The common ground is said to be the experience of a divine entity consummating a self-giving love, and of being saved by this love. This divine experience is the response to the deepest yearnings of the human spirit for transcendent meaning, purification, and illumination with the Savior.[461]

Coptic codices discovered in Nag Hammâdi (Egypt) provide insight into the beliefs and practices of various groups of early Egyptian Christians whose heterodox, gnostic views about God, Jesus, and the nature of the world and of humanity contrasted starkly with the ancient hegemonic Church of Rome. These Gnostics were typically ascetic and contemplative and affirmed the real possibility of mystical insight into our higher nature, the nature of God and of creation.[462]

My Personal Experiences of Higher States of Consciousness

The words of Stanislav Grof, Ron Krumpos, and those of the ancient mystics fully resonate with me. These writings have helped me comprehend my experiences of altered states of consciousness. This comprehension is particularly important when you are new to altered states of consciousness, as you have no language or conceptual framework to help you describe or comprehend the wide array of phenomena experienced. If you decide to explore altered states of consciousness, then you might wish to review the following referenced books.[463,464,465]

I have used the Ritual Meditation process, reverse-engineered from the ancient priesthood ritual fingerprint, on numerous occasions since December 21, 2012. In so doing, I have experienced Unity awareness of pure consciousness a number of times. I'd like to share some of these experiences with you.

In one of these experiences (on the winter solstice of 2014) my ego-body-space-time boundaries dissolved and my awareness appeared in a field of kaleidoscoping, colored energy waveforms as a meditating Buddha-like entity. My heart chakra opened, radiantly filling me with the most indescribable awareness of bliss-love, and in addition the awareness of being healed and forgiven left its impression in my consciousness. This Buddha-like awareness then dissipated into the black expanse of infinite nothingness (the metacosmic void) as my higher self's consciousness merged into Unity awareness with pure consciousness. After being aware of myself as the infinite void, this transitioned to my witnessing the birth and expansion of the Universe, also in Unity awareness. The experience of the metacosmic void and Universe expansion were imbued with the most indescribable feeling of bliss-love, witnessed for a seeming eternity. That was a truly mind-blowing experience.

In experiencing the birth and expansion of the Universe I was made aware of our species' destiny to evolve its consciousness and spiritually awaken en masse one day. This is a destiny we share with innumerable sentient species across the Universe. During my Unity awareness of pure consciousness I witnessed other species collective awakened consciousness, as the universe was shown to me in I am awareness. I know I'm part of pure consciousness' game plan to bring ancient, sacred ritual processes back to life so that we may fully realize our biological capability for accessing our higher states of consciousness. That was imprinted in my consciousness during the Ritual Meditation I conducted on the winter solstice of 2014.

Upon returning to this reality, all my unresolved anger from an abusive childhood, and all life's accumulated emotional traumas and their negative impressions simply vanished. That very day I reconnected by phone with my mother after decades of her being absent from my life, with love, compassion, forgiveness, and a deep gratitude in my heart. Two days later my mother came from the UK to visit me in Guatemala. I also mentally reconnected with my father, who had died in 2009. The same feelings overwhelmed me, and I knew that his spirit was responding in the same way. This experience opened a door and kindled a committed desire to heal and make progress in my life and relationships in a good and spiritual way.

On another of these experiences (summer solstice 2015) I began my Ritual Meditation by using my "I am" mantra. After some period of time, and a humble prayer asking for entry to Unity awareness of pure consciousness and to be healed and feel bliss-love, my ego-body boundaries dissolved and I emerged into a vista of kaleidoscoping, colorful waveforms with awareness of my eternal, higher self beyond my body and this earthly realm. In this higher self-awareness I asked, "Who am I?" This question arose automatically upon entry to the transcendental realm. An apparition appeared before me (ego consciousness) and I emphatically answered, "I am" (as awareness of my higher self) and "that is not I" ("that" being ego consciousness). This ego apparition dissolved before my higher self awareness, which then merged in Unity awareness with pure consciousness as the "Universal I am" for a seeming eternity (see section below: Consciousness, Self-Realization, and Healing).

I've experienced myself as the Universe and metacosmic void a number of other times as well, and Satcitānanda (Hindu Sanskrit; sublimely blissful experience of the boundless pure consciousness which is a glimpse of ultimate reality, or what I call bliss-love-awareness). I've witnessed a host of other phenomena including: chakra and kundalini activations, ego dissolution/death, mystical flight, time and space expansions, and awareness of my body energy field. On numerous occasions I've been aware of myself as a Buddha-like entity meditating with one or several chakras opening multiple times. I've communicated with Mayan spiritual forces at el Mirador (in Guatemala). I've also experienced an awareness of spirit entities wrapped in serpent coils, an unknown spirit being (deity?) inside the King's Chamber of The Great Pyramid, and other transcendental phenomena.

I've conducted Ritual Meditation where no transcendence has occurred, but in which deep revelations about my life have been provided. All this has catalyzed profound changes in my life, including transcendental self-realization, spiritual awakening, and profound healing. Most importantly, I've been able to forgive those who caused the abuse and deep pain I experienced in my childhood and struggled with and suffered from during my adulthood. Consequently, I have reopened doors to family and friends, and in turn I've felt the uplifting and healing impact of that in my life. I've eliminated the negative emotions and mind chatter from my mind. I rarely drink alcohol nowadays, whereas before I sometimes drank to excess and by myself.

Consciousness, Self-Realization, Healing, and the Meaning of Life

As a Ritual Meditation test pilot I have been fortunate to gain useful insight into consciousness and the mind, and I have witnessed profound states of consciousness, and I have made numerous journeys into the infinite and eternal realm of pure consciousness. This has given me an awareness of the process for accessing higher states of consciousness, and it's been impressed in my awareness by pure consciousness that I should share this so that you too may know. Sharing this insight is the purpose of Chapters 10 and 11.

I've been able to witness consciousness and its transformation — experiencing myself as pure "I am" awareness in and beyond space and time. Transcendental self-inquiry is how we answer the paradoxical riddle to the meaning of life. At some stage in the innumerable incarnations of our human spirit (higher self) we all have to come to understand who we really are. If I were to sum it up, I would say we must somehow create the opportunity via these karmic rebirths to transcendentally inquire as to "Who am I?" Because, unless you've self-realized, you're not who you think you are! This self-realization is done from the perspective of the higher self i.e., what some may call the soul, holy ghost, Atman, with ego dissolved, outside of space and time. In my case the question arose spontaneously upon transcending and I answered, "I am" my eternal higher self, and I profoundly felt this from my very core. My prior prayers and ritual intentions programmed my higher self. My I am mantra proved useful for answering the question! This was then followed by profound awareness of "that is not I," i.e., my ego apparition and consciousness is not who I am. You come to see an apparition of yourself as your ego self-image, and you witness this from your higher self (I am) in eternity and infinity while your awareness is bathed in this divine bliss-love-consciousness. Of course you can't help but be changed by such a profound experience!

When you experience transcendental self-inquiry and self-realization, however old you may be (age of your ego), you as an ego awareness pale into insignificance compared to your higher self as pure I am awareness in eternity. With this self-realization you become permanently (perhaps) transcended, that is, the higher self becomes your default window on consciousness instead of the ego, but your ego is still there albeit differently. You experience life through two windows on consciousness! Your life is never the same again, and in the most profound and peaceful of ways.

This is all still new to me, and is evolving week by week. What is obvious is that I am in the Now moment-by-moment, effortlessly silent in awareness. A deep joy, inner peace and tranquility, and a calmness and emptiness of the mind fill my day moment-by-moment. My crown chakra activation buzzes between my ears all day long, and in turn brings me effortlessly to the present moment. This chakra is where my awareness now seems to emanate from.

So, when you read about Ritual Meditation in the next two chapters, see it as a means of supplementing your own meditation (which, remember, is a gateway process), so that you may more readily access altered states of consciousness. You then have a choice: to conduct transcendental self-inquiry and become self-realized and healed, or just witness its teachings, healings, and profound experiences until you're ready for transcendental self-inquiry.

What is consciousness? According to my experiences it is single pointed self-reflective "I am" awareness within and beyond space and time. We are given three windows for witnessing consciousness; two inside this earthly realm (higher self, ego) and two beyond space and time (higher self, pure consciousness in Unity awareness). The higher self can be witnessed both inside and beyond space and time. You witness your higher self's window on consciousness in space and time by being present in the Now. It's always there and you do not need psychedelics to witness it, just effective meditation. Sacred rituals were a means of accessing higher states of consciousness beyond space and time, and the purpose was to use these experiences to transform and heal the mind. The concept of spiritual immortality is what transcendental self-realization is really about, in that you eliminate your future need for karmic rebirth after death.

The ego can be seen as a counterfeit window on consciousness, which overshadows the higher self from a young age, i.e., from about 2-3 years old. The higher self's consciousness exists silently alongside our ego consciousness, but we forgot this, and therefore live out the consequences of our ego until we awaken and shift the seat of consciousness back to the higher self (this *is* self-realization). Our higher self is our deep intuitive self in the Now, and its observing awareness simultaneously coexists alongside the pervasive ego consciousness. The higher self awaits our awakening, either in this life or a subsequent one. The higher self and pure consciousness are knowingly interconnected and eternal, whereas the ego is finite and perceives itself as separate, and is confined to this earthly realm.

When the seat of consciousness rests with the higher self in this earthly realm, consciousness is finite, but it is intuitively aware of its infinity, eternity, and capacity for unconditional love. When the seat of consciousness resides with the higher self upon ego dissolution it is deeply aware of its infinity and eternity, and connection with pure consciousness. The ego consciousness is impermanent, and only as old as you (that is, the corporeal you) are. So, when the ego consciousness' impermanence is reflected against the eternity of the higher self's consciousness outside of space and time, the higher self automatically regains the seat of consciousness and the ego realizes its days of pervasive influence are numbered. In relative terms, everything that happens in space and time is an illusion when reflected against eternity outside of space and time. Until you experience this, these are only words that I'm using to the best of my ability.

Our ego, in reality, is an impermanent window on a counterfeit consciousness, which develops early in our infancy and vanishes when you die. This ego consciousness obscures our coexistent higher self-consciousness, which will continue to exist after you die and seed your next life. The fragile ego of the very young child can be hurt by early life experiences (bad ones, at least), which shape our ego consciousness and its journey through space and time. Fortunately, the child, whose species prime directive is to survive, was gifted an inbuilt, self-healing capability triggered by transcendental self-inquiry. Our species' biological need to survive and our self-healing and transcendental self-realization capabilities are all linked to promote the evolution of consciousness to the higher self. Spiritual healing is in reality our doorway to spiritual awakening, i.e., discovering who we really are at the level of eternal consciousness. And who we *think* we are is a fundamentally different thing from who we really are!

Conducting sacred rituals allows us to know who we really are. We do this by dissolving our ego consciousness, which permits our expanded awareness to transcend the boundaries of our body-brain in space and time. This process exposes your coexistent, higher self-consciousness as the new primary window on consciousness.

The higher self is also awareness outside of space and time, and it can be more readily witnessed when the ego consciousness is dissolved. This higher self beyond space and time can merge with pure consciousness as Unity awareness. This fills your awareness with a deep sense of I am Oneness, and one and all in infinity and eternity, all bathed in bliss-love-awareness. This is experienced as the most profound thing that can be witnessed by your consciousness, and experienced in your heart, by your new seat of higher self-consciousness (crown chakra), and indeed by your entire being. You are Unity awareness of pure consciousness, and it is impressed upon you like no other experience that this is real, the truth, and when the short-lived or impermanent ego, with all its fictional dramas, is compared with this pure I am consciousness in eternity it simply dissolves, and you are liberated.

So, if you wish to become self-realized or enlightened, then you are going to need to ask, while in altered states of consciousness, "Who am I?" This is the most important question we can ever ask ourselves in this lifetime, and the question needs to be asked by your higher self when the ego consciousness has been dissolved. You will undergo this profound self-revelation of who you really are. You realize you are your higher self as I am awareness, both on earth and in eternity. Our bubble of counterfeit consciousness, propagated by the ego mind in space and time, must come face to face with the higher self. That higher self witnessing the ego from outside of space and time, and the transcendental self-realization (Who am I? I am my higher self), is what one's innumerable karmic rebirths have all been about. By asking, "Who am I?" the higher self is able to reject the ego consciousness and say "That is not I." In rejecting the ego the need to heal vanishes, simply because the perceived need to heal is an illusion of the ego mind (inside space and time), and is itself not real when viewed from the perspective of eternity by your higher self.

Undergoing transcendental self-realization means the seat of consciousness then changes to the higher self, and you become permanently transcended. This is what I term *transcendental self-realization through self-inquiry.* Whether the higher self remains the permanent seat on consciousness is unknown, but I am nonetheless effortlessly aware of my higher self in the Now most of the time two months after the summer solstice 2015. I have also become more aware of my ego mind and its arisings, because it still exists, albeit in a different way. For one thing it is significantly quieter in my mind and I am relearning new ways to be influenced by my higher self (I think this is how its working). Being in the Now is the key to our higher self-awareness and awareness of the ego. During such arisings I simply ask myself: which I is feeling, thinking, doing or saying that right now? Everything rapidly dissolves, stillness and peace imbue my mind once again, I smile inside at how I'm learning, and I continue to realize my journey is really just beginning.

So, to enable transcendental self-realization I have combined the Ritual Meditation process with a stripped-down version of Mooji's method of self-inquiry, which I then conduct in an altered state of consciousness.

Mooji[466,467] (a.k.a. Anthony Paul Moo-Young) is well recognized as a self-realized (or enlightened) person. I connected with the simplicity of his method of self-inquiry, and it made real sense and sort of clicked for me very quickly. During my summer solstice 2015 Ritual Meditation I used my "I am" mantra as I meditated into transcendence— that was the answer to the question, Who am I? The mantra "I am" was emblazoned on my consciousness during Unity awareness at my winter solstice 2014 Ritual Meditation, so I realized it would be important at some stage (which turned out to be the summer solstice of 2015). In fact, it was always my meditation mantra, and now I know why. Watching Mooji's method of self-realization made me realize that I needed to enact this self-inquiry in altered states of consciousness.

The truth is, the "Who am I?" question spontaneously arose from my higher self-perspective upon ego dissolution. My awareness as pure consciousness knew that my higher self was going to conduct transcendental self-inquiry, and this I believe is how the question arose. I think this is why setting ritual intentions and praying much beforehand is very important, and quite possibly constitutes a means for influencing the higher self in altered states of consciousness. My "I am" mantra was the answer to the self-inquiry: Who am I? In this state of awareness you transcendentally witness that "I am my higher self" and know that it's the real, eternal you. You feel it so deeply in your core that words simply cannot describe it. This is not a cognitive process, but has to be directly experienced for this self-realization to take place. Then you come to know who you really are!

More on the Ritual Meditation process in the next chapter.

Chapter 10

The Ritual Meditation Process

Introduction

This chapter discusses the full Ritual Meditation process that I reverse-engineered from my archaeological discoveries. In so doing, it provides you with knowledge on the ritual's preparation, and teaches you both how to meditate and how to conduct a Ritual Meditation. It also covers how to conduct a ceremonial fire and the opening of sacred space to transact your healing and spiritual intentions before conducting the Ritual Meditation. I cannot overstate the need for meditation in the ritual process, as well as meticulous and sacred preparation. Health, safety and legal responsibilities are discussed below, so please review this section before you begin using the Ritual Meditation process.

To date I have been unable to identify any other source of detailed information on sacred ritual processes involving sacredly timed meditation in conjunction with psychedelics. That's not to say such sources don't exist, because my instinct tells me they do, but I've not yet

The Ritual Meditation Process

been able to confirm this. The average person is simply not privy to that sort of know-how. Which is why I went to the ancient Sun god religions and pyramid cultures and found their ritual processes, from which I reverse-engineered the Ritual Meditation process.

While psychedelic literature and medical treatment protocols detailing methods for using psychedelics do exist, these typically refer to "set and setting" i.e., one's mindset and the place of psychedelic experience. I have found it hard to identify a consistent process with a basis in the biology of altered states of consciousness. Alternatively, medical treatment protocols conducted in a hospital or medical research environment tend to employ psychotherapy and counseling beforehand, generating familiarity between a healthcare professional and the study subject before treatment, whereupon the healthcare professional becomes the subject's spotter. Subjects close their eyes or have them covered, and often listen to specially selected music to assist the process for accessing altered states of consciousness. Little other preparation and process detail is specified. Importantly, the sacredness of the preparation and process, and the promotion of self-inquiry are not emphasized, at least not according to what I've reviewed.

My pharmaceutical innovation and development background, and my veterinarian's instinct for healing have been very useful to this journey. Once I achieved my discoveries, my mission became to refine a safe ritual process in order to help others transcendentally self-realize, spiritually awaken, and heal. Even without transcendental self-realization, which took me two and one-half years to achieve, the experience of Unity "I am" awareness of pure consciousness was profoundly healing. Such an experience will begin to awaken you spiritually, and over time you will regain awareness of your higher self in the Now. You can further propagate higher self-awareness with meditation and yoga. When the time is right, this awareness will occur naturally. That's just the way it works.

I'd like to share with you the Ritual Meditation process that I reverse- engineered from this shared ritual archaeological fingerprint. Ritual Meditation combined with transcendental self-inquiry allowed me to profoundly self-realize, end any perceived need to heal, and eventually led to my profound awakening and then living through the awareness of the higher self in the Now. In Chapter 11 I will show you how to integrate sacred rituals into a broader life and spiritual development plan, so as to accelerate your spiritual awakening and eliminate your need to heal. Remember though, where you end up is really just a new beginning.

Ensure Your Health and Safety (and Legal Responsibilities and Liabilities)

Before reading this section I request you please review the section Accepting Your Legal, Civil and Moral Responsibilities and Liabilit at the end of the book. This clearly draws your attention to your need to accept responsibility and liability for using Ritual Meditation and Mind Transformation Plan, and the basis upon which these are provided, because you are not under the author's direct supervisory or associated medical care. If you were, you would have medical and legal insurance, would have signed a legal and medical waiver, and would have undertaken full screening and a thorough ritual preparation beforehand.

Respect your country's laws: in many countries the use and/or possession of psychedelics are illegal. You will need to check this yourself. Respect this legal status or fully accept the legal risks for its contravention. I fully accept those risks for myself only.

Ensure your health & safety: If after considering the legal status of psychedelics, and choosing to pursue psychedelics and Ritual Meditation for healing and spiritual awakening, please understand that psychedelics have the potential to be dangerous to your health (and that of others). In providing this Ritual Meditation process and advice on its use, I provide it only for those people who consider themselves to be in good mental, emotional, and physical health. Please let common sense prevail—if you are not in good physical or mental health, or are on any form of medication prescribed by your physician or psychologist, then please avoid using psychedelics.

Potential dangers emerge if psychedelics are used improperly, or by people with certain preexisting medical conditions (whether they are under treatment or not), and even for no apparent reason. Preexisting medical conditions could include, but are not limited to, any cardiovascular (i.e., blood pressure disorders, arrhythmias, heart attack, stroke, etc.), central nervous system, or psychological conditions (bi-polar disorder, schizophrenia, etc.). Psychedelics should be avoided in conditions such as severe post-traumatic stress associated with extreme violence, or severe mood swings, emotional responses, or extreme personality and behavioral disorders. If you suspect that you might have one of these conditions, even if this has not yet been diagnosed or recognized, then please avoid psychedelics.

Avoid taking recreational drugs before, during, and after psychedelic use. If you take any prescription or over-the-counter medicines or herbal-health products, which are known to act on the heart, cardiovascular or central nervous system (please read the product label), then please avoid using psychedelics.

If you have (or suspect you have) any of the aforementioned medical or psychological conditions, or are being treated for such, please consult your physician and/or psychologist, and follow their advice. ***Their advice comes first.*** In any case, you are fully responsible for your own health and safety and that of others you interact with while under the influence of psychedelics, and also afterwards (during the after-glow effect). So please make sure you take the necessary precautions. ***Be Sacred and Safe, please.*** Get a health check first and consult with your physician about your plans to use psychedelics with Ritual Meditation, and follow their advice.

Use a spotter: if you've never used psychedelics before, make sure you have a good friend, or someone you deeply trust, present. This should be someone you can talk with at a deep and intimate level (before, during, and afterwards), and someone who understands you well. This person should not participate in using psychedelics, and they should keep their distance during the ritual unless you need them (and they should be strictly silent). Do not confuse sexual intimacy for intimacy of the mind, and avoid contaminating your sacred ritual with any sexual intimacy. You should also ensure that your spotter has the contact details for your physician, psychologist, or spiritual crisis network in case of a spiritual crisis. (Return to Some Words of Caution, My Mind Transformation Plan)

Ritual Meditation

At its simplest level Ritual Meditation involves an eyes-closed meditation technique, conducted in sensory silence at sacred time under the influence of entheogens. Preparation and the setting of one's ritual intention are important determinants of the ritual outcome. Conducting transcendental self-inquiry further specifies the ritual process, both in the ritual's intention and in the use of transcendental self-inquiry during the ritual (see below).

A key part of the Ritual Meditation process is planning. We must secure a supply of magic mushrooms, which means arranging for their purchase and delivery, and then give them time to grow. We also need to know where we will conduct our ritual, and we must ensure that we can clear the decks beforehand with regard to personal and professional responsibilities. We really need silence and being in nature for the final three days, and ideally for one to two days after the ritual for quiet reflection. This is important if we are to prepare properly for the ritual and have the necessary integration time afterwards. I can't emphasize enough how important preparation is for Ritual Meditation. Additionally, we would be wise to ensure that we are well practiced in our eyes-closed meditation technique beforehand. But no worries, the technique I teach here is really simple. You don't need to be elaborate, that I can promise you.

Early Preparation for Ritual Meditation

If you are serious about accessing altered states of consciousness using the Ritual Meditation technique, then you will need to do two things to prepare in good time. First, ensure that you have a supply of top quality magic mushrooms. Second, learn how to meditate.

At this phase in my journey, my preference is to use magic mushrooms (Psilocybin cubensis), simply because they work relatively dependably, are readily accessible, have a good safety record, create positive healing experiences (given good intentions and preparation), and have an extensive history of sacred ritual use in both ancient religions and present-day indigenous cultures. Additionally, they are a lot of fun to grow. Developing a loving, respectful relationship with them before you consume them is important. I am now learning to grow them from spore prints, which is more difficult than using grow kits. My standard magic mushroom dose is 50 grams wet weight or 5 grams dry.

I am using San Pedro cactus in my low dose/non-transcending sessions conducted on Sundays between the equinoxes and solstices. I use it because it lasts much longer, taking approximately six hours to reach its peak effect, and because it reveals and connects your awareness to everything including your higher self in this earthly realm. I cannot provide any insight for its use in accessing altered states of consciousness, but I can tell you it is some of the most horrible tasting plant material you can ever eat! Nevertheless, the level of stillness, connectivity and awe of nature it provides is very grounding. It's said the best sources of San Pedro come from southern Ecuador and northern Peru.

For readily accessing magic mushrooms you essentially have two options; using a magic mushroom grow kit, or purchasing ready to consume magic mushroom truffles. I purchase the strongest varieties in both cases. Both are available at online stores. Over recent years I have successfully purchased and had delivered magic mushrooms with a number of online retailers including Avalon Magic Plants, Zamnesia, Magic Truffles, and Shayanashop, but many other suppliers exist. I have grow kits delivered by courier to shorten transit time and prevent product spoilage. One really wants a rapid delivery to ensure the kit's contents don't perish in transit. Magic mushrooms are simple to grow, but like anything else, there's a learning curve. You may need to make or purchase an incubator, because magic mushrooms require an ambient temperature in the 23-27 degree Celsius range (73-82 degrees Fahrenheit).

The Ritual Meditation Process

It's best to allow 2 weeks for delivery and 2 weeks for growing, so factor this into your preparation timing. You can store grow kits in the fridge for some weeks (consult supplier) before cultivating. I will sometimes purchase both the grow kit and magic mushroom truffles (store in fridge or desiccate) to ensure I have a back-up plan should the magic mushroom grow kit not yield its crop of potent magic mushrooms.

For an extremely effective entheogen combination for accessing transcendental states of consciousness I use 50 grams of wet magic mushrooms (5 grams dry; moderate-strong potency) followed by 100 micrograms of LSD after approximately 30 minutes (I place the LSD on my thigh while I meditate so I can readily place it in my mouth when required). All my really profound experiences involving Unity awareness, the higher self, and self-inquiry involved this dose schedule and phasing.

Learning to Meditate

While meditation is often promoted as a mindfulness or spiritual practice or technique, I find it useful to understand specifically what we are trying to achieve with meditation. Meditation is an incredibly powerful practice that helps us become aware of our higher self in the present moment, while witnessing or observing the activities of our imposturous ego mind, that is, our arising feelings, emotions, and thoughts. In addition, it allows us to observe our body and its senses. This, over time, results in improved innate mindfulness and self-control.

If you know how to meditate (eyes closed) then you can skip this section. By knowing how to meditate I mean settling into direct awareness of your higher self (which is silently ever-present) and witnessing all arisings (i.e., feelings, thoughts, and senses), without attachment and in the Now. Your mind readily rests in silence, your breathing and heart rate are lowered, and you are simply present as unwavering awareness of the Now. If this describes your meditation (i.e., calm abiding) then you may skip this section if you wish.

My objective is to get you to a state of calm-abiding as efficiently as possible without a long learning curve. Why? Because meditation is the gateway process for directly accessing our higher states of consciousness, and you will need this for the Ritual Meditation process. Remember that there are many meditation methods, and what follows is essentially a technique I've developed from various sources and my own experiences.

Eyes-Closed Meditation Technique

This meditation technique was influenced by the Transcendental Meditation™ technique, as espoused by Maharishi Mahesh Yogi in his book *The Science of Being and Art of Living* [468] which is what I used when I

The Ritual Meditation Process

taught myself to meditate. My method omits a mantra unless it's required to help silence the mind. Ritual Meditation also includes an "I am" mantra for transitioning meditation to transcendental states of consciousness, when the intention for your ritual is self-inquiry (i.e., to ask and answer, Who am I?). The "I am" mantra is the answer to the self-inquiry question. There is merit in practicing this mantra during your meditation sessions close to the equinox and solstice Ritual Meditations, so that everything becomes instinctive during Ritual Meditation. Then you'll have those words right at the forefront of your consciousness. This mantra was inspired by my winter solstice 2014 Ritual Meditation where "I am" was emblazoned into my consciousness as I experienced Unity awareness.

Some important things to consider when bringing the mind to the Now, in silence and peace:

1) Find one or more comfortable, quiet spots (inside or out in nature), and alternate your locations as your inner voice directs you. Quiet is good, because it helps you silence the mind, especially when you are just learning to meditate.

2) Identify a comfortable sitting spot and technique. I prefer sitting on a comfortable chair with arm rests, but you can also sit on the ground connected to Mother Earth, or on a meditation cushion. Contorted leg positions with cramped circulation,

aching back and hips, and unusual hand positions are not necessary at this stage. The key is to be relaxed and comfortable, so that you may relax into your higher self-awareness. You wish to bring your awareness into the Now and use your aware but silent mind (higher self) to observe your senses, your body, and any ego arisings such as feelings, emotions and thoughts. That is meditation.

3) If you are seated, then place your feet shoulder width apart, with bare feet flat on the ground and relaxed. Watch with awareness for tensions in your calf muscles that might raise your heels. Place your hands on your thighs, and be nice and relaxed. My elbows are close to my hips but completely relaxed. Sometimes I might cross my hands with interlinked fingers and rest them between my upper thighs.

4) Face magnetic north (in the northern hemisphere) or magnetic south (in the southern hemisphere), particularly around the equinoxes, to assist the connection between earth's magnetic field and that of your own body. The exact position is 11 degrees east of true north, or west of true south.

5) Maintain a straight back; be relaxed and without discomfort. Hold your head up relatively straight but relaxed (eyes looking slightly down).

The Ritual Meditation Process

According to experts, you should be aiming for a straight line between the base of your skull and base of the spine, to align your energy meridians or chakras.

6) Close your eyes, and gently breathe via your nose (inspiration and expiration). Relax your abdominal muscles, feel your belly drop forward and gently breathe via your abdomen, and not your chest. Feel your abdomen gently rise and fall. Avoid overfilling or expanding your lungs and abdomen. Be gentle, slow, and aware of what is happening to your heart rate (you can feel it) as you breathe. If your heart rate increases, then gradually increase your breathing rate or depth of breath to return to a balance.

My mind's eye is focused simultaneously on the general region of my heart (heart chakra) and solar plexus, while placing my mind's attention on the inspiration and expiration phases of my breathing, as well as on the region behind the mid-forehead (crown chakra, or third eye). In my learning phase I practiced focusing on one region at a time, switching half way through the meditation to the other region, while always focusing on my breath. Fusing that awareness on both regions simultaneously then happens automatically, especially once you experience these chakras being activated during Ritual Meditation.

You will then come to appreciate these regions as places where consciousness arises during altered states of consciousness. The crown chakra also seems to be where my higher self-awareness rests during my awakened state, and is the place from which emanates the buzzing that brings me to a calm Now. Learn to become aware of the gap between the end of your expiration and the start of your inspiration, and do this while simultaneously focused on your heart-solar plexus region. I find the heart-solar plexus region is where my heart chakra opens, and my third eye is where the visuals are generally propagated from during meditation and Ritual Meditation. Moreover, when meditating I notice the gap between the end of expiration and the start of inspiration. By focusing on this gap we can rapidly relax into the Now—it's the quickest way I know how to achieve this.

When I meditate or focus on my breath in everyday life it reminds me to open my heart, to love, and to be appreciative of each moment in life, with the awareness that love emanates from our hearts. Meditation is "breathing awareness" and our breathing accompanies every new moment of life. This focused attention and concentration on our breath brings us to the present moment, from which awareness of our coexistent higher self can be realized. The Now is the only time you will have awareness of the higher self.

7) Your inspiration is generally longer than expiration when learning, but as you become more experienced the length of these breath phases tends to equalize. Avoid over-filling the lungs, and gently slow the breathing down, but not so much that you notice your heart rate speed up. My breathing rate is circa six full breaths (but not forced) per minute and inspiration/expiration phases are broadly of the same duration. I started with ten per minute 2½ years ago.

8) Our minds naturally wander and thoughts arise (ego fictions about our past or the future), but the more experienced we become the less this happens. The trick is to be aware of this and return to the Now, and avoid attaching to the thought by refocusing on your breath. Other meditation techniques can be useful to learn and alternate with this eyes-closed method, because they can specifically teach you to focus your attention and openly monitor your environment,

senses, body, and feelings in order to improve your mindfulness and ability to concentrate.

One technique that I use to improve my meditation concentration is as follows: once weekly I meditate in front of a mirror, focusing my opened eyes on my central forehead above the eyebrow level, with my awareness on my breath. This becomes a powerful means of binding breath with concentration. This concentration can then be transferred to your eyes-closed meditation technique to improve your meditation concentration, simply by following your breath. This concentration is useful when meditating with entheogens, at least until you have emerged into altered states of consciousness. This is because I find thoughts simply cease and I am readily able to stay in the awareness of altered states of consciousness.

9) Use a meditation app to provide a soft and gentle alarm. After each meditation I say a prayer to pure consciousness with gratitude for the good things in my life, the experiences of the previous day and my awakening to the new day, and the lessons I have been given. I dedicate my meditation to different groups of people who are suffering, to other life forms, and to Mother Earth who is

The Ritual Meditation Process

suffering because of our abuse of our home planet.

10) Open your eyes and gently relax your way back into your day. Start out by meditating for 5 minutes, and then extend 5 minutes every few days until you're doing a minimum of 30 minutes. The secret to persisting with meditation is in realizing how good, relaxed, energized, calm, peaceful, tranquil, and aware you feel afterwards. This, for me, is a really blissful awareness and feeling, and it's like a mind reboot that cleans up the ego mind-RAM. Remember that without meditation you're not going to be able to transcend.

11) I typically meditate 45-60 minutes a day. Quite often I meditate twice daily, at around sunrise and sunset. I also meditate in motion during the day when I can, i.e., while being in nature, watering the garden, sitting at my desk working, walking barefoot, motorbike riding, kayaking, diving, etc.

12) Now that you can meditate, try meditating using the "I am" mantra from time to time. Do this more frequently close to the solstices and equinoxes in order to practice for your Ritual Meditation and transcendental self-realization. The "I" is said mindfully but silently upon inspiration, and "am" is said mindfully and

silently upon expiration. "I am" becomes the answer to the question asked by your higher self, in the calm abiding state of meditation—Who am I? I am (my higher self consciousness). And that (my ego consciousness) is not I. You can practice saying these phrases from time to time while in deep meditation. Get into the habit during meditation of recognizing which I (ego or higher self) is observing your actions, feelings, thoughts, senses, and body awareness arisings. Make this self-awareness and observation instinctive, and you will be able to self-realize when you access altered states of consciousness.

13) Ideally it's best to start your meditation 30-60 minutes before sunrise (from autumn to spring equinox) or sunset (from spring to autumn equinox), in order to benefit from enhanced Schumann resonances. Likewise, if you can catch a new moon rise coinciding with sunrise/set then you can further augment the environment's impact on your meditation process, and go deeper. Meditating under the power of a full moon is also good, i.e., +/- 2 hours before its zenith. If time is short, just focus on the meditation, and keep it simple. See my free online meditation calendar (http://ritualmeditation.com/meditation-calendar/) for location-specific sun and moon rises/sets and moon phases to help you time your meditation.[469]

Stick with the meditation because it's the mind's gateway process for accessing altered states of consciousness, and if you really wish to transcend with Ritual Meditation then this is the ticket. Real motivation for meditation arrives once you've experienced altered states of consciousness.

Preparing and Conducting Ritual Meditation

My preparation for Ritual Meditation is flexible, and my ideas are not fixed. The basic principles I follow are to get my mind into a great spot and purify the emotion-body-mind system; to be positive, loving, quiet, compassionate, nature connected, and to deepen my relationship/intimacy with pure consciousness. I fast, which cleanses the gastrointestinal tract, helps weaken the ego's hold during the ritual (this is really important), and ensures a higher percentage of the entheogen payload gets to the brain during Ritual Meditation. I also switch off work and the outside world in general. In other words, I switch off people, communications, and all computer and online-related activities.

In my view, preparation makes a real difference, impacting the sacredness, safety, and profoundness of the transcendental experience. Some might advocate taking a higher entheogen dose to compensate for not fasting, but I'm not sure I agree with that. To reiterate, we are trying to quiet and purify the mind, rest in our higher self, and get ourselves into a sacred and nature-connected frame of mind. For me Ritual Meditation is sacred, and I wish to follow our ancestors' example, so I take preparation very seriously and I cast ritual intentions. In fact, the times I've failed to transcend were usually compromised by less than optimal preparation and/or low entheogen potency.

Preparation More Specifically:

1) One week before the ritual it is recommended to:

   a. Eat a healthy diet, with as much fresh fruit and vegetables as possible. Avoid eating pork, red meat, and dried cured meats. Foods like fresh fruit and vegetables, steamed fish, rice, whole grains, healthy breads, popcorn, vegetable soups, salads, herbs, herbal teas, and water are ideal.

   b. Stop all alcohol, drugs, all caffeine-containing drinks, cigarettes, and other brain stimulants.

   c. Avoid any sexual intimacy, including; sex, oral sex, masturbation, phone sex, and pornography.

2) Increase your eyes-closed meditation to at least two sixty-minute sessions daily during the last three days. I add some shorter meditation sessions as well to improve my focus-concentration capability, keeping my eyes open and focused on objects, or looking at the reflection of a spot between my eyes

in a mirror. I sometimes find the effect of the entheogens can make it hard to focus (ego struggling to let go) so that ability to continually refocus is crucially important, until you dissolve your ego-body-space-time boundaries.

3) Commence your fast three full days before the Ritual Meditation. This means strictly no food or calorific liquids. Only teas, broths and water. If you have a strong ego, you might wish to consider a dry fast for the first or second day of this final three days. Be careful about the risk of becoming too weak from dehydration and feeling lightheaded etc.

4) I consume passionflower tea 3-4 times daily during the final day. The passionflower tea is like a milder form Ayahuasca's Banisteriopsis caapi vine containing natural monoamine oxidase inhibitors (1/40th potency). Theoretically, this ensures a greater quantity of the entheogen's active ingredients gets to the brain. If you are assured of potent magic mushrooms then this step can be omitted.

5) I also stop working and online activities during these final three days, spending most of my time in nature strengthening my awareness of my connection to Earth and all its life forms, including plants, and deepening my awe for Mother Earth (this helps weaken the ego's hold).

The Ritual Meditation Process

6) Prayer (conversations with pure consciousness), reading spiritual books, and walking meditation also occupy my last few days. This is my time to quiet the mind and get into a great headspace for the Ritual Meditation! And I walk everywhere barefoot in order to feel the earth and become even more aware of my connection with Mother Earth.

Creating Sacred Space and Invocation

Opening a sacred circle and conducting a fire ceremony is one way to create sacred space in your mind, within which you can undertake healing and spiritual work. Creating a sacred circle with invocation and conducting a ceremonial fire transacts this intent. What follows is a framework for starters, and gives you scope to adapt to your situation or cultural and faith context.

I will conduct the fire ceremony the evening before the Ritual Meditation if it's an early morning ritual (winter solstice, equinoxes), or mid-afternoon for the summer solstice sunset. A ceremonial fire could be in one of three forms, depending on your circumstances. These forms are (1) a small candle fire ceremony held inside; (2) a small fire inside a fireplace; (3) a larger fire outside.

<u>Opening a Sacred Circle & Conducting a Ceremonial Fire:</u>

The Ritual Meditation Process

The following represents the principles and process for opening a sacred circle in which to conduct a ceremonial fire and invocation.

1) Organize your ceremonial fire materials around the place you will build the fire. Fire materials include incense blocks, small ceremonial candles (yellow, red, black, white, green, blue), flower petals (same colors), and offerings (sugar, candies, cigars, aromatic incenses). See Figure 11.1.

2) Ritual Cleansing: Each participant should anoint themselves, or each other, before the ritual with cleansing water that contains essential oils.

3) After cleansing, stand at the edge of an imaginary circle, around the ceremonial fireplace. If you are in a group, then hold hands. Close your eyes and visualize the energy flowing anticlockwise (Earth's direction of rotation & orbit) for a minute while saying "Only love may enter and love may leave." Be present in the Now and clear your mind of all thoughts and distracting emotions.

4) Conduct Smudging: Before entering the sacred space (the imaginary or bounded circle which will contain the fire) smudge yourself or each other with smoldering dried sage or sweet grass, while visualizing all negativity drifting away with the smoke. Immediately after smudging enter the

The Ritual Meditation Process

circle. You have now entered sacred space and should remain inside the circle until the fire is reduced to embers. If someone must leave, ask permission within yourself, cut an imaginary door at one of the cardinal points, step outside, and then immediately close it. Do the same upon your return and then say a silent thank you.

5) Conduct Invocation (see below). Calling for the presence and blessing of pure consciousness (God) by invoking the cardinal and solstice directions, the Sun, Moon, and stars, elements of life (earth, air, fire, water, and ether), ancestors and spirits, and animal and plant spirits, all of which have collectively created the building blocks and sustenance for all planetary life.

6) Assemble ceremonial fire, collectively or by assigning someone to this task. Assemble the blocks of incense in an anticlockwise manner at each cardinal point (NWSE, and at solstices midway between SE-NW, NE-SW), then place the colored candles on top of the incense. The color-direction pairings include; south-red, east-yellow, north-white, west-black, with inter-southeast-blue for the winter solstice sunrise, and inter-northwest-green for the summer solstice. Build the fire progressively outward to each cardinal point from

the fire's center. Light the candles on the fire when you are ready. Stand in silence as the fire is lit.

Figure 10.1 The Mayan Cross is cardinally-directed and solstice-demarcating. Each direction represents a grandfather and grandmother, and a cosmic force that is associated with characters, directions, colors, and qualities. East (red): father Sun, the way of the visionary. West (blue and black; blue was not available on this day): grandmother, moon, ocean, the way of the teacher. South (yellow): Mother Earth, the way of the healer. North (white): father sky, the way of the sacred warrior.[470] Flowers and candles aligned to a Mayan Cross at a shaman-led ceremony at Tak'alik Abaj (Olmec and Maya pyramid site Guatemala) on June 21, 2013. The central section is built of incense and food offerings (candies) in an anticlockwise fashion demarcating the solstices and marking the cardinal directions with different colored flowers. This is then set on fire. The shaman

reads the fire and communes with the spirit world through the whirling ebbs and flows of the smoke and flames.[471,472]

> For a candle fire ceremony held indoors I use four larger candles (clear, or yellow, red, black, white), or six (blue and green; solstice positions) and assemble these around a central basket of flowers and other offerings (cigars, candies, incense sticks). These are placed on the NSEW positions and inter-NW and inter-SE positions (solstices). Candles and incense are then lit.

Figure 10.2 A home-based candle ceremonial offering. Candles are placed around a circular area according to the cardinal positions, NSEW (and at the solstice positions if you can). A small tray or basket ladened with fresh flowers is placed in the center. Into this I also place my sacred objects. Incense can also

The Ritual Meditation Process

be lit, prayers offered, and ritual intentions requested during the day(s) before the Ritual Meditation.[473]

7) During the fire ceremony: offer prayers of gratitude and love to (as you see fit) pure consciousness (or your God), our ancestors, the Sun, Earth, Moon, and stars, the cardinal and solstice directions, the elements (earth, air, water, and fire), and human, non-earthly, and animal and plant spirits. Then make any requests and/or state clearly your Ritual Meditation intentions. This can be done silently or aloud. In between maintain silence, pray, and project your ritual intention(s) either silently or aloud while focusing on the fire. The flames will carry these between the realms. Most of all, respect the space and each other's silence, and collectively agree on any rules for this time upfront. An outside/inside ceremony typically lasts two hours, whereas a candle ceremony is shorter.

8) Close the circle: You should remain inside the sacred space until the fire is an ember, whereupon you should close the circle (see Invocation point 8 below).

Invocation

This is effectively your circle prayer. You can adapt this as you wish, and this is just a suggestion because I am without a formal religion or spiritual faith. I've

The Ritual Meditation Process

adapted North American Indian and Mayan Circle invocations because they are so beautiful and are aligned with my beliefs. Turn and face the horizon of each cardinal and solstice direction as you read or recite the invocation.

Pure consciousness (God): I (we) request your presence and blessing by invoking the cardinal & solstice directions, elements of life, ancestors and spirits, and animal and plant spirits, who we recognize have created the building blocks of all life which you pure consciousness have created. I (we) thank you, honor and worship you for this opportunity called my (our) life (lives). Please help me (us) transact this intent.

1) Guardian of the east, the great eagle, element of air and sacred breath–I (we) invite you in. Come to me (us) from the place of the rising sun and teach me (us) to fly wing to wing with the great spirit and illuminate my (our) destiny please, and teach me (us) to see through the eyes of my (our) heart(s). With each rising sun please bring me (us) continued lessons of new beginnings. Thank you.

2) Guardian of the south, great serpent, element of fire and sacred heart–I (we) invite you in. Wrap your golden coils of healing light around me (us) and teach me (us) to release my (our) past, and burn through my (our) illusions of separation from pure consciousness (God), purifying me (us) of my (our)

old ways which serve me (us) no more, so I (we) may transform anew. Thank you.

3) Guardian of the west, mother sister jaguar, element of water and sacred womb–I (we) invite you in. Come wash me (us) with your sea of compassion so I (we) may come from a place of grace, love, mindfulness, and compassion. Reveal my (our) path(s) to inner mastery and unconditional love, and teach me (us) the way of peace and integrity, to live fearlessly and impeccably and transact my (our) purpose in your gift of life. Thank you.

4) Guardian of the north, wise owl, element of earth, our sacred body–I (we) invite you in. Help me (us) remember ancient wisdoms, when to listen and when to speak, teach me (us) forgiveness and acceptance. Ancient ones, come and warm your hands by my (our) fire and receive my (our) offerings. I (we) honor the world you forged and those who have come before us. Teach me (us) to walk the sacred path; whisper to me (us) in the wind, in the crackle of the fire, and in the sacred space of my (our) heart(s). Thank you.

5) Mama Gaia, nurturing earth, rising from below to above. I (we) celebrate you and all your life forms, and thank you for creating and sustaining all life. In complete surrender of body, mind, and spirit, I (we) open myself (ourselves) to receive the mandala of

creation and your healing energies. I (we) deeply honor you. Thank you.

6) Father Sun and celestial heavens—thank you for bringing me (us) here to celebrate this moment. In complete surrender of body, mind, and spirit please deliver me (us) to you, so I (we) may know pure consciousness (your God) and heal in your presence, birthing anew so loving-kindness, compassion, and acceptance manifest in my (our) heart(s) forever more. Thank you.

7) Final: This is now a sacred space and to be within this circle is to be within the presence of pure consciousness (God). Only love may enter and love may leave. We are now free to meditate, pray, contemplate these words and project our ritual intentions, watch the flames and connect with the fire. If you wish, you can speak whatever is in your heart.

8) Closing a sacred circle: Sacred circles and fire ceremonies should finish by closing the circle once the embers fade away. You can say something like this aloud: pure consciousness whose presence and blessing was requested by invoking the elements, spirits, ancestors, and animal and plant spirits, you may now return from where you came; that is both your positive and negative polarities please. I (we) am (are) truly grateful for your presence and ask

you to continue looking after me(us) during our ritual and in my (our) life (lives). Thank you".

Setting Your Intentions and Praying

It is always a good idea to enter the Ritual Meditation and Transcendental Self-Inquiry with a specific intention. I start to consider my ritual intentions in the weeks leading up the Ritual Meditation, based on whatever mind material I'm currently focused on. This important mental seeding helps connect your healing and spiritual intent between your preparation and the outcome of your Ritual Meditation. At present I focus solely on healing, without being specific as to what I wish to experience during the Ritual Meditation.

For example, I do not ask for Unity consciousness, ego death/rebirth or chakra and kundalini activation, etc. Instead I will ask something like this:

"Pure consciousness, please look after me during my ritual and deliver me back safely and with more innate loving-kindness, compassion, acceptance, equanimity, inner peace, and generosity in all my feelings, thoughts, words, and actions forevermore. I trust you know what I need and I therefore submit myself fully to your realm and care. Please bring me to you and help me heal, awaken me to the real nature of who I am, and permanently open my heart so these spiritual qualities

The Ritual Meditation Process

are innately and eternally present, so I may be of benefit to other people, life and our planet. Thank you".

Or, more recently, during my (2015) summer solstice Ritual Meditation, I was targeting transcendental self-inquiry and self-realization as my ritual intention (inspired by Mooji). So my ritual intention was as follows:

"Dear pure consciousness, please may I come to you so that I may heal in your presence and witness the bliss-love awareness of Unity consciousness, and know my higher self. Please help me understand Who am I? Please dissolve my ego reality and reveal my higher self so that I may answer, "I am my higher self," Please help me shift the seat of consciousness to my higher self so that I may be permanently transcended. And I shall do good things with my life for the benefit of other people, for all life, and for our beloved Mother Earth. Thank you."

One day I will ask for a spirit guide who can teach me to become a useful shaman who can help others heal themselves, and expand my knowledge within the transcendental realm.

Alongside your intentions, saying lots of prayers in the days prior to and during the ceremonial fire is a very good thing to do. I think prayers are very personal, and I dedicate mine to my family, friends, and other people.

Particularly people who have suffered or are suffering in life as victims of physical, mental, emotional, or sexual abuse, or from war, famine, disease, and natural disasters. I ask that their suffering may cease and that doorways open to their own healing and spiritual awakening. I pray for the perpetrators of these acts of suffering, that they may awaken and desist from causing suffering, and find their own pathways to healing and spiritual awakening. I pray for our lovely planet and all her life forms, and that humanity will awaken *en masse* so that we may realize our evolutionary mission to spiritually awaken and become benevolent guardians of the planet. Rarely do I ask for anything for myself other than healing and spiritual qualities.

Conducting Ritual Meditation

Ritual Meditation is a form of eyes-closed meditation that includes a number of other defining characteristics aimed at improving the efficacy of the meditation process, thus enabling a person to access altered states of consciousness. Ritual Meditation represents a reverse-engineered ritual process, a process that was originally developed by priesthoods of the ancient Sun god religions, and which allowed them to access humankind's biologically enabled 4th state of consciousness.

In my view, sacred and well-prepared for, well-conducted, sacredly-timed meditation combined with entheogens gives one the best possible chance of accessing altered states of consciousness. And it places you in control.

Ritual Meditation has three main components in addition to its sacred preparation: 1) sacred space, 2) sacred time, and 3) the sacred ritual. The overarching theme is being **Sacred and Safe**.

Sacred Space: this embraces the space you will conduct your Ritual Meditation in. Ideally this should be dark and silent, and you would have accustomed yourself to meditating in it (a room, cupboard, basement) prior to the ritual date. Remember, we're trying to replicate the silence of the tunnels, chambers, and sanctums used by our ancestors. Sensory isolation permits you to significantly reduce sensory signals to the brain, helping to lower your overall brain activity, which is what meditation also achieves. Silence therefore helps the meditation process.

Make this place sacred and comfortable. In the days prior to the Ritual Meditation you can place a basket of freshly picked flowers, along with any sacred objects you possess, in your sacred space, and visit the latter frequently. I place four candles around this basket in the north, south, east and west positions and keep these lit while I'm around. Burn incense regularly throughout the day, and make prayers of gratitude and cast (silently or verbally) your intentions for the ritual as well. This is a really good way of connecting with your higher self, pure consciousness, Mother Earth, the Sun, Moon and heavens, our ancestors, and all the elements that constitute and support life.

I will align my body during the Ritual Meditation with magnetic north (in the Northern Hemisphere; and vice versa for the Southern Hemisphere) for the equinoxes, given Earth's magnetic field peaks in strength at this time. The idea being that we can benefit from this enhanced magnetic environment and facilitate magnetic field reconnections with the body's own magnetic fields in this alignment. According to principles of geomancy, this permits good cosmic energies to enter our being for a positive ritual affect. You will need a compass for this, and you must ensure that it's set for magnetic north (11 degrees east of north) or south (11 degrees west of south). For the solstices I face the direction of the rising or setting sun. You can observe the solstice sunrise/set direction in the days prior to know the specific direction to face.

Sacred Time: Typically I will time the start of my Ritual Meditation to coincide with one hour before sunrise or sunset, depending upon which solstice or equinox it is. This coincides with the timing of elevations in Schumann resonances. Sunrise and sunset timings are latitude specific, and you can determine these by clicking on my meditation calendar link (http://ritualmeditation.com/meditation-calendar/).

More specifically, for the winter solstice your Ritual Meditation should be timed for the sunrise, and at the summer solstice for the sunset. These timings are associated with peaks in Schumann resonances. If there is a new moon within one to two days of the winter solstice I will adjust my Ritual Meditation date to coincide with the sunrise and new moon rise. Likewise, if there is a new or full moon within one to two days of the summer solstice, I will adjust the ritual date to coincide the sunset with the new moon set, or full moon rise. The idea is based on bringing together as many sacred time events (sunrise, sunset, solstice, equinox, new and full moon rise/set) as possible for an enhanced sacred time impact on the ritual meditator's brain.

Generally I time my equinox Ritual Meditation for sunrise, but this will depend on the phase of the moon, and on my schedule. Remember the equinox is associated with enhanced magnetic fields and these are not sunrise or sunset dependent, but time of year (phase of Earth's solar orbit) dependent. This means there is some flexibility with the actual day of the ritual. If there is a new moon within one week of the equinox I will adjust my Ritual Meditation date to coincide the sunrise and new moon rise. Likewise, if there is a full moon

The Ritual Meditation Process

within one week of the equinox I will adjust the ritual date to coincide the sunset with the full moon rise.

Sacred Ritual: The timing for consuming your entheogens will depend upon whether you're taking magic mushrooms (Psilocybin cubensis) or San Pedro/Peyote. I consume the magic mushrooms and start my meditation straight away, and typically I feel their effects within 30-45 minutes. The goal is to bring together a deep state of meditation with the peak of the entheogens and peaks in Schumann resonances. You can either thoroughly chew your magic mushrooms, steep them in hot water (ground up) and drink them, or blend them with some cold passionflower tea or orange juice.

For transcendental self-inquiry I use my "I am" mantra for transitioning from deep meditation into altered states of consciousness. I also practice the self-inquiry ("who am I?", "I am", "And I am not that") during my meditation prior to the ritual until it becomes instinctive. You can do this self-inquiry practice using either the eyes-closed or eyes-open method for meditation (that is, prior to conducting Ritual Meditation).

Before consuming my entheogens I will say a prayer of gratitude and recast my ritual intentions. If you are doing this as a small group then one-to-one and group hugs are mandatory! Feel your love flow. My preference is to conduct Ritual Meditation in complete isolation, as

The Ritual Meditation Process

when I have conducted it in proximity to other people I haven't been able to transcend (because of noise, distractions). But it's good to meet up with your other ritual partners after your Ritual Meditation. Being in nature afterwards is always good.

In general, you'll know when your Ritual Meditation is finished. There's usually an urge to "come back" even though you will still be experiencing altered state of consciousness. This post-Ritual Meditation phase is a very special time to connect with other people who have conducted the Ritual Meditation with you, as well as for being in nature.

Before sharing experiences I like to be silent in this post-Ritual Meditation phase, because much insight and recall takes place. Initially you don't have a language for the transcendental realm, so finding the words can be very challenging. If you can think straight, it's good to write things down as soon as you can and is practical. It's a bit like recalling dreams: the further you are from the event, the harder it is to recall what happened in detail and its significance. I tend to do this outside, in nature, and just aim to be quiet, in love with nature, and show my gratitude to pure consciousness. As things come up or you recall what happened, write them down. I listed some books at the end of the previous chapter by Stanislav Grof and Ron Krumpos[474,475,476] that help provide a language for describing your experiences.

The Ritual Meditation Process

In the context of healing a lot of memories, thoughts, feelings, and emotions can surface. My advice is just let this naturally flow, and avoid trying to block it out or judging them. This is all good material for learning about oneself, even if it may not be pleasant. Trust me when I say any sad, sorrowful, painful, regretful, shameful feelings will all be replaced with an overwhelming sense of loving kindness, compassion, acceptance, and forgiveness toward yourself and the other people involved. It can often be helpful to record your thoughts, and/or have your spotter there to discuss and record material as it surfaces. Act positively upon these insights as your heart tells you; saying you're sorry is always a good step. I like to sit on things for a few days, the exception being when I called my Mother after decades of separation. You will also benefit from a day or two of staying at home and being isolated from other people after your ritual, as this is a time when insights and awareness emerge, and gives you space to integrate everything that's happened into your mind.

Once the Ritual Meditation is over you will be hungry! I tend to eat fresh fruit (such as melon, papaya, strawberries, and grapes) to reawaken my digestive system. Avoid eating heavy or processed foods, and too much too soon.

You can read two of my blogs detailing some of my profound experiences of altered states of consciousness (winter solstice 2014; http://tinyurl.com/nm3cbzo, spring equinox 2014; http://ritualmeditation.com/675/).

Chapter 11

A Mind Transformation Plan for Spiritually Awakening & Healing

Introduction

Having made this Ritual Meditation discovery, the big question for me became: what do I do with it?

My instincts told me that I must make my discovery available and be its champion, and that I must continue to experiment with and explore the Ritual Meditation process. And so I committed CEO suicide on the summer solstice in 2012 (see my biography), packed up my life and moved to my spiritual home at Lake Atitlan, Guatemala, which was calling me to begin the writing of this book. When I first visited Lake Atitlan in 1997 it touched me; I felt our connection and knew I would return. In August 2012 I returned to Guatemala in order to live there, and on December 21, 2012 I became a Ritual Meditation test pilot and developing shaman.

In creating this revised edition (2015) I have benefited tremendously from hindsight and the use of Ritual Meditation. The intervening period between first publishing this book in January 2014 and mid-2015 has been the most pivotal period of my life. Something profound definitely happened! My knowledge and experience have grown immensely, especially in the use of Ritual Meditation to experience altered states of consciousness, and in cognitive and transcendental healing. I also developed a scientific understanding of earthquakes, volcanism, global climate change, and Earth as a living biosystem orbiting its parental Sun. I was able to experience love and its impermanence, which opened my heart and mind and kindled my desire to heal and spiritually awaken. I travelled 20,000km on my motorcycle visiting pyramids in Central America, which further cemented the views and findings of this book. 2014 was the biggest year in my life, until 2015 came along, and the events of both years influenced the second edition of this book.

Ritual Meditation by itself is not likely to yield sustaining healing and awakening benefits, unless you manifest self-realization automatically. Ideally, Ritual Meditation should be integrated into a broader healing, spiritual, and lifestyle plan that supports self-inquiry and self-revelation. You come to understand that healing is synonymous with conducting transcendental self-inquiry and self-realization, and changing the seat of your consciousness to the higher self. When you experience transcendental self-realization it feels as if you solve a paradoxical self-identity riddle and awaken to the fact that you are in fact your eternal higher self, and not your space-time constrained ego awareness and the fictions it has created.

When I started my healing journey at the winter solstice sunrise of 2014, I knew nothing of the above. I intuitively developed a path to healing that was about helping paint my ego's self-image and identifying remedies to my ego's repetitive and counterproductive patterns of behavior. This defined who I was with brutal honesty and humility, the nature of my family and important relationships, and the big issues that required personal work. I call this cognitive self-inquiry and healing, and it's the slow train to healing. Spiritual healing makes the need for cognitive healing simply vanish, and it co-opts its own brain circuitries, which are different from the ego's default brain circuitries (i.e., the default mode network). I think this is how innate spiritual qualities such as loving-kindness, compassion, acceptance, forgiveness, non-judging, and equanimity can begin to innately manifest in your life after spiritual awakening.

Cognitive self-inquiry is an important part of this healing journey because it permits you to honestly elucidate your ego self-image, that is, who you really are in this earthly-ego realm. You must do this with honesty and humility because these are two of the most important attributes that a person must have in order to make this healing journey. Originally I thought healing was all about identifying my problematic and recurrent issues and developing new beliefs, behaviors, and knowledge to bring about cognitive change over time. Cognitive self-inquiry helps you connect very deeply with who you think you are (i.e., ego self image) and the reason you believe you need to heal. In transcendental states of consciousness you will then refute this ego image. This higher self-refutation of the ego consciousness, outside of space and time, leads to transcendental self-realization, that is, your spiritual awakening and healing.

I experienced a lot of abuse as a child, and this had a big impact on me. It gave me a bit of a defensive / offensive edge if emotionally triggered by significant or repeated disrespect, dishonesty, selfishness, abuse, trying to control me, breach of trust, etc. When provoked I tend to be direct and can shame, blame, become critical, and on big issues (important boundaries or values) I can be demanding or controlling. I have been known to sabotage important relationships in order to create my exit from unhealthy situations I have no control over. I came to realize that when others or I fail to respect my really important relationship values, I can become emotionally triggered which sets off a cascade of counterproductive behaviors. Something experienced in a recent intimate relationship made me feel deeply betrayed. This undermined trust for me in a most fundamental way and it triggered counterproductive emotional responses in both of us in the ensuing months that neither of us had any control over, which in turn snowballed and led to both our lives falling apart. An unimaginably deep desire to heal arose from this because my sadness was so profound.

Whatever happens, sooner or later we have to do the deep personal work, which means we need to lift the lid on the past, and look at the role of early life experiences and relationships on our lives and relationships today. These early life experiences impact our present-day, counterproductive, ego-driven beliefs and attitudes, which in turn shape our behaviors and emotional responses in our present-day relationships. This self-revelation is not rocket science, but I concede it's not easy either, and our egos can do a great job of finding excuses not to do this work. I've worked very hard to elucidate my past's influence on my life today, and I've reccived professional help to better understand and remedy this. Trust that your fears of looking deep within will evaporate if you approach them with self-love, compassion, forgiveness, and a commitment to heal. Fear is a trick of the imposturous ego mind as it tries to prevent you from awakening to your simultaneously ever-present higher self. Why is this so? Because the ego knows that its days of pervasive influence are numbered.

A Mind Transformation Plan for Spiritually Awakening & Healing

This chapter provides you with my *Mind Transformation Plan*, which integrates Ritual Meditation and Transcendental Self-Inquiry into a broader plan for healing and self-realization. This is designed to create a more connected, sacred, mind-nurturing, healthy context in which to undertake self-inquiry, spiritual awakening and healing. Whether you suffer from one of the various psychological issues already discussed, or you wish to spiritually awaken and evolve, we all have an ego, and our higher self is knowingly connected with pure consciousness in eternity. These windows on consciousness are there to be explored if we are to profoundly heal and spiritually awaken, i.e., transcendentally self-realize. The implication of transcendental self-realization is that you avoid the need for karmic rebirth after death, which means you will attain spiritual immortality.

Psychedelics have proven beneficial to people suffering death anxiety, psychological damage consequent to childhood abuse and trauma, depression and anxiety, and chemical addictions because they help us understand who we really are in eternity, and beyond the ego's temporary façade. We come to comprehend through direct experience our divinity, infinity, eternity, capacity for unconditional and infinite love, and how we are all One connected in Unity. In experiencing Satcitananda and heart and other chakra activations we experience unconditional and infinite love, and we become aware that we are the expression of that love and have the infinite capacity to create that same love in the life we manifest.

Through experiences of transcendental self-realization, unity awareness of pure consciousness, Satcitananda (being-consciousness-bliss), and chakra and kundalini activations we can profoundly heal and spiritually awaken. Knowing you are eternally and infinitely loved by pure consciousness anchors you like no other experience. The key is realizing how the ego consciousness develops and then hijacks our window on consciousness as young children, obscuring the higher self. Once you achieve this self-realization it's not hard to see why humans suffer from death anxiety, depression, anxiety, bipolar disorder, schizophrenia, personality and behavioral disorders, and why we develop chemical addictions.

Some Words of Caution

I would **strongly discourage anyone** jumping straight into Ritual Meditation and the use of high or transcending doses of psychedelics. Why? Because you **are best advised to test the waters with a low dose** (1-2 grams of dry psilocybin magic mushrooms, or 10-20 grams wet weight, always start at the lowest dose) of psilocybin magic mushrooms a couple of times in the months preceding your first Ritual Meditation. This helps to accustom you to their effects, develop the beginnings of a good relationship with them (prayers, intention, gratitude and general self-talk are useful for this), practice meditation under their influence, and allows us to process the surface psychological material from our past – what I call the low hanging fruit providing relatively simple issue resolutions (i.e., letting go of emotional issues, forgiveness, resolve to act positively in the future etc.). In my experience people tend to have more positive transcendental experiences once this initial material is processed, whereupon you can try the full blown Ritual Meditation.

I am an advocate of being fully responsible for my own health, be it physical, emotional, or psychological. My instinct as a veterinarian says we should seek professional help when required to ensure we receive the best possible medical or psychotherapeutic care we can afford. I take full responsibility for driving my own healing process, while deferring to the professional's expertise. I disclosed to various expert professionals (counselors, coaches) that I've worked with that I am on a quest to heal, and I let them know what I'm doing upfront.

In the context of healing and awakening, medical help or psychotherapy should be supplemented with a healthy and spiritual lifestyle that supports cognitive and transcendental self-inquiry and self-revelation. This lifestyle should ideally integrate meditation and yoga, and the unlearning of old dogma, beliefs and behaviors while acquiring new knowledge, attitudes, and behaviors. Why is this important? Because however we heal, we're going to need a new repertoire of beliefs, behaviors, and communication skills, while simultaneously defining and honoring our personal values. Perhaps we might also need to brush up on what constitutes successful relationship behaviors and attitudes. The ego also comes to know that I am now aware of its dramas—whereupon I ask, which I is thinking, doing, or saying that something in that specific moment? I laugh at myself more and more now!

I've noticed since my awakening that at this early stage innate, spiritual qualities manifest and emerge from a healthier and more loving, positive, and kinder mind. There's little drama going on in my mind anymore, which means I have deep inner peace and tranquility, and I am almost always in the Now. I have more time for people, I listen to them more and give of my time, and I have discovered patience where before there was little. The moment is, and I simply am, and I like how that is and feels. Re-education provides new options for creating your life after the seat of consciousness shifts to the higher self.

We are greatly assisted by opening ourselves to spiritual and psychology books and other media, and by working with professional psychotherapists, healers, and coaches. An open and flexible mind is useful, and is assisted greatly by psychedelics. By promoting a healthy body-mind-soul connection and obtaining professional help if required, while engaging in spiritual practices (meditation, yoga, etc.) we can begin to elucidate our imposturous ego mind's influence on our lives.

The medical and spiritual benefits of psychedelics, in my view, are generally not well understood, other than at the fringe of medical research or by those who have personally explored their use. I therefore provide you with a select list of medical psychedelic publication hyperlinks via [my website](http://tinyurl.com/otxoywj) (http://tinyurl.com/otxoywj), which you can review if you're interested. I believe there is a need for good information if one is to be empowered to make good decisions and choices. This is particularly important today, when physicians and psychotherapists are largely unaware of the promising and emerging clinical data associated with psychedelic treatments, let alone the pathways of spirituality. This is because clinical testing only recommenced in the last decade or so, and so this information is not yet in the medical mainstream.

One of the key issues we face today is a lack of medical and legal access to psychedelics. This sits over a mass of misinformation about their use (see The Significance Of The 1960s Psychedelic Era) and the medical benefits thereof. This lack of access to psychedelics is unlikely to change in the foreseeable future. What this means is that people do not have access to alternative or potentially superior treatment options for their psychological maladies. And likewise they don't have access to a process for the intended safe use of psychedelics, or for delivering mind and healing transformation benefits.

At this juncture I would like to clarify a few important things. I am not advocating that you should use psychedelics. I am instead advocating that you should seek professional help for your medical, psychological, or emotional condition(s) if they exist, and identify approaches to healing or best managing these conditions using conventional approaches. Whatever you may choose to do with psychedelics should be in addition to conventional approaches, or after you have no other treatment options left to you. The combination of the new intervention on top of an established standard of care is a basic principle of regulatory-directed pharmaceutical drug development, and makes good sense. Additionally, it can be beneficial to seek professional help to identify your repetitive patterns of counterproductive behaviors in relationships, which in turn helps you understand where you need to heal, and re-educate yourself.

Psychedelics have their place, but not without understanding of who you think you are (i.e., ego self-image, character, traits, behaviors, relationship outcomes, world view, etc.) as your first priority. You can promote a healing and awakening environment by living a healthy and spiritual lifestyle. If you are of the disposition to explore Ritual Meditation, have thoroughly researched the use of psychedelics as medicines, have comprehended and respected the health and safety principles outlined in Chapter 10, have understood your country's laws regarding psychedelic use and cultivation and fully accepted any legal risks you run for breaching those laws, Accepting Your Legal, Civil and Moral Responsibilities and Liabilities, and you then chose to use these medicaments-sacraments to spiritually awaken and profoundly heal, then this book can help you do that. **Please review** Chapter 10's section Ensure Your Health and Safety (and Legal Responsibilities and Liabilities).

Right now you have few, if any, options to access a safe process for using psychedelics should you wish to self-treat your psychological or emotional maladies or utilize sacred rituals to self-realize and spiritually awaken. That is a big problem and one I struggled with myself until I discovered Ritual Meditation and became its test pilot. To date I haven't witnessed or experienced a process for using psychedelics that is safe, effective, and repeatable, and applies a good understanding of the biology of altered states of consciousness other than as part of Ritual Meditation (as I practice it). Additionally, such experiences impart little process knowledge to the participant. The shaman or healer generally withholds process knowledge as a source of control and a means of making money, or else doesn't fully understand it. This is one of the reasons I sought to develop Ritual Meditation and share it—*to provide you with a standardized set of processes that you control.*

The bottom line is that we are all, each one of us, individually responsible for our own health and healing, and for managing our quality of life. We also each bare individual responsibility for contravening the laws of the country in which we reside when purchasing or growing magic mushrooms or other hallucinogens. That said, I must add that I wanted to heal so badly that no one was going to tell me what I could or could not do.

What my **Ritual Meditation** and **Transcendental Self-Inquiry** methods and my **Mind Transformation Plan** offers is access to a sacred ritual methods which ancient priesthoods and leaders once utilized to support great nation-states and empires over the course of thousands of years. Ritual Meditation and Transcendental Self-Inquiry transformed my mind, and as a result my need for profound healing simply vanished. I have been permanently transcended, more or less, since the summer solstice 2015 ritual, and my crown chakra buzzes 24/7. As I write this, some ten weeks after the ritual, my seat of consciousness still sits with my higher self (by default, by and large), and I am now aware of my ego arisings most of the time. This is a most joyous, peaceful, quieting experience of simply being, as I am (and identityless) awareness, in the Now moment-by-moment.

The Potential Benefits of Ritual Meditation To Society

What are the benefits of Ritual Meditation? The Ritual Meditation process has the potential to catalyze and accelerate one's spiritual awakening and profound healing.

Two categories of people can benefit from using psychedelics, ideally as part of a broader mind transformation plan (i.e., **Mind Transformation Plan**):

1) People with psychological maladies for which current treatments are largely ineffective. The clinical data developed between the 1950s and 1970s, prior to the banning of psychedelics, as well as that beginning to emerge from clinical studies conducted more recently, highlights a number of medical and clinical opportunities to better help broad segments of society.

   Such maladies of the mind include people suffering from death anxiety and its associated existential crisis. That is, those who ask themselves such questions as Who am I? (the most important question of our lives). What was the outcome of my life? What happens after death? Awareness of important relationship issues often emerges during death anxiety, and you come to realize you are offered important opportunities for forgiveness and resolution.

People suffering from psychological trauma associated with childhood physical, mental, and emotional abuse, sexual abuse, incest and rape, and post-traumatic stress can also potentially benefit from psychedelic treatment. Psychedelics have also alleviated chemical addictions and dysregulated emotions such as depression and anxiety. These conditions are obviously big issues that invariably become impediments in our lives, and which prevent honest and humble self-inquiry and the opportunity for self-realization. Right now the treatment options available underserve sufferers' needs.

It's beyond the scope of this new edition to fully explore the medical rationale for the use of psychedelics, but this does exist. A growing body of clinical data supporting the psychological healing role of psychedelics is slowly becoming available, now that clinical testing has resumed. This complements the pioneering work conducted from the 1950s to the 1970s. You might wish to review a **select list of medical publications** available via my website (http://tinyurl.com/otxoywj) to gain provisional insights into the potential for treatments using psychedelics.

2) People pursuing spiritual awakening and transcendental self-realization. People today are already attempting to change their consciousness using meditation and yoga practices, both within and outside organized faiths. An opportunity exists for meditators to consider other outcomes beyond calm abiding or mindfulness, and to understand that meditation can be supplemented (i.e., via sacred rituals) to access our higher states of consciousness so that we may conduct transcendental self-inquiry and self-realize.

Spiritual awakening is the same as spiritual healing, but without the belief in the need to heal. It is still self-inquiry, i.e., who am I? That is "I am consciousness" witnessed through three windows inside and outside of space and time. Two states of consciousness are real and the truth (higher self, pure consciousness as Unity awareness), while one is the counterfeit impostor to be revealed upon transcendental self-inquiry, and is what we call the ego mind. Your higher self has always been there, and you simply need to be quiet in order to discern it. Be in the Now! Meditation becomes a useful means of revealing your higher self in day-to-day life, but transcendental self-realization is the means for permanently shifting the window of consciousness to the higher self.

Ritual Meditation enables you to bypass the need for ultra-adept meditation skills to naturally access altered states of consciousness. This accelerates the learning curve for self-inquiry, self-revelation, and spiritual awakening, and ultimately eliminates the need for healing.

Ritual Meditation as Part of a Life Transformation Plan

Some Orienting Perspectives

In hindsight, there's merit in elaborating on how one might integrate the use of Ritual Meditation into one's life beyond simply accessing altered states of consciousness. I think my learning curve provides important examples worth sharing and learning from.

There is no information publically available to show us how we might integrate this profound sacred ritual know-how in our lives, nor a set of instructions on its use. This know-how was lost over time, and/or potentially hidden from our common human awareness by taboos, stigmas and misinformation. The good news is I've brought it back by reverse-engineering the ancient priesthoods' process for accessing altered states of consciousness. Ritual Meditation is that process, and can be used for accessing our higher states of consciousness, in which we undertake transcendental self-inquiry to self-realize, awaken, and eliminate our need to heal. Even without transcendental self-realization the psychological healing benefits are impressive in terms of how much forgiveness can be achieved, both for you and others who are in need of it.

As a Ritual Meditation test pilot I would like to share my discoveries and growing knowledge, so that others may benefit in a similar, profound manner. A lot happened to me within a very short space of time, beginning in 2012 and then especially since my 2014 winter solstice Ritual Meditation experience. During this Ritual Meditation it was impressed into my Unity aware consciousness that being self-realized en masse was the destiny of every sentient species throughout the Universe. During my summer solstice 2015 Ritual Meditation, and upon self-realizing that I am my higher consciousness, I was made aware that this self-realization was the highest accomplishment a human being could achieve and was the raison d'etre for evolving life.

A Vision for Self Realization, Healing and Awakening

Why would we wish to spiritually awaken and transform our lives? In order, ultimately, to become self-realized (and know that I am my higher self and not my ego consciousness), profoundly heal, and to stop our ego-induced suffering. Upon achieving self-realization you become spiritually immortal after death, that is you escape the need for future karmic rebirth.

In using psychedelics (both low and higher transcending doses) we are afforded an opportunity to accelerate the self-realization of our higher self consciousness (I am). The need, desire, and intention to heal, with deep humility and self-honesty, are the most essential requirements for this journey. Spiritual healing is transcendental self-inquiry (who am I?) followed by self-revelation that I am my higher self, witnessed from outside of space and time, and I am not that, i.e., my imposturous ego consciousness which exists only until we die. In refuting the impermanent ego illusion from the perspective of your eternal higher self in altered states of consciousness, it dawns on you there is nothing to heal.

As we do our cognitive self-inquiry in normal states of consciousness, between sacred times, we should be reminded that our eternal higher self is already awake, witnessing our ego-driven life, and that the higher self is silently ever-present and unchanging. Being in the present moment (the "Now") is important to being aware of your higher self inside space and time. Actually, the Now is the only moment of time you'll experience it. Effective meditation is a very useful way of witnessing your higher self. It brings you into the Now through mindful awareness of your breath, of all your senses, of your body and emotional arisings, and the general environment. You simply rest in that composite awareness of the comings and goings of things, and you witness their impermanence without attachment. In that Now moment I am pure awareness without identity, simply observing everything and it feels like bliss.

Ritual Meditation takes meditation to a whole new level, by ritually dissolving the ego awareness to reveal awareness of your higher self. Depending on your experience, this can be both inside and outside space and time. From this higher self perspective, outside of space and time, merging in Unity awareness is possible. The profound nature of this experience, accompanied by an indescribably intense bliss-love-awareness for a seeming eternity, literally transforms your mind and you experience great healing. You surely know you are unconditionally loved, and that bliss-love is unimaginably indescribable and beyond all known earthly love.

The partial promise of psychedelics is to accelerate self-awareness and yield a more flexible and adaptive mind for the unlearning of the old while learning the new. You need to make reading and self-education a daily event to make the most of this period of flexibility. In my view, cognitive self-adjustment via the unlearning/learning offered by books, media, counseling, and teachers, is ineffective for deep intransigents like myself, and is unlikely to lead to transcendental self-revelation and changing the seat of consciousness to the higher self. Why? Because it's incredibly hard to change old, counterproductive habits of behavior while our ego is in control of our consciousness. This is especially true within the aspiring and stressful lives we lead, or with the maladies of the mind from which some of us suffer. Change is particularly difficult if our ego minds were programmed during an abusive and traumatic childhood (like my own). Ultimately, in such circumstances, our tenacious egos will sabotage our attempt at transformation.

Psychedelics, if properly used, are not an escape, but offer us a chance to peek deep inside our minds, and transcendentally self-inquire (Who am I?) and spiritually awaken. Depending on a person's willingness and capacity to view their ego's self-image, we are offered powerful tools to cognitively self-inquire. Intransigent people like me need extraordinary help, which is probably why I was motivated to develop and explore the Ritual Meditation process. Ritual Meditation literally transformed my mind in the space of four hours. This was the amount of time that passed from the moment I started my Ritual Meditation to my exiting the meditation room with a transformed mind. I am permanently (perhaps) transcended now, which is a rather blissful, joyous, peaceful, and tranquil state of mind, and my mind is silent and effortlessly present in the Now; I realize I simply am. From this perspective on consciousness it's hard to even conceive of wishing to have my ego return to the seat of consciousness.

Ritual Meditation and low dose psychedelics should be combined with cognitive and transcendental self-inquiry in order to help you define who you really are. At the cognitive level this self-enquiry should, ideally, adopt two approaches. First, you can focus on cognitive self-revelation and unlearning/learning to help you define your ego self-image and identify remedies for repetitive counterproductive patterns of behavior. You should realize, however, that this is not spiritual healing. Second, as you gain experience, during sacred time you can focus on conducting transcendental self-inquiry during Ritual Meditation. There are no promises, but perhaps you will transcendentally self-realize. The cognitive process partially mitigates the risk that it may take time for you to experience transcendental self-revelation and profound healing. At least progress can still be made in one's life and relationships, as this learning is all good material for positive change.

My Ritual Meditation learning curve took two and one-half years before I experienced this ultimate transcendental self-realization, though only six months from the winter solstice of 2014 by means of a good process, directed intentions, and some serious dedication to healing.

My Mind Transformation Plan

Ritual Meditation is best combined with both cognitive and transcendental self-inquiry. You wish to know your ego self-image in all its naked glory: Who am I? Over time, by using Ritual Meditation, you will have the opportunity to refute this ego self-image ("that is not I") from the perspective of your higher self. You come to automatically realize that your ego self-image is an impermanent impostor when viewed outside of space and time by the higher self. The seat of consciousness changes, and it dawns on your awareness that *there is nothing to heal*. Healing is an illusion of ego consciousness and the fictions it creates.

Coming to that realization is the ultimate goal for Ritual Meditation, Transcendental Self-Inquiry and my Mind Transformation Plan.

To further Ritual Meditation's ultimate goal we need to create an environment throughout the year that is conducive to self-exploration and healing. You need to recognize who you are (ego, self-image) with honesty, humility, love, and compassion, because you are going to refute this ego image from the perspective of your higher self while in a transcendental state. You must also really desire to end your suffering, and know this from your very core—this is ***the most essential quality*** that a person who wishes to self-realize and heal must possess.

Having a good guru is invaluable too, because such a person usually became self-realized or enlightened without psychedelics. Find someone you can connect with (see this list[477]). These gurus have wise words, methods, and ways that we can all learn from. Gurus sit on the other side of a metaphorical Grand Canyon bridging a vast yet subtle divide in awareness.

A guru's predicament can be understood by someone who has experienced all three windows or eyes of consciousness, and has transcendentally self-realized. He or she then becomes permanently transcended, such that consciousness rests with the higher self. The concept that three windows on consciousness (ego, higher self, pure consciousness) are available to us is crucial to our spiritual awakening (see Chapter 9, "Consciousness, Healing, and the Meaning of Life").

I recently started watching Mooji, or Anthony Paul Moo-Young[478], a well-recognized, self-realized (i.e., enlightened) person, and I connected with the simplicity of his method of self-inquiry. In fact I only came to listen to Mooji on the day of my summer solstice 2015 Ritual Meditation. However, I connected with his methods via a friend for a few months prior to the summer solstice 2015. For this Ritual Meditation I adapted Mooji's method of self-inquiry and asked, Who am I? As it happened, for me the question naturally arose and it spontaneously greeted me on entry (from deep meditation) to the transcendental realm, and the answer was my mantra—I am. I adapted my ritual intention for transcendental self-inquiry, healing, and my wish was granted (thank you).

What follows is a set of important principles underpinning the *Mind Transformation Plan* for spiritual awakening-transformation and profound spiritual healing.

1) **Make the decision to stop the suffering:** Get into the mindset that you are responsible for your own life and the suffering and pain you have experienced in it, irrespective of what others have done or may do to you. It's not always an easy thing to accept, I know, but it's an important key to the healing journey and its ultimate revelation. That is, your ego mind's emotional beliefs and responses, feelings, thoughts, words, and behaviors, consequent to what has happened to you in life, are the real source from which your suffering arises.

   Making the decision to stop the suffering you cause, with deep humility, and feeling

that from your very core, is the first big step you must take.

By virtue of the gift of life we are all empowered to this end. We should avoid giving control of our mind to other people such as priests, shamans, gurus, friends, or partners. Why? Well, ask yourself honestly, how many people really operate from their higher self, know how to access their higher self, and don't have their own self-interest at heart?

Take control of your life and decide that you will become your authentic spiritual self, aligned with your deep inner heart-wisdom and higher self. That becomes a very powerful seed of intention that your higher self and pure consciousness will eventually germinate.

2) **Identify who you think you are:** To start with you really want to know "who am I?" and you want to know this from two perspectives, the ego's and the higher self. One day you might witness your higher self after dissolving your ego consciousness, and come to know who you really are. You will come to realize that there were always two coexistent windows on consciousness available to the human mind in this earthly realm, in space and time, but that one was long ago forgotten. The higher self is typically hidden from awareness by the

imposturous and pervasive ego, beginning in our early childhood.

Before you realize this, you're going to first have to identify who you believe you are, using cognitive self-inquiry. That is, who you really are in this earthly realm (i.e., your ego self-image, your relationships, your perceived issues, your worldview, etc.). Why? So that during transcendental self-inquiry your higher self will know with absolute honesty, humility, and forgiveness who in its entirety will be refuted.

The preparatory part of self-inquiry, i.e., the cognitive self-image and remedies for your counterproductive cycles of behavior, will require you to be honest with yourself, and could involve psychological or relationship counseling to reveal the core issues that are causing you to suffer. Use all this learning to help you make good decisions about your healing and spiritual development. Be the champion of your own healing, and make it happen. Such efforts will always pay dividends in your life. Life crises, such as the end of an intimate relationship, bereavement, a personal trauma, or an existential crisis, can open you to higher levels of self-awareness and provide a great catalyst for personal transformation. Life crises in reality are hidden gems for self-inquiry and self-revelation.

Such crises are often short-lived—so use these gifts wisely while they last!

There's an expression I am growing to like (although its hard to accept at times): **When you point the finger in blame at someone else, there's always three pointing back at you.** What that means is when another person or a situation is causing you emotional pain, i.e., triggers you, ask yourself "What does this teach me about myself and the demanding beliefs I have underpinning my strong emotions?" This really helps you to see yourself in a different light, and you begin to laugh at yourself and your ego dramas.

Invariably we find something that was perceived as traumatic, controlling, deficient, or suddenly removed in our childhood or youth. This could be the withholding or absence of love, physical-mental-emotional-sexual abuse, or repeated transgressions of important personal boundaries by a member of your family, a guardian, or someone else. All of these early life events shape our ego-bound beliefs and attitudes that we are often blind to as adults, and these can impact our adult emotional responses.

At some stage during early childhood development (circa 2-3 years of age) our innate higher self becomes veiled from our awareness. The ego mind develops out of its emerging self-identity and its illusion of separateness from the world around it. Out of our childhood need for self-preservation we develop fixed beliefs and attitudes after hurtful events. Being demanding (i.e., insisting that another person should or should not do something) can be a consequence, or perhaps our thinking becomes black and white, or we may exaggerate the effect of someone else's actions or words. This unresolved or unprocessed emotional damage can be re-triggered in later life by relationships and other life events. By understanding what triggers your emotions you learn what needs to be cognitively healed, and you also help to elucidate your ego self-image.

The practice of non-judgment and acceptance can also be very helpful to stem the tide of the ego's influence before you begin to spiritually awaken and heal. You begin to realize that your proclivity for unconscious judging is the root cause of your ensuing emotional responses and suffering.

I have found that low dose psychedelics (in LSD psychotherapy this is referred to as a psycholytic dose) are very powerful tools for helping in ego self-revelation. This can help us become aware of what we've done or said to others, or had done or said to us by others (and especially by family), and we tend to do so with more empathy, love, forgiveness and compassion than we could otherwise achieve. Similarly, we can begin to understand how an event in our earlier lives, for example, trauma, abuse, conflicts etc., can impact our relationships and lives today. Additionally, we become more aware of the positive-negative balance of our thoughts, words, and behaviors and their impact on other people and our own being.

Low-dose psychedelics also make it possible to switch off the mind to a much greater degree, be present in the moment with a heightened sense of awareness and connectivity, and at the same time allow us to witness consciousness through the higher self in the Now. Glimpsing this higher self is important because it will come as no shock later when you connect with this awareness outside of space and time, while in altered states of consciousness. A healthy and spiritual lifestyle becomes a natural part of this healing and awakening journey, and you feel much better for this.

During the latter part of my healing journey (March-May 2015), I consumed low-dose psychedelics (San Pedro cactus, magic mushrooms, or LSD) three Sundays per month, and combined this with long periods of meditation (different techniques), inner revelation work and silently being present in the Now in nature. However, I avoid psychedelics one month before conducting Ritual Meditation at the solstices or equinoxes, because frequent psychedelic use can create accumulated brain tolerance. This is especially so with magic mushrooms.

Even without profound Unity and higher self-awareness, psychedelics will provide an afterglow effect that creates an expanded mind effect or outcome in the days, weeks, and months after their initial effect—i.e., inner peace, reduced anxiety, positivity toward the future, mindfulness, adaptability, diminished addictions, etc. No other medicinal drugs confer this positive afterglow effect.

Low-dose psychedelics are not for everyone and can precipitate mild sadness and anxiety. Understanding your sadness and angst is how self-revelations actually happen. This angst may hang over you for days or weeks as you process arising psychological material and begin to transform your outlook on life. In my experience, this angst dissolves when I become aware of it and embrace its lessons. Sometimes, we can't understand our difficult emotions or angst, and so simply by saying; "I don't understand my pain, please help me"[479] is enough to invite in the help of our higher self and pure consciousness.

The truth is, we all need to make peace with ourselves and with the people we've wronged or who have wronged us (be they dead or alive). I don't mean that we have to make direct contact with such people, although that can be helpful. I mean that we should mentally recognize the issue and person involved, drop any judgment, forgive them and yourself, and apologize for our part in co-creating the traumatic circumstances that linger in our minds. Your higher self and pure consciousness will automatically do the rest. We can then release ourselves from the pain we hold. We either do this now, or when we die; the choice is yours and there's not really any escape from it, especially not when it comes to the big issues.

In my view, forgiveness does not mean you need to have future contact with that person (but it might). It means that you forgive yourself and the other person, and that you simply let go of the need to judge, while accepting the situation and its lessons for what they are. Cherish it and let it go.

I have found forgiving one of the hardest things to do in my life. I went a lifetime holding on to my anger before I could forgive. The good news is that psychedelics, if approached sacredly, safely, and sparingly with good intentions, simply wipe the ego slate clean—even without transcendental self-realization. The forgiveness I found was instant and effortless (the need for self-awareness and honesty excepted). I know I would not have achieved that level of profound forgiveness and acceptance within such a short timeframe without Ritual Meditation, Transcendental Self-Inquiry and low-dose psychedelics.

Be kind and loving to yourself and all others. I find this is starting to become more innate in myself since self-realization. And especially so since my childhood anger simply vanished at the winter solstice sunrise 2014 Ritual Meditation, to be replaced by forgiveness and love[480]. I find unconditional love toward myself and others happening with a greater intensity and innateness since the summer solstice 2015. The helpful thing to remember is that we all make mistakes, and while other people are generally trying their best, they will not always meet our needs—and that's OK. Being reminded of this helps us undermine emotion-triggering beliefs and to become aware of our habit for judging, while at the same time generating acceptance.

Cognitive therapy (i.e., Rational Emotive Behavior Therapy[481]) provides methods for undermining emotional triggering beliefs and helping you to release and better manage difficult emotions. We cannot change the past, all we can do is understand it, remove our judgments, forgive and accept it and ourselves, and then move on. If we adopt that attitude toward ourselves, we are more likely to do so with other people. I can state from direct experience that pure consciousness (God) forgives and loves everyone and everything, whether we realize it or not. I know this because several times now I've experienced the most indescribable bliss-love-awareness and forgiveness indelibly impressed into my consciousness for an eternity while in Unity awareness of pure consciousness. I now know what unconditional love feels like, and it's hard not to be moved by these experiences.

And it's okay to cry too! Crying releases our painful memories. I was brought up that boys and men don't cry, but now I know that's not true. Crying is a very powerful act of releasing and healing. So very powerful!

3) **Unlearning the old and learning the new:** We need to do this for two main reasons; first to help our cognitive or ego self-inquiry and self-revelation, and second because we need to learn new beliefs, attitudes, and behaviors in order to help us create the rest of our lives. Reading,

listening to, and watching both spiritual and psychological media is really important, because it helps us correctly orient the mind spiritually, and gives us practical cognitive tools (psychotherapy, counseling, new beliefs and knowledge) to assist change.

Spiritual wisdom (i.e., Eastern and monotheistic religions' mystic traditions) orients you to your higher self and what constitutes a spiritual way of life, while psychological education can help us better understand our emotional triggers, behaviors, and relationship dynamics. Understanding our emotional triggers and learning new psychotherapy tools, e.g., dialectical behavior therapy and rational emotive behavior therapy, is invaluable for this cognitive healing journey. Seeking professional psychotherapy (difficult emotions, addictions, depression, anxiety etc.) and relationship counseling is also helpful.

Having a good spiritual guide or guru is invaluable (see this list[482]), but I caution that such people are incredibly rare. If the person is not a recognized guru, then observe first: does he or she display spiritual qualities innately? And with equanimity? Important qualities spiritual guides should possess innately, if they are self-realized, would include loving-kindness, compassion, generosity, and spiritual and mind insight. Sometimes gurus talk an abstract language that makes them hard to comprehend. Try to find someone you can really connect with, who you can connect with to their teachings, and who provides you with practical, easy-to-comprehend tools that support your spiritual self-inquiry.

By and large I am cautious of spiritual healers who claim to channel healing or guidance from the spirit world, and who say they can modulate your emotional or other energy fields to heal you. They exist, but they are very, very rare. Why? Because this type of healing does not involve the expansion of your consciousness so that you become aware of your higher self, witnessed both inside and outside of space and time. Without the expansion of consciousness any healing will likely be short-lived, and possibly even be nothing more than a placebo effect.

Avoid confusing someone's self-professed spiritual or healing capabilities and their use of spiritual language with genuine enlightenment. Ask that person whether have they accessed altered states of consciousness, and if they have, how did they achieve this? Likewise, just because someone is a meditation or yoga instructor does not mean that person operates from the higher self. Bad advice and guidance will lead you astray and take you years or even many lifetimes to awaken to and overcome.

4) **Develop a healthy lifestyle**: This embraces eating a healthy diet as much as possible, doing some exercise and yoga as often as you practically can, and avoiding or at least minimizing your consumption of toxic or addictive substances. Start off by doing what you can, observe the effects, and then expand on that until it becomes your lifestyle.

   a) **Healthy diet**: Drink more fresh water than you currently do. Try to eat as much raw fruit and vegetables as possible to help you reestablish more alkaline body chemistry and give your body the full nutritive value of the food. Minimize your consumption of processed foods, too many complex carbohydrates, simple sugars, and artificial ingredients. Try eating less animal protein that involves the killing and/or cruelty to animals. Be more aware that when you do eat meat or animal protein that the animal while alive was also connected to pure consciousness. I use this more and more to guide my food menu and recipe choices, and I feel much healthier and vital for eating less animal protein.

b) **Develop an exercise regime**: Perform a variety of exercises that make you feel good and you enjoy. Focus on working the muscles and heart, and on developing flexibility while being careful not to injure the joints (impact damage). Be mindful when you are doing them.

c) **Yoga**: Yoga is integral to the spiritual practice of Eastern traditions. Yoga means union of our limited individual self with our supreme, unlimited, and universal self. Yoga is a lifestyle embracing a clean and healthy diet, good exercise, meditation and the daily practice of asanas (or yoga postures). There are many different categories of Yoga: Raja Yoga, Karma Yoga, Jnana Yoga, Bhakti Yoga, Kriya Yoga, Kundalini Yoga, etc. Yoga works mainly on our nervous system, and will automatically help bring to the surface (for dissolution) all of the trapped, neurotic energy patterns that are lodged inside of our emotional or astral bodies i.e., the ethereal bodies invisibly supporting our physical bodies. This trapped energy makes our minds restless, and causes us to feel anxiety. Yoga postures can help us establish unity within our bodies so that we feel more quiet and peaceful, and have an easier time meditating.

Ideally we should do yoga before our meditation.

d) **Minimize toxic consumptions**: Alcohol and addictive drugs do not mix well with consciousness development, and can be destructive in one's life and relationships. I know this only too well. Psychologists have stated that our drug and alcohol addictions and consumptions are our intuitive clamoring to experience altered states of consciousness, and stem as well from a lack of unconditional love in our lives. What I discovered was that intermittent transcending and low-dose psychedelics almost switched off my appetite for alcohol.

If its altered states of consciousness you clamor for, then get the real thing. If it's your perception of a lack of unconditional love in your life; know you are already unconditionally loved by pure consciousness. Better still, why not experience pure consciousness using Ritual Meditation so that you can have that indelibly emblazoned in your consciousness forevermore—I am unconditionally loved and am the reflection of that love, on Earth, in all that I feel, think, say and do! This experience plants an incredibly powerful seed that begins to positively transform your mind.

5) **Daily Meditation**: While meditation is often promoted as a mindfulness or spiritual practice or technique, I find it useful to understand specifically what we are trying to achieve with meditation. Meditation is an incredibly powerful practice that helps us become aware of our higher self in the present moment, while witnessing or observing the activities of our imposturous ego mind, that is, our arising feelings, emotions, and thoughts. In addition, it allows us to observe our body and its senses. This, over time, results in improved mindfulness and self-control. As a result of this understanding, you can actually be washing the dishes or watering the garden and be meditating as well. Meditation is not about specific postures and breathing exercises; these are simply an effective means of achieving higher self-awareness in the Now.

A friend of mine[483], a self-realized guru who was present for my awakening, always asked me, "Which I is saying or doing that right now? Is that the higher self "I" or the "I" driven by the ego? I found this a very good question for provoking self-inquiry and self-awareness; it also makes me laugh at myself when I see my ego mind's fictions and dramas arising. Without higher self-realization and the seat of consciousness changing from the ego to the higher self, then you will need to work on stabilizing your awareness of the higher self in the present moment. This is where formal meditation is very helpful.

Learn and practice daily meditation because you will need it for conducting Ritual Meditation (on the solstices and equinoxes) and the development of mindfulness. In my view meditation should be taught to every child from a very young age. This is not about religion-spirituality, but the development of emotional intelligence (mindfulness), that is, self-awareness, self-regulation, empathy, effective communication skills, and motivation for life above the norm.

Please seek expert guidance when learning to meditate, and read books and observe experts. Assess a teacher's expertise by asking if they have ever transcended using meditation. Observe if they radiate with equanimity great exemplary spiritual qualities such as mindfulness, loving-kindness, compassion, and acceptance. Do they have a peaceful tranquility about them, innately in their words and actions? I have only met one meditation instructor who had routinely transcended, and he's the friend who guided me toward self-inquiry to discern my higher self during meditation and in day-to-day Now moments. You become present and ask which I is doing or saying that in that moment (i.e., ego or higher self)? Others whom I've quizzed never considered altered states of consciousness as a possible outcome for meditation. So I am cautious of what is taught by others, and of any claimed meditation expertise.

Please read *Learning to Meditate* in Chapter 10 if you'd like to learn how to do it. I started to learn meditation the day I nearly drowned (autumn equinox 2012) and underwent a near-death experience (at Lake Atitlan, Guatemala). I first transcended three months later using the Ritual Meditation process on the winter solstice of 2012 (end of the Mayan calendar).

I do not consider myself an expert, however I have self-developed my own meditation skills, and learned more through my own natural inclination for observing details, listening to my deep intuitive voice, and through possessing a mind attuned to innovation and process development. This has been further augmented by meditation guidance (higher self) received during altered states of consciousness. This guidance was used to help generate chakra and kundalini activations, and assist my crown chakra activation during transcendental self-realization.

I most commonly use an eyes-closed technique, adapted from the Transcendental Meditation™ technique espoused by Maharishi Mahesh Yogi[484] and detailed in Chapter 10. I use this adaptation of his meditation technique (base technique) both with and without a mantra. If I use a mantra, it's only to silence my thoughts, and I use "I Am," "Let Go," or "I Love" 'I or Let' upon inspiration, 'Am, Go, or Love' upon expiration. The "I am" mantra is important to practice during meditation, so that you may use it in transcendental self-inquiry while in altered states of consciousness. I also use an eyes-open meditation variant of this base technique. Both eyes-open and eyes-closed meditations involve a number of variations such as 'focused attention". That is, focused on a visible object or your breath. When I focus on my breath I am best aware of gap between inspiration and expiration over your heart base/solar plexus region. I find that by focusing on the gap between my breaths is the quickest way to arrive at the present moment, which is where we witness the higher self.

Once a week I will use an eyes-open technique, sitting in front of a mirror looking between and slightly above my eyes in the third eye region. An 'open monitoring' technique involves meditating with your eyes open while monitoring a wider field of vision than a solitary object, and monitoring all five senses without attachment. I also use emotion-feeling and body awareness meditation for a few minutes before or after my base meditation technique, or as I feel like. These body-mind awareness meditations help me become more self-aware and/or quell any arising emotions (i.e., negative mind chatter about someone or something, etc.).

Eyes-closed meditation is the form you'll use for your Ritual Meditation (see below). The consequence of meditation is being aware of your higher self in the Now, and mindfulness as your experience progresses, i.e., improved self-awareness, self-regulation, empathy, and communication skills, as well as. If you become very adept at meditation you might even be able transcend without psychedelics.

6) **Conducting Ritual Meditation (see Chapter 10):** Please read the seventh principle on Ensure Your Health and Safety (and Legal Responsibilities and Liabilities) and respect this; this places *sacredness and safety foremost in our minds.*

Ritual Meditation is best conducted at sacred time. According to the concept of sacred time i.e., that the solstices and equinoxes naturally enhance alpha brainwave voltages emanating the frontal brain, we are offered four times a year when we may optimally conduct Ritual Meditation. We might also conduct Ritual Meditation at other times like at special full and new moons, and at eclipses. In my view, we should not force the exploration of the transcendental realm by conducting Ritual Meditation too frequently, and we should be grateful for all of our experiences. Everything is provided perfectly just when it's needed, so trust in how pure consciousness works. Its mission is to help you evolve your consciousness, so fully trust in this and it will be.

These are profoundly powerful experiences and take time to integrate into our day-to-day lives. We are trying to reveal, or allow to be revealed, our higher self by dissolving our ego consciousness. The next step is to stabilize the higher self's ever-present awareness as the seat of consciousness in the Now. If you achieve transcendental self-realization and your seat of consciousness permanently shifts, then you will permanently witness life through your higher self-consciousness.

Always remember that access to altered states and Unity states of consciousness is still by the grace of pure consciousness (God). These states of consciousness are not our God-given right to experience, though we are biologically programmed to experience these higher states of consciousness. I believe we have the best chance of experiencing these profound states of consciousness when we do the following:

Developing and communicating to pure consciousness a strong desire to heal (felt in our core), with deep humility, honesty, and a sacred intention, is the most important quality of a person wishing to transcendentally self-realize and heal. Then we must integrate all these principles to the best of our ability, and focus our good intentions on healing and our consciousness development on the betterment of other humans, other life, and our planet; and prepare for the Ritual Meditation properly (see Chapter 10).

I need to make an important emphasis. Ritual Meditation should really only be used up to four times a year (perhaps additional lunar related sacred times). However, before Ritual Meditation is ever used my preference is to "take it slow" and become acquainted with low doses of magic mushrooms (in nature, meditation, observing) first.

This permits you to make your connection with the magic mushrooms, become acquainted with your higher self (meditation), and learn to practice meditation under their influence.

I am sharing a set of principles that have the potential to help you heal and spiritually awaken. Transcendental self-inquiry and self-revelation are crucial to these outcomes. This is the reason we've marched through all these lifetimes accumulating our karmic baggage–to learn who we really are–and it's the most profound experience any sentient being can ever have. It's different from who you think you are!

It's worth emphasizing that Ritual Meditation should always be subordinate to a healthy and spiritual life style, and to cognitive self-inquiry and self-revelation. The above **Mind Transformation Plan** embraces all these mind and life-transforming principles.

I need to emphasize something here. I'm not talking about the cognitive adjustment of one's mind to the higher self consciousness, but real direct experience of our higher self through meditation, yoga, and by accessing altered states of consciousness. Arguably, a lot of self-help literature and media promotes a cognitive adjustment of the mind in order to realize one's higher self, i.e., you are instructed or advised on how to perceive, act, behave, think, or feel. This invariably comes from someone who had an epiphany or spontaneous enlightenment without fully knowing how it happened. Without a step-by-step process for achieving awareness of your higher self by dissolving your ego consciousness (which makes it easier to witness the higher self), you are very unlikely to achieve this state of self-realization, or enlightenment. It's such a rare event in a population or within a faith. When I read such books about enlightenment or listen to such media, it feels like I'm being called to from across the metaphorical Grand Canyon, but no one is giving me the bridge by which I can walk across that expansive yet very subtle divide.

Being instructed, coached or advised on how I must feel, think, speak, and behave has simply never created lasting healing or personal transformation in my life. Perhaps it's because I'm half a century old, and suffered a lot of abuse in my early life, which was compounded by some of my adult life experiences (i.e., relationships, addictions, and repetitive, counterproductive patterns of behavior). I was quite an intransigent before I discovered Ritual Meditation and low dose psychedelics, and started to get my act together (see my **Mind Transformation Plan**). I now reject the notion that it's impossible to change adult behavior and mindsets. In my view it's dangerous when people wrongly educate us that we cannot change our behaviors (as adults), because you simply give up trying (my case). Psychedelic experience tells us that we can indeed change. Change the seat of consciousness to the higher self, then brain circuitries supporting spiritual qualities will innately manifest.

As a consequence of these Ritual Meditation discoveries, i.e., the sacred ritual process, transcendental self-inquiry method, and self-realization, we now have access to ancient spiritual methods that can help us spiritually awaken and heal wounds of the mind. When we emerge back in this earthly realm, with the seat of consciousness shifted to the higher self, we can then comprehend the subtle divide between the higher self and ego when witnessed in the Now.

Here it is in a nutshell. To comprehend the paradox of this very subtle divide and to spiritually awaken, you need to witness consciousness through each of its three windows. Two windows of consciousness simultaneously coexist in the earthly body (higher self, ego), two windows are outside of space and time (higher self, pure consciousness). The higher self window on consciousness bridges space and time, resting as One in eternity, and in the earthly body for as long as it lives. The dawning realization there are two windows on consciousness witnessed via this earthly body is a truly profound revelation i.e., rapturous ecstasy.

I knew the ego, and I could witness the higher self using low-dose psychedelics and in meditation, but prior to 2015 I had not discerned my higher self as a discreet window on consciousness. Guy Finley[485] and Mooji introduced me to the concept of the higher self-consciousness, while the summer solstice 2015 Ritual Meditation helped me become experientially aware of all three windows on consciousness. In our earthly realm one window on consciousness is real and eternal (higher self), and one is a time-bound counterfeit window on consciousness (ego) which developed during infancy. Self-realization is about experientially witnessing all three windows on consciousness and refuting the impermanent ego in the transcendental realm from the perspective of your higher self outside of space and time. Innumerable rebirths and lifetimes have happened for that one self-realization: I am my eternal higher self.

To help achieve this outcome, two powerful sacred ritual processes, a mind transformation plan, and a set of mind-adjusting tools (psychedelics, cognitive learning) are offered to help you shift your seat of consciousness to the higher self. This is where all of those spiritual gurus reside i.e., Eckhart Tolle, Bernadette Roberts, Mooji, Gangaji, etc.[486] If you are unable to switch the seat of consciousness in transcendental states of consciousness then you will need to work on stabilizing your higher self's presence in your day-to-day life. But at least you will have glimpsed your higher self and will know that there are two windows on consciousness in this earthly realm, and that's a great start.

Chapter 12

A Bigger Perspective

Recapping the Discovery of Ritual Meditation

At the start of this book I asked if you would like to know one of humankind's best-kept secrets. This profound secret consisted of the sacred ritual processes used by the Sun god religions' priesthoods for accessing higher states of consciousness. In my view, these ritual processes were the basis upon which all society-coalescing religions and spiritual faiths were founded, prior to the birth of today's global monotheistic religions.

A number of fundamental assumptions were made from the outset. First, I assumed that ancient priesthoods, as catalyzing leaders of religions, were in the business of accessing altered states of consciousness by using sacred ritual processes, and telling time by using pyramid alignments to assist their society's ritual and agricultural agendas. These ancient Sun god religion priesthoods understood that sacredly-timed meditation conducted in sensory silence under the influence of

Chapter 12 A Bigger Perspective

entheogens provided a predictable means for accessing altered states of consciousness.

These priestly skills called for the ability to accurately tell sacred time, to create sacred space which was silent for the conduct of meditation-based rituals, and to be able to access floral, fungal, and/or fauna-based hallucinogens as rich sources of brain chemicals (dopamine, serotonin-5HT2a). All of these elements were coordinated as a sacred ritual process that put meditation at center stage. The meditation process was supplemented with sacred time via the latter's impact on increasing alpha brainwave voltages (over the frontal brain), and also by using entheogens as concentrated sources of the same brain chemicals produced by the brain during meditation and altered states of consciousness. This was required to trigger a switch in the state of consciousness from being in deep meditation to altered states of consciousness.

Priesthoods had a specific job to do, and operated in a political context that necessitated a source of power. This power and influence came from the priests' ability to accurately tell time (enabling rituals, agriculture-fertility calendars, etc.), as well as from their development and control of sacred ritual processes for accessing altered states of consciousness. This in turn helped create a partnership with leaders and the elite that served to organize and control society for the "greater good". Every ancient Sun god religion society was built on this foundation.

This priestly role created a need for a communicating medium to illustrate and pass on ritual or esoteric know-how, while at the same time controlling access to that information's unveiling. Deity art and icons addressed that need very well because they embedded symbolic information that could be revealed during the ritual discussion. This ritual fingerprint (a triad of deity or leader, sacred time, and entheogen symbols) is in evidence from the beginning to the end of each of these great religions, indicating its central importance to all of them. This ritual know-how has only recently been rediscovered by me, after being in front of our eyes for a very long time.

The underlying assumptions discussed above, and the need for a communicating medium to help with the ritual's instruction, compelled me to search the pyramid and temple art-icon image databases (Wikimedia and others), ancient site museums, and academic publications for clues regarding where and how information was encoded beyond the written language. In the same vein, an understanding that the majority of pyramids and temples were aligned with the equinox sunrises/sets, and the winter solstice sunrise/summer solstice sunset, and that these times constituted the Sun

Chapter 12 A Bigger Perspective

god religions' most important sacred ritual dates, was an important coincidence that needed to be understood.

Recall from Chapter 6 that solar terrestrial processes ultimately defined sacred time. That is, sacred time is the optimal time to conduct sacred rituals for accessing altered states of consciousness, due to peaks in Earths magnetic fields (i.e., at the equinoxes) and Schumann resonances, especially 7.8 hertz (at the winter solstice sunrise/summer solstice sunset). Sacred time was utilized to enhance meditation's alpha brainwave-generating processes, which are located in specific structures of the frontal brain. Enhanced alpha brainwave voltages over the forehead region is the most important brainwave signature associated with deep meditation and altered states of consciousness. Moreover, this brainwave voltage signature can be naturally supplemented via brainwave entrainment. Sacredly-timed rituals permit meditation's processes to be supplemented to promote a switch in the state of consciousness. Peaks in both Schumann resonances (solstices) and Earth's magnetic fields (equinoxes) also naturally enhance frontal alpha brainwave voltages.

It's important to understand that meditation is a "gateway process" controlling access to our higher states of consciousness. Meditation can be supplemented via sacred rituals (embracing sacred time and psychedelics) to enhance the prospects of accessing

Chapter 12   A Bigger Perspective

altered states of consciousness. This understanding was missing when psychedelics were introduced into Western society in the 1960s. Only recently have brain-imaging studies begun to highlight the fact that meditation and psychedelics operate, broadly speaking, on the same parts of the brain.

Interestingly, the most important brain chemicals supporting deep meditation and altered states of consciousness are the same ones depicted in Sun god deity art that is, dopamine (i.e., metabolized nuciferine via pink lotus, blue and white water lilies) and 5-hydroxytryptamine-2a serotonin (i.e., magic mushrooms, San Pedro cactus, Anadenanthera colubrina, bufotenin stimulators.

How do we know meditation was a key part of the ritual process? Firstly, we can see this with Hindu's Trimurti deities sitting in a meditation posture atop upside-down lotus flowers. We also see the pharaohs of ancient Egypt seated with eyes closed and hands on knees, facing the winter solstice sunrise in front of the temple (for example, the statue of Ramese II at Abu Simbel, and the statues of Memnon at the Temple of Amenhotep III in Luxor). If possible, make it a point to visit the museums or review the online image databases associated with these ancient sites. You will often see icons (especially religious icons of ancient Mesoamerica, Egypt, India) that depict people meditating. Additionally, Hinduism and its Buddhist offshoot still retain meditation (and yoga) as their core ritual process. We also know it's possible for highly adept spiritual and meditation practitioners to transcend directly without entheogens, thereby fully displaying the human potential for transcendence via meditation. Indirectly, I deduced that meditation was integral to the ritual because these religions conducted their sacred rituals in sacred spaces offering places of sensory silence (tunnels, pyramid chambers, temple sanctums). After all, we know that sensory silence quiets the brain's average brainwave frequency, just as meditation does.

It's worth mentioning the regional sacred real estate clustering pattern because this was possibly the most intriguing part of the project, and led to some very big questions. How could such long distance pyramid clustering alignments over distances between 100 and 1,000km be achieved? This led to the following question: Can humans communicate non-locally in altered states of consciousness by simultaneously accessing these higher states of consciousness?

The regional sacred real estate map depicted in Figure 6.14 highlights that between 60 and 97% percent of these Sun god religions' sacred sites were clustered within 2-to-7-minute-wide time-bandwidths, as delineated by the day-night boundary's overhead passage on the winter solstice sunrise and summer

Chapter 12 A Bigger Perspective

solstice sunset. This clustering alignment is observed over distances of 100-1,000km. As a result, sacred sites belonging to a society's religion would have simultaneously experienced the same enhanced Schumann resonances (7.8 hertz) overhead on the solstices. This raises the possibility that non-local communication networks created by the simultaneous access to altered states of consciousness (i.e., group consciousness) actually existed.

The association of these religions with lightning centers, solar terminators, fault lines, and volcanoes indicates an awareness of the ritual benefit of these cyclically (i.e., lightning, solar terminators) and intermittently (fault lines and volcanic activity) enhanced electromagnetic and magnetic fields.

In many ways this project felt like I was building a bridge connecting the archaeology, via some priestly assumptions devoid of religious dogma, to the sciences associated with altered states of consciousness.

The reason for emphasizing the above "but devoid of religious dogma" is complex. Higher self-realization is attainable by everyone. I believe there's merit in offering less religious people, and those jaded by the world religion has helped create, an alternative pathway to access their higher states of consciousness. You can integrate your faith into this process if you wish, but you don't have to.

Focusing on the last two millennia of religious and spiritual experience, we observe that the average human being hasn't learned how to access higher states of consciousness. That capability for accessing altered states of consciousness is our pure consciousness or God-gifted biology, and yet most of us are oblivious to this. In my view, whenever you permit another human (i.e. shaman, priest, guru) or a religious institution to be placed between your awakened state and access to altered states of consciousness and higher states of consciousness, you become a victim of the power, control and ignorance that those people and institutions exert. And that for me is a big problem, and why I went in search of this ritual process know-how and then decided to share it.

The Significance Of The 1960s Psychedelic Era

It's worth placing the 1960s psychedelic experiment in context, because I do not believe that society, governments, religions, and the scientific community fully comprehend the significance of what actually happened during this social experiment. It's worth understanding this experiment a little more deeply, especially in light of our inherent capacity to experience altered states of consciousness. Allow me to explain.

At the heart of this misunderstanding was a general lack of awareness that meditation was the central ritual

Chapter 12 A Bigger Perspective

process which ancient priesthoods supplemented with entheogens and sacred time to assist meditation's natural biological outcome, i.e., to access altered states of consciousness and higher self awareness outside of space and time. Meditation rituals effectively supplemented alpha brainwave voltages and brain chemical levels, such that specific brain thresholds could be reached, which in turn manifested as a switch in one's state of consciousness. This full ritual process was missing in the 1950s and 1960s.

Let's just recap on the potted history of what actually happened. Gordon Wasson (see Chapter 4) retrieved magic mushrooms from Maria Sabina (a Mexican shaman) while conducting private research (as an amateur ethnomycologist) in Mexico, and then provided samples to Albert Hoffman, who isolated psilocybin and psilocin from them. Hofmann subsequently went on to manufacture LSD based on other research. Timothy Leary, Ram Dass, and other maverick social scientists then spawned the 1960s psychedelic era driven by LSD and magic mushrooms. Perhaps the CIA was involved more than we generally understand.[487] Anyway, this ultimately led to the prohibition of psychedelics.

In essence, magic mushrooms and, subsequently, LSD were being used completely out of their ancient ritual context. The part of the sacred ritual process involving sacredly timed meditation, in sensory silence,

Chapter 12 A Bigger Perspective

and preceded by sacred ritual preparation, was not retrieved by Gordon Wasson (or anyone else). In my view "Set and Setting," (i.e., one's mindset and the setting in which the user has the experience) as the process that evolved from the 1960's psychedelic era, does not reflect the ancient use of entheogens in sacredly-timed meditation, nor does it promote transcendental self-inquiry. Oftentimes during this era, psychedelics were combined with alcohol and recreational drugs as a means of escape. This goes on today as well.

As a consequence of the psychedelic era, society lost the opportunity to fully explore some incredibly valuable medicines and spiritual awakening-transformation tools. Not only that, but this psychedelic experiment added further to the mountain of historical misinformation, stigmas, and taboos that regarded psychedelics as witches' poisons, and associated them with the ancient European pagan religions which Christianity eventually suppressed. The misinformation, stigmas, taboos, and the lack of awareness that meditation was a gateway process to altered states of consciousness together helped create a misinformed 21st century society. In addition, today's drug regulatory agencies and government legislative bodies pose significant hurdles to the legal reintroduction of psychedelics.

Chapter 12 A Bigger Perspective

Now, imagine if entheogens had been introduced to Western society, accompanied by the full sacred ritual process and preparation, which placed meditation rather than psychedelics at the heart of the ritual. Can you imagine how that might have changed our world in a very different way?

The question I therefore ask is "how can psychedelic and patient advocate groups best work to ensure these valuable healing and spiritual tools become available once again?"

It's not an easy question to answer. The mass of misinformation and the need to reeducate people are two significant impediments, to which you can then add the legislative and pharmaceutical regulatory agencies of any country. Conducting clinical studies with psychedelics within academia is a great start and indicates government, healthcare, and people in general are harkening to societies' needs and the clinical data already in hand. In my view, if good clinical data is generated in significant populations then positive change will naturally happen. I'm an advocate of Big Pharmaceutical (Pharma) sponsoring a regulatory-directed approach supporting a synthetic product (LSD, mescaline, psilocybin/psilocin) for numerous sizable and definable subpopulations, but I think this would be strategically off limits to them. (Return to Chapter 11 Some Words of Caution)

Chapter 12 A Bigger Perspective

To give you further context on why big Pharma are unlikely to get involved in this therapeutic category, a typical pharmaceutical product and manufacturing development investment cost would be in the region of $250-$500 million, and it would require that someone accept that risk in a phased manner upfront. Big Pharma does not typically accept such large risks (i.e., legal and regulatory) upfront, at least not without a clear path to an approvable and reimbursable product with good sales potential. Legal change will happen in time if a persuasive case can be made for the medical benefit of psychedelics in important subpopulations, much as it has with marijuana. The good news is that magic mushrooms and other psychedelics are already available online, so a quality product supply precedent already exists, at least so long as these remain legal and people continue to accept personal risk.

What do people in medical or spiritual need do while waiting for the lifting of psychedelic prohibition and for medicine to advance?

Simple. Find another way to access psychedelics (i.e., online retailers) and an effective process for their safe use. By combining Ritual Meditation with quality assured magic mushrooms purchased online (check online suppliers for delivery to your country and the legal status of this in your country[488]), you can gain access to an A to Z method for accessing higher states of

Chapter 12 A Bigger Perspective

consciousness that you control. By undertaking Ritual Meditation as a sacred process you improve the prospects for both positive experiences and your own safety.

Human psychological conditions that respond poorly to current treatment options are most interesting, because many of these conditions are known to respond well to psychedelics. The body of scientific evidence showing the efficacy of treatment with psychedelics is expanding, and it tells us that psychedelics provide significant benefits in treating psychological conditions that afflict sizable human populations (discussed in Chapter 11, see an extensive list of medical publications via hyperlinks on my website http://ritualmeditation.com). There are also people who might wish to explore meditation outcomes beyond calm abiding or mindfulness.

While awaiting change, a process is available which gives you new tools for accessing altered states of consciousness and exploring methods for self-realization and ending any need to heal. The consequences of this are innately living from your higher self thereafter, becoming liberated and enlightened, and becoming spiritually immortal after death. How this will then impact your preexisting condition of the mind is unknown, other than as indicated in the clinical studies cited above.

Remember that whether we have maladies of the mind and emotional scars or not, we all have three naturally gifted windows on consciousness to be explored if we so wish. In experiencing the higher self and pure consciousness, with or without transcendental self-realization, profound healing and forgiveness are natural consequences. It has been my experience that profound bliss-love and healing always result from Unity awareness of pure consciousness, transcendental self-realization, and chakra and kundalini activations. In the afterglow period of these experiences and with higher self realization we can positively reshape our minds by subordinating the ego and learning to operate from the higher self in the Now. We must end up using different parts of the brain and mind, rather than the ego. As these spiritual qualities naturally manifest, peace and tranquility pervade the mind, and by maintaining our awareness in the Now the ego is rendered unable to dominate events. For me today, being mindfully aware in the Now happens rather effortlessly, whereas before the summer solstice 2015 I had to meditate or consume low dose psychedelics to achieve that state of being.

Final Thoughts

If you choose to use **Ritual Meditation, Transcendental Self-Inquiry, and the Mind Transformation Plan**, please use them in their sacredly-intended way, and above all *be sacred and safe*. Please,

Chapter 12   A Bigger Perspective

only use this knowledge as part of a healing and/or spiritual-consciousness-life development process. Learn wisdom and knowledge from within or outside of your faith, and particularly from the mystic and eastern traditions.

Use it to benefit your consciousness evolution, and bring a positive transformative impact to the lives of your family and friends, as well as to your community and, if you can, to positively impact our wider humanity. And use this wisdom to honor Mother Earth and all her life. Pay homage to our ancestors; both those who are known and remembered, and those who forged our species' journey out of deep time. Remember that they forged our world against great odds and in much harsher times. We should honor that from the very depths of our hearts.

This is serious stuff and not without the potential for serious risks and mental discomforts. Therefore please be careful, be sacred and safe, and reflect the broader **Mind Transformation Plan**. If this is your path, find the right people to help and support you in this process in a healthy and safe manner i.e., spotter, psychologist, empathic counselor, spiritual guide / teacher.

If you do choose to pursue Ritual Meditation or psychedelics, my hope is that you will find this process and plan helpful to that pursuit. I have been unable to find any other comprehensive ritual process involving

Chapter 12 A Bigger Perspective

psychedelics, be it religious, cultic, shamanic, or out of the mystic school tradition, that is publically available. While books on psychedelics and hallucinogens do exist, they do not contain the same level of process detail from A to Z as does Ritual Meditation and Transcendental Self-Inquiry methods, and the Mind Transformation Plan.

If you are going to invest your time, energy, mind, and life being involved in religion and spirituality, and living under its influence, then it makes sense to ensure that this endeavor delivers access to your higher states of consciousness. We should remember that the mystic founders of today's global faiths were people who ritually or spontaneously accessed their higher states of consciousness and transformed their minds. One day perhaps it will be more generally accepted that spiritual awakening and healing are the natural consequences of ritually accessing altered states of consciousness and transcendentally self-realizing. The combination of Ritual Meditation combined with transcendental self-inquiry makes this a real possibility.

Something very important, beyond words and language, was indelibly impressed into my awareness during my experience of Unity consciousness on the winter solstice of 2014, and similarly on the summer solstice of 2015, and these experiences are something I will never forget (see also Chapter 9).

Chapter 12 A Bigger Perspective

According to this imparted awareness, every sentient species throughout the Universe has an evolutionary mission to spiritually awaken, and to do so en masse. The evolution of consciousness is the inexorable journey of our human species, and of the Universe. It was impressed upon my consciousness that transcendental self-realization is the most profound experience a human can ever have, and is the reason why we are karmically reborn innumerable times. The ego's development in early childhood and its imposturous domination of our consciousness thereafter blinds us to our eternal higher self. Ultimately sentient life fully awakens, and naturally becomes the benevolent guardian of its planet and of all that planet's life.

Perhaps Jiddhu Khrishnamurti's profoundly impacting question (*"What will it take for humankind to spiritually awaken?"*), indelibly impressed into my consciousness from this project's outset, influenced my Unity experiences. Perhaps Khrishnamurti's question and my finding the sacred ritual process were my qualifying ticket to those experiences. None the less, the impression left in awareness as Unity consciousness was of the need to share these ancient ritual processes to help others have the possibility of self-realizing and healing.

Remember that Ritual Meditation is simply a ritual means of supplementing meditation's gateway process for accessing altered states of consciousness. Accessing

Chapter 12   A Bigger Perspective

altered states of consciousness is a natural, but infrequently experienced, part of our biology. Accessing altered states of consciousness is a means by which we can dissolve our ego-body-space-time boundaries and witness our eternal higher self and pure consciousness. Ritual Meditation is simply an eyes-closed meditation method carried out at sacred time under the influence of magic mushrooms, and undertaken in a sacred and safe manner. Integrate Ritual Meditation, Transcendental Self-realization, and the Mind Transformation Plan in a sacred and safe manner and witness life from your higher self!

If you'd like to explore **Ritual Meditation, Transcendental Self-Realization** and **Mind Transformation Coaching** on a **One-to-One or a Retreat basis**, then please contact me via my website contact form (http://ritualmeditation.com/contact/). Please join my blog (http://ritualmeditation.com/category/blog/) for updates and helpful advice, and sign up on my social media platform at www.ritualmeditation.com. You can also access a free online meditation calendar (http://ritualmeditation.com/meditation-calendar/) and know the sun/moon rise or set anywhere in the world. You can also download a Google Earth pyramid tour (http://tinyurl.com/qz488ll) of 450 pyramids and temples and view their sunrise and sunset and alignments.

Chapter 12   A Bigger Perspective

Thank you for reading this book. My hope is that you too will be able to realize profound psychological healing and your spiritual awakening, and complete your spiritual journey for self-realization in this lifetime.

Would you please write me a review on Amazon (http://tinyurl.com/pj5tlpl) and Goodreads (http://tinyurl.com/pq5b79u) if merited? These reviews are like gold dust and they really help.

My best wishes to you. Thank you.

Carlton Brown

Please connect with Carlton via www.ritualmeditation.com: to enquire about Ritual Meditation coaching, retreats and eLearning, as well as to schedule potential media interviews and speaking engagements, to access meditation resources, and for blog and social media sign-up links.

.

Accepting Your Legal, Civil and Moral Responsibilities and Liabilities

If you decide to explore Ritual Meditation and Transcendental Self-Inquiry methods, the Mind Transformation Plan, and psychedelics for deep inner self-exploration, healing and spiritual awakening, then please realize that you run the **risk of permanent mind changes** (hopefully good ones, but bad experiences might also happen), and that you do so at your own risk and liability. I am simply providing a sacred ritual process reverse-engineered and deduced from my archaeological research and Ritual Meditation test piloting. I provide the Ritual Meditation (Transcendental Self-Inquiry methods, Mind Transformation Plan) and everything I have learned in the spirit of sharing knowledge with the best of my intentions and wishes. This is provided on an as is basis and with no legal recourse to the author.

Please: you must accept full responsibility and legal, civil, and moral liability for using Ritual Meditation and Transcendental Self-Inquiry methods and the Mind Transformation Plan ("processes"). You are not under the author's direct supervisory or associated medical care. If you were, you would have

medical and legal insurance, would have signed a legal and medical waiver, undergone full medical and psychological screening and undertaken a thorough ritual preparation beforehand. Additionally, i can not be held responsible for the content of your mind and how Consciousness and psychedelic based ritual s interacts with that.

You must be very aware that **permanent changes to the mind can and most likely will take place**. No person (you, me, anyone else) has any control over what is experienced during altered states of consciousness. What you experience reflects the totality of your mind and life experience, your intentions, ritual preparation and experience, etc., so it would be unrealistic to expect others to assume or accept responsibility for this. My experiences have been mind transformingly positive and profoundly healing, but that does not mean negative outcomes or experiences are not possible for others or for myself in the future.

I provide these processes on an as is basis with my best, most sacred, and safest set of intentions and wishes for you. To the best of my knowledge and intention I provide you a reverse-engineered ritual process deduced from the shared archaeological fingerprint discussed in this book, and I have added to this based upon my own learning. This is provided at a time when we, the public, have no medical option available for treating our maladies of the mind with psychedelics (despite the [clinical data indicating putative benefits](http://tinyurl.com/otxoywj) http://tinyurl.com/otxoywj). Nor do we have publically available processes or protocols for the intended safe use of psychedelics (medical, spiritual, or other). The Ritual Meditation and Transcendental Self-Inquiry processes and the Mind Transformation Plan are provided as an alternative to the current state of affairs. That is you now have, where you did not beforehand, a sacred (safety intended) ritual process for using psychedelics, with its pedigree of use by the ancient Sun god religion priesthoods.

If you use these processes to explore new treatment options or further explore your spirituality then you do so at your own risk and you fully accept all legal, civil, and moral responsibility and liability for whatever happens to you or to another party or property. In using these processes you waive any and all legal, civil and moral right to pursue the author for any liability for your use of psychedelics, the processes provided herein, and any adverse medical, psychological, or other outcomes experienced by you.

Appendices

Biography: A Path Less Trodden

Born in the UK and raised in New Zealand, Carlton has led an interesting, eclectic, adventurous, and purposeful life—a road less travelled with good purpose intended.

Carlton is a veterinarian, biotech entrepreneur, vaccine innovator, hobby archaeologist, and private researcher, as well as the author of Discovering Ritual Meditation. His lifetime fascination with pyramid archaeology and cultures, ancient priesthood ritual knowledge, lost civilizations, and humankind's history through the Holocene, is augmented by his researches into the science of altered states of consciousness. More recently, his interests have expanded to understanding the story lurking behind global climate change. Carlton lives in Guatemala, his spiritual home, overlooking the beautiful Lake Atitlan and its cluster of inspiring volcanoes, right in the heartland of the ancient Maya.

Carlton earned an MBA from the London Business School (1997), and was the founding CEO of Immune Targeting Systems Ltd (2003-12), which was recently (2015) sold to Altimmune Inc. During his CEO tenure, Carlton raised GBP£23 million of investment funding, developed a biotechnology company and technology de novo, and led a team that successfully validated novel vaccine solutions for mutating viruses, thus solving a multi-decade industry and technology bottleneck (vaccines promoting cellular immunity). In 2012 he stepped down as CEO to pursue his career as an author.

If you wish to learn more about the author please visit his [LinkedIn profile](http://tinyurl.com/ov65393).

Appendices

Dedication

To You

The reader of this book, and those whose interest you spark

To our Ancestors

Who forged our world and upon whose shoulders we all stand

To God and all God's mystic avatars in every religion throughout time

To planet Earth, our mother provider, and all her life forms

A hope that humankind will awaken to our collective responsibility of looking after you better than we have in recent times

To an eternal abundance of enlightened souls all over our Planet to help that aim

To a world in eternal peace and harmony

To our part in that, we can all make a difference

To all that sacred rituals promise, it is literally up to us

Self-realization, enlightenment, liberation anyone?

In this lifetime, or perhaps another

What are you going to chose?

Carlton Brown

Appendices

Copyright Notice

Discovering Ritual Meditation

Transcendental Healing and Self-Realization

By Carlton Brown

Copyright© 2008 Carlton Brown, All Rights Reserved

Except as provided by the Copyright Act, as amended from time to time, and that provided for by the figure image permissions, no part of this publication may be reproduced, stored in a retrieval system, be used to create other media, be used to create media or services to derive revenues, sales, profit or charity (and/or deprive the copyright holder of such rights), or be transmitted in any form or by any means without the prior written consent of the author and copyright holder, Carlton Brown or his successor(s).

More specifically, important discoveries and findings of this book are the ancient priesthood ritual methods for accessing Consciousness (the higher self and pure consciousness within and beyond objective reality). From these discoveries the ritual processes were reverse engineered and further optimized into the following methods: **(1) Ritual Meditation**: that is Meditation (as the central ritual method), conducted in sensory silence (or not), and supplemented with sacred time (or not) and entheogens (psychedelics), with the meditator aligned with Earth's magnetic axis (or not). **(2) Transcendental Self-Inquiry**: where self-inquiry (asking "Who am I?" and replying "I am") is conducted during altered states of consciousness (within or beyond objective reality) during Ritual Meditation, specifically so (s)he may become self-realised (enlightened). Such ritual methods were (are to be) conducted in a sacred manner with sacred preparation to help generate grace and ensure the Ritual Meditator's safety.

As an individual you are freely permitted to use this copyrighted information and know-how for personal use if you have purchased this book and have fully comprehended the appended section "Accepting Your Legal, Civil and Moral Responsibilities and Liabilities" and comply with it. To utilize this copyrighted know-how to create media or services to derive revenues, sales, profit or charity please contact the author and copyright holder for permission (via http://ritualmeditation.com).

Permission to use any figures or images should be sought from their originators detailed in the book's Bibliography. This Book (print and ebook) is licensed for the purchaser's use only. Thank you for respecting the author's hard work and proprietary rights.

Appendices

Bibliography & Figure Attributions

Thank you to everyone referenced in this book, and to those who provided images. Every best endeavor has been made to respect the original authorship and contribution of research and graphical-image resources used in developing this book. Despite final quality control, it is possible errors have occurred. In this event, please accept my sincere apologies and make contact with me and I shall rectify this.

Most of these scientific publications and books are hyperlinked to an online source via my website (Library resources, http://ritualmeditation.com/resource-library/), and where possible I have sourced free copies for you.

[1] Earths 3 rotations: original work by Dennis Nilsson / Wikimedia Commons / CC-BY-3.0. http://commons.wikimedia.org/wiki/File%3AAxialTiltObliquity.png

[2] Earth's Pole Star pointing: original image by Tau'olunga / Wikimedia Commons / Public Domain-CC0 1.0 Universal. http://en.wikipedia.org/wiki/File:North_season.jpg

[3] Composite image created by Carlton Brown / Public Domain. Composed of; (A & B) Cropped images repositioned to accentuate V47 solstice angle, with additional annotation overlays. Original images by Tom Ruen (Full Sky Observatory) / Wikimedia Commons (Public Domain), http://en.wikipedia.org/wiki/File:Seasonearth.png.

[4] Composite image created by Carlton Brown / Public Domain. Composed of; (A & B) Tom Ruen (Full Sky Observatory) / Wikimedia Commons / Public Domain. http://en.wikipedia.org/wiki/File:Seasonearth.png.

[5] Carlton Brown / Public Domain

Appendices

6. Composite image created by Carlton Brown / Public Domain. Composed of one of an images 4 subimages (cropped) used to accentuate the solstice solar terminator, with additional annotation overlays by the author. Original images by Tom Ruen (Full Sky Observatory) / Wikimedia Commons / Public Domain. http://en.wikipedia.org/wiki/File:Seasonearth.png.

7. Composite image created by Carlton Brown / Public Domain. of Uaxactun alignments comprising a number of modified pieces of original work (cropped); (A&B) Carlton Brown / Public Domain.

8. Charles Hapgood; The Path of the Pole: Cataclysmic Pole Shift Geology. By Adventures Unlimited Press; New Ed edition (2 April 2010). ASIN: B003F7PEFG.

9. Christopher Dunn. The Giza Power Plant: Technologies of Ancient Egypt. Bear & Company (1 Aug 1998), ISBN: 1879181509.

10. Composite image created by Carlton Brown / Public Domain. of Mayan cave & Egyptian pyramid chamber comprising a number of modified pieces of original work (cropped); (A&B) Carlton Brown / Public Domain.

11. Composite image created by Carlton Brown of Mesoamerican site alignments comprising modified original works (annotations, cropping); (A) Teotihuacan: a modified image created by Carlton Brown / Wikimedia / CC-BY-SA-3.0. original work by JOMA-MAC / Wikimedia Commons / CC BY-SA 3.0. http://commons.wikimedia.org/wiki/File:Teotihuac%C3%A1n_2012-09-28_00-07-11.jpg. (B) Cholula: a modified image created by Carlton Brown / Wikimedia / CC-BY-SA-3.0. original work by Jflamenco / Wikimedia Commons / CC BY-SA 3.0. http://commons.wikimedia.org/wiki/File:Cholula-puebla1.jpg.

12. Composite image created by Carlton Brown of Mesoamerican site alignments comprising modified original works (annotations, cropping); (A) Chichen Itza: a modified image created by Carlton Brown / Public Domain. original work by NASA Earth Observatory / Public Domain. http://eoimages.gsfc.nasa.gov/images/imagerecords/5000/5349/chichenitza_iko_2001064_lrg.jpg. (B) Giza: a modified image created by Carlton Brown / Public Domain. original work by NASA Earth Observatory / Public Domain. http://earthobservatory.nasa.gov/IOTD/view.php?id=79253.

Appendices

13 Composite image created by Carlton Brown of V47 superstructure architecture comprising modified original works (annotations, cropping); (A) Brahma temple: a modified image created by Carlton Brown / Public Domain. original work by Coolsangamithiran / Wikimedia Commons / CC-BY-SA-3.0. http://commons.wikimedia.org/wiki/File%3ABrahma_temple.jpg. (B) Meroe: a modified image created by Carlton Brown / CC-BY-SA-2.0. original work by Fabrizio Demartis / Wikimedia Commons / CC-BY-SA-2.0. http://commons.wikimedia.org/wiki/File:Sudan_Meroe_Pyramids_30sep2005_16.jpg. (C) a modified image created by Carlton Brown / Wikimedia / CC-BY-SA-3.0-2.5-2.0-1.0. original work by Roland Unger / Wikimedia Commons / CC-BY-SA-3.0-2.5-2.0-1.0. http://commons.wikimedia.org/wiki/File:Meidum97NorthSide.jpg.

14 Giza graphical depiction of the annual sunrise progression: Carlton Brown / Public Domain.

15 Anthony F. Aveni, Archaeoastronomy in the ancient Americas. Journal of Archaeological Research, 11:2 (June 2003).

16 Tonina: Composite image created by Carlton Brown / Public Domain. Composed of; (all images) Carlton Brown / Public Domain.

17 Composite image created by Carlton Brown / Wikimedia Commons / CC BY-SA 3.0. of Mesoamerica comprising modified original works (cropping); (A) original images by Fabienkhan / Wikimedia Commons / CC-BY-SA-3.0. http://commons.wikimedia.org/wiki/File:Map_Olmec_sites.png, (B) original images by Kaufman, Terrence / Wikimedia Commons / CC BY-SA 3.0. http://commons.wikimedia.org/wiki/File:Mayan_Language_Migration_Map.svg.

18 Composite image created by Carlton Brown of Mesoamerican sites relative to the solstice terminators comprising a number of modified pieces of original work (annotations, cropping, formatting; by the author); (A&B) a modified image created by Carlton Brown / Public Domain using satellite imagery by NASA World Wind / Public Domain.

19 Composite image created by Carlton Brown of South American sites relative to the solstice terminators comprising a number of modified pieces of original work (annotations, cropping, formatting; by the author); (A&B) a modified image created by Carlton Brown / Public Domain using satellite imagery by NASA World Wind / Public Domain.

20 Composite image created by Carlton Brown of South American sites relative to the solstice terminators comprising a number of modified pieces of original work (annotations, cropping, formatting; by the author); (A&B) a modified image created by Carlton Brown / Public Domain using satellite imagery by NASA World Wind / Public Domain.

21 Composite image created by Carlton Brown of South American sites relative to the solstice terminators comprising a number of modified pieces of original work (annotations, cropping, formatting; by the author); (A&B) a modified image created by Carlton Brown / Public Domain using satellite imagery by NASA World Wind / Public Domain.

Appendices

22 J. A. Belmonte, M. Shaltout,; Keeping Ma'at: An astronomical approach to the orientation of the temples in ancient Egypt. Advances in Space Research, 46 (2010) 532–539.

23 Composite image created by Carlton Brown. Temple of Amun (Egypt). Composed of; (A, B & C) cropped images created by the following originators with additional annotation overlays by the author. (A) Modified image created by Carlton Brown / Public Domain. Comprising; Markh at the English Wikipedia project / Wikimedia Commons / Public Domain. http://commons.wikimedia.org/wiki/File:Temple_of_amun_karnak.jpg. (B) Modified image created by Carlton Brown / CC-BY-2.0. Original image created by Arian Zwegers / Wikimedia Commons / CC-BY-2.0. http://commons.wikimedia.org/wiki/File:Karnak,_Temple_of_Amun_(6201367717).jpg (C) Furlong, D - Egyptian Temple Orientation - http://www.kch42.dial.pipex.com/egyptarticle_temple_orient1.html.

24 Composite image created by Carlton Brown / Wikimedia Commons / CC-BY-SA-3.0. Temple of Hatshepsut (Egypt). Composed of cropped original images from the following contributors, with additional annotation overlays by the author. (A) Nowic talk /Wikimedia Commons / CC-BY-SA-3.0-2.5-2.0-1.0. http://commons.wikimedia.org/wiki/File:Tempel_der_Hatschepsut_(Deir_el-Bahari).jpg. top left sub-figure; Markh / Wikimedia Commons / CC-BY-SA-3.0. http://commons.wikimedia.org/wiki/File:Mentuhotep_Deir_el-Bahri.jpg. (B) Aligatorek / Wikimedia Commons / CC-BY-SA-3.0. http://commons.wikimedia.org/wiki/File:Alig_Deir_el_Bahari_314.jpg.

25 Composite image created by Carlton Brown (Public Domain) of the Temples Amenhotep III Temple & the Colossi of Memnon. Comprising; (A) a modified image created by Carlton Brown / Wikimedia / Public Domain. original image by Markh / Wikimedia Commons / Public Domain. http://commons.wikimedia.org/wiki/File:Amenhotep_III_mortuary_Temple.jpg. (B) Modified image created by Carlton Brown / Wikimedia Commons / CC-BY-SA-2.5-poland. Roweromaniak / Wikimedia Commons / CC-BY-SA-2.5-poland. http://commons.wikimedia.org/wiki/File:Teby_Kolosy_Memnona_C18-24.jpg

26 Composite image created by Carlton Brown of the Great Temple of Rameses II at Abu Simbel (Egypt). Comprising 3 modified (annotations; author) pieces of original work; (A) a modified image created by Carlton Brown / Wikimedia / CC BY-SA 2.0. original work by Dennis Jarvis / Wikimedia Commons / CC BY-SA 2.0. http://commons.wikimedia.org/wiki/File:Flickr_-_archer10_(Dennis)_-_Egypt-10C-063.jpg. (B) a modified image created by Carlton Brown / Wikimedia / CC BY-SA 1.0. original work by NebMaatRe from wikipedia.de / Wikimedia Commons / CC BY 1.0. http://commons.wikimedia.org/wiki/File:Tempelplan_Abu_Simbel.png. (C) a modified image created by Carlton Brown / Wikimedia / Public Domain. original work by Brooklyn Museum / Wikimedia Commons / Public Domain. http://commons.wikimedia.org/wiki/File:Abu_Simbel_1900.jpg.

Appendices

27 Composite image created by Carlton Brown of the Temples at Edfu & Deir el-Hagar (Egypt). Comprising a number of modified pieces of original work (annotations, cropping; by the author); (A) a modified image created by Carlton Brown / Wikimedia / CC BY-SA 2.5. original work by Dunning, H.W. / Wikimedia Commons / CC BY-SA 2.5. http://commons.wikimedia.org/wiki/File:The_Temple_of_Edfu_(1905)_-_TIMEA.jpg. (B) a modified image created by Carlton Brown / Wikimedia / CC-BY-SA-3.0-2.5-2.0-1.0. original work by Roland Unger / Wikimedia Commons / CC-BY-SA-3.0-2.5-2.0-1.0. http://commons.wikimedia.org/wiki/File:DeirHagarPronaos.jpg.

28 Jeremy Naydler. Shamanic Wisdom in the Pyramid Texts: The Mystical Tradition of Ancient Egypt. Inner Traditions (9 Dec 2004), ASIN: B00702M6U8.

29 Jeremy Naydler. Shamanic Wisdom in the Pyramid Texts: The Mystical Tradition of Ancient Egypt. Inner Traditions (9 Dec 2004), ASIN: B00702M6U8.

30 Composite image created by Carlton Brown / Public Domain. Overhead the Giza Plateau (Egypt). Composed of NASA Earth Observatory image cropped with additional annotations overlayed by the author; All images are in the Public Domain. Satellite image by: http://earthobservatory.nasa.gov/IOTD/view.php?id=79253.

31 Composite image created by Carlton Brown (Public Domain) of the Giza and Red Pyramids (Egypt). Comprising a number of modified pieces of original work (annotations, cropping; by the author); (A) Carlton Brown / Public Domain. (B) Chipdawes / Wikimedia Commons / public domain. http://en.wikipedia.org/wiki/File:RedPyramid.JPG.

32 Composite image created by Carlton Brown / Wikimedia Commons / CC-BY-SA-3.0. of the Pyramid of Ahmose (Egypt) comprising a number of modified pieces of original work (annotations, cropping; by the author); (A) a modified image created by Carlton Brown / Wikimedia / CC BY-SA 3.0. original work by GDK / Wikimedia Commons / CC-BY-SA-3.0. http://commons.wikimedia.org/wiki/File:Ahmose_Pyramid.png. (B) a modified image created by Carlton Brown / Wikimedia / CC BY-SA 3.0. original work by Wannabe Egyptologist / CC-BY-SA-3.0 / Wikimedia Commons. http://commons.wikimedia.org/wiki/File:Pyramid_of_Ahmose,_Abydos,_1998.png.

33 Composite image created by Carlton Brown / Wikimedia Commons / CC-BY-SA-3.0. of the Pyramid of Meidum (Egypt) comprising a number of modified pieces of original work (annotations, cropping; by the author); (A) a modified image created by Carlton Brown / Wikimedia / CC BY-SA 3.0. original work by GDK / Wikimedia Commons / CC-BY-SA-3.0. http://commons.wikimedia.org/wiki/File:Meidum_Pyramid_Complex.png. (B) a modified image created by Carlton Brown / Wikimedia / CC-BY-SA-3.0-2.5-2.0-1.0. original work by Roland Unger / Wikimedia Commons / CC-BY-SA-3.0-2.5-2.0-1.0. http://commons.wikimedia.org/wiki/File:Meidum97NorthSide.jpg.

Appendices

34 JA Belmonte, M. Shaltout Et al. JHA, xli (2010); On the orientation of Egyptian temples – testing the theory in middle Egypt and Sudan.

35 Composite image created by Carlton Brown / Wikimedia Commons / CC-BY-SA-3.0. of the Pyramids at Meroe (Sudan) comprising a number of modified pieces of original work (annotations, cropping; by the author); (A) a modified image created by Carlton Brown / Wikimedia / CC-BY-SA-1.0. original work by B N Chagny / Wikimedia Commons / CC-BY-SA-1.0. http://commons.wikimedia.org/wiki/File:Sudan_Meroe_Pyramids_2001.JPG. (B) a modified image created by Carlton Brown / Wikimedia / CC-BY-SA-2.0. original work by Fabrizio Demartis / Wikimedia Commons / CC-BY-SA-2.0. http://commons.wikimedia.org/wiki/File:Sudan_Meroe_Pyramids_30sep2005_16.jpg.

36 Anthony F. Aveni, Archaeoastronomy in the ancient Americas. Journal of Archaeological Research, 11:2 (June 2003.

37 Ivan Šprajc, Carlos Morales-Aguilar, and Richard D. Hansen, Early Maya astronomy and urban planning at El Mirador. Guatemala: Peten, 2009.

38 Anthony F. Aveni; Archaeoastronomy in the Ancient Americas. Journal of Archaeological Research, 11:2 (June 2003).

39 Composite image created by Carlton Brown / Wikimedia Commons / CC-BY-SA-3.0. of site maps for Teotihuacan and Uxmal (Mexico) comprising a number of modified pieces of original work (annotations, cropping; by the author); (A) a modified image created by Carlton Brown / Wikimedia / CC-BY-SA-3.0. original work by Aceofhearts1968 / Wikimedia Commons / CC-BY-SA-3.0. http://commons.wikimedia.org/wiki/File:TEOTIHUACAN_CALZADA_DE_LOS_MUERTOS-plan-of-the-city-SIGN.jpg. (B) a modified image created by Carlton Brown / Wikimedia / CC-BY-SA-3.0-2.5-2.0-1.0. original work by HJPD / Wikimedia Commons / CC-BY-SA-3.0-2.5-2.0-1.0. http://commons.wikimedia.org/wiki/File:Uxmal_Plan.jpg.

40 Anthony F. Aveni, Archaeoastronomy in the Ancient Americas. Journal of Archaeological Research, 11:2 June 2003.

41 W. Ashmore, Site planning principles and concepts of directionality among the ancient Maya. Latin American Antiquity, 2: 199–226 (1991).

42 Ivan Šprajc, Carlos Morales-Aguilar, Richard D. Hansen, Early Maya astronomy and urban planning at El Mirador. Gusatemala: Peten, 2009.

43 Anthony F. Aveni; Archaeoastronomy in the Ancient Americas, Journal of Archaeological Research, 11:2 (June 2003).

44 R. H. Fuson, The orientation of Maya ceremonial centers. Annals of the Association of American Geographers, 59: 494, 511 (1969).

45 John B. Carlson. Lodestone Compass: Chinese or Olmec Primacy? Multidisciplinary analysis of an Olmec hematite artifact from San Lorenzo, Veracruz, Mexico. Science 5 September 1975: Vol. 189 no. 4205 pp. 753-760. DOI: 10.1126/science.189.4205.753.

Appendices

46 Jaroslav Klokoníka: Pyramids and Ceremonial Centers in Mesoamerica and China: Were They Oriented Using a Magnetic Compass? 2011 3rd International Conference on Environmental Science and Information Application Technology (ESIAT 2011). Procedia Environmental Sciences 10 (2011) 255 – 261.

47 http://kansas.academia.edu/DavidKaufman/Papers/898720/Did_Ancient_China_Influence_Olmec_Mexico

48 Composite image created by Carlton Brown / Wikimedia Commons / CC-BY-SA-3.0. of site maps for Teotihuacan (Mexico) comprising a number of modified pieces of original work (annotations, cropping; by the author); (A) a modified image created by Carlton Brown / Wikimedia / CC-BY-SA-3.0. original work by JOMA-MAC / Wikimedia Commons / CC BY-SA 3.0. http://commons.wikimedia.org/wiki/File:Teotihuac%C3%A1n_2012-09-28_00-07-11.jpg. (B) a modified image created by Carlton Brown / Wikimedia / CC-BY-SA-3.0. original work by Juan Carlos Jaime / Wikimedia Commons / CC BY-SA 3.0. http://commons.wikimedia.org/wiki/File:Calzada_de_los_Muertos,_Teotihuac%C3%A1n,_M%C3%A9xico.JPG.

49 NF. Declercq et al A theoretical study of special acoustic effects caused by the staircase of the El Castillo pyramid at the Maya ruins of Chichen-Itza in Mexico. J. Acoust. Soc. Am. Volume 116, Issue 6, pp. 3328-3335 (2004).

50 Composite image created by Carlton Brown / Public Domain of the Pyramid of Kukulkan at Chichen Itza (Mexico) comprising a number of modified pieces of original work (annotations, cropping; by the author); (A) a modified image created by Carlton Brown / Public Domain. original work by; NASA Earth Observatory / Public Domain. http://eoimages.gsfc.nasa.gov/images/imagerecords/5000/5349/chichenitza_iko_2001064_lrg.jpg. (B) Carlton Brown /Public Domain.

51 Composite image created by Carlton Brown / Wikimedia Commons / CC-BY-SA-3.0. Images of Uxmal (Mexico) comprising a number of modified pieces of original work (annotations, cropping; by the author); (A & B) originals by Carlton Brown / Wikimedia / CC-BY-SA-3.0.

Appendices

52 Composite image created by Carlton Brown of San Andres (El Salvador) comprising a number of modified pieces of original work (annotations, cropping; by the author); (A) a modified image created by Carlton Brown / Wikimedia / CC-BY-SA-3.0. original work by Mariordo (Mario Roberto Durán Ortiz) / Wikimedia Commons / CC-BY-SA-3.0. http://commons.wikimedia.org/wiki/File:ES_SanAndres_06_2011_Estructuras_1_y_2_La_Acropolis_2186.jpg. (B) a modified image created by Carlton Brown / Public Domain. original work by Efegé / Wikimedia Commons / Public Domain. http://commons.wikimedia.org/wiki/File:Volc%C3%A1n_San_Salvador_.JPG. (C) a modified image created by Carlton Brown / Wikimedia / Public Domain. original work by Lee Siebert (Smithsonian Institution) / Wikimedia Commons / Public Domain. http://commons.wikimedia.org/wiki/File:Ilopango_caldera.jpg.

53 Composite image created by Carlton Brown of Great Pyramid of Cholula & Volcan Iztaccihuatl (Mexico) comprising a number of modified pieces of original work (annotations, cropping; by the author); (A) a modified image created by Carlton Brown / Wikimedia / CC-BY-SA-3.0. original work by Jflamenco / Wikimedia Commons / CC BY-SA 3.0. http://commons.wikimedia.org/wiki/File:Cholula-puebla1.jpg. (B) a modified image created by Carlton Brown / Wikimedia / CC-BY-SA-3.0. original work by Hajor / Wikimedia Commons / CC BY-SA 3.0. http://commons.wikimedia.org/wiki/File:Mexico.Pue.Cholula.Pyramid.03.jpg.

54 Personal observation. Composite image created by Carlton Brown / Public Domain. Composed of; (A) Satellite image by NASA World Wind / Public Domain. (B) Other smaller images; Eneas De Troya / Wikimedia / CC BY 2.0. http://commons.wikimedia.org/wiki/File:Pico_de_Orizaba_desde_Xalapa.jpg, Jose Alonso / Wikimedia / CC BY 3.0. http://commons.wikimedia.org/wiki/File:Malinche.jpg, AlejandroLinaresGarcia / Wikimedia Commons / CC-BY-SA-3.0-2.5-2.0-1.0. http://commons.wikimedia.org/wiki/File:PopoAmeca.JPG, Jflamenco / Wikimedia Commons / CC BY-SA 3.0. http://commons.wikimedia.org/wiki/File:Cholula-puebla1.jpg.

55 Composite image created by Carlton Brown at Tikal. Composed of; (A) Tikal Temple II & III, Carlton Brown / Public Domain, (B) Tikal Temple IV, Carlton Brown / Public Domain.

Appendices

56 Composite image created by Carlton Brown of Mesoamerican volcano alignments comprising a number of modified pieces of original work (annotations, cropping, formatting; by the author); (A) a modified image created by Carlton Brown / Public Domain using Satellite imagary by NASA World Wind / Public Domain, and other smaller volcano images include; original works by Eneas De Troya / Wikimedia / CC BY 2.0. http://commons.wikimedia.org/wiki/File:Pico_de_Orizaba_desde_Xalapa.jpg, Jose Alonso / Wikimedia / CC BY 3.0. http://commons.wikimedia.org/wiki/File:Malinche.jpg, AlejandroLinaresGarcia / Wikimedia Commons / CC-BY-SA-3.0-2.5-2.0-1.0. (B) a modified image created by Carlton Brown / Public Domain using Satellite imagary by NASA World Wind / Public Domain, and other smaller volcano images include; original works by; Norm Banks / Wikimedia Commons / Pubic Domain. http://commons.wikimedia.org/wiki/File:Volcan_Tajumulco_1987.jpg, Stan Shebs / Wikimedia Commons / CC-BY-SA-3.0. http://commons.wikimedia.org/wiki/File:Guatemala_Volcano_Fuego.jpg, Derick Leony / Wikimedia Commons / CC-BY-SA-2.0. http://commons.wikimedia.org/wiki/File:Volcan_de_Agua_in_Guatemala.jpghttp://commons.wikimedia.org/wiki/File:PopoAmeca.JPG, Jflamenco / Wikimedia Commons / CC BY-SA 3.0. http://commons.wikimedia.org/wiki/File:Cholula-puebla1.jpg.

57 Andean Archaeology III: North and South, Volume 3, Edited by William Isbell, Helaine Silverman. Chapter 2: America's First City? The Case of Late archaic Caral, Ruth Shady Solis.

58 The origin of States Societies in South America; Annu. Rev. Anthropol. 2001. 30:41–64 Charles Stanish; Department of Anthropology, University of California, Los Angeles, Los Angeles,California 90095–1553.

59 The origin of States Societies in South America; Annu. Rev. Anthropol. 2001. 30:41–64 Charles Stanish; Department of Anthropology, University of California, Los Angeles, Los Angeles,California 90095–1553.

60 Pre-Columbian Landscapes of Creation and Origin, edited by John Staller. Chapter 9: Dimensions of Place: The Significance of Centers to the Development of Andean Civilization: An Exploration of the Ushnu Concept.

61 Jeffrey Quilter; Moche Politics, Religion, and Warfare, Journal of World Prehistory, Vol. 16, No. 2, June 2002.

62 Pre-Columbian Landscapes of Creation and Origin, edited by John Staller. Chapter 9: Dimensions of Place: The Significance of Centers to the Development of Andean Civilization: An Exploration of the Ushnu Concept.

63 Pre-Columbian Landscapes of Creation and Origin, edited by John Staller. Chapter 9: Dimensions of Place: The Significance of Centers to the Development of Andean Civilization: An Exploration of the Ushnu Concept.

Appendices

64 Composite image created by Carlton Brown / Wikimedia / CC-BY-SA-3.0. Of Caral (Peru) comprising a number of modified pieces of original work (annotations, cropping; by the author); (A) a modified image created by Carlton Brown / Wikimedia / CC-BY-SA-3.0. original work by Xauxa / Wikimedia Commons / CC-BY-SA-3.0 . http://commons.wikimedia.org/wiki/File:PeruCaral01.jpg. (B) a modified image created by Carlton Brown / Wikimedia / CC-BY-SA-3.0. original work by By Ssola (Own work) [CC BY-SA 3.0 (http://creativecommons.org/licenses/by-sa/3.0) or GFDL (http://www.gnu.org/copyleft/fdl.html)], via Wikimedia Commons. https://commons.wikimedia.org/wiki/File%3APir%C3%A0mide_i_pla%C3%A7a_de_Caral.jpg.

65 Andean Archaeology III: North and South edited by William Isbell, Helaine Silverman: Missing Links, Imaginary Links: Staff God Imagery in the South Andean Past William H. Isbell and Patricia J. Knobloch.

66 Ivan Ghezzi and Clive L. N. Ruggles. The social and ritual context of horizon astronomical observations at Chankillo. Oxford IX International Symposium on Archaeoastronomy Proceedings IAU Symposium No. 278, 2011.

67 Composite image created by Carlton Brown / Wikimedia / CC-BY-SA-3.0. Of Caral (Peru) comprising a modified image created by Carlton Brown / Wikimedia / CC-BY-SA-3.0. original work by David Edgar / Wikimedia Commons / CC-BY-SA-3.0. http://commons.wikimedia.org/wiki/File:ThirteenTowersOfChanquilloFromFortress.JPG.

68 Composite image created by Carlton Brown of Sechin Alto (Peru) comprising a number of modified pieces of original work (annotations, cropping, formatting; by the author); (A) a modified image created by Carlton Brown / Public Domain using Satellite imagery by NASA World Wind / Public Domain. (B) Sylvain2803 / Wikip(m)edia / CC-BY-SA-3.0-2.5-2.0-1.0. http://en.wikipedia.org/wiki/File:Sechin_casma_valley.JPG.

69 Jeffrey Quilter; Moche Politics, Religion, and Warfare, Journal of World Prehistory, Vol. 16, No. 2, June 2002.

70 Composite image created by Carlton Brown / Wikimedia / CC-BY-SA-3.0. Of the Huacas del Luna y Sol (Moche; Peru) comprising modified original works (annotations, cropping; by the author); (A) a modified image created by Carlton Brown / Wikimedia / CC-BY-SA-2.0. original work by Carl Ottersen / Wikimedia Commons / CC-BY-2.0. http://commons.wikimedia.org/wiki/File:Huaca_del_Sol_090323_018_Moche.jpg.

Appendices

71 Composite image created by Carlton Brown / Wikimedia / CC-BY-SA-3.0. Of the Huacas del Luna y Sol (Moche; Peru) comprising modified original works (annotations, cropping; by the author); (A) a modified image created by Carlton Brown / Wikimedia / CC-BY-SA-3.0. original work by Ingo Mehling / Wikimedia Commons / CC-BY-3.0. http://en.wikipedia.org/wiki/File:Templo_del_Sol_1.jpg. (B) a modified image created by Carlton Brown / Wikimedia / CC-BY-SA-3.0. original work by Ingo Mehling / Wikimedia Commons / CC-BY-3.0. http://en.wikipedia.org/wiki/File:Piramida_con_Rampa_1.jpg.

72 Composite image created by Carlton Brown / Wikimedia / CC-BY-SA-3.0. of Machu Piccu (Peru) comprising modified original work (annotations, cropping; by the author); (A) a modified image created by Carlton Brown / Wikimedia / CC-BY-SA-3.0. original work by Lqgoldfish / Wikimedia Commons / CC-BY-SA-3.0. http://commons.wikimedia.org/wiki/File:Macchu_picchu_panoramic.jpg.

73 Chapter 14 South American Cultures.

74 Personal research on 30 of the UK's largest stone circles: These depict alignments with the solstice and equinox sunrises and sunsets, define midday and midnight (sun & moon zeniths) permitting their use as calendars, clocks & stellar observatories.

75 Composite image created by Carlton Brown / Wikimedia / CC-BY-SA-3.0. of Tiwanaku (Bolivia) comprising modified original work (annotations, cropping; by the author); (A) Carlton Brown / Public Domain. (B) a modified series of images created by Carlton Brown / Wikimedia / Public Domain. original work by Mhwater at the wikipedia project / Wikimedia Commons / Public Domain. http://commons.wikimedia.org/wiki/File:Plein_Tiwanaku.jpg. (Other embedded figures within (B)) original works by Mhwater / at the wikipedia project / Wikimedia Commons / Public Domain. http://commons.wikimedia.org/wiki/File:Zonnepoort_tiwanaku.jpg & http://commons.wikimedia.org/wiki/File:Tiwanaku_VerzonkenTempel.jpg.

76 Percy Brown. Indian Architecture (Buddhist And Hindu Period). Upton Press (November 15, 2010), ISBN-10: 1446513963.

77 Subhash Kak; Space and Cosmology in the Hindu Temple—presented at the International Symposium on Science and Technology in Ancient Indian Monuments, New Delhi, November 16-17, 2002. http://www.ece.lsu.edu/kak/Time2.pdf.

78 Dagens, Bruno (1986): Mayamata - An Indian Treatise on Housing Architecture and Iconography. New Delhi. Sitaram Bhartia Institute of Scientific Research.

79 Kramrisch, Stella (2002): The Hindu Temple (Volume I/II). Delhi - Motilal Banarsidas Publishers Private Limited.

Appendices

80 Composite image created by Carlton Brown / Wikimedia / CC-BY-SA-3.0. of Machu Piccu (Peru) comprising modified original work (annotations, cropping; by the author); (A) Carlton Brown / Public Domain. (B) a modified image created by Carlton Brown / Wikimedia / CC-BY-SA-3.0. original work by Muthukumaran pk / CC-BY-SA-3.0 / Wikimedia Commons. http://commons.wikimedia.org/wiki/File%3AVaradarajaperumal_temple%2C_Thirubuvanai%2C_Puducherry%2C_India_(7).JPG. (C) a modified image created by Carlton Brown / Wikimedia / CC-BY-SA-3.0. original work by Rathishkrishnan / Wikimedia Commons / CC-BY-SA-3.0. http://commons.wikimedia.org/wiki/File:Varadharaja_Perumal_Temple_Gopuram_View_At_Night.jpg.

81 Composite image created by Carlton Brown of Hindu Divya Desam Temples (India) comprising modified original work (annotations, cropping; by the author); (A) a modified image created by Carlton Brown / Wikimedia / CC0 1.0. original work by Krishna Kumar Subramanian / Wikimedia Commons / CC0 1.0. http://commons.wikimedia.org/wiki/File%3AParimala_Ranganathar_Temple.jpg. (B) a modified image created by Carlton Brown / Wikimedia / CC-BY-SA-3.0. original work by YVSREDDY / Wikimedia Commons / CC-BY-SA-3.0. http://commons.wikimedia.org/wiki/File%3ASri_Ranganathaswamy_Temple%2C_Galigopuram%2C_Nellore_YS.JPG. (C) a modified image created by Carlton Brown / Wikimedia / CC-BY-SA-3.0. original work by Rathishkrishnan / Wikimedia Commons / CC-BY-SA-3.0. http://commons.wikimedia.org/wiki/File:Varadharaja_Perumal_Temple_Gopuram_View_At_Night.jpg.

82 Composite image created by Carlton Brown / Wikimedia Commons / CC-BY-SA-3.0 / of Hindu Divya Desam Temples (India) comprising modified original worka (annotations, cropping; by the author); (A) a modified image created by Carlton Brown / Wikimedia / CC-BY-SA-3.0. original work by Thamizhpparithi Maari / Wikimedia Commons / CC-BY-SA-3.0. http://commons.wikimedia.org/wiki/File%3A%22A_Majestic_Brihadisvara_Temple_of_Gangaikonda_Cholapuram%22.JPG. B) a modified image created by Carlton Brown / Wikimedia / CC-BY-SA-3.0. original work by Muthukumaran pk / CC-BY-SA-3.0 / Wikimedia Commons. http://commons.wikimedia.org/wiki/File%3AVaradarajaperumal_temple%2C_Thirubuvanai%2C_Puducherry%2C_India_(7).JPG.

83 Composite image created by Carlton Brown / Wikimedia Commons / CC-BY-SA-3.0-2.0. of Prambanan temple & Ankor Wat comprising modified original works (annotations, cropping; by the author); (A) a modified image created by Carlton Brown / Wikimedia / CC-BY-SA-3.0. original work by Gunawan Kartapranata / Wikimedia Commons / CC-BY-SA-3.0. http://commons.wikimedia.org/wiki/File:Prambanan_Complex_2.jpg. (B) a modified image created by Carlton Brown / Wikimedia / CC-BY-SA-2.0. original work by Sam Garza / Wikimedia Commons / CC-BY-2.0. http://commons.wikimedia.org/wiki/File:Buddhist_monks_in_front_of_the_Angkor_Wat.jpg.

Appendices

84 Composite image created by Carlton Brown / Wikimedia Commons / CC-BY-SA-3.0-2.0. of Sun god deity art comprising modified original works (annotations, cropping; by the author); (A) a modified image created by Carlton Brown / Wikimedia / CC-BY-SA-3.0. original work by Indian poet / Wikimedia Commons / CC-BY-SA-3.0. http://commons.wikimedia.org/wiki/File:SURYA_GOD.JPG. (B) a modified image created by Carlton Brown / Wikimedia / Public Domain CC-BY-SA-3.0. original work by Walters Art Museum / Wikimedia Commons / Public Domain CC-BY-SA-3.0. http://commons.wikimedia.org/wiki/File:Egyptian_-_Pectoral_-_Walters_42199.jpg.

85 Handbook of Hindu Mythology, by George M. Williams.

86 Flipside of Hindu Symbolism (Sociological and scientific linkages in Hinduism) by Narayan M.K.V. Fultus Corporation (April 20, 2007), ISBN-10: 1596821175.

87 Handbook of Hindu Mythology, by George M. Williams.

88 Flipside of Hindu Symbolism (Sociological and scientific linkages in Hinduism) by Narayan M.K.V. Fultus Corporation (April 20, 2007), ISBN-10: 1596821175.

89 Handbook of Hindu Mythology, by George M. Williams.

90 Flipside of Hindu Symbolism (Sociological and scientific linkages in Hinduism) by Narayan M.K.V. Fultus Corporation (April 20, 2007), ISBN-10: 1596821175.

91 Composite image created by Carlton Brown / Wikimedia Commons / CC-BY-SA-3.0-2.0. of ancient Hindu Gods comprising modified original works (annotations, cropping; by the author); (A) a modified image created by Carlton Brown / Wikimedia / CC-BY-SA-2.0. original work by 23 dingen voor musea from Nederland (Suryabeeldje) / Wikimedia Commons / CC-BY-SA-2.0. http://commons.wikimedia.org/wiki/File:WLANL_-_23dingenvoormusea_-_Suryabeeldje.jpg. (B) a modified image created by Carlton Brown / Wikimedia / CC-BY-SA-2.0. original work by ptwo (originally posted to Flickr as 057) / Wikimedia Commons / CC-BY-2.0 / Wikimedia Commons. http://commons.wikimedia.org/wiki/File:Indra_Ellora.jpg. (C) a modified image created by Carlton Brown / Wikimedia / CC-BY-SA-3.0-2.5-2.0-1.0. original work by Benjamín Preciado, Centro de Estudios de Asia y África de El Colegio de México / Wikimedia Commons / CC-BY-SA-3.0-2.5-2.0-1.0. http://commons.wikimedia.org/wiki/File:Bhuvanesvar_3024.jpg.

92 Flipside of Hindu Symbolism (Sociological and scientific linkages in Hinduism) by Narayan M.K.V. Fultus Corporation (April 20, 2007), ISBN-10: 1596821175.

Appendices

[93] Composite image created by Carlton Brown of Trimurti Hindu Gods comprising modified original works (annotations, cropping; by the author); (A) a modified image created by Carlton Brown / Wikimedia / CC-BY-SA-3.0-2.5-2.0-1.0. original work by Benjamín Preciado, Centro de Estudios de Asia y África de El Colegio de México / Wikimedia Commons / CC-BY-SA-3.0-2.5-2.0-1.0. http://commons.wikimedia.org/wiki/File:Prajapati.JPG. (B) a modified image created by Carlton Brown / Wikimedia / CC-BY-SA-3.0. original work by David Monniaux / Wikimedia Commons / CC BY-SA 3.0. http://commons.wikimedia.org/wiki/File:Vishnu_p1070271.jpg. (C) a modified image created by Carlton Brown / Wikimedia / CC-BY-SA-2.0. original work by mdemon / Wikimedia Commons / CC-BY-SA-2.0. http://commons.wikimedia.org/wiki/File:Hoysala_stone_sculpture.jpg.

[94] Flipside of Hindu Symbolism (Sociological and scientific linkages in Hinduism) by Narayan M.K.V. Fultus Corporation (April 20, 2007), ISBN-10: 1596821175.

[95] Acharya S. Suns of God: Krishna, Buddha and Christ Unveiled. Adventures Unlimited Press (September 1, 2004), ISBN-10: 1931882312.

[96] Acharya S. Suns of God: Krishna, Buddha and Christ Unveiled. Adventures Unlimited Press (September 1, 2004), ISBN-10: 1931882312.

[97] Kersey Henry Graves. The World's Sixteen Crucified Saviours: Christianity Before Christ. Forgotten Books (November 7, 2007), ISBN-10: 1605061034.

[98] Anacalypsis (Volume 2 of 2) by Godfrey Higgins. Digireads.com (January 1, 2007), ISBN-10: 1420929933.

[99] Sarah E. Titcomb and Charles Morris. Aryan Sun Myths: The Origin of Religions (p.128). Cosimo Classics (April 15, 2007), ISBN-10: 1602062226.

[100] Sarah E. Titcomb and Charles Morris. Aryan Sun Myths: The Origin of Religions (p.128). Cosimo Classics (April 15, 2007), ISBN-10: 1602062226.

[101] Acharya S. Suns of God: Krishna, Buddha and Christ Unveiled. Adventures Unlimited Press (September 1, 2004), ISBN-10: 1931882312.

[102] Jan Assmann. The Search for God in Ancient Egypt. Cornell University Press (15 Feb 2001), ISBN-13: 978-0801487293.

[103] Jeremy Naydler. Shamanic Wisdom in the Pyramid Texts: The Mystical Tradition of Ancient Egypt. Inner Traditions (9 Dec 2004), ASIN: B00702M6U8.

[104] Jeremy Naydler. Shamanic Wisdom in the Pyramid Texts: The Mystical Tradition of Ancient Egypt. Inner Traditions (9 Dec 2004), ASIN: B00702M6U8.

Appendices

[105] Composite image created by Carlton Brown of important ancient Egyptian deities (Ennead) comprising modified original works (annotations, cropping; by the author); (A) a modified image created by Carlton Brown / Wikimedia / CC-BY-SA-3.0-2.5-2.0-1.0. original work by Atum: https://en.wikipedia.org/wiki/File:Atum.svg. Jeff Dahl / Wikimedia Commons / CC-BY-SA-3.0-2.5-2.0-1.0. (B) a modified image created by Carlton Brown / Wikimedia / CC-BY-SA-3.0-2.5-2.0-1.0. original work by Jeff Dahl / Wikimedia Commons / CC-BY-SA-3.0-2.5-2.0-1.0. https://en.wikipedia.org/wiki/File:Shu_with_feather.svg. (C) a modified image created by Carlton Brown / Wikimedia / Public Domain. original work (Shu & Geb) photographed by the British Museum /Wikimedia Commons / Public Domain. https://en.wikipedia.org/wiki/Nut_%28goddess%29#/media/File:Geb,_Nut,_Shu.jpg.

[106] Composite image created by Carlton Brown / Wikimedia / CC-BY-SA-3.0-2.5-2.0-1.0. of important ancient Egyptian deities (Ennead) comprising modified original works (annotations, cropping; by the author); (A) a modified image created by Carlton Brown / Wikimedia / CC-BY-SA-3.0-2.5-2.0-1.0. original work by (Osiris) Jeff Dahl / Wikimedia Commons / CC-BY-SA-3.0-2.5-2.0-1.0. (B) a modified image created by Carlton Brown / Wikimedia / CC-BY-SA-3.0-2.5-2.0-1.0. original work by (Isis): Jeff Dahl / Wikimedia Commons / CC-BY-SA-3.0-2.5-2.0-1.0. (C) a modified image created by Carlton Brown / Wikimedia / CC-BY-SA-3.0-2.5-2.0-1.0. original work by (Set) Jeff Dahl / Wikimedia Commons / CC-BY-SA-3.0-2.5-2.0-1.0. (D) a modified image created by Carlton Brown / Wikimedia / CC-BY-SA-3.0-2.5-2.0-1.0. original work by (Nepthys) Jeff Dahl / Wikimedia Commons / CC-BY-SA-3.0-2.5-2.0-1.0. http://en.wikipedia.org/wiki/Ennead.

[107] Composite image and modified original images created by Carlton Brown / Wikimedia / CC-BY-SA-3.0-2.5-2.0-1.0. of important ancient Egyptian deities (Ra & his namesake evolution) comprising modified original works (annotations, cropping; by the author); (A) Re-Horakhty: original work by Jeff Dahl / Wikimedia Commons / CC-BY-SA-3.0-2.5-2.0-1.0, https://en.wikipedia.org/wiki/Ra#/media/File:Re-Horakhty.svg. (B) Atum: original work by Jeff Dahl / Wikimedia Commons / CC-BY-SA-3.0-2.5-2.0-1.0 https://en.wikipedia.org/wiki/Atum#/media/File:Atum.svg. (C) Horus: original work by Jeff Dahl / Wikimedia Commons / CC-BY-SA-3.0-2.5-2.0-1.0, https://en.wikipedia.org/wiki/Horus#/media/File:Horus_standing.svg. (D) Amun: original work by Jeff Dahl / Wikimedia Commons / CC-BY-SA-3.0-2.5-2.0-1.0, https://en.wikipedia.org/wiki/Amun#/media/File:Amun.svg.

[108] Jan Assmann. The Search for God in Ancient Egypt. Cornell University Press (15 Feb 2001), ISBN-13: 978-0801487293.

Appendices

[109] Composite image created by Carlton Brown / Wikimedia / CC-BY-SA-3.0-2.5-2.0-1.0. of important ancient Egyptian deities (Osiris, Isis & Horus) comprising modified original work (annotations, cropping; by the author); (A) original work by Jon Bodsworth (photo) / Wikimedia Commons / Public domain. http://commons.wikimedia.org/wiki/File:BD_Hunefer.jpg.

[110] Composite image created by Carlton Brown / Wikimedia Commons / Public Domain of important ancient Egyptian Sun goddesses (Isis & Hathor) comprising modified original works (annotations, cropping; by the author); (A) a modified image created by Carlton Brown / Wikimedia Commons / Public Domain. original work by Louvre_042007_57 / Wikimedia Commons / Public domain. http://commons.wikimedia.org/wiki/File:Louvre_042007_57_b.jpg. (B) a modified image created by Carlton Brown / Wikimedia Commons / CC-BY-SA-3.0. original work by Ben Pirard / Wikimedia Commons / CC-BY-SA-3.0. http://commons.wikimedia.org/wiki/File:Dodentempel_Ramses_II_Medinet_Haboe.JPG.

[111] H. Brugsch. Thesaurus Inscriptionum Aegyptiacarum.

[112] D. M. Murdock and Acharya S. Christ in Egypt: The Horus-Jesus Connection by (Feb 28, 2009), Stellar House Publishing, LLC (February 28, 2009). ISBN-13: 978-0979963117.

[113] Normandi Ellis; Feasts of Light - Celebrations for the Seasons of Life based on the Egyptian Goddess Mysteries, Quest Books (March 1, 1999), ISBN-13: 978-0835607445.

[114] Ramona Louise Wheeler Walk Like an Egyptian. A modern guide to the religion and philosophy of ancient Egypt. Expanded and 3rd Edition. Published by Wildside Press.

[115] Normandi Ellis; Feasts of Light - Celebrations for the Seasons of Life based on the Egyptian Goddess Mysteries, Quest Books (March 1, 1999), ISBN-13: 978-0835607445.

[116] Hilton Hotema. Secret of Regeneration. Publisher - SOS Free Stock, ISBN-13: 978-0787304294.

[117] Walk Like an Egyptian by Ramona Louise Wheeler. A modern guide to the religion and philosophy of ancient Egypt. Expanded and 3rd Edition. Published by Wildside Press.

Appendices

[118] Composite image created by Carlton Brown / Wikimedia Commons / CC-BY-SA-3.0-2.5-2.0-1.0. of important ancient Egyptian Sun goddesses (Isis & Hathor) comprising modified original works (annotations, cropping; by the author); (A) Ptah: a modified image created by Carlton Brown / Wikimedia Commons / CC-BY-SA-3.0-2.5-2.0-1.0. original work by Jeff Dahl / Wikimedia Commons / CC-BY-SA-3.0-2.5-2.0-1.0., (B) Thoth: a modified image created by Carlton Brown / Wikimedia Commons / CC-BY-SA-3.0-2.5-2.0-1.0. original work by Jeff Dahl / Wikimedia Commons / CC-BY-SA-3.0-2.5-2.0-1.0. (C) Bastet: a modified image created by Carlton Brown / Wikimedia Commons / CC-BY-SA-3.0. original work by Gunkarta / Wikimedia Commons / CC BY-SA 3.0. http://en.wikipedia.org/wiki/File:Bastet.svg.

[119] Ramona Louise Wheeler. Walk Like an Egyptian. A modern guide to the religion and philosophy of ancient Egypt. Expanded and 3rd Edition. Published by Wildside Press.

[120] Original Papers Read Before the Syro-Egyptian Society of London. https://archive.org/details/originalpapersre00syro

[121] Ramona Louise Wheeler. Walk Like an Egyptian. A modern guide to the religion and philosophy of ancient Egypt. Expanded and 3rd Edition. Published by Wildside Press.

[122] Paul R. Steele. Handbook of Inca Mythology. Published by ABC-CLIO (December 8, 2004), ISBN-10: 1576073548.

[123] Religion in the Andes: Vision and Imagination in Early Colonial Peru, MacCormack, Sabine, published by Princeton University Press (May 17, 1993), ISBN-10: 0691021066.

[124] Native American Religious Beliefs and Practices_Draft_Academia.edu.

[125] Isbell, W. and P. Knobloch. 2006. Missing links, imaginary links: staff god imagery in the south Andean past. In H. Silverman and W. Isbell, editors, Andean Archaeology III, pp. 307-351. Springer Science+Business Media: New York.

[126] Paul R. Steele. Handbook of Inca Mythology. Published by ABC-CLIO (December 8, 2004), ISBN-10: 1576073548.

[127] Composite image created by Carlton Brown of important Inca dieties (Viracocha & Inti) comprising modified original works (annotations, cropping; by the author); (A) a modified image created by Carlton Brown / Wikimedia Commons / CC BY-SA 2.5. original work by Mhwater / Wikimedia Commons / CC BY-SA 2.5, https://upload.wikimedia.org/wikipedia/commons/c/c1/Zonnepoort_tiwanaku.jpg. (B) Orionist / Wikimedia Commons / CC BY-SA 3.0. http://en.wikipedia.org/wiki/File:Jos%C3%A9_Bernardo_de_Tagle_Inti.svg.

[128] Paul R. Steele. Handbook of Inca Mythology. Published by ABC-CLIO (December 8, 2004), ISBN-10: 1576073548.

[129] Paul R. Steele. Handbook of Inca Mythology. Published by ABC-CLIO (December 8, 2004), ISBN-10: 1576073548.

Appendices

[130] Native American Religious Beliefs and Practices_Draft_Academia.edu.

[131] Paul R. Steele. Handbook of Inca Mythology. Published by ABC-CLIO (December 8, 2004), ISBN-10: 1576073548.

[132] Lewis Spence. The Myths of Mexico and Peru. Dover Publications (January 1, 1995), ISBN-10: 0486283321.

[133] Paul R. Steele. Handbook of Inca Mythology. Published by ABC-CLIO (December 8, 2004), ISBN-10: 1576073548.

[134] Brian Bauer. Legitimization of the State in Inca Myth and Ritual; American Anthropologist (1996; 98 (2): 327-37).

[135] T. Inomata and L. Coben. Other Cuzcos: Replicated Theaters of Inca Power. In Archaeology of Performance, Theatres of Power, Community and Politics, New York: Altamira Press (2006).

[136] Referenced dissertation: http://www.academia.edu/1299708/Ritual_and_Performance_in_Andean_Plazas.

[137] Paul R. Steele. Handbook of Inca Mythology. Published by ABC-CLIO (December 8, 2004), ISBN-10: 1576073548.

[138] Lewis Spence. The Myths of Mexico and Peru. Dover Publications (January 1, 1995), ISBN-10: 0486283321.

[139] Paul R. Steele. Handbook of Inca Mythology. Published by ABC-CLIO (December 8, 2004), ISBN-10: 1576073548.

[140] Lewis Spence. The Myths of Mexico and Peru. Dover Publications (January 1, 1995), ISBN-10: 0486283321.

[141] John Frederick Schwaller. The History of the Catholic Church in Latin America: From Conquest to Revolution and Beyond. Pub; NYU Press (February 22, 2011), ISBN-10: 0814740030.

[142] M.Y Sánchez. Tiwanaku: Papers from the 2005 Mayer Center Symposium at the Denver Art Museum. Denver Art Museum, (2009). ISBN 0-8061-9972-5.

[143] Lewis Spence. The Myths of Mexico and Peru. Dover Publications (January 1, 1995), ISBN-10: 0486283321.

[144] Thomas B. F. Cummins. Toasts with the Inca: Andean Abstraction and Colonial Images on Quero Vessels. University of Michigan Press (May 15, 2002), ISBN-10: 0472110519.

[145] MacCormack, Sabine. Religion in the Andes: Vision and Imagination in Early Colonial Peru. Princeton University Press (May 17, 1993), ISBN-10: 0691021066.

[146] Paul R. Steele. Handbook of Inca Mythology. Published by ABC-CLIO (December 8, 2004), ISBN-10: 1576073548.

[147] Irene Marsha Silverblatt. Moon, Sun and Witches. Princeton University Press (May 1, 1987), ISBN-10: 0691022585.

Appendices

[148] South and Meso-American Mythology A to Z, by Ann Bingham, Jeremy Roberts. Pub; Facts on File Inc. (31 May 2004), ISBN-13: 978-0816048892.

[149] Reiko Ishihara. Deities of the ancient Maya: A guide for the 3rd Maya at the Playa workshop (2009), Dumbarton Oaks Research Library and Collection Washington, D.C.

[150] Karl A. Taube. Aztec and Maya Myths (Legendary Past). Published by University of Texas Press; 1 edition (1993), ISBN-10: 029278130X.

[151] Karl A. Taube. Aztec and Maya Myths (Legendary Past). Published by University of Texas Press; 1 edition (1993), ISBN-10: 029278130X.

[152] Reiko Ishihara. Deities of the ancient Maya: A guide for the 3rd Maya at the Playa workshop (2009), Dumbarton Oaks Research Library and Collection Washington, D.C.

[153] 2002 Maya Creator Gods. Mesoweb: www.mesoweb.com/features/bassie/CreatorGods/CreatorGods.pdf

[154] Karl A. Taube. Aztec and Maya Myths (Legendary Past). Published by University of Texas Press; 1 edition (1993), ISBN-10: 029278130X.

[155] Composite image created by Carlton Brown of Mayan cosmology comprising modified original works (annotations, cropping; by the author); (A) a modified image created by Carlton Brown / Wikimedia Commons / CC BY-SA 3.0. original work by CyArk / Wikimedia Commons / CC-BY-SA-3.0. http://commons.wikimedia.org/wiki/File:Balakanche1_cyark.jpg. (B) a modified image created by Carlton Brown / Wikimedia Commons / CC BY-SA 2.0. original work by Steve Jurvetson / Wikimedia Commons / CC-BY-2.0 . http://commons.wikimedia.org/wiki/File:Under_the_Milky_Way.jpg.

[156] Karl A. Taube. Aztec and Maya Myths (Legendary Past). Published by University of Texas Press; 1 edition (1993), ISBN-10: 029278130X.

[157] Karl A. Taube. Aztec and Maya Myths (Legendary Past). Published by University of Texas Press; 1 edition (1993), ISBN-10: 029278130X.

[158] Deities of the ancient Maya: A guide for the 3rd Maya at the Playa workshop (2009), Reiko Ishihara, Dumbarton Oaks Research Library and Collection Washington, D.C.

[159] Merideth Paxton. The Cosmos of the Yucatec Maya: Cycles and Steps from the Madrid Codex. University of New Mexico Press (November 6, 2001), ISBN-10: 0826322921.

[160] 2002 Maya Creator Gods. Mesoweb: www.mesoweb.com/features/bassie/CreatorGods/CreatorGods.pdf.

[161] Reiko Ishihara. Deities of the ancient Maya: A guide for the 3rd Maya at the Playa workshop (2009), Dumbarton Oaks Research Library and Collection Washington, D.C.

[162] 2002 Maya Creator Gods. Mesoweb: www.mesoweb.com/features/bassie/CreatorGods/CreatorGods.pdf.

Appendices

[163] Karl A. Taube. Aztec and Maya Myths (Legendary Past). Published by University of Texas Press; 1 edition (1993), ISBN-10: 029278130X.

[164] Reiko Ishihara, Deities of the ancient Maya: A guide for the 3rd Maya at the Playa workshop (2009), Dumbarton Oaks Research Library and Collection Washington, D.C.

[165] Robert Sharer and Loa Traxler. The Ancient Maya, 6th Edition, Stanford University Press; 6 edition (October 7, 2005). ISBN-10: 0804748179.

[166] Karl Taube. Flower Mountain: Concepts of Life, Beauty, and Paradise among the Classic Maya. Res 45: 69-98 (2004).

[167] A Study of Classic Maya Rulership; PhD thesis in Anthropology by Mark Alan Wright August 2011. http://www.academia.edu/781885/A_Study_of_Classic_Maya_Rulership.

[168] Carolyn Elaine Tate. Yaxchilan: The Design of a Maya Ceremonial City. University of Texas Press; 1st edition (1992). ISBN-10: 0292770413.

[169] Reiko Ishihara. Deities of the ancient Maya: A guide for the 3rd Maya at the Playa workshop (2009), Dumbarton Oaks Research Library and Collection Washington, D.C.

[170] Ann Bingham, Jeremy Roberts. South and Meso-American Mythology A to Z. Pub; Facts on File Inc. (31 May 2004), ISBN-13: 978-0816048892.

[171] Karl A. Taube. Aztec and Maya Myths (Legendary Past). Published by University of Texas Press; 1 edition (1993), ISBN-10: 029278130X.

[172] Ann Bingham and Jeremy Roberts. South and Meso-American Mythology A to Z. Pub; Facts on File Inc. (31 May 2004), ISBN-13: 978-0816048892.

[173] Itzamna & Ix Chel: original work by Salvador alc / Wikimedia Commons/ CC-BY-SA-3.0. http://commons.wikimedia.org/wiki/File:Itzamna_e_Ixchel.JPG.

[174] Karl A. Taube. Aztec and Maya Myths (Legendary Past). Published by University of Texas Press; 1 edition (1993), ISBN-10: 029278130X.

[175] Ann Bingham, Jeremy Roberts. South and Meso-American Mythology A to Z. Pub; Facts on File Inc. (31 May 2004), ISBN-13: 978-0816048892.

[176] Composite image created by Carlton Brown Wikimedia Commons / CC BY-SA 3.0 of Mayan Sun deities comprising modified original works (annotations, cropping; by the author); (A) Kinich Ahau: a modified image created by Carlton Brown / Wikimedia Commons / CC BY-SA 3.0. original work by Aguilardo / Wikimedia Commons / CC-BY-SA-3.0. http://commons.wikimedia.org/wiki/File:Mascar%C3%B3n_de_Kinich_Ahau.jpg. (B) Kukulkan: a modified image created by Carlton Brown / Wikimedia Commons / CC BY-SA 3.0. original work by BoNoMoJo / Wikimedia Commons / CC-BY-SA-3.0. http://en.wikipedia.org/wiki/File:Head_of_serpent_column.jpg.

[177] 2002 Maya Creator Gods. Mesoweb: www.mesoweb.com/features/bassie/CreatorGods/CreatorGods.pdf.

Appendices

[178] Merideth Paxton. The Cosmos of the Yucatec Maya: Cycles and Steps from the Madrid Codex. University of New Mexico Press (November 6, 2001), ISBN-10: 0826322921.

[179] Martin Brennan. The Hidden Maya: A New Understanding of Maya Glyphs, Bear and Company (June 1, 1998), ISBN-10: 187918124X.

[180] Madrid Codex: Simon Burchell / Wikimedia Commons / CC-BY-SA-3.0. http://commons.wikimedia.org/wiki/File:Madrid_Codex_19.jpg.

[181] Carolyn Elaine Tate. Yaxchilan: The Design of a Maya Ceremonial City. University of Texas Press; 1st edition (1992), ISBN-10: 0292770413.

[182] F. D. Duran. Book of the Gods and Rites and the Ancient Calendar. Published; University of Oklahoma Pr (June 1977), ISBN-10: 0806112018.

[183] http://www.allabouthistory.org/huitzilopochtli-faq.htm

[184] Dan Furst. Dance of the Moon: Celebrating the Sacred Cycles of the Earth. Llewellyn Publications (July 8, 2009), ISBN-10: 0738715107.

[185] Composite image created by Carlton Brown of the Sun god´s favorite flowers comprising modified original works (annotations, cropping; by the author); (A) Sacred pink Lotus: 余文麟 / Wikimedia Commons / CC-BY-SA-3.0-2.5-2.0-1.0. http://commons.wikimedia.org/wiki/File%3A%E4%B8%AD%E8%88%88%E6%96%B0%E6%9D%91%E8%8D%B7%E8%8A%B1%E5%AD%A3.JPG. (B) Blue water lily: Fernandograu / Wikimedia Commons / CC-BY-3.0. http://commons.wikimedia.org/wiki/File:Nymphaea_cultivar_flowering,_Sanya_city_in_Hainan_island.jpg. (C) White water lily: Anne Burgess / Wikimedia Commons / CC-BY-SA-2.0. http://commons.wikimedia.org/wiki/File%3AWhite_Water-lily_(Nymphaea_alba)_-_geograph.org.uk_-_1341457.jpg.

[186] Composite image created by Carlton Brown of entheogens associated with ancient religions comprising modified original works (annotations, cropping; by the author); (A) Syrian rue: Kurt Stüber / Wikimedia Commons / CC-BY-SA-3.0. http://commons.wikimedia.org/wiki/File:Peganum_harmala1.jpg. (B) Angel trumpets in my garden (datura): Carlton Brown / Public Domain. (C) Mandrake depiction: William Turner (1508-1568) / Wikimedia Commons / Public domain. http://commons.wikimedia.org/wiki/File%3AMandrake_-_William_Turner's_Herbal.jpg.

[187] Composite image created by Carlton Brown of entheogens associated with ancient religions comprising modified original works (annotations, cropping; by the author); (A) Syrian rue: Kurt Stüber / Wikimedia Commons / CC-BY-SA-3.0. http://commons.wikimedia.org/wiki/File:Peganum_harmala1.jpg. (B) Angel trumpets in my garden (datura): Carlton Brown / Public Domain. (C) Mandrake depiction: William Turner (1508-1568) / Wikimedia Commons / Public domain. http://commons.wikimedia.org/wiki/File%3AMandrake_-_William_Turner's_Herbal.jpg.

[188] Bourguignon, E., ed. 1973. Religion, altered states of consciousness, and social change. Ohio University Press, Columbus.

[189] MD Merlin. Archeological evidence for the tradition of psychoactive plant use in the Old World. The New York Botanical Garden Press, Bronx, NY 10458-5126 U.S.A. Economic Botany 57(3) pp. 295–323. 2003.

[190] Philippe de FÉLICE. Poisons sacrés. Ivresses divines. Essai sur quelques formes inférieures de la mystique (1936). Published by Albin Michel (11 Jun 1970) in French. ISBN-10: 222604504X.

[191] Weston La Barre. The Ghost Dance: Origins of Religion. Published by Allen and Unwin (1st Ed 3 Aug 1972). ISBN-10: 0042110033.

[192] Gordon Wasson. The hallucinogenic fungi of Mexico: An inquiry into the origins of the religious idea among primitive peoples. Published by Botanical Museum of Harvard University (1961), ASIN: B0007FV1G0.

[193] Albert Hofmann and Jonathan Ott. Pharmacotheon: Entheogenic Drugs, Their Plant Sources and History. Publisher: Published by Natural Products Company (2nd Ed Feb 1993), ISBN-10: 0961423498.

[194] Schultes R.E. An Overview of Hallucinogens in the Western Hemisphere. 1972.

[195] Weston La Barre PhD. Shamanic Origins of Religion and Medicine. Journal of Psychedelic Drug Vol. 11 (1-2) Jan-Jun, 1979.

[196] Weston La Barre PhD. Shamanic Origins of Religion and Medicine. Journal of Psychedelic Drug Vol. 11 (1-2) Jan-Jun, 1979.

[197] Michael J. Harner. Hallucinogens and Shamanism. Published by OUP USA (15 Nov 1973), ISBN-10: 0195016491.

[198] Weston La Barre PhD. Shamanic Origins of Religion and Medicine. Journal of Psychedelic Drug Vol. 11 (1-2) Jan-Jun, 1979.

[199] MD Merlin. Archeological evidence for the tradition of psychoactive plant use in the Old World. The New York Botanical Garden Press, Bronx, NY 10458-5126 U.S.A. Economic Botany 57(3) pp. 295–323. 2003.

[200] Benny Shannon. Biblical Entheogens: a Speculative Hypothesis by Time and Mind - The Journal of Archaeology Consciousness and Culture. Volume 1, Issue 1, March 2008, pp. 51–74.

[201] R. Gordon Wasson, Albert Hofmann, Carl A. P. Ruck. The Road to Eleusis (Unveiling the Secret of the Mysteries) by. Published by A Harvest / HBJ Book (1st Ed 1978), ASIN: B000I1T69C.

[202] MD Merlin. Archeological evidence for the tradition of psychoactive plant use in the Old World. The New York Botanical Garden Press, Bronx, NY 10458-5126 U.S.A. Economic Botany 57(3) pp. 295–323. 2003.

[203] Terence Mckenna. Food of the Gods. Published by Bantam USA; Bantam Trade Pbk. Ed edition (5 Oct 1998), ISBN-10: 0553371304.

Appendices

[204] Sachidananda Padhy and Santosh Kumar Dash. The Soma Drinker of Ancient India: An Ethno-Botanical Retrospection by J. Hum. Ecol. 15(1): 19-26 (2004).

[205] MD Merlin. Archeological evidence for the tradition of psychoactive plant use in the Old World. The New York Botanical Garden Press, Bronx, NY 10458-5126 U.S.A. Economic Botany 57(3) pp. 295–323. 2003.

[206] Robert Gordon Wasson. Soma: Divine Mushroom of Immortality, Published by Harcourt (April 1972), ISBN-10: 0156838001.

[207] David Flattery. Haoma and Harmaline: The Botanical Identity of the Sacred Hallucinogen 'Somo' and Its Legacy in Religion, Language. Published by Univ of California Pr (May 1989), ISBN-10: 0520096274.

[208] Terence Mckenna. Food of the Gods. Published by Bantam USA; Bantam Trade Pbk. Ed edition (5 Oct 1998), ISBN-10: 0553371304.

[209] David L. Spess. Soma: The Divine Hallucinogen. Park Street Press; First Edition edition (August 1, 2000), ISBN-10: 0892817313.

[210] David L. Spess. Soma: The Divine Hallucinogen. Park Street Press; First Edition edition (August 1, 2000), ISBN-10: 0892817313.

[211] Carod-Artal FJ. Hallucinogenic drugs in pre-Columbian Mesoamerican cultures. Published in Neurologia. 2011 Sep 3.

[212] William Emboden. Transcultural use of narcotic water lilies in ancient Egyptian and Maya drug ritual. Journal of Ethnopharmacology, 3 (1981).

[213] Gordon Wasson. The hallucinogenic fungi of Mexico: An inquiry into the origins of the religious idea among primitive peoples. Published by Botanical Museum of Harvard University (1961), ASIN: B0007FV1G0.

[214] Dobkin de Rios, Marlene. The influence of psychotropic flora and fauna on Maya religion. Published in Current Anthropology, Vol 15(2), Jun 1974, 147-164.

[215] Schultes, R. E. 1939. Plantae Mexicanae II. The Identification of Teonanácatl, a Narcotic Basidiomycete of the Aztecs. Published by Botanical Museum Leaflets, Harvard University 7:37–56.

[216] Carod-Artal FJ. Hallucinogenic drugs in pre-Columbian Mesoamerican cultures. Published in Neurologia. 2011 Sep 3.

[217] Gaston Guzman. Hallucinogenic mushrooms in Mexico: An overview. Published by The New York Botanical Garden Press, Economic Botany, 62(3), 2008, pp. 404–412.

[218] Andrew McDonald and Brian Stross. Waterlily and cosmic serpent: equivalent conduits of the Maya spirit realm. Journal of Ethnobiology 32(1): 74–107 (2012).

[219] Carod-Artal FJ. Hallucinogenic drugs in pre-Columbian Mesoamerican cultures. Published in Neurologia 2011 Sep 3.

Appendices

[220] Composite image created by Carlton Brown of entheogens associated with ancient Mesoamerican Sun god religions comprising modified original works (annotations, cropping; by the author); (A) Morning glory flower: Fg2 / Wikimedia Commons / Public domain / Wikimedia Commons. http://commons.wikimedia.org/wiki/File:Edit_Turbina_corymbosa.jpg. (B) Peyote cactus: Frank Vincentz / Wikimedia Commons / CC-BY-SA-3.0. http://commons.wikimedia.org/wiki/File:Lophophora_williamsii_ies.jpg. (C) Bufo marinus toad: Eli Greenbaum/ Wikimedia Commons / CC BY-SA 2.5. http://en.wikipedia.org/wiki/File:Bufo_marinus01e.jpg.

[221] Carod-Artal FJ. Hallucinogenic drugs in pre-Columbian Mesoamerican cultures. Published in Neurologia. 2011 Sep 3.

[222] Schultes, R. E. 1939. Plantae Mexicanae II. The Identification of Teonanácatl, a Narcotic Basidiomycete of the Aztecs. Published by Botanical Museum Leaflets, Harvard University 7:37–56.

[223] Gordon Wasson. The hallucinogenic fungi of Mexico: An inquiry into the origins of the religious idea among primitive peoples. Published by Botanical Museum of Harvard University (1961), ASIN: B0007FV1G0.

[224] Isbell, W. and P. Knobloch. 2006. Missing links, imaginary links: staff god imagery in the south Andean past. In H. Silverman and W. Isbell, editors, Andean Archaeology III, pp. 307-351. Springer Science+Business Media: New York.

[225] Bonnie Glass-Coffin. Shamanism and San Pedro through Time: Some Notes on the Archaeology, History, and Continued Use of an Entheogen in Northern Peru. Anthropology of Consciousness, Vol. 21, Issue 1, pp. 58–82.

[226] Rainer W Bussmann and Douglas Sharon. Traditional medicinal plant use in Northern Peru: tracking two thousand years of healing culture. Journal of Ethnobiology and Ethnomedicine 2006, 2:47.

[227] San Pedro cactus: MacAllenBrothers / Wikimedia Commons / CC-BY-SA-2.0. http://commons.wikimedia.org/wiki/File:Echinopsis-pachanoi-peru.jpg.

[228] Bonnie Glass-Coffin. Shamanism and San Pedro through Time: Some Notes on the Archaeology, History, and Continued Use of an Entheogen in Northern Peru. Anthropology of Consciousness, Vol. 21, Issue 1, pp. 58–82.

[229] Andean Archaeology III: North and South edited by William Isbell, Helaine Silverman: Missing Links, Imaginary Links: Staff God Imagery in the South Andean Past William H. Isbell and Patricia J. Knobloch.

[230] Composite image created by Carlton Brown of entheogens associated with ancient South American Sun god religions comprising modified original works (annotations, cropping; by the author);(A) João Medeiros (Anadenanthera colubrina) / Wikimedia Commons / CC-BY-2.0. http://commons.wikimedia.org/wiki/File:Anadenanthera_colubrina_tree.jpg.

(B) Anadenanthera colubrina seed pods: João Medeiros (Anadenanthera colubrina) / Wikimedia Commons / CC-BY-2.0. http://commons.wikimedia.org/wiki/File%3AAnadenanthera_colubrina_fruits.jpg.

Appendices

[231] Composite image created by Carlton Brown of entheogens associated with Ancient Egypt's art depicted hallucinogens comprising modified original works (annotations, cropping; by the author); (A) Blue water lily: Fernandograu / Wikimedia Commons / CC-BY-3.0. http://commons.wikimedia.org/wiki/File:Nymphaea_cultivar_flowering,_Sanya_city_in_Hainan_island.jpg. (B) Datura: dalbera / Wikimedia Commons / CC-BY-2.0. http://commons.wikimedia.org/wiki/File%3ADaturas_(4334808682).jpg. (C) Opium flower & poppy: tanja niggendijker / Wikimedia Commons / CC-BY-2.0. http://commons.wikimedia.org/wiki/File:Papaver_somniferum_flowers.jpg. (D) Magic mushrooms: Mädi / Wikimedia Commons / CC-BY-SA-3.0. http://commons.wikimedia.org/wiki/File:Golden_teacher_kookoskuidussa.jpg.

[232] Rosalie David. The art of healing in ancient Egypt: a scientific reappraisal. The Lancet, Volume 372, Issue 9652, 22–28. November 2008, Pages 1802–1803.

[233] W. B. J. Harer. Nymphaea: Sacred Narcotic Lotus of Ancient Egypt? JSSEA XIV, no. 4 (1984), 100-102;, 'Pharmacological and Biological Properties of the Egyptian Lotus,' JARCE XXII (1985), 49-54.

[234] Kasia Szpakowska. A Delta-man in Yebu: Occasional Volume of the Egyptologists' Electronic Forum No. 1. Altered States: An inquiry into the possible use of narcotics or alcohol to induce dreams in Pharaonic Egypt. Universal Publishers (September 15, 2003), ISBN-10: 158112564X.

[235] M. D. Merlin. Archaeological Evidence for the Tradition of Psychoactive Plant Use in the Old World. Economic Botany, 57(3):295-323. 2003 published by The New York Botanical Garden.

[236] William A. Emboden, Jr. Ethnobotanical Tools in the Ancient Near East.

[237] Fertile Crescent: Nafsadh / Wikimedia Commons / CC-BY-SA-3.0-2.5-2.0-1.0. http://en.wikipedia.org/wiki/File:Map_of_fertile_cresent.svg.

[238] Ioanna A Ramoutsaki, Helen Askitopoulou, Eleni Konsolaki. International Congress Series: Volume 1242, December 2002, Pages 43–50. The history of anesthesia, Pain relief and sedation in Roman Byzantine texts: Mandragoras officinarum, Hyoscyamos niger and Atropa belladonna.

[239] Dr Pulok K. Mukherjee, Debajyoti Mukherjee, Amal K. Maji, S. Rai, Michael Heinrich. Review: The sacred lotus (Nelumbo nucifera)—phytochemical and therapeutic profile. Published by the Journal of Pharmacy and Pharmacology, 2009, 61: 407–422.

[240] Wang X, Liu J, Geng Y, Wang D, Dong H, Zhang T. Preparative separation of alkaloids from Nelumbo nucifera Gaertn by pH-zone-refining counter-current chromatography. J Sep Sci. 2010 Mar;33(4-5):539-44.

[241] Zheng Z, Wang M, Wang D, Duan W, Wang X, Zheng C. Preparative separation of alkaloids from Nelumbo nucifera leaves by conventional and pH-zone-refining counter-current chromatography.

Appendices

[242] Xu X, Sun CR, Dai XJ, Hu RL, Pan YJ, Yang ZF. LC/MS guided isolation of alkaloids from lotus leaves by pH-zone-refining counter-current chromatography.

[243] http://www.natureproduct.cn/EN/abstract/abstract8639.shtml: Xiao Juan; Fu Xiao-yan; Yang chao; Li Hai-long; Chen Lin; Wang Zhi-hui; Nan Nan; Sun Zhida. Analysis and Determination of Alkaloids in the Inedible Parts of Nelumbo nucifera Gaertn.

[244] A Review Paper: Distribution, Structures and Pharmacological Activities of Aporphine Alkaloids in various plant families by Wei Wang et al. Published by http://www.topclassglobaljournals.org: Journal of Herbal Medicine Vol. 1(1) Pp. 001-028, 26 November, 2012.

[245] S. K. Bhattacharya, R. Bose, P. Ghosh, V. J. Tripathi, A. B. Kay, B. Dasgupta. Psychopharmacological Studies on Nuciferine and Its Hofmann Degradation Product Atherosperminine. Journal of Psychopharmacology 59, 29-33 (1978) by Springer-Verlag.

[246] Pramipexole (Parkinson's disease): http://www.nlm.nih.gov/medlineplus/druginfo/meds/a697029.html.

[247] Ropinirole (Parkinsons disease): http://www.nlm.nih.gov/medlineplus/druginfo/meds/a698013.html.

[248] Cabergoline (hyperprolactinemia): http://www.nlm.nih.gov/medlineplus/druginfo/meds/a612020.html

[249] Blue water lily extract. http://sxkesheng.en.alibaba.com/product/898178458-215918456/Blue_Lotus_Flower_Extract_Nymphaea_Caerulea.html, http://www.chemkind.com/chemicals-p_3278630_blue-lotus-leaf-extract.htm, http://au.alibaba.com/product/620498131-Blue-Lotus-Flower-Extract-Nymphaea-Caerulea.html.

[250] S. K. Bhattacharya, R. Bose, P. Ghosh, V. J. Tripathi, A. B. Kay, B. Dasgupta. Psychopharmacological Studies on Nuciferine and Its Hofmann Degradation Product Atherosperminine. Journal of Psychopharmacology 59, 29-33 (1978) by Springer-Verlag.

[251] William Emboden. The sacred narcotic lily of the Nile—Nymphaea caerulae. Economic Botany, 32(4), 1978, pp. 395-407 1979, by the New York Botanical Garden, Bronx, NY 10458.

[252] William Emboden. Transcultural use of narcotic water lilies in ancient Egyptian and Maya drug ritual. Journal of Ethnopharmacology, 3 (1981).

[253] William Emboden. The sacred narcotic lily of the Nile—Nymphaea caerulae. Economic Botany, 32(4), 1978, pp. 395-407 1979, by the New York Botanical Garden, Bronx, NY 10458.

[254] W. B. J. Harer. Pharmacological and Biological Properties of the Egyptian Lotus. JARCE XXII (1985), 49-54.

Appendices

[255] Composite image created by Carlton Brown of Pharoah icons comprising modified original works (annotations, cropping; by the author); (A) Ramesses II: a modified image created by Carlton Brown / Wikimedia Commons / Public Domain. original work by Than217 / Wikimedia Commons / Public domain. http://commons.wikimedia.org/wiki/File%3ACloseup_Ramesses_II_Colossus.jpg. (B) Tutankhamun's mummy: Erik Hooymans / Wikimedia Commons / CC BY-SA 2.5. http://commons.wikimedia.org/wiki/File:Tutankhamun_Mask.JPG.

[256] Uxmal (Mexico): Carlton Brown / Public Domain.

[257] Composite image created by Carlton Brown of Surya comprising modified original works (annotations, cropping; by the author); (A) (23 dingen voor musea (Suryabeeldje) / Wikimedia Commons / CC-BY-SA-2.0. http://commons.wikimedia.org/wiki/File:WLANL_-_23dingenvoormusea_-_Suryabeeldje.jpg.

[258] Composite image created by Carlton Brown of important Hindu Sun gods comprising modified original works (annotations, cropping; by the author); (A) Surya: a modified image created by Carlton Brown / Wikimedia Commons / CC BY-SA 3.0. original work by Sailko / Wikimedia Commons / CC-BY-SA-3.0. http://commons.wikimedia.org/wiki/File:Rajastan,_surya,_ix-x_sec.JPG. (B) Vishnu: a modified image created by Carlton Brown / Wikimedia Commons / CC BY-SA 3.0. original work by David Monniaux / Wikimedia Commons / CC BY-SA 3.0. http://commons.wikimedia.org/wiki/File:Vishnu_p1070271.jpg. (C) Brahma: a modified image created by Carlton Brown / Wikimedia Commons / CC-BY-SA-3.0-2.5-2.0-1.0. original work by Benjamín Preciado, Centro de Estudios de Asia y África de El Colegio de México / Wikimedia Commons / CC-BY-SA-3.0-2.5-2.0-1.0. http://commons.wikimedia.org/wiki/File:Prajapati.JPG.

[259] Composite image created by Carlton Brown of Surya comprising modified original works (annotations, cropping; by the author); (A) Surya: a modified image created by Carlton Brown / Wikimedia Commons / CC BY-SA 2.0. original work by 23 dingen voor musea (Suryabeeldje) / Wikimedia Commons / CC-BY-SA-2.0. http://commons.wikimedia.org/wiki/File:WLANL_-_23dingenvoormusea_-_Suryabeeldje.jpg. (B) Surya: a modified image created by Carlton Brown / Wikimedia Commons / CC BY-SA 3.0. original work by Jonathan Cardy / Wikimedia Commons / CC-BY-SA-3.0. http://commons.wikimedia.org/wiki/File:Surya_at_V%26A.jpg.

[260] Composite image created by Carlton Brown of Surya comprising modified original works (annotations, cropping; by the author); (A) Surya: a modified image created by Carlton Brown / Wikimedia Commons / CC-BY-SA-3.0-2.5. original work by G-u-t / Wikimedia Commons / CC-BY-SA-3.0-2.5. http://commons.wikimedia.org/wiki/File%3ASunspot_butterfly_graph.gif. (B) original work by NASA / Wikimedia Commons / Public domain. http://en.wikipedia.org/wiki/File:Traceimage.jpg.

[261] Composite image created by Carlton Brown of Brahma comprising modified original works (annotations, cropping; by the author); (A) Brahma: a modified image created by Carlton Brown / Wikimedia Commons / CC-BY-SA-3.0-2.5-2.0-1.0. original work by Benjamín Preciado Centro de Estudios de Asia y África de El Colegio de México / Wikimedia Commons / CC-BY-SA-3.0-2.5-2.0-1.0. http://commons.wikimedia.org/wiki/File:Prajapati.JPG. (B) Brahma: a modified image created by Carlton Brown / Wikimedia Commons / CC0 1.0. original work by Wmpearl / Wikimedia Commons / CC0 1.0. http://commons.wikimedia.org/wiki/File:Vishnu_Brahma_My_Son_E1.jpg.

[262] Composite image created by Carlton Brown of Vishnu comprising modified original works (annotations, cropping; by the author); (A) Vishnu: original work by Leon Meerson / Wikimedia Commons / CC-BY-SA-2.0. http://commons.wikimedia.org/wiki/File:Munneswaram_Vishnu.jpg. (B) Vishnu & Consorts: a modified image created by Carlton Brown / Wikimedia Commons / CC0. original work by Hiart / Wikimedia Commons / CC0. http://commons.wikimedia.org/wiki/File:WLA_haa_Vishnu_with_Consorts_Lakshmi_and_Sarasvati_Bengal.jpg.

[263] Composite image created by Carlton Brown of Shiva comprising modified original works (annotations, cropping; by the author); (A) Shiva: a modified image created by Carlton Brown / Wikimedia Commons / CC-BY-SA-3.0-2.5-2.0-1.0. original work by Benjamín Preciado Centro de Estudios de Asia y África de El Colegio de México/ Wikimedia Commons / CC-BY-SA-3.0-2.5-2.0-1.0. http://commons.wikimedia.org/wiki/File:MADRAS36.JPG. (B) Shiva: a modified image created by Carlton Brown / Wikimedia Commons / CC BY-SA 3.0. original work by QuartierLatin1968 / Wikimedia Commons / CC BY-SA 3.0. http://commons.wikimedia.org/wiki/File:Ellora_Kailash_temple_Shiva_panel.jpg. http://commons.wikimedia.org/wiki/File:Shiva_statue_at_Parmarth_Niketan,_Muni_ki_Reti,_Rishikesh.jpg.

[264] Composite image created by Carlton Brown of Old Kingdom Pharaohs comprising modified original works (annotations, cropping; by the author); (A) Khafre: a modified image created by Carlton Brown / Wikimedia Commons / CC-BY-SA-2.5. original work by José-Manuel Benito Álvarez / Wikimedia Commons / CC-BY-SA-2.5. http://commons.wikimedia.org/wiki/File:Khafra_-_Queft%C3%A9n.jpg. (B) Menkaure: a modified image created by Carlton Brown / Wikimedia Commons / CC-BY-SA-2.5. original work by Keith Schengili-Roberts / Wikimedia Commons / CC BY-SA 2.5. http://en.wikipedia.org/wiki/File:MenkauraAndQueen_MuseumOfFineArtsBoston.png. (C) Sahure: a modified image created by Carlton Brown / Wikimedia Commons / CC-BY-SA-2.5. original work by Keith Schengili-Roberts / Wikimedia Commons / CC-BY-SA-2.5. http://commons.wikimedia.org/wiki/File%3ASahureAndNomeGod-CloseUpOfSahure_MetropolitanMuseum.png.

Appendices

[265] Composite image created by Carlton Brown of New Kingdom Pharaohs comprising modified original works (annotations, cropping; by the author); (A) Akhenaten: a modified image created by Carlton Brown / Wikimedia Commons / Public Domain. original work by qwelk / Wikimedia Commons / Public domain. http://commons.wikimedia.org/wiki/File:Akenaton.jpg. (B) Ahmenhotep III: a modified image created by Carlton Brown / Wikimedia Commons / Public Domain. original work by Chasuble / Wikimedia Commons / Public domain. http://commons.wikimedia.org/wiki/File%3ASeated_statue_of_Amenhotep_III%2C_British_Museum.jpg. (C) Rameses II: a modified image created by Carlton Brown / Wikimedia Commons / CC-BY-SA-3.0-2.5-2.0-1.0. original work by Steve F-E-Cameron / Wikimedia Commons / CC-BY-SA-3.0-2.5-2.0-1.0. http://commons.wikimedia.org/wiki/File:S_F-E-CAMERON_EGYPT_2006_FEB_00671.JPG.

[266] Composite image created by Carlton Brown of the Aten and its Elite associations comprising modified original works (annotations, cropping; by the author); (A) Akhenaten-Aten: a modified image created by Carlton Brown / Wikimedia Commons / Public Domain. original work by RickK / Wikimedia Commons Public Domain. http://commons.wikimedia.org/wiki/File:Aten_disk.jpg. (B) Queen Nefertiti-Aten: a modified image created by Carlton Brown / Wikimedia Commons / CC-BY-SA-2.5-2.0-1.0. original work by Captmondo / Wikimedia Commons / CC-BY-SA-2.5-2.0-1.0. http://commons.wikimedia.org/wiki/File:NefertitiRelief_SmitingSceneOnBoat-CloseUp.png.

[267] William Emboden. The sacred narcotic lily of the Nile—Nymphaea caerulae. Economic Botany, 32(4), 1978, pp. 395-407 1979, by the New York Botanical Garden, Bronx, NY 10458.

[268] William Emboden. Transcultural use of narcotic water lilies in ancient Egyptian and Maya drug ritual. Journal of Ethnopharmacology, 3 (1981).

[269] William A. Emboden, Jr Ethnobotanical Tools in the Ancient Near East.

[270] Re-Horakhty-Lady Taperet "communion": UnknownRama / Wikimedia Commons / CC-BY-SA-2.0-fr. http://commons.wikimedia.org/wiki/File:Taperet_stele_E52_mp3h9201.jpg.

[271] William Emboden. The sacred narcotic lily of the Nile—Nymphaea caerulae. Economic Botany, 32(4), 1978, pp. 395-407 1979, by the New York Botanical Garden, Bronx, NY 10458.

[272] Jeremy Naydler. Shamanic Wisdom in the Pyramid Texts: The Mystical Tradition of Ancient Egypt. Inner Traditions (9 Dec 2004), ASIN: B00702M6U8.

[273] Composite image created by Carlton Brown of Egyptian temple art comprising modified original works (annotations, cropping; by the author); (A) Papyrus of Ani: original work by Jon Bodsworth (www.egyptarchive.co.uk) / Wikimedia Commons / Public domain. http://commons.wikimedia.org/wiki/File:Hieratic_Book_of_the_Dead_of_Padiamenet.jpg. (B) Re-Horakhty: original work by Musée du Louvre / Wikimedia Commons / Public Domain. http://commons.wikimedia.org/wiki/File:Ra-harphist.jpg.

[274] William Emboden. Transcultural use of narcotic water lilies in ancient Egyptian and Maya drug ritual. Journal of Ethnopharmacology, 3 (1981).

[275] Composite image created by Carlton Brown of Egyptian temple art comprising modified original works (annotations, cropping; by the author); (A) Semenkhara relief: dalbera / Wikimedia Commons / CC-BY-2.0. http://commons.wikimedia.org/wiki/File%3ACouple_royal_dans_un_jardin_(Neues_Museum%2C_Berlin)_(6098971245).jpg. (B) Re-Horakhty and Lady Djedkhonsuiwesankh "communion": original work by Oriental Institute, the University of Chicago / Wikimedia Commons / Public domain. http://commons.wikimedia.org/wiki/File:Re-Horakhty_Stela.jpg.

[276] William Emboden. Transcultural use of narcotic water lilies in ancient Egyptian and Maya drug ritual. Journal of Ethnopharmacology, 3 (1981).

[277] Deity & Pharoah headgear: Composite image created by Carlton Brown of Egyptian temple art comprising modified original works (annotations, cropping; by the author); (A) Hedjet: https://upload.wikimedia.org/wikipedia/commons/thumb/9/9e/Hedjet.svg/512px-Hedjet.svg.png, By fi:Käyttäjä:kompak (self-made drawing) [GFDL (http://www.gnu.org/copyleft/fdl.html), CC-BY-SA-3.0 (http://creativecommons.org/licenses/by-sa/3.0/) or CC BY 2.5 (http://creativecommons.org/licenses/by/2.5)], via Wikimedia Common. (B) Deshret: https://upload.wikimedia.org/wikipedia/commons/f/fe/Deshret.svg, By fi:Käyttäjä:kompak (self-made drawing) [GFDL (http://www.gnu.org/copyleft/fdl.html), CC-BY-SA-3.0 (http://creativecommons.org/licenses/by-sa/3.0/) or CC BY 2.5 (http://creativecommons.org/licenses/by/2.5)], via Wikimedia Commons. (C) Pschent (Double Crown): https://commons.wikimedia.org/wiki/File:Double_crown.svg, By Jeff Dahl (Own work) [GFDL (http://www.gnu.org/copyleft/fdl.html) or CC BY-SA 4.0-3.0-2.5-2.0-1.0 (http://creativecommons.org/licenses/by-sa/4.0-3.0-2.5-2.0-1.0)], via Wikimedia Commons. (D) Atef: https://upload.wikimedia.org/wikipedia/commons/f/fc/Atef_crown.svg, By Jeff Dahl (Own work) [GFDL (http://www.gnu.org/copyleft/fdl.html) or CC BY-SA 4.0-3.0-2.5-2.0-1.0 (http://creativecommons.org/licenses/by-sa/4.0-3.0-2.5-2.0-1.0)], via Wikimedia Commons.

[278] Stephen R. Berlant. The entheomycological origin of Egyptian crowns and the esoteric underpinnings of Egyptian religion,. Journal of Ethnopharmacology 102 (2005) 275–288.

Appendices

[279] Stephen R. Berlant. The entheomycological origin of Egyptian crowns and the esoteric underpinnings of Egyptian religion,. Journal of Ethnopharmacology 102 (2005) 275–288.

[280] Fergus Fleming and Alan Lothian Ancient Egypt's Myths and Beliefs (World Mythologies (Rosen)). Rosen Publishing Group (December 15, 2011), ISBN-10: 1448859948.

[281] Egyptian Mythology: A Guide to the Gods, Goddesses, and Traditions of Ancient Egypt by Geraldine Pinch. Oxford University Press, USA; First Edition (April 8, 2004), ISBN-10: 0195170245.

[282] Composite image created by Carlton Brown of ancient Egyptian temple art comprising modified original works (annotations, cropping; by the author); (A) Osiris: a modified image created by Carlton Brown / Wikimedia Commons / Public Domain. original work by mursal / Wikimedia Commons / Public Domain. http://commons.wikimedia.org/wiki/File:Osiris-tomb-of-Nefertari.jpg. (B) Carlton Brown / Public Domain. (C) original work by Rémih / Wikimedia Commons / CC-BY-SA-3.0-2.5-2.0-1.0. http://commons.wikimedia.org/wiki/File:Wall_relief_Kom_Ombo13.JPG.

[283] Stephen R. Berlant. The entheomycological origin of Egyptian crowns and the esoteric underpinnings of Egyptian religion,. Journal of Ethnopharmacology 102 (2005) 275–288.

[284] Dobkin de Rios, Marlene. The influence of psychotropic flora and fauna on Maya religion. Published in Current Anthropology, Vol 15(2), Jun 1974, 147-164.

[285] Gordon Wasson. The hallucinogenic fungi of Mexico: An inquiry into the origins of the religious idea among primitive peoples. Published by Botanical Museum of Harvard University (1961), ASIN: B0007FV1G0.

[286] Gaston Guzman. Hallucinogenic mushrooms in Mexico: An overview. Published by The New York Botanical Garden Press, Economic Botany, 62(3), 2008, pp. 404–412.

[287] Peter T. Furst. Hallucinogens and Culture. Published by Chandler & Sharp Publishers, 1976. ISBN: 0-88316-517-1.

[288] William A Emboden. The mushroom and the water lily. Literary and pictorial evidence for Nymphaea as a ritual psychotogen I Mesoamerica. Journal of Ethnopharmacology, 5 (1982) 139 -148.

[289] Mayan Sacred Mushroom Stones (cropped): NIDA / Wikimedia Commons / Public domain. http://commons.wikimedia.org/wiki/File:Psilocybe_Mushrooms_statues.jpg.

[290] William A Emboden. The mushroom and the water lily. Literary and pictorial evidence for Nymphaea as a ritual psychotogen I Mesoamerica. Journal of Ethnopharmacology, 5 (1982) 139 -148.

[291] Andrew McDonald and Brian Stross. Waterlily and cosmic serpent: equivalent conduits of the Maya spirit realm. Journal of Ethnobiology 32(1): 74–107 (2012).

Appendices

[292] Karl A. Taube. Aztec and Maya Myths (Legendary Past). Published by University of Texas Press; 1 edition (1993), ISBN-10: 029278130X.

[293] Waterlily Jaguar: Originally published in McDonald and Stross 2012, used with permission. Andrew McDonald and Brian Stross. Waterlily and cosmic serpent: equivalent conduits of the Maya spirit realm. Journal of Ethnobiology 32(1): 74–107 (2012). V47 degree overlay by Carlton Brown.

[294] Andrew McDonald and Brian Stross. Waterlily and cosmic serpent: equivalent conduits of the Maya spirit realm. Journal of Ethnobiology 32(1): 74–107 (2012).

[295] Waterlily serpent: Originally published in McDonald and Stross 2012, used with permission. Andrew McDonald and Brian Stross. Waterlily and cosmic serpent: equivalent conduits of the Maya spirit realm. Journal of Ethnobiology 32(1): 74–107 (2012).

[296] Quadripartite God: Originally published in McDonald and Stross 2012, used with permission. Andrew McDonald and Brian Stross. Waterlily and cosmic serpent: equivalent conduits of the Maya spirit realm. Journal of Ethnobiology 32(1): 74–107 (2012).

[297] Composite image created by Carlton Brown of Kukulkan comprising modified original works (annotations, cropping; by the author); (A) Governors Palace Uxmal: HJPD / Wikimedia Commons / CC-BY-SA-3.0-2.5-2.0-1.0. http://en.wikipedia.org/wiki/File:Uxmal_Gobernador_Ecke.jpg. (B) Mixco Viejo: Simon Burchell / Wikimedia Commons / CC BY-SA 3.0. http://en.wikipedia.org/wiki/File:Mixco_Viejo_ballcourt_marker.jpg. (C) Nunnery Quadrangle Uxmal (Mexico): Carlton Brown / Public Domain.

[298] Dobkin de Rios, Marlene. The influence of psychotropic flora and fauna on Maya religion. Published in Current Anthropology, Vol 15(2), Jun 1974.

[299] William Emboden. Transcultural use of narcotic water lilies in ancient Egyptian and Maya drug ritual. Journal of Ethnopharmacology, 3 (1981).

[300] Andrew T. Weil, Wade Davis. Bufo alvarius: a potent hallucinogen of animal origin. Published in the Journal of Ethnopharmacology 41 (1994) 1-8.

[301] Carod-Artal FJ. Hallucinogenic drugs in pre-Columbian Mesoamerican cultures. Published in Neurologia. 2011 Sep 3.

[302] Photograph © Justin Kerr. All rights reserved. Figure reproduced with the permission of the copyright holder.

[303] Isbell, W. and P. Knobloch. 2006. Missing links, imaginary links: staff god imagery in the south Andean past. In H. Silverman and W. Isbell, editors, Andean Archaeology III, pp. 307-351. Springer Science+Business Media: New York.

[304] Rebecca Stone-Miller. Art of The Andes (March 1996). Thames and Hudson (March 1996), ISBN-10: 0500202869.

Appendices

[305] Bonnie Glass-Coffin. Shamanism and San Pedro through Time: Some Notes on the Archaeology, History, and Continued Use of an Entheogen in Northern Peru. Anthropology of Consciousness, Vol. 21, Issue 1, pp. 58–82.

[306] Composite image created by Carlton Brown of Raimondi Stella & Viracocha comprising modified original works (annotations, cropping; by the author); (A) Raimondi Stela: a modified image created by Carlton Brown / Wikimedia Commons / Public Domain. original work by Antonio Raimondi: The book "El Perú" 1875) / Wikimedia Commons / Public domain. http://commons.wikimedia.org/wiki/File:Raimondi_Stela_%28Chavin_de_Huantar%29.png. (B) Gate of the Sun - Viracocha (Tiwanaku): a modified image created by Carlton Brown / Wikimedia Commons / Public Domain. original work byArthur Posnansky / Wikimedia Commons / Public Domain. http://commons.wikimedia.org/wiki/File:Centro_de_la_puerta_1903-1904.jpg.

[307] Andean Archaeology III: North and South edited by William Isbell, Helaine Silverman: Missing Links, Imaginary Links: Staff God Imagery in the South Andean Past William H. Isbell and Patricia J. Knobloch.

[308] Isbell, William H. and Patricia J. Knobloch. 2006 Missing Links, Imaginary Links: Staff God Imagery in the South Andean Past. In Andean Archaeology Vol. III: North and South, edited by William H. Isbell and Helaine Silverman, pp. 307-351. Springer, New York.

[309] Andean deity icons: Original drawings by Dr. Patricia Knobloch in Andean Archaeology Vol. III. Isbell, William H. and Patricia J. Knobloch. 2006 Missing Links, Imaginary Links: Staff God Imagery in the South Andean Past. In Andean Archaeology Vol. III: North and South, edited by William H. Isbell and Helaine Silverman, pp. 307-351. Springer, New York. V47 angle and entheogen annotations by Carlton Brown.

[310] Composite image created by Carlton Brown of Sun surface activity comprising modified original works (cropping; by the author); NASA/SDO/AIA / Wikimedia Commons / Public domain. http://commons.wikimedia.org/wiki/File%3AA_burst_of_solar_material_leaps_off_the_left_side_of_the_sun.jpg.

[311] Composite image created by Carlton Brown of Sun spot activity comprising modified original works (cropping, annotations; by the author); both images (1 magnified) by Ben-Zin at de.wikipedia / Public domain / Wikimedia Commons. http://commons.wikimedia.org/wiki/File:Sunspotcloseinset.png.

[312] Composite image created by Carlton Brown of solar activity cycles comprising modified original works (cropping by the author); (A) NASA, Marshal Space Flight Center, Solar Physics / Wikimedia Commons / Public domain. http://en.wikipedia.org/wiki/File:Sunspot_butterfly_graph.gif.

[313] http://science.nasa.gov/heliophysics/focus-areas/magnetosphere-ionosphere/.

[314] Original works by NASA / Public Domain. http://www.nasa.gov/mission_pages/sunearth/science/magnetosphere2.html.

Appendices

[315] H. Schreiber. On the periodic variations of geomagnetic activity indices Ap and ap. J. Ann. Geophysicae 16: 510-517 (1998) © EGS - Springer-Verlag 1998.

[316] A. Yoshida. Physical meaning of the equinoctial effect for semi-annual variation in geomagnetic activity. Published by Ann. Geophys., 27, 1909–1914, 2009.

[317] S. R. C. Malin, D. E. Winch, and A. M. I‚sıkara. Semi-annual variation of the geomagnetic field. Published in Earth Planets Space, 51, 321–328, 1999.

[318] Composite image created by Carlton Brown / Public Domain. of Earth´s varying magnetocusp position comprising modified original works (cropping, annotations, thematically positioning; by the author); (A) original works by NASA / Public Domain. http://nasasearch.nasa.gov/search/images?utf8=%E2%9C%93&sc=0&query=magnetosphere&m=false&affiliate=nasa&commit=Search.

[319] H. Schreiber. On the periodic variations of geomagnetic activity indices Ap and ap. J. Ann. Geophysicae 16: 510-517 (1998) © EGS - Springer-Verlag 1998.

[320] S. R. C. Malin, D. E. Winch, and A. M. I‚sıkara. Semi-annual variation of the geomagnetic field. Published in Earth Planets Space, 51, 321–328, 1999.

[321] E. M. Apostolov1, D. Altadill1, and M. Todorova. The 22-year cycle in the geomagnetic 27-day recurrences reflecting on the F2-layer ionization. Published in Annales Geophysicae (2004) 22: 1171–1176.

[322] Northern Lights: Nick Russill / CC-BY-2.0 / Wikimedia Commons. http://commons.wikimedia.org/wiki/File:Northern_Lights,_Greenland.jpg.

[323] A. Yoshida. Physical meaning of the equinoctial effect for semi-annual variation in geomagnetic activity. Published by Ann. Geophys., 27, 1909–1914, 2009.

[324] L. Svalgaard1, E. W. Cliver2, A. G. Ling. The semiannual variation of great geomagnetic storms. published in Geophysical Research Letters, Vol. 29, No. 16, 1029/2001GL014145, 2002.

[325] S. R. C. Malin, D. E. Winch, and A. M. I‚sıkara. Semi-annual variation of the geomagnetic field. Published in Earth Planets Space, 51, 321–328, 1999.

Appendices

[326] Composite image created by Carlton Brown / Public Domain. of sunspot cycles and geomagnetic activity comprising modified original works (cropping, annotations, legends, data reproduction; by the author); (A) original works by Joe H Allen (Ret NOAA), Dan Wilkinson (NOAA-- NGDC). Spacecraft Charging: The and Now Spacecraft charging technology conference, Albuquerque NM, 20-24 September 2010. Figure reproduced with the permission of the NOAA/National Geophysical Data Center. http://www.ngdc.noaa.gov/stp/geomag/ApStardescription.pdf, (B) http://www.ngdc.noaa.gov/stp/satellite/anomaly/2010_sctc/docs/ 1-1_JAllen.pdf. (A&B) National Geophysical Data Center (NGDC), National Oeanic and Atmospheric Administration (NOAA) / Public Domain (USA).

[327] Composite image created by Carlton Brown / Public Domain. of Earth´s ionosphere comprising modified original works (cropping, annotations, additions; by the author); (A) a modified image created by Carlton Brown / Wikimedia Commons / Public Domain. original work by NASA / Wikimedia Commons / Public Domain. http://commons.wikimedia.org/ wiki/File:The_Earth_seen_from_Apollo_17_with_white_background.jpg. (B) original work by Naval Postgraduate School / Wikimedia Commons / Public Domain. http://commons.wikimedia.org/wiki/ File:IonosphereLayers-NPS.gif.

[328] Composite image created by Carlton Brown / Wikimedia Commons / Public Domain. of Earth´s ionosphere waveguide comprising modified original works (cropping, annotations, additions; by the author); (A) original work by NASA / Wikimedia Commons / Public Domain. http:// commons.wikimedia.org/wiki/ File:The_Earth_seen_from_Apollo_17_with_white_background.jpg.

[329] A. Melnikova. Influence of solar terminator passages on Schumann resonance parameters. Published in the Journal of Atmospheric and Solar-Terrestrial Physics 66 (2004) 1187– 1194.

[330] M. Füllekrug, A. C. Fraser-Smith and K. Schlegel. Global ionospheric D-layer height monitoring. Published in Europhysics Letters 2002. 59, 626– 629.

[331] N. Cherry. Schumann Resonances, a plausible biophysical mechanism for the human health effects of Solar / Geomagnetic Activity (2002). Lincoln University, New Zealand. http://www.salzburg.gv.at/ cherry_schumann_resonances.pdf.

[332] A. Melnikova. Influence of solar terminator passages on Schumann resonance parameters. Published in the Journal of Atmospheric and Solar-Terrestrial Physics 66 (2004) 1187– 1194.

[333] Neil Cherry. Review: Schumann Resonances, a plausible biophysical mechanism for the human health effects of Solar/Geomagnetic Activity. Environmental Management and Design Division, Lincoln University, Canterbury, New Zealand, 9/8/2001.

Appendices

[334] Composite image created by Carlton Brown / Wikimedia Commons / CC-BY-SA-3.0. of the Schumann resonance spectrum comprising modified original works (cropping, annotations; by the author); (A) original work by AdmiralHood / Wikimedia Commons / CC-BY-SA-3.0. http://commons.wikimedia.org/wiki/File:Schumann_resonance_spectrum.gif.

[335] A. Melnikova. Influence of solar terminator passages on Schumann resonance parameters. Published in the Journal of Atmospheric and Solar-Terrestrial Physics 66 (2004) 1187– 1194.

[336] Neil Cherry. Review: Schumann Resonances, a plausible biophysical mechanism for the human health effects of Solar/Geomagnetic Activity. Environmental Management and Design Division, Lincoln University, Canterbury, New Zealand, 9/8/2001.

[337] Satori, G.; Williams, E.; Mushtak, V. Response of the Earth-ionosphere cavity resonator to the 11-year solar cycle in X-radiation. Journal of Atmospheric Solar Terrestrial Physics, 2005, 67, 553–562.

[338] Kulak, A.; Kubisz, J.; Michalec, A.; Zięba, S.; Nieckarz, Z. Solar variations in extremely low frequency propagation parameters, and Observations of Schumann resonances and computation of the ELF attenuation parameter. Published by the Journal of Geophysical Research: Space Physics, Volume 108, Issue A7, July 2003.

[339] SS. De. Analysis of Schumann resonance spectra from Kolkata and their possible interpretations. Published in The Indian Journal of Radio and Space Physics, Vol 38, August 2009. pp208-214.

[340] C. Clark / Public domain / Wikimedia Commons. http://commons.wikimedia.org/wiki/File:Lightning_NOAA.jpg.

[341] Composite image created by Carlton Brown / Wikimedia Commons / Public Domain. of the Schumann resonance generators comprising modified original works (cropped); (A) original work by C. Clark / Wikimedia Commons / Public Domain. http://commons.wikimedia.org/wiki/File:Lightning_NOAA.jpg. (B) original work by Tom Ruen (Full Sky Observatory) / Wikimedia Commons / Public Domain. http://en.wikipedia.org/wiki/File:Seasonearth.png.

[342] The Encyclopaedia of World Climatology by John E. Oliver. Published by Springer (August 1, 2005), ISBN-10: 1402032641.

[343] Victor P. Pasko. Three-dimensional finite difference time domain modeling of the diurnal and seasonal variations in Schumann resonance parameters. Published in RADIO SCIENCE, VOL. 41, RS2S14, doi. 10.1029/2005RS003402, 2006.

[344] Global lightning centers: Citynoise at en.wikipedia / Wikimedia Commons / CC BY-SA 3.0. http://en.wikipedia.org/wiki/File:Global_lightning_strikes.png.

Appendices

[345] H. Yang & V.P. Pasko. Three-dimensional finite difference time domain modelling of the diurnal and seasonal variations in Schumann resonance parameters. Published by Radio Science (a Wiley publication), Vol. 41, RS2S14, doi:10.1029/2005RS003402, 2006.

[346] Hugh J. Christian, Richard J. Blakeslee, Dennis J. Boccippio, William L. Boeck, Dennis E. Buechler, Kevin T. Driscoll, Steven J. Goodman, John M. Hall, William J. Koshak, Douglas M. Mach, Michael F. Stewart. Global frequency and distribution of lightning as observed from space by the Optical Transient Detector. published in Journal of Geophysics Research, 108 (D1), 4005, doi:10.1029/2002JD002347, 2003.

[347] M. Hayakawa, M Sekiguchi and A.P Nickolaenko. Diurnal variation of electric activity of global thunderstorms deduced from OTD data. Published in J. Atmos. Electr., 25, 55–68, 2005.

[348] M. Sekiguchi, M. Hayakawa, A. P. Nickolaenko, and Y. Hobara: Evidence on a link between the intensity of Schumann resonance and global surface temperature. J. Ann. Geophys., 24, 1809–1817, 2006.

[349] M. Sekiguchi, M. Hayakawa, A. P. Nickolaenko, and Y. Hobara: Evidence on a link between the intensity of Schumann resonance and global surface temperature. J. Ann. Geophys., 24, 1809–1817, 2006. Figure reproduced with the permission of the copyright holder Copernicus Publications on behalf of the European Geosciences Union.

[350] Composite image created by Carlton Brown / Public Domain. of the Sun god religions 3D positioning relative to the solstice solar terminators comprising modified original works (cropping, annotations, additions; by the author); (A-D) original works by NASA World Wind / Public Domain.

[351] A. Melnikova. Influence of solar terminator passages on Schumann resonance parameters. Published in the Journal of Atmospheric and Solar-Terrestrial Physics 66 (2004) 1187–1194.

[352] Possible Mechanism of the Observed Schuman Resonance Diurnal Amplitude Variations by O. Pechony and C. Price. http://www.ursi.org/proceedings/procGA08/papers/EGHp7.pdf (NASA Goddard Institute for Space Studies, and Tel Aviv University respectively.

[353] Masashi Hayakawa, Katsumi Hattori, Kenji Ohta. Monitoring of ULF (ultra-low-frequency) Geomagnetic Variations Associated with Earthquakes. Published in Sensors 2007, 7, 1108-1122.

[354] N Borisova, V Chmyreva, S Rybachekb. A new ionospheric mechanism of electromagnetic ELF precursors to earthquakes. Journal of Atmospheric and Solar-Terrestrial Physics 63 (2001) 3–10.

[355] Hayakawa, M.; Sue, Y.; Nakamura, T. The effect of earth tides as observed in seismo-electromagnetic precursory signals. Nat. Hazards Earth Syst. Sci., 9, 1733–1741, 2009.

Appendices

[356] Chatterjee, Achintya K, Bari, Washimul, Choudhury, Asit K. Anomalous behavior of D-layer formation time of the ionosphere due to earthquake. Published in Indian Journal of Radio and Space Physics Vol, 38, June 2009 pp138-142.

[357] Masashi Hayakawa, Katsumi Hattori and Kenji Ohta. Monitoring of ULF (ultra-low-frequency) Geomagnetic Variations Associated with Earthquakes. Published in Sensors 2007, 7, 1108-1122.

[358] Y Fujinawa, K Takahashi, T Matsumoto, H Iitaka, S Yamane, T Nakayama, T Sawada, H Sakai. Electromagnetic Field Anomaly Associated with the 1998 Seismic Swarm in Central Japan. published in Physics. Chem. Earth, Vol. 25. No. 3, pp. 247-253, 2000.

[359] Masashi Hayakawa, Katsumi Hattori and Kenji Ohta. Monitoring of ULF (ultra-low-frequency) Geomagnetic Variations Associated with Earthquakes. Published in Sensors 2007, 7, 1108-1122.

[360] Konig, H.L., Krueger, A.P., Lang, S. and Sonning, W. (198 1). Biological Effects of Environmental Electromagnetism. New York: Springer-Verlag.

[361] Human biological clock: original work by YassineMrabet / Wikimedia Commons / CC-BY-SA-3.0-2.5-2.0-1.0. http://en.wikipedia.org/wiki/File:Biological_clock_human.PNG.

[362] J. lipkova and J. Cechak. Human electromagnetic emission in the ELF band. MEASUREMENT SCIENCE REVIEW, Volume 5, Section 2, 2005.

[363] J. Lipkova and J. Cechak. Existence of Electromagnetic Radiation in Humans in ELF Band. Presentation; Progress In Electromagnetics Research Symposium 2005, Hangzhou, China, August 22-26.

[364] A. G. Kolesnik, A. S. Borodin, S. A. Kolesnik, S. V. Pobachenko. Resonant mechanisms of solar-terrestrial relationships. Published in the Russian Physics Journal, Vol. 46, No. 8, 2003.

[365] Composite image created by Carlton Brown / Wikimedia Commons / CC-BY-SA-3.0. of human brainwaves and the Schuman resonance spectrum comprising modified original works (cropping, image fusion, legends, annotations; by the author); (A) Brainwaves alpha to gamma: original work by Hugo Gamboa / Wikimedia Commons / CC-BY-SA-3.0. http://commons.wikimedia.org/wiki/File:Eeg_alpha.svg, http://commons.wikimedia.org/wiki/File:Eeg_beta.svg, http://commons.wikimedia.org/wiki/File:Eeg_delta.svg, http://commons.wikimedia.org/wiki/File:Eeg_gamma.svg, http://commons.wikimedia.org/wiki/File:Ecg_theta.svg. (B) AdmiralHood / Wikimedia Commons / CC-BY-SA-3.0. http://commons.wikimedia.org/wiki/File:Schumann_resonance_spectrum.gif.

[366] Irena Ćosić, Dean Cvetković , Qiang Fang, Emil Jovanov, Harry Lazoura. Human Electrophysiological Signal Responses to ELF Schumann Resonance and Artificial Electromagnetic Fields. FME Transactions (2006) 34, 93-103.

Appendices

[367] Irena Ćosić, Dean Cvetković, Qiang Fang, Emil Jovanov, Harry Lazoura. Human Electrophysiological Signal Responses to ELF Schumann Resonance and Artificial Electromagnetic Fields. FME Transactions (2006) 34, 93-103.

[368] T.S. Tenforde. Biological interactions of extremely-low-frequency electric and magnetic fields. Published in Journal of Bioelectrochemistry and Bioenergetics, 25 (1991) 1-17.

[369] J. Lipkova and J. Cechak. Existence of Electromagnetic Radiation in Humans in ELF Band. Presentation; Progress In Electromagnetics Research Symposium 2005, Hangzhou, China, August 22-26.

[370] Composite image (cropping, labels, border) created by Carlton Brown / Wikimedia Commons / Public Domain. Original drawing of the human brain, from the National Institute for Aging, National Institutes of Health, United States Department of Health and Human Services. https://commons.wikimedia.org/wiki/Category:Anatomical_plates_and_drawings_of_the_human_brain#/media/File:NIA_human_brain_drawing.jpg / Public Domain.

[371] Schienle A, Stark R, Kulzer R, Klöpper R, Vaitl D. Atmospheric electromagnetism: Individual differences in brain electrical response to simulated sferics. International Journal of Psychophysiology 21 (1996) 177-188.

[372] D. Cvetkovic and I. Cosic. Alterations of human electroencephalographic activity caused by multiple extremely low frequency magnetic field exposures. Published in the Med Biol Eng Comput (2009) 47:1063–1073.

[373] Capone F, Dileone M, Profice P, Pilato F, Musumeci G, Minicuci G, Ranieri F, Cadossi R, Setti S, Tonali PA, Di Lazzaro V. Does exposure to extremely low frequency magnetic fields produce functional changes in human brain? published in the J Neural Transm (2009) 116:257–265.

[374] A. G. Kolesnik, A. S. Borodin, S. A. Kolesnik, and S. V. Pobachenko. Resonant mechanisms of solar-terrestrial relationships. Published in the Russian Physics Journal, Vol. 46, No. 8, 2003.

[375] S. V. Pobachenko, A. G. Kolesnik, A. S. Borodin, and V. V. Kalyuzhin: The Contingency of Parameters of Human Encephalograms and Schumann Resonance Electromagnetic Fields Revealed in Monitoring Studies. Journal of Biophysics, 2006, Vol. 51, No. 3, pp. 480–483.

[376] A. G. Kolesnik, A. S. Borodin, S. A. Kolesnik, and S. V. Pobachenko. Discussion paper: An electromagnetic mechanism of solar-terrestrial relations. Published in the International Journal of Geomagnetism and Aeronomy Vol. 6, GI1004, doi:10.1029/2004GI000096, 2005.

[377] With kind permission from Springer Science+Business Media: The Contingency of Parameters of Human Encephalograms and Schumann Resonance Electromagnetic Fields Revealed in Monitoring Studies. Journal of Biophysics, 2006, Vol. 51, No. 3, pp. 480–483. S. V. Pobachenko, A. G. Kolesnik, A. S. Borodin, and V. V. Kalyuzhin. Figure 2.

[378] With kind permission from Springer Science+Business Media: Resonant mechanisms of solar-terrestrial relationships. Published in the Russian Physics Journal, Vol. 46, No. 8, 2003. A. G. Kolesnik, A. S. Borodin, S. A. Kolesnik, and S. V. Pobachenko. Figure 3.

[379] A. G. Kolesnik, A. S. Borodin, S. A. Kolesnik, and S. V. Pobachenko. Resonant mechanisms of solar-terrestrial relationships. Published in the Russian Physics Journal, Vol. 46, No. 8, 2003.

[380] Elchin S. Babayev, Aysel A. Allahverdiyeva. Effects of geomagnetic activity variations on the physiological and psychological state of functionally healthy humans: Some results of Azerbaijani studies. Published in Advances in Space Research 40 (2007) 1941–1951.

[381] Mulligan, Bryce P.; Hunter, Mathew D.; Persinger, Michael A. Effects of geomagnetic activity and atmospheric power variations on quantitative measures of brain activity: Replication of the Azerbaijani studies. Published in Advances in Space Research 45 (2010) 940–948.

[382] Advances in Space Research 40 (2007). Elchin S. Babayev, Aysel A. Allahverdiyeva. Effects of geomagnetic activity variations on the physiological and psychological state of functionally healthy humans: Some results of Azerbaijani studies. Pages 1941–1951. Figures 1 & 2. © 2007. Figures reproduced with permission from Elsevier.

[383] Newberg AB, Iversen J. The neural basis of the complex mental task of meditation: neurotransmitter and neurochemical considerations. Medical Hypotheses (2003) 61(2), 282–291.

[384] Travis F, Tecce J, Arenander A, Wallace RK. Patterns of EEG coherence, power, and contingent negative variation characterize the integration of transcendental and waking states. Biological Psychology 61 (2002) 293–319.

[385] Fell J, Axmacher N, Haupt S. From alpha to gamma: Electrophysiological correlates of meditation-related states of consciousness. Medical Hypotheses 75 (2010) 218–224.

[386] Travis F, Shear J. Focused attention, open monitoring and automatic self-transcending: Categories to organize meditations from Vedic, Buddhist and Chinese traditions. Consciousness and Cognition 19 (2010) 1110–1118.

[387] B. Rael Cahn Meditation States and Traits: EEG, ERP, and Neuroimaging Studies. Psychological Bulletin, 2006, Vol. 132, No. 2, 180–211.

[388] Travis F. Autonomic and EEG patterns distinguish transcending from other experiences during Transcendental Meditation practice. Int J Psychophysiol. 2001 Aug;42(1):1-9.

[389] Eckhart Tolle. The Power of Now: A Guide to Spiritual Enlightenment. Published by New World Library, 6 Oct. 2010. ASIN B002361MLA.

[390] Fred Travis, Joe Tecce, Alarik Arenander, R. Keith Wallace. Patterns of EEG coherence, power, and contingent negative variation characterize the integration of transcendental and waking states. Biological Psychology 61 (2002). Pages 293–319.

[391] Fred Travis, Joe Tecce, Alarik Arenander, R. Keith Wallace. Patterns of EEG coherence, power, and contingent negative variation characterize the integration of transcendental and waking states. Biological Psychology 61 (2002). Pages 293 -319.

[392] Reprinted from the Biological Psychology 61 (2002). Fred Travis, Joe Tecce, Alarik Arenander, R. Keith Wallace. Patterns of EEG coherence, power, and contingent negative variation characterize the integration of transcendental and waking states. Pages 293 -319, figure 2. Copyright 2002, with permission from Elsevier.

[393] B. Rael Cahn. Meditation States and Traits: EEG, ERP, and Neuroimaging Studies. Psychological Bulletin, 2006, Vol. 132, No. 2, 180 –211.

[394] Yamamoto S, Kitamura Y, Yamada N, Nakashima Y, Kuroda S. Medial Prefrontal Cortex and Anterior Cingulate Cortex in the Generation of Alpha Activity Induced by Transcendental Meditation: A Magnetoencephalographic Study. Acta Med. Okayama, 2006. Vol. 60, No. 1, pp. 55-58.

[395] Newberg AB, Wintering N, Waldman MR, Amen D, Khalsa DS, Alavi A. Cerebral blood flow differences between long-term meditators and nonmeditators. Consciousness and Cognition xxx (2010).

[396] Travis F, Tecce J, Arenander A, Wallace RK. Patterns of EEG coherence, power, and contingent negative variation characterize the integration of transcendental and waking states. Biological Psychology 61 (2002) 293 -319.

[397] Brefczynski-Lewis JA, Lutz A, Schaefer HS, Levinson DB, Davidson RJ. Neural correlates of attentional expertise in long-term meditation practitioners. PNAS July 3, 2007 vol. 104 no. 27 11483–11488.

[398] Original work by Paul H. Levine, J Russell Herbert, Christopher Haynes, Urs Strobel. EEG Coherence during the Transdendentalmeditation technique. Copyright 1975 by the Maharishi European Research University, Weggis, Switzerland. Composite image created from this publication by Carlton Brown (no rights) of meditation and alpha brainwaves comprising modified original works (cropping, legends, and annotations by the author).

[399] Cooper NR, Croft RJ, Dominey SJ, Burgess AP, Gruzelier JH. Paradox lost? Exploring the role of alpha oscillations during externally vs. internally directed attention and the implications for idling and inhibition hypotheses. International Journal of Psychophysiology 47 (2003) 65–74.

[400] Travis F, Shear J. Focused attention, open monitoring and automatic self-transcending: Categories to organize meditations from Vedic, Buddhist and Chinese traditions. Consciousness and Cognition 19 (2010) 1110–1118.

[401] B. Rael Cahn. Meditation States and Traits: EEG, ERP, and Neuroimaging Studies,. Psychological Bulletin, 2006, Vol. 132, No. 2, 180 –211.

Appendices

[402] Travis F, Tecce J, Arenander A, Wallace RK. Patterns of EEG coherence, power, and contingent negative variation characterize the integration of transcendental and waking states. Biological Psychology 61 (2002) 293 -319.

[403] Travis F, Shear J. Focused attention, open monitoring and automatic self-transcending: Categories to organize meditations from Vedic, Buddhist and Chinese traditions. Consciousness and Cognition 19 (2010) 1110–1118.

[404] Newberg AB, Iversen J. The neural basis of the complex mental task of meditation: neurotransmitter and neurochemical considerations. Medical Hypotheses (2003) 61(2), 282–291.

[405] Troels W. Kjaera, Camilla Bertelsena, Paola Piccinib, David Brooksb, Jørgen Alvingc, Hans C. Loua. Increased dopamine tone during meditation-induced change of consciousness. Cognitive Brain Research 13 (2002) 255 –259.

[406] Composite image created by Carlton Brown /Wikimedia / Public Domain (subject to all attributions). of entheogen symbolisms comprising modified original works (cropping, annotations; by the author); (A) a modified image created by Carlton Brown / Wikimedia Commons / Public Domain. original work by RickK / Wikimedia Commons / Public Domain. http://commons.wikimedia.org/wiki/File:Aten_disk.jpg. (B) a modified image created by Carlton Brown / Wikimedia Commons / CC-BY-SA-2.0. original work by 23 dingen voor musea (Suryabeeldje) / Wikimedia Commons / CC-BY-SA-2.0. http://commons.wikimedia.org/wiki/File:WLANL_-_23dingenvoormusea_-_Suryabeeldje.jpg. (C) a modified image created by Carlton Brown / Wikimedia Commons / Public Domain. original drawing by Antonio Raimondi: The book "El Perú" 1875) / Wikimedia Commons / Public domain. http://commons.wikimedia.org/wiki/File:Raimondi_Stela_%28Chavin_de_Huantar%29.png. (D) a modified image created by Carlton Brown / Wikimedia Commons / Public Domain. original work by NIDA (cropped image) / Wikimedia Commons / Public Domain. http://commons.wikimedia.org/wiki/File:Psilocybe_Mushrooms_statues.jpg.

[407] AB. Newberg and J. Iversen. The neural basis of the complex mental task of meditation: neurotransmitter and neurochemical considerations. Medical Hypotheses (2003) 61(2), 282–291.

[408] Travis F. Autonomic and EEG patterns distinguish transcending from other experiences during Transcendental Meditation practice. Int J Psychophysiol. 2001 Aug;42(1):1-9.

[409] Cooper NR, Croft RJ, Dominey SJ, Burgess AP, Gruzelier JH. Paradox lost? Exploring the role of alpha oscillations during externally vs. internally directed attention and the implications for idling and inhibition hypotheses. International Journal of Psychophysiology 47 (2003) 65–74.

[410] Stanislav Grof. A Brief History Of Transpersonal Psychology. The International Journal of Transpersonal Studies Volume 27, 2008.

Appendices

[411] Niko Kohls and Harald Walach. Exceptional experiences and spiritual practice: a new measurement approach. Spirituality and Health International 7: 125–150 (2006).

[412] Jeff Levin, PhD, MPH and Lea Steele, PhD. Review: The Transcendent Experience: Conceptual, Theoretical, and Epidemiological Perspectives. Explore 2005; 1:89-101.

[413] Michael Harner. The Way of the Shaman. HarperOne; 10 Anv edition (26 July 2011). ASIN: B005AJWUF4.

[414] Stanislav Grof. Healing Our Deepest Wounds: The Holotropic Paradigm Shift. Stream of Experience Productions (28 Jun 2012).

[415] Michael A Persinger (1983) Religious and Mystical Experiences as Artifacts of Temporal Lobe Function: A General Hypothesis. Perceptual and Motor Skills: Volume 57, Issue , pp. 1255-1262.

[416] Thomas L, Cooper PE. Incidence and psychological correlates of intense spiritual experiences. J Transpersonal Psychol. 1980;12:75-85.

[417] Stanislav Grof. LSD: Doorway to the Numinous: The Groundbreaking Psychedelic Research into Realms of the Human Unconscious. M.D. Park Street Press; 4 edition (12 Feb 2009). ASIN: B003GDFROM.

[418] Stanislav Grof. LSD: Doorway to the Numinous: The Groundbreaking Psychedelic Research into Realms of the Human Unconscious. M.D. Park Street Press; 4 edition (12 Feb 2009). ASIN: B003GDFROM.

[419] Stanislav Grof. LSD: Doorway to the Numinous: The Groundbreaking Psychedelic Research into Realms of the Human Unconscious. M.D. Park Street Press; 4 edition (12 Feb 2009). ASIN: B003GDFROM.

[420] Spiritual emergencies: Understanding and treatment of psychospiritual crises, by Stanislav Grof. Internet based article found at; http://www.realitysandwich.com/spiritual_emergencies.

[421] Stanislav Grof. LSD: Doorway to the Numinous: The Groundbreaking Psychedelic Research into Realms of the Human Unconscious. M.D. Park Street Press; 4 edition (12 Feb 2009). ASIN: B003GDFROM.

[422] Stanislav Grof. LSD: Doorway to the Numinous: The Groundbreaking Psychedelic Research into Realms of the Human Unconscious. M.D. Park Street Press; 4 edition (12 Feb 2009). ASIN: B003GDFROM.

[423] Stanislav Grof. LSD: Doorway to the Numinous: The Groundbreaking Psychedelic Research into Realms of the Human Unconscious. M.D. Park Street Press; 4 edition (12 Feb 2009). ASIN: B003GDFROM.

[424] Stanislav Grof. LSD: Doorway to the Numinous: The Groundbreaking Psychedelic Research into Realms of the Human Unconscious. M.D. Park Street Press; 4 edition (12 Feb 2009). ASIN: B003GDFROM.

[425] Stanislav Grof. LSD: Doorway to the Numinous: The Groundbreaking Psychedelic Research into Realms of the Human Unconscious. M.D. Park Street Press; 4 edition (12 Feb 2009). ASIN: B003GDFROM.

Appendices

[426] Toward a more culturally sensitive DSM-IV. Psychoreligious and psychospiritual problems, by D Lukoff et al. J Nerv Ment Dis. 1992 Nov; 180(11):673-82. http://www.ncbi.nlm.nih.gov/pubmed/1431819.

[427] Dr. Nicki Crowley. Psychosis or Spiritual Emergence? Consideration of the Transpersonal Perspective within Psychiatry.http://www.rcpsych.ac.uk/pdf/Nicki%20Crowley%20%20Psychosis%20or%20Spiritual%20Emergence.pdf.

[428] Stanislav Grof. Spiritual emergencies: Understanding and treatment of psychospiritual crises. Internet based article found at; http://www.realitysandwich.com/spiritual_emergencies.

[429] Dr. Nicki Crowley. Psychosis or Spiritual Emergence? Consideration of the Transpersonal Perspective within Psychiatry. http://www.rcpsych.ac.uk/pdf/Nicki%20Crowley%20%20Psychosis%20or%20Spiritual%20Emergence.pdf.

[430] Niko Kohls and Harald Walach. Exceptional experiences and spiritual practice: a new measurement approach. Spirituality and Health International 7: 125–150 (2006).

[431] Katherine A. MacLean, Jeannie-Marie S. Leoutsakos, Matthew W. Johnson, Roland R. Griffiths. Factor Analysis of the Mystical Experience Questionnaire: A Study of Experiences Occasioned by the Hallucinogen Psilocybin. Journal for the Scientific Study of Religion (2012) 51(4):721–737.

[432] Stanislav Grof, M.D. Psychology of the Future: Lessons from Modern Consciousness Research (Holotropic Experiences and Their Healing and Heuristic Potential).

[433] Jeff Levin. Esoteric healing traditions: a conceptual overview. Explore (NY). 2008 Mar-Apr;4 (2):101-12. doi: 10.1016/j.explore.2007.12.003.

[434] David Grinstead. Religious Traditions: East and West. A Contrast of the Mystical Elements of Buddhism, Taoism, Judaism, and Christianity at Atlantic University.

[435] David Grinstead. Religious Traditions: East and West. A Contrast of the Mystical Elements of Buddhism, Taoism, Judaism, and Christianity at Atlantic University.

[436] Jeff Levin. Esoteric healing traditions: a conceptual overview. Explore (NY). 2008 Mar-Apr; 4 (2):101-12. doi: 10.1016/j.explore.2007.12.003.

[437] Antoon Geels. Altered Consciousness in Religion. http://www.academia.edu/1405697/Altered_Consciousness_in_Religion.

[438] R.D. Krumpos. The greatest achievement in life: Five traditions of mysticism, Mystical approaches to life. http://www.suprarational.org/.

[439] R.D. Krumpos. The greatest achievement in life: Five traditions of mysticism, Mystical approaches to life. http://www.suprarational.org/.

[440] Jeff Levin. Esoteric healing traditions: a conceptual overview. Explore (NY). 2008 Mar-Apr; 4 (2):101-12. doi: 10.1016/j.explore.2007.12.003.

Appendices

[441] Antoon Geels. Altered Consciousness in Religion. http://www.academia.edu/1405697/Altered_Consciousness_in_Religion.

[442] David Grinstead. Religious Traditions: East and West. A Contrast of the Mystical Elements of Buddhism, Taoism, Judaism, and Christianity at Atlantic University.

[443] R.D. Krumpos. The greatest achievement in life: Five traditions of mysticism, Mystical approaches to life. http://www.suprarational.org/.

[444] David Steindl-Rast. The Mystical Core of Organized Religion. http://www.hofmann.org/.

[445] David Steindl-Rast. The Mystical Core of Organized Religion. http://www.hofmann.org/.

[446] James A Wiseman. To be with god: the autotheistic sayings of the mystics, Theological Studies 51 (1990).

[447] Jeff Levin. Esoteric healing traditions: a conceptual overview. Explore (NY). 2008 Mar-Apr;4 (2):101-12. doi: 10.1016/j.explore.2007.12.003.

[448] Jeff Levin. Esoteric healing traditions: a conceptual overview. Explore (NY). 2008 Mar-Apr;4 (2):101-12. doi: 10.1016/j.explore.2007.12.003.

[449] Antoon Geels. Altered Consciousness in Religion. http://www.academia.edu/1405697/Altered_Consciousness_in_Religion.

[450] R.D. Krumpos. The greatest achievement in life: Five traditions of mysticism, Mystical approaches to life. http://www.suprarational.org/.

[451] Prof. David Loy. Enlightenment in Buddhism and Advaita Vedanta: Are Nirvana and Moksha the Same?

[452] Prof. David Loy. Enlightenment in Buddhism and Advaita Vedanta: Are Nirvana and Moksha the Same?

[453] http://viewonbuddhism.org/buddha.html

[454] Prof. David Loy. Enlightenment in Buddhism and Advaita Vedanta: Are Nirvana and Moksha the Same?

[455] Stanislav Grof M.D. LSD: Doorway to the Numinous: The Groundbreaking Psychedelic Research into Realms of the Human Unconscious. Park Street Press; 4 edition (12 Feb 2009). ASIN: B003GDFROM.

[456] James M. Nelson. Psychology, Religion, and Spirituality. Springer; 2009 edition (February 27, 2009), ISBN-10: 0387875727.

[457] Prof. David Loy. Enlightenment in Buddhism and Advaita Vedanta: Are Nirvana and Moksha the Same?

[458] Religious Traditions: East and West. A Contrast of the Mystical Elements of Buddhism, Taoism, Judaism, and Christianity David Grinstead at Atlantic University.

[459] R.D. Krumpos. The greatest achievement in life: Five traditions of mysticism, Mystical approaches to life. http://www.suprarational.org/.

Appendices

460 Kanz Philosophia: A Journal for Islamic Philosophy and Mysticism. Volume 2. Number 1. June 2012. ISSN 2088-8511.

461 David Grinstead. Religious Traditions: East and West. A Contrast of the Mystical Elements of Buddhism, Taoism, Judaism, and Christianity at Atlantic University.

462 Jeff Levin. Esoteric healing traditions: a conceptual overview. Explore (NY). 2008 Mar-Apr;4 (2):101-12. doi: 10.1016/j.explore.2007.12.003.

463 Stanislav Grof. LSD: Doorway to the Numinous: The Groundbreaking Psychedelic Research into Realms of the Human Unconscious. M.D. Park Street Press; 4 edition (12 Feb 2009). ASIN: B003GDFROM.

464 Stanislav Grof. Healing Our Deepest Wounds: The Holotropic Paradigm Shift. Stream of Experience Productions (28 Jun 2012).

465 R.D. Krumpos. The greatest achievement in life: Five traditions of mysticism, Mystical approaches to life. http://www.suprarational.org/..

466 http://enlightened-people.com/2014/10/mooji/

467 http://www.mooji.org/biography.html

468 Maharishi Mahesh Yogi. The Science of Being and Art of Living. http://www.amazon.com/Science-Being-Living-Maharishi-Mahesh-ebook/dp/B0061YCTYE

469 http://carltonbrownv47.com/meditation-calendar/

470 http://www.mayancross.com/reference-glossary-four-directions.

471 The Tak´alik Abaj archaeological site, http://english.takalik.com/.

472 Carlton Brown / Public Domain.

473 Image created by Carlton Brown / Public Domain

474 Stanislav Grof. LSD: Doorway to the Numinous: The Groundbreaking Psychedelic Research into Realms of the Human Unconscious. M.D. Park Street Press; 4 edition (12 Feb 2009). ASIN: B003GDFROM.

475 Stanislav Grof. Healing Our Deepest Wounds: The Holotropic Paradigm Shift. Stream of Experience Productions (28 Jun 2012).

476 R.D. Krumpos. The greatest achievement in life: Five traditions of mysticism, Mystical approaches to life. http://www.suprarational.org/..

477 http://enlightened-people.com/2014/10/mooji/

478 http://enlightened-people.com/2014/10/mooji/

479 Guy Finley. The Secret of Letting Go. Published by Llewellyn Publications; 2 Rev Exp edition (October 8, 2007), ISBN-13: 978-0738711980. Location 2504.

480 http://ritualmeditation.com/winter-solstice-ritual-meditation-witnessing-the-birth-of-the-universe-in-unity-states-of-consciousness/

481 http://albertellis.org/rebt-cbt-therapy/. http://www.amazon.com/Practice-Rational-Emotive-Behavior-Therapy/dp/0826122167.

Appendices

[482] http://enlightened-people.com/2014/10/mooji/

[483] http://www.onandoffthebeatenpath.org

[484] Maharishi Mahesh Yogi. The Science of Being and Art of Living. http://www.amazon.com/Science-Being-Living-Maharishi-Mahesh-ebook/dp/B0061YCTYE

[485] Guy Finley. The Secret of Letting Go. Published by Llewellyn Publications; 2 Rev Exp edition (October 8, 2007), ISBN-13: 978-0738711980. Location 2504.

[486] http://enlightened-people.com/2014/10/mooji/

[487] Martin Lee and Bruce Shlain. Acid Dreams: The Complete Social History of LSD: The CIA, the Sixties, and Beyond.

[488] The author has had good experiences in final delivery of magic mushroom grow kits, their storage, and growth yielding potent magic mushrooms from the following online retailers; Avalon Magic Plants, Zamnesia, Magic Truffles, and Shayanashop. Please review the legal status of your country and follow the supplier's advice for growth, preparation and dose, and any other instructions that ensure your safety.

www.ingramcontent.com/pod-product-compliance
Lightning Source LLC
Chambersburg PA
CBHW071137300426
44113CB00009B/999